PC SOFTWARE

PC SOFTWARE

by

Satish Jain

B.Sc., B.E.(IISc), M.E.(IISc), M.Tech.(IIT Kanpur),
Professor of Information Technology,
Institute of Information Technology & Management
GGS Indraprastha University, Delhi.

Dr. Shalini Jain

M. Geetha

BPB PUBLICATIONS

B-14, CONNAUGHT PLACE, NEW DELHI - 110 001

FIRST EDITION 2010

Copyright © BPB Publications, New Delhi

ISBN : 978-81-8333-389-4

Distributors:

COMPUTER BOOK CENTRE
12, Shrungar Shopping Centre, M.G. Road,
BANGALORE-560001 Ph: 25587923, 25584641

MICRO BOOKS
Shanti Niketan Building, 8, Camac Street
KOLKATA-700017 Ph: 22826518/9

BUSINESS PROMOTION BUREAU
8/1, Ritchie Street, Mount Road,
CHENNAI-600002 Ph: 28410796, 28550491

MICRO MEDIA
Shop No.5, Mahendra Chambers, 150 D.N. Rd,
Next to Capital Cinema V.T. (C.S.T.) Station,
MUMBAI-400001 Ph: 22078296, 22078297

DECCAN AGENCIES
4-3-329, Bank Street,
HYDERABAD-500195 Ph: 24756400, 24756967

BPB PUBLICATIONS
B-14, Connaught Place, NEW DELHI-110001
Ph: 23329760, 23723393, 23737742

BPB BOOK CENTRE
376, Old Lajpat Rai Market, DELHI-110006
Ph: 23861747

INFOTECH
G-2, Sidhartha Building, 96, Nehru Place,
NEW DELHI-110019
Ph: 26438245, 26415092, 26234208

INFOTECH
Shop No.2, F-38, South Extention Part-1
NEW DELHI-110049
Ph: 24691288

Published by Manish Jain for BPB Publications, B-14, Connaught Place, New Delhi-110001 and Printed by him at Akash Press, New Delhi.

Dedicated to

Sri Raja Rajeshwari and Sai Baba

who bless Immense Power of Knowledge

BOOKS *by Prof. Satish Jain*

'O' Level made simple Books (According to DOEACC Syllabus effective from July, 2010 Examination)

➤ IT Tools and Business Systems *(covering M1-R4 and A1-R4 papers)*
➤ Internet Technology and Web Design *(covering M2-R4 and A2-R4 papers)*
➤ Programming and Problem Solving through 'C' language *(covering M3-R4 and A3-R4 papers)*
➤ Application of .Net Technology *M4.1-R4*
➤ Introduction to Multimedia *M4.2-R4*
➤ Introduction to ICT Resources *M4.3-R4*
➤ BPB 'O' Level Course (Covering: IT Tools and Business Systems, Internet Technology & Web Design and Programming and Problem Solving through 'C'Language) (Also covering A1-R4, A2-R4 & A3-R4 papers)

'A' Level made simple Books (According to DOEACC Syllabus effective from July, 2010 Examination)

➤ Computer System Architecture *(covering A4-R4 paper)*
➤ Structured System Analysis & Design *(covering A5-R4 paper)*
➤ Data Structure Through C++ *(covering A6-R4 paper)*
➤ Introduction to Database Management Systems *(covering A7-R4 paper)*
➤ Basics of OS, UNIX and Shell Programming *(covering A8-R4 paper)*
➤ Data Communication and Network Technologies *(covering A9-R4 paper)*
➤ Introduction to Object Oriented Programming through Java *(covering A10.1-R4 paper)*
➤ Software Testing and Quality Management *(covering A10.2-R4 paper)*

'O' & 'A' Level Ques. & Ans. Series (According to DOEACC Syllabus effective from July, 2010 Examination)

➤ 'O' Level Question and Answer–IT Tools and Business Systems, Internet Technology & Web Design and Programming & Problem Solving through 'C' language *(Also covering A1-R4, A2-R4 & A3-R4 papers)*
➤ 'A' Level Question and Answer–Computer System Architecture and Structured System Analysis & Design *(A4-R4 & A5-R4 papers)*
➤ 'A' Level Question and Answer–Data Structure through C++ and Introduction to Database Management Systems *(A6-R4 & A7-R4 papers)*
➤ 'A' Level Question and Answer–Basics of OS, UNIX & Shell Programming and Data Communication and Network Technologies *(A8-R4 & A9-R4 papers)*
➤ 'A' Level Question and Answer–Introduction to Object-Oriented Programming through Java *(A10.1-R4 paper)*
➤ 'A' Level Question and Answer–Software Testing and Quality Management *(A10.2-R4 paper)*

For B.E., MCA, M.Sc.(IT), B.Sc.(IT), BCA, PGDCA, and other IT Related Examinations for leading Indian Universities and Engineering Colleges

➤ Introduction to Database Management
➤ Systems Analysis, Design and Management Information System
➤ Computer Networks

PREFACE

This book covers the syllabus of Personal Computer Software course prescribed by Gujarat University. Our objective is to explain to students this highly technical subject in an easy-to-understand manner through many examples and diagrams. It is felt that most of the books available in the market do not cover the entire syllabus for the course to meet the needs of the students. The syllabus provided by Gujarat University is very comprehensive and needs very thorough study of computer science and PC software packages. For this reason, we have pressed into service all our practical experience in computer engineering as well as in academics by bringing out this book to meet the needs of students of all streams.

We have observed that the syllabus at the outset appears to be very simple and can be easily covered. But when it comes to answering the question papers, one realizes how thorough the student has to be in the study of *PC software Packages*. To make students realize this point, we have added a set of question papers appeared in earlier examinations and added them at the end of this book. The readers wil find them very useful to prepare themselves for the examination in future.

We have made this book user friendly by adding Glossary of technical terms at the end of book. This will be specially helpful to the reader in clarifying the subject matter. A comprehensive Index is also given at the end of the book, which will be very handy for locating page numbers of topics discussed in this book.

A special feature of this book is that the important information has been shown with a (☞) mark to draw attention of the reader.

We shall feel highly obliged to the readers if they send us their critical opinion of the presentation, readability and coverage in this book as well as suggestions to improve the subject matter.

7th July, 2010   Authors

BOOKS *by Prof. Satish Jain* (Contd...)

- ➤ Computer Organization and Architecture
- ➤ Data Structures *Made Simple*
- ➤ Advanced Computer Networking
- ➤ Wireless Communications and Networking
- ➤ Software Testing and Quality Management
- ➤ PC Software *made simple*
- ➤ *Guide to* Digital Electronics and Devices *(Ques. & Ans.)*
- ➤ *Guide to* Computer Networks and Data Communications *(Ques. & Ans.)*
- ➤ *Guide to* Systems Analysis, Design and MIS *(Ques. & Ans.)*
- ➤ *Guide to* Data Structures *(Ques. & Ans.)*
- ➤ *Guide to* Database Management Systems *(Ques. & Ans.)*

For MBA, PGDBM and other Business Related Examinations for leading Indian Universities and Management Colleges

- ➤ Computers in Business Management *Principles and Practice*
- ➤ *Guide to* Computers in Business Management *(Ques. & Ans.)*

'O' Level CHM (Computer Hardware Maintenance) Made Simple (According to DOEACC Syllabus)

- ➤ Electronics Components and PC Hardware *(covering CHM–O1 paper)*
- ➤ Computer Peripherals and Networking *(covering CHM–O3 paper)*
- ➤ System Software, Dignostics and Debugging Tools *(covering CHM–O4 paper)*

Training Guides for Application Packages

- ➤ CorelDRAW-10, 12
- ➤ Photoshop CS3
- ➤ PageMaker-6.5, 7.0

ACKNOWLEDGEMENTS

We gratefully acknowledge the contribution made by the following persons in bringing out the book in this form:

- Shashank Jain

- Dr. Madhulika Jain

- Kratika

Syllabus

PC Software

BCA Semester-I

1. Operating Systems:

Concept of Operating System, Examples of Operating System
What is an operating system? Why is it required? Different types of Operating System available.

CUI Operating System
DOS
Booting process DOS features, comparison with GUI, file naming, Convention, wildcard characters, purpose of commands: DIR, MD, RD, CD, COPY, TYPE, DEL, PROMPT, DATE, TIME, CLS, VER, MOVE.

GUI Operating System
WINDOWS 98/2000
Concept of windows, General features of windows: Desktops, Icon My Computer, my Documents, Network neighourhood, recycle bin, Start menu, Taskbar Windows explore, Control panel, creating folder, finding files and folders, copying and moving files, deleting files, creating shortcuts, Scan Disk, Defragmentation, Importances of DOS within Windows, difference between Server and workstation, introduction of Client/Server.

2. Word Processing Package:

Create, edit, save, navigating documents, different views, formatting, Cut-Copy and Paste, find and replace, word wrap, alignment, tabs, inserting-Tables-hyperlink-pictures-charts-Autotext-header-footer-footnote- endnote-Comments-bookmark, Autocorrect, spell checking, theasurus, protecting a document, mail merge, macros, templates.

3. Presentation Package:

Creating-editing-printing slides, different views, using text, drawings, Tables, pictures, charts and other objects in slide, Custom and preset Animation, slide transition effects, Running slide shows, custom shows, Rehearse timing, pack and Go, Speaker notes, pen.

4. Spreadsheet Packages:

Concept of workbook-worksheet-workspace, Cell, range, Types of data, Formatting, conditional formatting, Fill series, Entering formula, Absolute-Relative-Mixed addressing, cut-copy-paste special, Hyperlink, Function: SUM, COUNT, MIN, MAX, AVERAGE, TODAY, NOW IF, SUMIF, COUNTIF, UPPER, LOWER, ROUND, VLOOKUP, HLOOKUP, DAYS360, Creating charts, protecting and hiding data, data filtering: Autofilter-Advanced filter-Dataforms-validation consolidation, whatif Analysis: Goal seek-Scenario-Data table, import-export of data, charts, Types of Erros.

5. Outlook Express:

Introduction, Creating account, sending, receiving, Managing and Organizing e-mail, Address Book

6. Computer Viruses:

Introduction to Computer Virus, types of Virus, Prevention and Cure.

CONTENTS

PC Software

Chapter 2. Word Processing Package   51

Chapter 4.   Spreadsheet Package   **163**

Chapter 5. Outlook Express   240

CHAPTER 1

Operating Systems

After this chapter the reader will be able to understand
- Concept of Operating System
- Types of Operating Systems
- DOS commands
- Features of Windows 98

1.1 CONCEPT OF OPERATING SYSTEM

An Operating System (OS) is a software that controls the internal activities of the computer hardware and provides user interface. All application programs need to be programmed in such a way that they talk with the operating system for interacting and use hardware resources.

It is the first program loaded (copied) into the computer's memory after the computer is switched on. Popular operating systems are Windows XP Windows vista, OS/2 and Unix. IBM Mainframe computer uses MVS, VM or DOS/ VSE operating system.

☞ *One of the primary jobs of the Operating System is to provide an interface between the user and the hardware. This interface enables a user to use hardware resources efficiently.*

Operating System (OS) is primarily concerned with allocating and deallocating computer resources to one or more jobs. In fact, it can be looked upon as a cover on the hardware. Thus, an OS is an important part of every computer system.

Operating systems that support a single user at a time is a single-user operating system such as Windows XP. Some, like Linux, Unix etc. support multiple users at a time.

An operating system performs the following functions:

(a) *Processor Management*: The operating system assigns processors (if a computer has more than one processor) to the different tasks that must be performed by the computer system.

(b) *Memory Management*: It (OS) allocates the main memory and secondary memory to the system programs, user programs and data.

(c) *Input/Output Management*: It carries out the input/output management and co-ordinates and assigns different input and output devices.

(d) *File Management*: It manages files on various storage devices and the transfer of these files from one storage device to another. It also allows all files to be easily changed and modified through the use of text editors or some other file manipulation software packages.

(e) *Scheduling*: It establishes and enforces the job priority. That is, it determines and maintains the order in which jobs are to be executed in the computer system.

(f) *Timesharing*: It co-ordinates and assigns compilers, assemblers, utility programs, and other software packages to various users working on the computer system.

(g) *Security Management*: It establishes data security and integrity. That is, it keeps different programs and data in such a manner that they do not interfere with each other. Moreover, it also protects data from being destroyed by any other user.

(g) It produces dumps, traces, error messages, and other debugging and error-detecting codes.

(i) It maintains internal time clock and log of system usage for all other users.

(j) It facilitates easy communication between the computer system and the computer operator (human).

The main functions of an operating system, in short, can be categorized as follows:

(a) Resource Management (Processor management, Memory management, device management)

(b) Process Management (Job scheduling, Task management)

(c) Data Management (File management and Input/Output management)

(d) Security management

☞ *Some of the popular operating systems are MS-DOS, WINDOWS XP, VISTA, UNIX, LINUX, SOLARIS and OS/2.*

All operating systems can be classified into four categories:

(a) *Single User Operating System*: Operating system which allows only one user to work on a computer at a time is known as single user operating system. Examples include DOS, Windows, etc.

(b) *Multiuser Operating System*: A Multiuser operating system allows a number of users to work together on a single computer. Each user will be provided a terminal connected to a single computer. Examples include Linux, Unix, Windows 2000, etc.

(c) *Single tasking Operating System*: Operating system which can execute only a single task at a time is known as single tasking operating system. eg. DOS.

(d) *Multitasking Operating System*: Multitasking operating system supports execution of more than one job at a time. Most of today's operating systems such as Windows 2000, OS/2, UNIX, LINUX etc. support multitasking.

1.1.1 Why OS is required?

User interacts with the application programs but the application programs do not access the hardware resources directly. Hardware resources include input/output devices, Primary Memory, secondary Memory (like Hard Disk, etc.) and the microprocessor. Therefore, an operating system is required to access and use these resources. The application programs are so created that they talk with the operating system to get access to the resources. (See Figure 1.1)

☞ *An Operating System (OS) is the first program that is loaded (copied) into the computer's main memory, when a computer is switched on. The efficiency of any operating system measured in terms of its throughput, turn around time and response time.*

The two primary objectives of an operating system are:

(a) To enable running of Application programs.

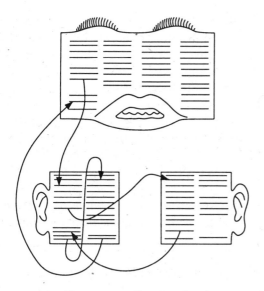

Programs talk to each other

Figure 1.1   Program talks with an Operating System loaded in a computer

(b) To manage the different computer resources.

1.1.2 Examples of Operating Systems

Different Types of Operating System

An overview of the different types of operating systems are:

(a) Single-user Operating System
(b) Multiuser Operating System
(c) Single-tasking Operating System
(d) Multitasking Operating System
(e) Real-time Operating System
(f) Multiprogramming
(g) Network Operating System
(h) Distributed Operating System

Single-user Operating System

Operating system which allows only one user to work on a computer at a time is known as single user operating system. Examples include MS-DOS, Windows etc.

Multiuser Operating System

A Multiuser operating system allows a number of users to work together on a single computer. UNIX is a multiuser operating system. It is not that all users will bump on a computer at the same time. Each user will be provided with a terminal and all such terminals will be connected to the single computer. Examples of multiuser operating systems are Linux, Unix, Windows 2000.

> ☞ *Multiuser operating system running on a computer will manage the work of all users, without letting them know that they all are actually working on a single computer.*

Single-tasking Operating System

Operating system which can execute a single job at a time is known as Single-tasking operating system. For example, MS-DOS is a single tasking operating system because you can open and run only one application in DOS, at one time.

Multitasking Operating System

Multitasking operating system allows the user to perform more than one job at the same time on a computer. Most of today's operating systems such as Windows, OS/2, UNIX, LINUX etc. support multitasking. For example, when you open MS-Word and Internet Explorer at the same time, the Windows operating system is doing multitasking. The operating system is able to keep track of where you are in each of these applications and switch from one to another without losing track.

Real Time vs Time Sharing Operating Systems

Time Sharing System *Time Sharing* is a mode of processing in which more than one user uses the CPU time. It is so named because the processor time is shared among multiple users. Time sharing uses multiprogramming.

☞ *Development of time sharing operating system was motivated by the desire to provide fast response to user requests.*

Thus, time sharing is a term used to describe a computer system that has a number of independent, relatively low speed, on-line, simultaneously usable terminals. Each terminal provides direct access to the CPU. In other words, time sharing refers to the allocation of computer resources in a time-dependent fashion to several users simultaneously. Main purpose of a time sharing system is to provide a large number of users direct access to the computer for problem solving.

Time sharing is accomplished by providing a separate terminal to each user. All these terminals are connected to the main computer system. Thus, a time sharing system has many terminals linked up to the same computer at the same time. This is shown in Figure 1.2. In time sharing, the CPU time is divided among all the users on a scheduled basis.

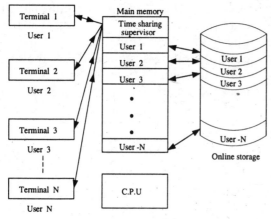

Figure 1.2 Concept of a time sharing system

Realtime System   Realtime Systems are online computer systems which provide immediate processing and also respond to user's commands immediately. They can respond to *transactions* by updating the corresponding master files right away. Although the term is commonly used in reference to business applications, it is most appropriately used in process control and scientific processing like airplane control and space vehicle operations.

☞ *Realtime also refers to simulated operations that are performed in the same timeframe as a real operation.*

Multiprogramming

Most medium and large computers use multiprogramming operating systems. Multiprogramming is the name given to the interleaved execution of two or more different and independent programs by the same computer. In multiprogramming several programs are processed by a computer simultaneously. Usually a CPU is much faster as compared to I/O devices. While I/O devices are performing certain tasks the CPU may not be doing any task, it may be lying idle. To keep CPU busy for most of the time, it is desirable to process a number of programs concurrently. This is achieved by overlapping CPU and I/O operations when several programs are running simultaneously.

Scheduling various tasks such as Input/Output, processing etc are an important activity of an operating system (OS). As the processor is very fast compared to the speed of the Input/Output devices, the expensive processor will be kept idle during the Input/Output procedures. Hence operating systems have been developed which can supervise the processing and manage the Input/Output and memory allocations of more than one program simultaneously.

Such OS are called multiprogramming OS. Let program A, B and C be concurrently processed by a computer. Suppose that program A processes a file and at time t, it needs some input. The OS instructs the input device to transfer the required data. During this time the processor is free and the OS starts executing the second program B. When B needs some Input or Output, if A is ready, the processor is switched back to A and if not is switched to C. The Figure 1.3 explains this procedure clearly.

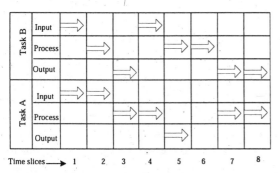

Figure 1.3 Concept of multiprogramming system

The input data are collected in Buffers while other task is being processed. The buffers can receive input at the speed of the input devices and release them at electronic speed to the processor. Similarly, output data are collected in output buffers which receives data at high speed and release them at the speeds of the output device. Such multiprogramming requires highly sophisticated OS compared to the single program OS. OS software for PCs used to be single task OS while concurrent and timesharing OS were available for bigger machines. Nowadays multi-user operating systems are available for PCs also.

Network Operating System (NOS)

Network Operating System (NOS) is an operating system specifically designed to support interconnection of several computers. NOS provides support for multiuser operations as well as administrative, security and network management functions. Some examples of NOSs are Novell's Netware, Microsoft's Windows NT, Artisoft's LANtastic etc.

☞ *A network operating system has to acknowledge and respond to requests from many workstations, managing network access, resource allocation and sharing, data protection as well as error control. It provides for printer, file-system, database and application sharing.*

Distributed Operating System

A Distributed Operating System hides the existence of multiple computers (interconnected by a network) from the user. That is, the user remains unaware of the fact that many computers are being used to process the data. These computers may be located at many places around the globe. Distributed Operating System provides single-system image to its users. Each computer in a distributed computing system processes a part of the global distributed operating system. All these computers work in close coordination with each other. Processes and system resources are managed globally, and controlled from specific locations.

☞ *Users view the complete system as a "virtual uniprocessor" and not as a collection of machines. The distributed operating system works towards generating this illusion.*

☞ *Degree of autonomy of individual computers in an environment that uses network operating system is very high whereas the degree of autonomy of individual computers in an environment that uses distributed operating system is considerably low.*

Input/Output Bound Programs The programs perform very little computations but handle a huge amount of data and information. The commercial data processing and educational data processing environment the input and output data in large amount but computations are very little. Therefore, such programs that utilize maximum time in I/O operations are called I/O bound programs.

CPU Bound Programs The program, which needs very little time for I/O operations but requires large amount of time to calculate are called CPU bound programs. The operating speed of CPU is much faster than that of I/O operation therefore the CPU can provide the services to several programs instead of remaining idle when one program is busy with input/out operations.

On-line Processing/Random Access Processing

On-line processing premits transaction data to be fed, under CPU control, directly into secondary on-line storage devices from the point where data originates. These data may be keyed in by the use of a typewriter-like terminal, or they may be produced by a variety of other data collection and transaction recording devices. The access to, and retrieval of, any record in quick and direct. Thus, on-line processing systems feature random and rapid input of transactions and immediate and direct access to record contents as and when needed. A simplified concept of on-line processing is illustrated in Figure 1.4.

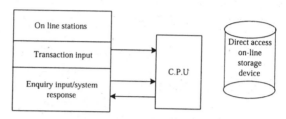

Figure 1.4 On-line processing

Multiprocessing Operating System

Multiprocessing is simultaneous processing with two or more processors in one computer or two or more computers that are processing together. When two or more computers are used, they are tied together with a high-speed channel and share the general workload between them. In the event one fails to operate, the other takes over automatically. Some large computers and powerful minicomputers contain two or more CPUs. These CUPs operate in parallel under the integrated control of an operating system to handle one task or job.

Embedded System

The operating systems designed for being used in embedded computer systems are known as embedded operating systems. They are designed to operate on small machines like PDAs with less autonomy. They are able to operate with a limited number of resources. They are very compact and extremely efficient by design. Windows CE, FreeBSD and Minix 3 are some examples of embedded operating systems.

The operating systems thus contribute to the simplification of the human interaction with the computer hardware. They are responsible for linking application programs with the hardware, thus achieving an easy user access to the computers.

1.2 CHARACTER USER INTERFACE (CUI)

Character User Interface or CUI is like Graphical User Interface which is used for input and output of the data in the computer, except in the graphical user interface (GUI) apart from text there are also graphical contents present, in CUI there is only use of text typed one after other just as commands used in MS DOS.

1.2.1 DOS (DISK OPERATING SYSTEM)

MS-DOS (Microsoft Disk Operating System) is an operating system supplied by Microsoft Corporation of U.S.A. Latest operating system (OS) available from Microsoft Corporation is Windows 2000, Windows XP and Windows 7.

DOS is a disk operating system based on MS-DOS and it operates on all IBM compatible personal computers. A *system file* contains low-level information that DOS needs to be able to configure and use specific hardware devices. DOS's own two system files **IO.SYS** and **MSDOS.SYS** include the essential programmes that DOS needs to be able to communicate with any of your computer's hardware. Another system file— **CONFIG.SYS**—contains valuable configuration information for your computer. Most system files, however, are DEVICE DRIVERS that contain instructions that tell DOS how to manipulate specific devices. Those files usually have the .SYS extension, such as **MOUSE.SYS**, **RAMDRIVE.SYS**, **HIMEM.SYS**, etc.

☞ *DOS is a single user single tasking operating system that can support only one user and only one task at a time.*

1.2.2 Booting Process

Boot means start or make the computer system ready so that it can take our instructions. The word "boot" comes from "bootstrap," since bootstraps helps you to get your boots on; likewise booting the computer helps it to get its Read Only Memory (ROM) instructions loaded in its main memory. In a personal computer, there is a small bootstrap routine in a ROM chip that is automatically executed when the computer is turned on or reset. The bootstrap routine searches for the operating system, loads it and then passes control over to it. You can boot your computer system in two ways: one is called *cold booting*, when the computer is first turned on; and the other is called *warm booting*, when the computer is already on and is being reset. With personal computers using single tasking operating systems, it is usually necessary to reset the computer after it crashes. For example in IBM PC compatible machines, you can do the warm booting by pressing the (Ctrl), (Alt) and (Del) keys together. In this way it will not do initial checks like memory checks etc. which it will do only when it is switched on for the fist time.

DOS Features

The key features of DOS are given below.

(a) **Simplicity and transparency**–DOS is simple and very transparent. You always know what your computer is doing.

(b) Low hardware requiremetns–DOS has extremely low hardware needs. It runs on every PC. What is even better is the fact that, when compared to Windows, the same tasks can run on much weaker hardware.

If you are new to DOS, use DOS version 6.2. It is even possible to play audio files on a 486 or Pentium class computer.

Reason not to use DOS that is:
(a) Application software did not evolve.
(b) No Javascript capable browser
(c) No good PDF viewer.

1.2.3 Comparison with Graphical User Interface (GUI)

The CUI is an acronym for **Character User Interface**. It is a type of display format used with most of the DOS based application packages that enables a user to choose commands and see list of files and other options by pointing to drop down menus using mouse or keyboard keys. The familiar

example is the CUI used with FoxPro package for DOS.

GUI (pronounced "gooey") is an acronym for **G**raphical **U**ser **I**nterface. It is a type of display format that enables the user to choose commands start programs, and see list of files and other options by pointing to pictorial representations (icons) and lists of menu items on the screen. Choices can generally be actived either with the keyboard or with a mouse. GUI offers an environment of what you see what you get. Table 1.1 will help to illustrate the major advantages and disadvantages of each of the interfaces.

Table 1.1 Advantages and disadvantages of CUI and GUI

Command Line (CUI)	GUI
Because of the memorization and familiarity needed to operate a command line interface new users find it much more difficult to successfully navigate and operate a command line interace.	Although new users may have a difficult at time learning to use the mouse to operate and use a GUI most user pick up this interface much easier when compared to a command lne interface.
User have much moe control of their file system and operating system in a command line interface. For example, users can easily copy a specific type of file from one location to another with a one-line command.	Although a GUI offers plenty of control of a file system and operating system ofen advance users or users who need to do spcific task may need to resort to a command line to complete that task.
Although many command line environments are capable of multitasking they do not offer the same ease and ability to view multiple things at once on one screen.	GUI users have windows that enable a user to easily view, control and manipulate multiple things at once and is commonly much faster to do when compared to a command line.
Because command line user only need to use their keyboards to navigate a command line interface and often only need to execute a few line to perform a task an advanced command ine interface user would be able to get something done faster than an advance GUI user.	A GUI may be easier to use because of the mouse. However, using a mouse and/or keyboard to navigate and contol your operating system for many things is going to be much slower than somone who is workng in a command line evironment.
A computer that is only using the command line takes a lot less of the computers resources.	A GUI will require a lot more system resources because of each of the elements that need to be loaded such as icons, fonts, etc. In addition video drivers, mouse drivers, and other drivers that need to be loaded will also take additional resources.

A command line interace enables a user to easily script a sequence of commands to perform a task or execute a program	Although a GUI enables a user to create shortcuts, tasks, or other similar actions to complete a task or run a program it does not even come close in comparison to what is available through a command line.

1.2.4 File Naming Conventions

The filename is the system's key for unlocking file contents and without friendly names the user will have trouble handling large numbers of files. Reading file contents requires considerable disk access especially for large files. Filenames, on the other hand, are stored separately from their contents in system files called allocation tables and can be loaded with minimal disk access. Meaningful filenames provide software developers with the ability to write programs that can manage and process large numbers of files quickly because the key information is in the filenames. The PC hardware benefits too from the reduced number of disk access operations.

Filenames

A filename is composed of two parts. The first part is the name and the second part is the extension. The extension is normally used to specify the type of the file. In general, there are two different types of files. The first type is binary files such as program files (EXE) and dynamic link libraries (DLL), and the second type is ASCII files such as batch files (BAT), text files (TXT) and delimited files (CSV). Filenames are listed in system files called allocation tables (file allocation table "FAT" for DOS, and NT file system "NTFS" for Windows). Each entry in these tables corresponds to a single file and has a number of fields including filename, file attributes ("A" for archive and "H" for hidden) and the address of the file contents.

Filenames are limited in size. Compression, especially in DOS, may be required in order to place required key information in the filename. Compression is the art of representing a long sequence of information with a brief sequence of codes. Certain ASCII characters (such as " ? / \ < > * | :) can not be used in naming files. Applying compression methods could produce non-valid filenames. To eliminate this problem an alternate code set is assigned to the ASCII characters that can be used in naming files. The alternate code set is normally called the filename character set.

A Windows filename can be up to 253 characters long (11 for DOS) and a filename character can be any one of 245 ASCII codes (52 for DOS). DOS filenames are compatible with Windows but such filenames are not always compatible with DOS. Compatibility is lost either when the filename is longer than 11 characters or when any character in the filename is assigned an ASCII value outside the DOS range. For example: when saving the file "HELLO_MY_FRIEND.TXT" to Disk, it is renamed to "HELLO_^1.TXT" which follows the DOS naming convention. If a sequence of other filenames also begins with the characters "HELLO_" then the 10th file in the sequence is named "HELLO^10.TXT".

Naming Conventions

A number of TSD (time sequence data) naming conventions are in use today. These formats are organized in three classes. The classes are called associated, coded, and sequenced. The filename extension defines the type of data storage format. For example, the extensions "HDR", "CFG", "DAT", and "INF" are used to indicate that the file contents are compatible with the IEEE COMTRADE standard. The non-extension part of an associated filename or the name is left at the discretion of the user and could be assigned in a coded or sequenced way.

1.2.5 Wildcard Characters

A wildcard character is a keyboard character such as an asterisk (*) or a question mark (?) that is used to represent one or more characters when you are searching for files, folders, printers, computers etc. Wildcard characters are often used in place of one or more characters when you do not know that the real character is or you do not want to type the entire name. Uses of Wildcard character are disscussed in Table 1.2.

Table 1.2 Wildcard character and its uses

Wildcard character	Uses
	Use the asterisk as a substitute for zero or more characters. If you are looking for a file that you know starts with "gloss" but you cannot remember the rest of the file name, type the following:
	gloss*
Asterisk (*)	This locates all files of any file type that begin with "gloss" including Glossary.txt, Glossary.doc, and Glossy.doc. To narrow the search to a specific type of file, type:
	gloss*.doc
	This locates all files that begin with "gloss" but have the file name extension as doc, such as Glossary.doc and Glossy.doc.

Question mark (?)	Use the question mark as a substitute for a single character in a name. For example, if you type gloss?.doc, you will locate the file Glossy.doc or Gloss1.doc but not Glossary.doc.

1.3 DOS COMMANDS

DOS commands can be broadly classified into two categories. One category of commands are in-built into the DOS's system file and thus can be executed *automatically*. Whereas the other category of commands are executed only if corresponding program files are copied into the system. These two types of commands are termed as *internal* commands and *external* commands respectively.

☞ *The entire set of commands available in DOS can be divided into Internal commands and External commands.*

1.3.1 Internal commands

Internal commands are such programs in DOS which get loaded in the memory of a PC automatically at the time of booting or starting of a computer. These commands are made available so long as the PC is kept **ON**. Some of the internal commands that you will be using very often are **dir, del, rename, copy, type** etc.

1.3.2 External commands

External commands are such short programs or utilities which are available on your floppy/hard disk. These get loaded in the memory of the PC when specially asked for. Some of the external commands that you will often use are **format, chkdsk, print** and **diskcopy.**

1.4 FILE MANAGEMENT COMMANDS

File management commands are specially designed to manage and operate different kinds of files stored in disks and directories. Various commands that can operate on files are explained in the following sections.

1.4.1 Copy

The Copy command in DOS copies and also combines the files. The syntax is:

```
COPY source:\path\file(s)
target:\path\file(s) /switches
```

Alternative syntax for combining files is:

```
COPY source file(s) + source
file(s) target \path\fi-
le(s)/switches
```

The different switches used with copy command are as follows:

Switch	Action
/A	Indicates that the files are to be treated as ASCII files.
/B	Indicates that the files are to be treated as binary files.
/V	Instructs DOS to perform a validity check on the target files after they are copied.

Example 1

```
C:\COPY B:*.* A:  (Enter)
```

This command would copy all files on the current drive, i.e. B drive to disk drive **A**.

```
C:\COPY A:*.TXT *.BAK /A/V  (Enter)
```

This command would copy all files with extension **.TXT** to file with the same name but with extension **.BAK** from floppy disk in drive **A** to current drive (i.e. C).

```
B:\COPY B:*.TXT \BACKUP /V  (Enter)
```

The above command copies all files with extension **.TXT** to a subdirectory named **BACKUP** on the same drive.

```
C:\COPY A:*.TXT  (Enter)
```

The above command copies all files on drive **A** with the extension **.TXT** to the currently logged drive, i.e. **C:**.

```
C:\COPY START.FIL + MIDDLE.FIL +
END.FIL COMPLETE.FIL  (Enter)
```

The above command combines the files **START.FIL**, **MIDDLE.FIL** and **END.FIL** into one file called **COMPLETE.FIL**.

```
C:\COPY A:LETTER.TXT > PRN  (Enter)
```

The above command copies a file to the printer, for printing. Be sure your printer is switched on and is online.

1.4.2 Xcopy

The command selectively copies files. The syntax is:

```
C:\XCOPY  source:\path\file(s)
target:\path\file(s) /switches
```

The **xcopy** command requires a source file name, which may include wildcard characters (such * or ?) plus optional drive letter and subdirectory path. You may provide a target parameter which may be another file name, drive letter, subdirectory path or combination of the three. If you do not include a target drive, XCOPY will attempt to copy the source files on to the currently logged drive and subdirectory.

The source and target parameters cannot be duplicated with the same file name and location. In other words, the XCOPY command will not copy a file on to itself.

If you use wildcard characters (such as * or ?) to indicate multiple source files and the target does not include a file name, then copies of each file matching the source specification will be made in the target location.

☞ *If you indicate multiple source files and the target file name also includes wildcard characters, DOS will attempt to rename the target files in accordance with the wildcard conventions that you indicate.*

The options available with **XCOPY** makes it more flexible than the **COPY** command.

Different switches available in **xcopy** command are mentioned in the Table 1.3.

Table 1.3 Xcopy command

Switch	Action
/A	Copies only those files matching the source specification that also have their archive bit set.
/D:*date*	Copies files that were modified on or after the specified date. The exact format of the *date* parameter depends on the COUNTRY setting you are using.
/E	Creates subdirectories on the target location, even if there are no files in them. This switch is valid only when used in conjunction with the /S switch.
/M	Resets (turns off) the archive bit in a file after making the copy.
/P	Issues a prompt asking you to confirm the copy of each source file.
/S	Copies files matching the source specification that are found in sub directories nested below the source subdirectory.
/V	Performs a verification check against the image of the file in memory.
/W	Causes XCOPY to pause before making copies allowing you an opportunity to change disks in the source drive if necessary.

Example 2

XCOPY C:\REPORTS*.TXT A: (Enter)

Copies all files in the C:\REPORTS subdirectory with the extension .TXT to drive A.

XCOPY C:\REPORTS*.TXT A: /S/D: 10/26/97 (Enter)

copies all files in the **C:\REPORT** subdirectory, as well as any located in sub directories nested below **C\REPORTS** with the extension **.TXT**, provided that they have been modified on or after October 26, 1997. The copies are placed on drive **A**.

In addition to being more flexible than COPY, XCOPY can handle larger number of files more efficiently, because it reads as many files as it can into the main memory before writing them onto disk. This decreases the number of disk accesses. If you copy many smaller files, then this method can save you time and reduce wear and tear of the disk.

1.4.3 Del or Erase Command

These commands erase data or program files. The syntax is:

DEL drive:\path\file(s) /switches
ERASE   drive:\path\file(s) /switches

DEL command requires the name of a file to be deleted. You can use wildcard characters (such as *, ?) to erase groups of files. You may also specify a drive letter and subdirectory path to delete files. If you specify a subdirectory path without file names, DOS 6 assumes that you want to delete all the files in the subdirectory. In this case, DOS will ask you:

All file in directory will be deleted! Are you Sure (Y/N)?

If you really intend to delete all the files, enter Y in response to this prompt. If you enter N, the command is cancelled. The switch available is given in the following table.

Switch	Action
/P	Instructs DOS to display each file that matches the file name parameter and prompts, "Delete (Y/N)?" If you enter Y, the file is deleted.

Example 3

`C:\DEL EXAMPLE.TXT` (Enter)

Deletes the file **EXAMPLE.TXT**.

`C:\DEL *.BAK` (Enter)

Deletes all files on the current subdirectory with the extension **BAK**.

`C:\DEL A: *.*` (Enter)

Deletes all files in the root directory on drive A. Prompts for confirmation first.

`C:\DEL C:\BACKUP\*.BAK/P` (Enter)

Displays each file of the **C:\BACKUP** subdirectory with the extension **.BAK**, and prompts for confirmation before deleting it.

1.4.4 Rename (REN)

This command would give a new name to a file.

The syntax for this command is:

`RENAME drive:\path\oldfile drive:\path\newfile`

The REN command requires an old file name and the new file name. When invoked, the command changes the old file name to the new file name. Wildcard characters may be used to rename groups of files, but the wildcard specification must match between the old name and the new name.

If the old file is not located in the current drive or subdirectory, you may specify the drive and path name as part of the old file name as a parameter. It is not necessary to repeat the drive and path names with the new file name. DOS will rather keep the renamed file in its original location.

You can only rename files on the same disk. You can also rename group of files using **RENAME** command. For example to rename all the files having extension **.BAK** to take extension **.DOC**, type the following command.

`C:\>RENAME *.BAK *.DOC` (Enter)

Example 4

`REN REPORT.TXT SALES.RPT` (Enter)

This command changes the name **REPORT.TXT** to **SALES.RPT**.

`REN C:\WORD\*.BAK *.OLD` (Enter)

Changes the names of all files with the extension **.BAK** on the **C:\WORD** subdirectory so that they will now have the extension **.OLD**.

1.4.5 Attrib

The Attrib command changes the characteristics of files. Files can be declared *read-only, read-write, archived*. In DOS 6, attributes of directories may also be changed. The syntax is:

`ATTRIB modes drive:\path\file\(s) /switches`

ATTRIB requires a file name parameter. The file name may contain wildcard characters. If called without parameters, ATTRIB will display the attributes of all files matching the indicated file name.

The different switches associated with this command are as follows:

Switch	Action
/S	Used with file names that contain wildcard characters or subdirectory names without file names. This option will include matching files in sub directories nested below the current subdirectory.
– R	Changes specified file(s) to read write which means, the file may be overwritten or erased.
+ R	Changes specified file(s) to read-only which means the file(s) cannot be overwritten or erased.
+ A	changes file setting(s) to archived.

(Contd...)

Switch	Action
– A	Changes file setting(s) to Not Archived.
+ H	Changes specified file(s) to hidden, which means the file(s) will not be visible to most DOS Operations.
– H	Makes hidden file (s) visible again.
+ S	Marks specified file(s) as DOS system file(s).
– S	Removes DOS system-file setting.

You cannot use more than one mode of options at one time.

Example 5

```
C:\ATTRIB FILE.EXE  [Enter]
```
will display the attributes of the file **FILE.EXE**.

```
C:\ATTRIB\ +R C:\DOS\*.* /S  [Enter]
```
will change all the files on the **C:\DOS** subdirectory, and sub directories nested below **C:\DOS**, to read-only.

1.4.6 Backup

This command backs up and restores files. This command can overwrite or erase data. So be very careful!

The syntax for this command is:

```
MSBACKUP specfile /switches
```

Example 6

```
C:\MSBACKUP MYFILES.SET [Enter]
```
Starts the backup program using (or creating) a specification file called **MYFILES.SET**.

Various switches available with this command are given below:

Switch	Action
/TF	(Type = full) Backs up all files named in the specification.
/TI	(Type = Incremental) Backs up all files

(Contd...)

Switch	Action
	named in the specification file that have changed since the last backup.
/TD	(Type = Differential) Backs up all files named in the specification file that have changed since the last full backup.
/BW	Starts MSBACKUP in black-and-white for monitors that have trouble displaying the screen in colours.

1.4.7 Restore

This command restores files from disks made by using the BACKUP command from earlier versions of MS-DOS. The syntax for this command is:

```
RESTORE source drive: target
 drive:\path\file(s)] [/switches]
```

RESTORE command requires two parameters: a source drive (a floppy-diskdrive), where the backup files are located, and a target drive (usually a hard disk), where the restored files are to be located.

RESTORE is used only to restore files that were backed up using the BACKUP command. DOS 6.0 does not include a BACKUP command. This utility is present only for compatibility with earlier versions of DOS.

☞ *BACKUP remembers the original subdirectory locations of the files it backed up. RESTORE command restores the backup files to the same subdirectory.*

Example 7

```
C:\RESTORE A:  [Enter]
```

restores those files from the backup disk in drive **A** that originally resided on the currently logged subdirectory.

```
RESTORE A: C: /S /B:05-01-02
/E:13:00:00  [Enter]
```

Restores files from backup disk in drive **A:** to the root directory of drive **C**, plus all files below the root directory, except those on the target drive that were modified on or after May 1, at 1:00 p.m. 2002.

Different switches available with this command are:

Switch	Action
/A:*mm-dd-yy*	Restores only those files that were modified on or after the specified date, where *mm* is the month, *dd* is the day and *yy* is the year.
/B:*mm-dd-yy*	Restores only those files that were modified on or before the specified date, namely mm-dd-yy.
/D	Displays file name(s) on the backup disk but does not restore them.
/E:*hh-mm-ss*	Restores those files modified *at* or *earlier* than the specified time, where *hh* is the hour (in 24 hour format), *mm* is the minutes after the hour, and *ss* is the seconds. This switch is effective when used with the date parameter.
/L:*hh: mm: ss*	Restores only those files that were modified *at* or *after* the specified time. The switch effects only when used with the time parameter.
/M	Restores files that were modified since the last backup was made.
/N	Restores files that were deleted since the last backup.
/P	Prompts to confirm the restoration of files that were changed since the last backup or marked as read-only files. Without this parameter all files on the target drive with names identical to the backup files will be overwritten.
/S	Restores files in sub directories nested below the specified target subdirectory.

1.4.8 Type

This command displays the contents of a text file. The Syntax is:

TYPE drive:\path\file

TYPE command requires the name of a file. You may include a drive and directory name if the file is not in the currently logged drive and subdirectory. Wildcard characters are not allowed in the file name. This command is useful to display contents of a text file or a file in ASCII format.

Example 8

TYPE REPORT.TXT ⌨Enter⌨

Displays the contents of a file named **REPORT.TXT** on the screen.

TYPE REPORT.TXT | MORE ⌨Enter⌨

displays the contents of the file one screen at a time and pauses the display after each screen of information.

TYPE REPORT.TXT > PRN ⌨Enter⌨

sends the contents of **REPORT.TXT** file to the standard printer device.

1.4.9 Date

This command displays or sets the system date. The Syntax is:

DATE date ⌨Enter⌨

If you invoke the DATE command without parameters, DOS displays the current system date and prompts you to enter another. Dates are accepted using the format **mm/dd/yy**, where *mm* is the month (1-12), *dd* is the day (1-31) and *yy* is the year from 1980 to 2079(80-79).

Example 9

C:\DATE ⌨Enter⌨

displays the current date and prompts you to enter another date.

To leave the date unchanged, press ⌨Enter⌨.

DATE .5-26-07 (Enter)

changes the current date to May 26, 2007.

1.4.10 Time

This command displays and allows changes to the system time. The Syntax is:

TIME hh:mm:ss.cc

If you invoke TIME without parameters, it displays the current system time and prompts you to enter a new time. If you do not want to change the current time, press (Enter). Otherwise, enter the new time, where *hh* is the hour of the day in 24 hour format, *mm* is the minutes after the hour, *ss* is the seconds after the minutes, and *cc* is hundreds of a second.

☞ *Only the hours parameter (followed by a colon) is required to set a new time, other time values are optional. If you include the desired time on the command line, the system time is changed without prompting you.*

Example 10

  C:\TIME 22:30 (Enter)

  C:\TIME 10:30:15.21 (Enter)

Either of the above example changes the time to 10:30 p.m.

1.4.11 Prompt

This DOS command lets you change the DOS SYSTEM PROMPT, and (if **ANSI.SYS** is installed in your **CONFIG.SYS** file) lets you manipulate the colours, position, and attributes of the text on your screen.

The Syntax is:

  PROMPT [string]

The switches available are as follows:

Switch	Action
PROMPT	Without any parameters, PROMPT

                                        (Contd...)

Switch	Action
	resets the DOS prompt to its default setting, the current drive followed by the > symbol.
String	Specifies the text that you want to display as your system prompt. It can be any text (except the reserved DOS characters |, >, <, or =) and the following special $ symbols:
$$	$(dollar sign)
$_	Carriage return/linefeed
$B	| (bar, pipe symbol)
$D	Current date
$e	Escape code (note that character e must be lowercase)
$G	> (greater-than symbol)
$H	Backspace (erases the preceding character)
$L	< (less-than symbol)
$N	Current drive
$P	Current drive name and path name
$Q	= (equal sign)
$T	Current time
$V	System DOS version number

Example 11

To create a prompt that includes current date and a dollar ($) sign, type the following command:

  PROMPT $D$$ (Enter)

It creates the prompt, Sat 11/23/2002$_.

1.5 DIRECTORY COMMANDS

Directory commands are specific to view the contents of the hard disk/floppy disk. These commands are also used for creating directory and sub-directory on the storage device such as hard disk/floppy disk.

1.5.1 The DIR Command

To find out what files are on a disk you can use the *dir* command. To display directory, type the following at the DOS prompt:

  C:\>dir (Enter)

A list of files and directories in *root* directory i.e. *main* directory of your disk drive such as C:\ drive will be displayed.

Example 12

To display only *one* screen of information at a time, type the following at the command prompt:

`dir/p` [Enter]

One screen of information would appear on your monitor. At the bottom of the screen, you will see the following message:

`press any key to continue...`

To view the next screen of information, press any key on your keyboard. Repeat this step until the command prompt appears at the bottom of the monitor screen.

To see a list of files widthwise or in a wide format, type the following at the command prompt:

`dir /w` [Enter]

The directory list appears, with the file names listed widthwise on the screen.

☞ *In width wise option, only file names are listed. Information about the files size or date and time of creation will not appear.*

You can also combine the **/p** and **/w** options together along with dir command.

`dir/w/p` [Enter]

➡ **To display hidden files do this:**

`C:\>dir\h` [Enter]

➡ **To display system files do this:**

`C:\>dir\s` [Enter]

You can also display files of some other directory or subdirectory, by specifying the full path of the directory after the DIR command. For example, to display a list of files present in **<DOS>** directory from the current or the root directory do this:

`C:\>dir\dos` [Enter] **or**

`C:\>dir dos` [Enter]

To display the directory listing of drive A, type the following command at the command prompt:

`C:\>dir a:` [Enter]

1.5.2 MD (Make Directory)

This command creates a new directory on the hard disk or floppy disk. The syntax is:

`MD drive:\path directory` **or**

`MKDIR drive:\path directory`

MD command requires that you provide a subdirectory name on the command line. If the subdirectory name is preceded by a backslash (/) it will be created one level below the root directory. If the name is preceded by a space it will be created one level below the currently logged subdirectory.

If you include an existing subdirectory path, the new subdirectory will be created one level below the indicated path.

If you include a drive letter, the subdirectory will be created on the existing drive.

Example 13

`MD \TEXT` [Enter]

The above command will create a subdirectory named **TEXT** one level below the root directory.

`C:\>MD \DATA\TEXT` [Enter]

The above command will create a subdirectory named **TEXT** one level below the **DATA** subdirectory if the **DATA** subdirectory already exists.

`C:\>MD \DATA\TEXT` [Enter]

The above command will create a subdirectory named **TEXT** one level below the **DATA** subdirectory if the **DATA** subdirectory already exists.

1.5.3 RD or RMDIR (Remove Directory)

This command removes empty sub directories. The syntax for the command is:

```
RD drive:\path\subdirectory
```

```
RMDIR drive:\path\subdirectory
```

RD command requires that you supply the name of a subdirectory that does not contain any files. You cannot remove the currently logged subdirectory. If the subdirectory that you want to remove is located on a different drive or nested below other sub directories, you must include the full subdirectory path for the unwanted directory on the command line.

Example 14

```
RD OLDDIR
```

Removes an empty subdirectory named **OLDDIR** located on a level just below the current subdirectory.

```
C:\>RD WORD\OLDDIR
```

removes an empty subdirectory named **OLDDIR** located one level below the **WORD** subdirectory, which is located just below the root directory on drive C:.

☞ *Directories that contain hidden or system files may appear empty, but cannot be removed until the hidden files are deleted or moved from the directory. To remove such directory first, delete the hidden files and then only delete the directory.*

1.5.4 Tree

This command displays the subdirectory structure of a drive. The syntax is:

```
TREE drive:\path/switches
```

Switch	Action
/F	Includes the file names in each subdirectory.
/A	Displays the subdirectory using standard ASCII characters rather than graphic characters.

Example 15

```
TREE | MORE
```

displays the subdirectory structure of the currently logged drive with pauses after each screen of information.

```
TREE C: /F/A > PRN  [Enter]
```

Displays the subdirectory structure of drive C, includes the file names in each subdirectory and sends the output to the standard printing device in ASCII format .

1.5.5 Path Command

This command specifies a list of sub directories (the *search path*) where DOS is to look for executable program files. The syntax is:

```
PATH drive:\path : drive:\path...
```

If used without parameters, **PATH** command displays the current search path. If you want to create or change the search path, invoke **PATH** followed by a list of the drives and sub directories where you want DOS to look for program files. Drive letters must be followed by colons. Subdirectory names must be preceded by a backslash (****).

If you do not include a drive letter, DOS will assume that the subdirectory is on the currently logged drive. Otherwise, it always looks for the subdirectory on the specified drive. The entire **PATH** command can include up to 127 characters.

Example 16

```
C:\>PATH  [Enter]
```

displays the search path or the message "No path" if path is not found.

The following command,

```
C:\>PATH C:\DOS:C:\WORD:C;\LOTUS;
C:\SYS;C:\ [Enter]
```

instructs DOS to look for program files on drive **C:** on sub directories **\DOS, \WORD, \LOTUS; \SYS;** and the root directory.

C:\>PATH **\DOS; \WORD; \LOTUS; \SYS; ** (Enter)

instructs DOS to look for program files on the same set of sub directories as in the previous example; however, DOS will look for them on whatever drive is currently logged.

☞ *The* **PATH** *command creates a search path for program files only. Program files have the extensions.* **.EXE, .COM,** *or* **.SYS**.

1.6 DOS UTILITY COMMANDS

OOS Utility commands are helpful in performing various operations on the files such as moving the files from one location to other, deleting files, etc.

1.6.1 Move

Move command moves files to different locations. It can also rename sub directories. This command can overwrite or delete data. The Syntax is:

MOVE source:\path\file(s) target:\path\file(s)

MOVE requires that you specify the name of a source file or files. You can include a drive letter or directory path if the source file is not on the currently-logged directory. Wildcards are allowed and will move groups of files that match the wildcard specification.

MOVE is the same as copying a file to a new location and then deleting the file in the original location, in a single command. You can rename a file as you move it by specifying a new name for the file. You can specify only one file as the source if you are renaming it at the same time. If you do not specify a *target* location, DOS attempts to move the source file to the currently logged directory.

Example 17

Let us learn what the following command does?

C:\MOVE C:\TEMP C:\NEWLOCA (Enter)

If **C:\TEMP** is a file, it is moved from the root directory to the **C:\NEWLOCA** directory. If **C:\TEMP** is a directory, it is renamed as **C:\NEWLOCA**

1.6.2 Scandisk

The directory tree and the *File Allocation Table* (FAT) stored on a disk are essential to access the data on the disk. If either one becomes damaged, you could lose contact with some–and perhaps– all of your files. This vital system information can become damaged in many ways. Malfunctioning hardware, pwer fluctuations, viruses, and not waiting for the drive light to go out before rebooting are just some of the possibilities.

DOS includes a program called SCANDISK that analyzes the FAT and directory structure, reports problems, and repairs most of the problems it finds. In addition, it test the surface of the disk for physical flaws and rescues any data from flawed areas. "CHKDISK and SCANDISK," are the two maintenance facilites that you should run on a regular basis to keep your hard disk in good running order. For example,

SCANDISK D:*.*

Displays a fragmentation report for all the files in the root directoy of drive D.

1.6.3 CLS

Cls is a command that allows a user to clear the complete contents of the screen and leave only a prompt. The cls command is an internal command. Running the cls command at the command prompt would clear your screen of all previous text and only return the prompt.

1.6.4 VER

Displays the version of MS-DOS. The ver command is an internal command.

1.7 GRAPHICAL USER INTERFACE (GUI)

Graphical User Interface abbreviated GUI is a graphics-based user interface that allows users to select files, programs, or commands by pointing to pictorial representation on the screen rather than by typing long, complex commands from a command prompt. Applications execute in windows, using a consistent set of pull-down menus, dialog boxes, and other graphical elements, such as scroll bars and icons. This consistency among interface elements is a major benefit for the user, because as soon as you learn how to use the interface in one program, you can use it in all programs running in the same environment. GUIs have emerged for most operating environments including Windows, Windows 7, UNIX and the OS/2 Desktop.

1.8 CONCEPT OF WINDOWS 98 OPERATING SYSTEM

Microsoft Windows 98 is the worlds largest selling Operating System for PCs. As soon as you switch on the power supply, Windows operating system program starts loaded in PC and takes over. It provides the communication link between your computer hardware and the software that you see. For example, when you tell your spreadsheet software to save a file, the operating system tells the computer system how and where to save it.

However, Windows 98 is more than an operating system. It provides functions that let you manage many program simultaneously, customize it, and do many of the maintenance taks associated with a PC. It also comes with many accessories, software programs, such as utilities and media player, etc.

1.8.1 What Does Microsoft Windows 98 Do?

Windows 98 takes care of PC and does many things in the background that are not visible to you. It keeps busy behind the scenes managing your software packages and hardware working. Windows 98 does the following jobs:

- Provides ways for you to start programs.

- Runs more than one program at a time. This is called multitasking and it means that you can run, for example, both a word processing program and spreadsheet program open at the same time and switching between them.

- Provides a way for you to manage files. Files are documents that you create, namely, letters, memos, and worksheets. Use Windows Explorer, the file management program that comes with Windows 98, to *copy, move, organize, delete,* and otherwise work with files.

- Helps you to set up Internet access. The Internet Connection wizard will help you set up an account with an Internet service provider if you do not already have one. Once you have an account, use Internet Explorer that comes with Windows, to surf the Web.

- Windows comes with Outlook Express which is an e-mail program. Use this program to send and receive electronic mail.

- Windows 98 comes with a number of useful accessory programs, such as WordPad a word processing program. It has a text editor called Notepad for typing notes, etc and other small documents.
- It Provides a way for you to customize the desktop and other screen areas of the monitor.

1.8.2 General Features of Windows 98

Analyzed bit by bit, Windows 98 is not a major upgrade as from Windows 3.x to Windows 95 was. It has many refinements, add-on, conveniences, and some important networking and administrative enhancements. Some features that are new to Windows 98 and not found in Windows 95 are the following:

- **Window Tune-Up Wizard:** A new program in the System Tools group keeps the operating system and hard disk in peak condition by defragmenting the hard disk, removing unnecessary startup commands, deleting unnecessary *temp, setup,* and *Internet files,* and checking a hard disk for errors. This results in faster program execution and more disk space.
- **Windows System Update:** This feature ensures that you have the latest system software such as drivers and system files that are available. You can access the Microsoft Web-based service over the Internet.
- **System File Checker Utility:** Along the same lines as the Windows System Update, which works on-line. This new utility works off-line when you are not connected to the Internet to verify if your Windows 98 system files (***.dll, *.com, *.vxd, *.drv, *.ocx, *.inf, *.hlp,** and so on) are altered, dead, or missing.

- **Disk Defragmenter Optimization Wizard:** Uses the process of disk defragmentation to increase the speed with which your applications run. Thus, the wizard creates a log file, which identifies your most commonly used programs. Once this log file has been created, it can be used by the disk defragmenter to store the files associated with those programs. By storing all of the files associated with a given application in the same location on your hard disk, this wizard optimizes the speed with which your application runs.
- **Enhanced Dr. Watson Utility:** This is a tool for capturing information about the system at the time of a program or system malfunction. Dr. Watson reports which program corrupted records the relevant details, such as state of the system, and can display it and/or save it on disk for later perusal.
- **New Backup Program:** The supplied backup program now supports SCSI tape devices, and has general enhancements so that backing up your data is simpler and faster.
- **Support for New Generation of Hardware:** Since Windows 95 came out, lots of new types of hardware has came up eg. Universal Serial Bus (USB), IEEE 1394, Accelerated Graphics Port (AGP), Advanced Configuration and Power interface (ACPI), and Digital Video Disc (DVD), and some new video conferencing devices. Windows 98 has drivers, controls, and software programs for these new hardware devices.
- **Support for Intel MMX Processors:** Provides support so that third parties can build software that exploits the Intel Pentium Multimedia Extensions (MMX) for fast audio and video support on the Intel Pentium processors.

- **ActiveMovie:** ActiveMovie is a new media-streaming architecture for Windows that delivers high-quality video playback while exposing an extensible set of interface upon which multimedia applications and tools can be built.

- **Display Setting Enhancements:** We can dynamically change our screen resolution and color depth without having to reboot Windows as in earlier versions

- **FAT 32:** FAT32 is an improved version of the FAT (File Allocation Table) file system that allows disks over two gigabytes to be formatted as a singe drive. FAT32 also uses smaller clusters than FAT drives, resulting in a more efficient use of space on large disks.

- **FAT32 Conversion Utility:** For added flexibility, Windows 98 includes a graphical FAT32 conversion utility, which can quickly and safely convert a hard drive from the original version of FAT to FAT32.

- **Multiple Display Support:** Multiple Display Support allows you to use multiple monitors and/or multiple graphics adapters on a single PC. This can be beneficial for doing work such as: desktop publishing, Web development, video editing, and for playing computer games.

- **Support for Multilink Channel Aggregation.** That means you can connect multiple modems together (assuming you have multiple dial-up phone lines available) to get higher transfer speeds to the Internet, other dial-up services, or remote computers.

- **Advanced Internet Browsing Functionality:** With Windows 98 (via Internet Explorer) surfing the Web has become easier due to advanced browsing capabilities such as AutoComplete, enhanced Web searching, improved Favorites list, navigation history on the Forward/Back buttons, and improved printing.

- **Tools for Internet Communication:** Windows 98 also contains rich tools for online communication including Outlook Express, Microsoft NetMeeting, Personal Web Server and the Web Publishing Wizard.

- **Client Support for Point-to-Point Tunneling Protocol (PPTP):** The Point-to-Point Tunneling Protocol (PPTP) provides a way to use public data networks, such as the Internet, to create virtual private networks connecting client PCs with servers.

- **Windows Scripting Host:** Windows 98 supports direct script execution from the user interface or the command line (a script is a series of commands that can be automatically executed). This support is provided via the Windows Scripting Host (WSH) and allows administrators and/or users to save time by automating many user interface actions such as creating a shortcut, connecting to a network server, disconnecting from a network server, etc.

- **Distributed Component Object Model (DCOM):** The Component Object Model (COM) allows software developers to create component applications. Now, Distributes COM (DCOM) in Windows 98 (and Windows NT 4.0) provides the infrastructure that allows DCOM applications (the technology formally known as Network OLE) to communicate across networks without needing to redevelop applications.

- **32-bit Data Link Control (DLC):** The Data Link Control (DLC) protocol is used primarily to access IBM Mainframe and IBM AS/400 computers. The 32-bit DLC protocol software built-in to Windows 98 enables a network administrator to add support for 32-bit and 16-bit DLC programs.

1.8.3 Starting Windows 98

Windows 98 startup logo appears when you switch on your PC and then, the Windows sign-on dialog box appears as seen in Figure 1.5. It asks you to type user's name and the password.

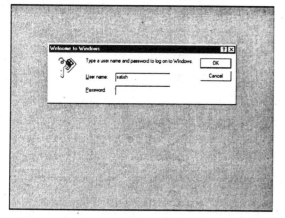

Figure 1.5 Welcome to Windows Dialog box

You may enter the user name and the password or press (Esc) or click Cancel button if you do not want to use the password. Thereafter, Windows opening screen appears as seen in Figure 1.6.

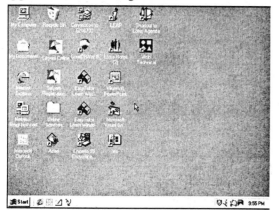

Figure 1.6 Windows 98 Opening Screen

The Windows operating system uses both mouse and keyboard as input devices. Interaction with Windows or any Windows application works most efficiently when options are chosen with a mouse and characters are entered *via* the keyboard.

1.8.4 Using the Mouse

A *mouse* is a very convenient hand-held pointing device which is used to control the position of the on-screen pointer. As you move the mouse on your desk or mouse pad, the pointer moves on the screen corresponding to the mouse movement. Using the mouse, you can *select menus, commands, text, graphic objects,* or *windows,* etc.

Main mouse actions are as follows:

Click

Press and release the left mouse button quickly as you point to an item. Clicking is used to reposition the insertion point in text, or to select a menu, or to choose a command from a menu, or select an option from a dialog box.

Double-click

As you point to the pointed item on the screen, press and release the left mouse button twice quickly. By double-clicking an icon or file name, you can open an application or window related icon or a file.

Right click

Position the tip of the mouse pointer at the desired location on a document or toolbar and then click the right mouse button.

(Shift)+click

Press and hold down the (Shift) key as you click. You use this method to select many consecutive file names, or to select text between the current insertion point and the location where you press (Shift)+click.

Ctrl +*click*

Press and hold down the Ctrl key as you click. This is used to select many nonconsecutive file names or item of choices.

Dragging

Dragging is moving objects on the PC's screen and it is similar to moving objects on a desk. For example, clicking and dragging an icon is like physically picking up a pencil with your hand on a desk and putting the pencil in a new location. Similarly, to move objects on your PC's screen, you first position the mouse pointer on the object. Next, you "pick up" the object by pressing and holding down the *left* mouse button. While you are still holding down the mouse button, move the mouse pointer to where you want to "drop" the object and then release the mouse button.

➡ **To select an object or menu item using the mouse, do this:**

1. Move the mouse so that the tip of the mouse pointer on the screen is on the *command, graphic object,* or *text* that you want to select.
2. Now without moving the mouse, press and release the left mouse button quickly.

➡ **To *drag* with the mouse, do this:**

1. Move the mouse so that the tip of the mouse pointer is on the object or at the beginning of the text to be selected. (See Figure 1.7) (Note that over text, the pointer appears as an I-beam.)
2. Press and hold down the left mouse button.
3. Holding down the mouse button, move the mouse slowly to the right or left and up or down. This is called *dragging*.
4. Release the mouse button.

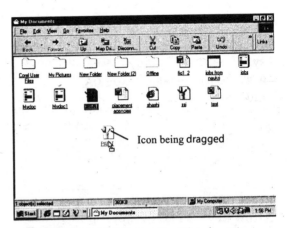

Figure 1.7 Moving an Icon by dragging

1.8.5 Using the Keyboard

The mouse and the keyboard work as a team for controlling the Windows 98 operations. Some tasks can be performed more easily with the mouse and some with the keyboard.

Keyboard Terminology

The following conventions are followed throughout the book while using the keyboard.

- A comma (,) sign between keystrokes indicates that you release the first key before pressing the second key say for example — Alt , Space bar means press and release the Alt key and then press Space bar .

- A plus (+) sign between keystrokes indicates that you press and hold down the first key and then press the second key say for example — Alt +Esc means press and hold down the Alt key and press the Esc key.

- Alt , **letter key:** Press and release the Alt key and then press the corresponding letter key. This action opens a menu without choosing a command.

- **Alt+letter key:** Press and hold down the Alt key and press the underlined letter key. This action opens a *menu* or selects an *option* in a dialog box.
- **Letter key:** Press the letter in the command that is <u>underlined</u> in the menu on-screen to choose a command in a menu (this book shows the letter you are to press in **<u>bold and underlined</u>**). Press **C**, for example, to choose the **C**opy command.
- **Arrow key:** Press the appropriate directional arrow key say for example, ⬆ ⬅ ⬇ ➡ arrow keys.

1.9 ELEMENTS OF WINDOWS SCREEN

The different parts of the Windows screen are as marked in Figure 1.8 and discussed in the following paragraphs.

1.9.1 The Desktop

The Desktop is work area on a Windows screen where you work in Windows. It is called the Desktop because Windows uses your whole screen in a way that is similar to the way you use the top of a desk. As you work in Windows, you move items on the Desktop, retrieve and put away items and perform many other day-to-day tasks.

1.9.2 Icons and their types

An icon is a graphic object that shows something on your monitor. The different types of icons are described below.

System Icons

System icons are displayed along left edge of the screen. These objects are created automatically by Windows 98 during its installation. The five system icons are explained in the following table.

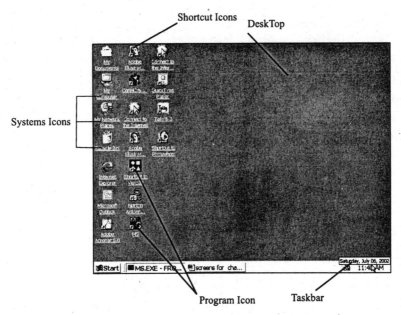

Figure 1.8 Different parts of the Windows Screen

System Icon	Function
My Computer	This icon lets you browse through the resources connected to your computer.
My Documents	This icon represents a folder that is used by many programs as a default location for starting the documents.
Internet Explorer	This icon starts Internet Explorer.
Network Neighborhood	This icon opens a Windows Explorer Window displaying the names of each server or computer in your own work group.
Recycle Bin	This icon provides temporary storage for files and folders that you delete.

Shortcut Icons

These are the icons with small arrows in the lower left corner. A shortcut icon provides easy access to some objects on your system, such as a *program*, a *document*, or a *printer*, etc. The shortcut icon only contains information about the location of the object but not the object itself.

☞ *Deleting a shortcut icon does not delete the program from the hard disk for that shortcut.*

Program, Folder and Document Icons

These are non–system icons without arrows and they represent the actual objects they describe.

☞ *Thus, if you delete such an icon you are deleting the object itself, from the hard disk. So be very careful!*

1.9.3 The Taskbar

The taskbar can be seen along the side or the top of the screen. The different parts of the taskbar are explained in the following table.

Taskbar Element	Function
Start button	It is located at the left end of the taskbar. Clicking the start button brings up the start menu as seen in Figure 1.9.
Toolbars	Toolbars represent a set of related icons for an easy access of mouse. For example, the Quick launch toolbar provides icons for launching Internet Explorer and Outlook Express. Windows provides several toolbars which you can use as per your convenience.
Task buttons	*Task buttons* are displayed in the center portion of the Taskbar. A button appears for each program you have started or each document you have opened. You can click these buttons to move from one open Program or Folder to another.
Notification Area	The right corner of the Taskbar has the notification area in which Windows provides information about the status of your system. To see the description of the icon appearing in the notification area, position the mouse pointer on the icon and the Screen Tip appears to give a brief description. The notification area also includes clock. The clock also works as a calendar, to display the current date. (See Figure 1.8) Position the mouse pointer over the clock and the current date appears.

1.10 VARIOUS TYPES OF WINDOW IN WINDOWS 98

There are three types of windows namely, *application window, document window* and *folder window*. Details of each type is given in the following sub sections.

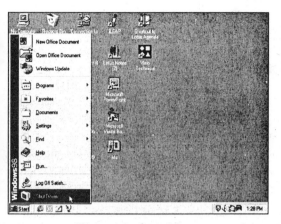

Figure 1.9 Start Menu

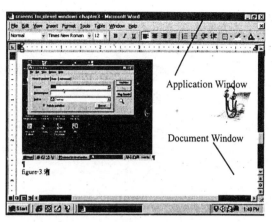

Figure 1.10 An application Window (Document Open in Microsoft Word)

1.10.1 Application window

Application windows are those windows that contain a program which you are running and working with, namely, Microsoft Word, Excel, Paint, etc. Most of the work that you do will be in application windows. Figure 1.10 shows a typical application window, also called a *parent window.*

1.10.2 Document Window

Document window is the those window that contain a document you are working on within an application window. Most of the applications allow you to have multiple document windows open at the same time (See in Figure 1.11).

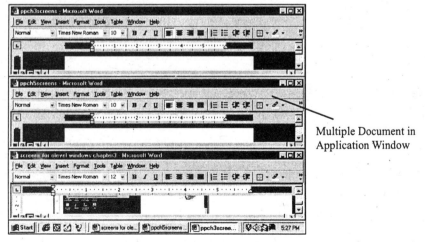

Figure 1.11 An application Window with Multiple Document Windows

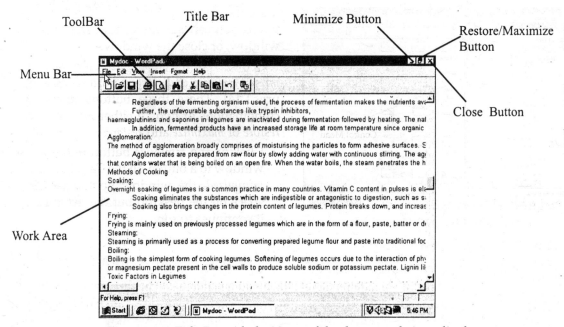

Figure 1.12   Title Bar with the Name of the document being edited

1.11   ELEMENTS OF A WINDOW

Most of the windows have the following similar elements and these are shown in Figure 1.12.

- Borders
- Title bar
- Control box
- Close button
- Minimize, Restore/Maximize button
- Menu bar
- Toolbar
- Work area

The use of all these elements is discussed in the following sections.

1.11.1   Borders

The four edges that define the perimeter of a window are called borders. Borders also gives a way to change the size of the window.

1.11.2   The Title Bar

Just below the top border of the window is the Title bar. It displays the name of the program or the document. For example, in Figure 1.12, Wordpad's Title bar shows the name of the document being edited. It is also used for moving the window.

➡ **To move a window do this:**

1. Position the mouse pointer in the Title bar of the window to be moved.
2. Now drag the Title bar i.e press and hold the left mouse button and move the pointer to reposition the window. The Title bar also indicates which window is active.

1.11.3   The Control Box

The Control box is the small icon located on the left side of the Title bar. The Control box performs two functions namely,

- It opens the Control menu as seen in Figure 1.13 whenever you click the Control

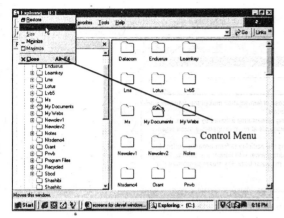

Figure 1.13 Control box menu

bar. In most of the programs the commands on a Control menu lets you control the size of the window. But some programs may have special items on their control menus.

- Control box for a program or document will close the window that terminates the program or closes the document when you double click it.

☞ *Pressing* (Alt)+(-) *keys opens the Control box of the active document window.* (Alt)+(Spacebar) *opens the Control box of the active application window.*

Close Button

At the right edge of the Title bar is a square containing an × called the Close button. Clicking the Close button closes a *document* or folder, or terminates a program. (See Figure 1.14)

Minimize, Maximize and Restore Buttons

The three small buttons at the right end of the Title bar as in Figure 1.14 with small graphics in them are the *Minimize* button, *Maximum* or *Restore* button, and the *Close*

buttons. These are control buttons with which you can quickly change the size of a window, or close the window.

To the left of the close button are the *Minimize, Maximize* and *Restore* buttons (See Figure 1.14). These three buttons appear in combinations of two i.e either *minimize* and *restore* or *maximize* and *restore*.

- Clicking the *minimize* button reduces the window to a button on the Task bar. Once *minimized*, the window no longer takes space on the desktop but the program in it continues to run.
- Clicking the *maximize* button enlarges the window to occupy the whole Desktop. When the window is *maximized*, the *minimized* and *restore* button appear.
- Clicking the restore button causes a window to assume an intermediate size i.e neither minimized nor maximized. In this case, the *minimized* and *maximized* button appear.

1.11.4 Scroll Bars, Scroll Boxes and Scroll Buttons

If a window is not long enough to display its contents completely, *vertical scroll bar* appears along the right edge. If the window is not wide enough, a *horizontal scroll bar* appears along the bottom of the window.

Scroll bars offer an easy way to navigate through a window with the mouse. They also provide useful information about the contents of the window.

Scroll bars have small rectangular boxes called scroll box (See Figure 1.15). The position of this box within the scroll bar tells you where you are within the window itself. If the scroll box is at the top of the scroll bar means you are at the top of the document.

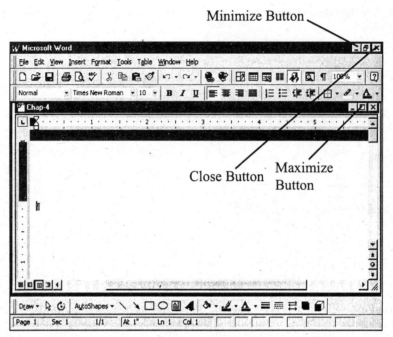

Figure 1.14 Minimize, Maximize and Close buttons

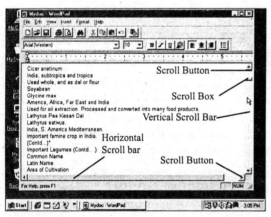

Figure 1.15 Scroll bars, Scroll boxes and Scorll buttons

Scroll buttons appear along the top and bottom edges of the vertical scroll bar and along the left and right edges of the horizontal scroll bar.

1.11.5 The Menu Bar

The row of words just below the Titlebar constitute the *Menubar*. The *Menubar* appears only in an application window and not in a document window. Each word on the Menubar represents a menu which opens up when you click it (See Figure 1.16). The names of the menus may vary from program to program but they have some common headings such as File, Edit, Window, and Help.

Choosing Menu Commands

Choosing a menu command involves two steps:

- Click to open it.
- Selecting the required command form the menu.

➡ To open a menu do this:

Using the mouse click the menu name. Or using the keyboard press Alt+(underlined letter in the menu name). For example, to open the Edit menu press Alt+E.

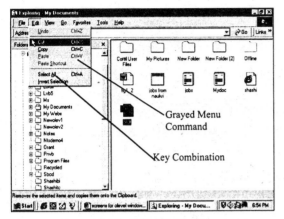

Figure 1.16 Edit Menu Open

1.11.6 Shortcut Menus

Pressing the right mouse button brings up a small menu related to the currently selected object or the one, the mouse is pointing to. This menu is at times also referred to as *pop up* menu. For example, if you right click the Taskbar, you get a menu of commands relating only to the Taskbar. (See Figure 1.17)

1.11.7 Dialog Boxes

A Dialog box will appear when you select a command with an ellipsis(...) after it. Dialog boxes appear on your screen when Windows or the Windows Application program you are using needs more information to execute the command.

1.11.8 Dialog box tabs

Some of the dialog boxes (See Figure 1.18) have multiple option pages. You select the

- By typing the underlined letter in the command name (e.g. **t** for cut in Figure 1.16)
- By clicking on a command's name.
- By pressing the ⬇ arrow or ⬆ arrow keys to highlight the desired command name and then pressing Enter.

To close a menu without selecting any command, press the Esc key or click anywhere outside the menu.

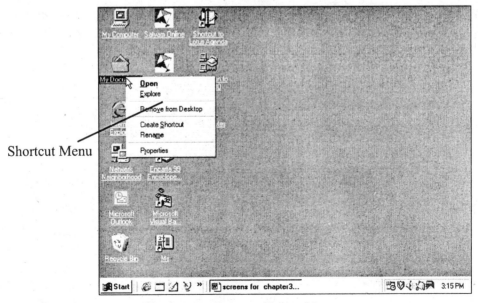

Figure 1.17 Shortcut/Popup Menu

page you are interested in by clicking its icon at the top of the dialog box. Using the keyboard, press (Ctrl)+(tab) to flip through the option pages.

Moving between Dialog Box Elements

Dialog boxes often have several sections in them as seen in Figure 1.18. You can move between the sections in three ways:

- By clicking on the section you want to change.
- Using the keyboard, you can press the (Tab) key to move between sections and press the (Spacebar) to select them. Or
- Press the (Alt)+underlined letter of the section name you want to jump to.

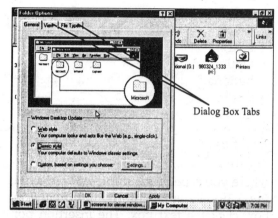

Dialog Box Tabs

Figure 1.18   Dialog box Tabs

Entering Information in a Dialog Box

The dialog boxes have following eight different types of sections where you need to enter information (See Figure 1.19).

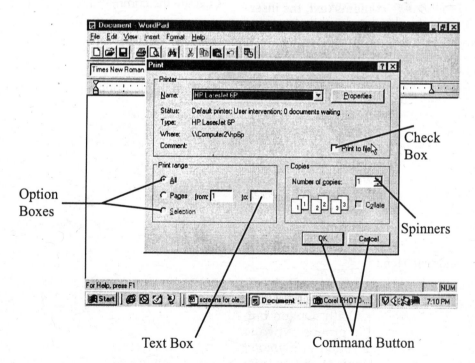

Figure 1.19   Different section of a dialog box

- Text boxes
- Check boxes
- Option buttons
- Command buttons
- List boxes
- Drop-down list boxes
- Sliders
- Spinners

Text Boxes

Text box is also called an *Edit box* and it is where you type in the information (See Figure 1.19). To enter information in the text box, click the text box. The insertion point appears in the text box. The insertion point indicates the place where the character you type will appear.

- If the text box is empty, the insertion point appears at the left side of the box.
- If the box already contains text, the insertion point appears at the point where you clicked the mouse.

Check Boxes Check boxes are small square boxes (See Figure 1.19). Each check box is independent of all other check boxes in the dialog box. To select a check box item, click the box or anywhere in the text next to the box and similarly, to deselect repeat the same procedure. A check box when selected displays an (×) or (✔) within the box. Some check boxes have three states — *checked, unchecked,* and *partly checked.* A gray (in place of a black) check mark means that certain condition applies to it and some of the selections do not apply.

Option Buttons These are also called *radio buttons* and present a set of mutually exclusive options (See Figure 1.19). Option buttons are always present in groups of two or more and may either be round or diamond shaped. You may select any one option from the group but not more than one. To select the option click the button or any where in the text next to the button.

Command Buttons Command buttons are like option buttons and are used to execute a command immediately. They are rectangular and not square or circular in shape. An example of a command button is the OK button found on almost every dialog box. (Figure 1.20)

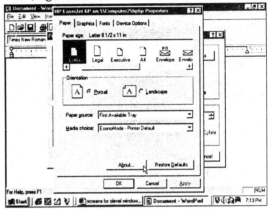

Figure 1.20 Command Button with Ellipses(...)

List Boxes A List box presents a list of options or items from which you can choose. To make a selection from a list box, using the mouse, click on it or using the keyboard highlight the desired option and then press (Enter) to choose it.

Drop-Down List Boxes A *Drop down list box* looks like a text box with a downward pointing arrow to the right. When you click the downward-pointing arrow (or press (Alt)+(↓)), a list box opens up. It works just like a normal list box and has scroll bars. If there are a lot of options, then Drop-down list boxes are used.

Sliders A slider works like a sliding control. Moving it in one direction increases some value, moving it in the other direction decreases the same value.

Spinners A spinner is a pair of arrows used to increase or decrease the value in a text box. (See Figure 1.20). To increase the value in the text box, click the up arrow and to decrease the value click the down arrow.

1.12 THE MY COMPUTER ICON

The My Computer icon lets you browse through all the resources attached to your PC. When you click on My Computer icon, a Windows Explorer window similar to the one shown in Figure 1.21 appears. Windows Explorer is a program that Windows uses to display folder contents. This window includes icons for each of the computer's disk drives (floppy, hard disk, CD-ROM,) and network directories if you have connected your PC to a network. It also shows additional *system folders*, providing access to the Windows Control Panel, printers, Dial-Up Networking, and a folder that manages scheduled tasks.

☞ *To change the name, of My Computer Icon, right-click the icon. Choose Rename from the context menu, type the name you want to use and then press* (Enter) *key.*

Figure 1.21 My Computer in Windows Explorer window

1.13 MY DOCUMENTS

Folders can contain many different types of files, such as documents, music, pictures, videos, and programs. You can copy and move files from other locations, such as another folder, computer, or the Internet, to folders you create. You can even create folders within folders.

For example, if you are creating and storing files in the My Documents folder, you can make a new folder within My Documents to contain the files. If you decide that you want to move the new folder to a different location, you can easily move it and its contents by selecting the folder and dragging it to the new location.

1.14 NETWORK NEIGHBORHOOD

Network Neighborhood is the gateway to all available network resources, just as My Computer is the gateway to all the resources stored on PC system. Launching Network Neighborhood opens a Window of your immediate workgroup.

☞ *If your computer is not part of a network, the Network Neighborhood icon would not appear on your desktop.*

1.14.1 Using Network Neighborhood to Find Network Files

Opening the Network Neighborhood icon provides a Windows Explorer window displaying the names of each server or computer in your workgroup. In addition, the Network Neighborhood folder includes an Entire Network icon, which you can use to access other workgroups on your network.

In addition to entries for each workstation in your workgroup, the Network Neighborhood folder includes an entry labeled Entire Network. Launching Entire Network opens a folder that displays a top-level view of the entire network.

1.15 THE RECYCLE BIN

Files and folders deleted from your hard drives are not actually deleted but transferred to the *Recycle bin*. The Recycle Bin icon appears on the desktop and looks like a waste paper basket. When you open the icon, a Folder window opens, displaying the files and folders that have been deleted since the Recycle Bin was last emptied. In effect the Recycle Bin works like a folder.

☞ *Unlike a folder, the Recycle Bin is not contained on a single drive. Each of your computer's hard drives maintains its own Recycle folder, and the contents of all of the Recycle folders are visible whenever you open the Recycle Bin. (See Figure 1.22)*

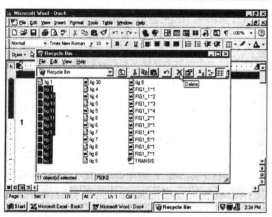

Figure 1.22 Recycle Bin with files being deleted

1.16 WORKING WITH FILES AND FOLDERS

Files and folders are two of the most fundamental concepts of the Windows operating system. You create and organize files and folders as soon as you save your work in a PC.

1.16.1 File

A file is any collection of related information that is given a name and stored on a disk so that it can be read and manipulated whenever required.

☞ *A file can contain any kind of information: a program or application or a document; a part of a document, such as a table or a graphic; a sound or a piece of music, etc.*

1.16.2 Folder

As you work in Windows you would see that a hard disk contains hundreds of files even before you start creating your own files. It would be impossible to keep a track of all these files if they are not arranged properly. In Windows 98 the fundamental device for managing files is the *folder*.

☞ *A folder is a special kind of file that contains a list of other files or subfolders. The files on the list are said to be in the folder, and each file is allowed to be in only one folder at a time.*

A folder can be either open or closed. When it is closed, all you see is its name and the folder icon (See Figure 1.23). When a folder is open, it has its own window, and the files contained in the folder are shown in the window.

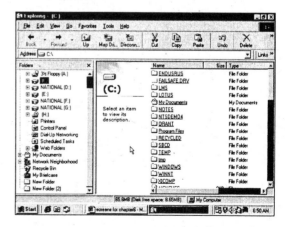

Figure 1.23 Folder Name with Folder Icon

1.16.3 The Folder Tree

The arranging power of the folder system lies in the fact that it is hierarchical, similar to a family.

☞ *Hierarchical means that folders can contain other folders. This feature allows you to organize and keep track of a large numbers of folders.*

If Folder *A* is *inside* Folder *B*, then Folder *A* is a *subfolder* of *B*. Any folder can contain as many subfolders as you want, but each sub-folder (like each file) is contained in only one folder. And so, a diagram showing which folders are contained in which other folders looks something like a family tree. This diagram is called the *folder tree*, or the *folder hierarchy*. Windows Help calls it the *folder list*.

At the top of the folder tree is the founder of the Folder family, namely the desktop. Next to the desktop are *My Computer*, etc. and additional files and folders that you might have copied to the desktop. (See Figure 1.23)

Underneath My Computer are icons representing all of your system's storage media: *hard drives, floppy drives, CD-ROMs,* and so on.

Basic file and folder operations are the following:

- Selecting
- Creating
- Naming
- Opening

1.16.4 Selecting Files and Folders

Windows works on the rule, *select* and *do*. It means, you first have to select the file or folder you want to use. Files and folders are represented in Folder and Windows Explorer windows by icons, with the name of the file or folder printed underneath its icon.

➡ **To select and open a file or folder do this:**

- In *Web style* view, to select a file or folder, move the cursor over its icon. When the icon appears highlighted, the object is selected. To open the file or folder, single-click the icon.
- In *Classic style*, to select an object single click the object that you want. To open an object double click it.

☞ *To select more than one object, select the first object, and then press the* (Ctrl) *key while selecting other objects.*

➡ **To select all the items in a folder do this:**

1. Open a Folder or Windows Explorer window.
2. Click the <u>E</u>dit menu and choose **Select All**. Or press (Ctrl)+(A) keys together on the keyboard.

1.16.5 Creating Files and Folders

➡ **To create a new File/Folder do this:**

1. In the Windows Explorer or Folder window click the <u>F</u>ile menu and choose <u>N</u>ew. *Alternatively*, right click an empty area of the Desktop and choose <u>N</u>ew.
2. In both the cases a submenu listing the new objects you can create: *folders, short-cuts,* and a variety of types of files (see Figure 1.24).
3. Select an element of this list. Windows 98 creates the selected object.

Naming and Renaming Files and Folders

➡ **To rename a file or folder, do this:**

1. Select the file/folder in the Explorer window you want to rename. Click the <u>F</u>ile menu and choose re<u>n</u>ame. *Alternatively*, right click the file/folder and choose Rena<u>m</u>e from the context menu.

2. A box appears around the current name, and the entire name is selected. Type the new name in the box and press (Enter) (See Figure 1.25).

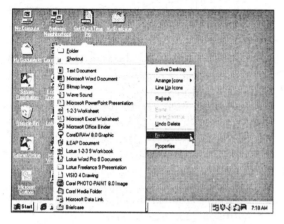

Figure 1.24 Submenu Indicating the News Objects that can be created

In Classic style, you can also rename by selecting an object, and then clicking the name text of the icon. A box appears around the current name. Now follow as in step 2 above.

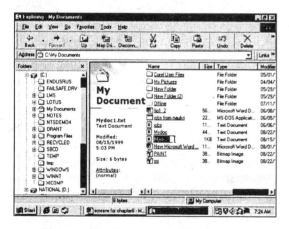

Figure 1.25 Renaming a file Mydoc1

To edit the old name instead of typing the new one, Click inside the name-box at the place where you want to begin typing or deleting.

Opening Files and Folders

Any object in a Windows Explorer or Folder window can be opened by single-clicking (*in Web style*) or double-clicking (*in Classic style*) its icon.

Moving or Copying Folders, Files

To move or copy an object in the Windows Explorer window, right-drag it from its current position to its destination. When you release the mouse button, the shortcut menu appears, as seen in Figure 1.26 From this Shortcut menu, choose *Copy Here, Move Here,* or *Create Shortcut(s) Here.* Make the selection, you need.

Figure 1.26 Shortcut menu

☞ *If you open a file of a known file type, Windows opens it with the application associated with that file type. However, if you open a file in a Windows Explorer or Folder window, and Windows 98 does not recognize its file type, or if that file type has no associated application, Windows would open with a box asking you to identify an application to use for opening the file.*

Dragging-and-Dropping Files and Folders

Drag-and-drop is the simplest way to move or copy objects from one drive or folder to another, or between a folder and the desktop. You can also delete objects by dragging-and-dropping them onto the Recycle Bin icon.

➡ To drag-and-drop files or folders do this:

1. Set up the window(s) so that you can see both the *source* and the *target* in a Windows Explorer window. Open the source folder in one window. In the other window, you can either open the target folder, or simply have its icon visible.
2. Select the icons of the objects that you want to drag-and-drop.
3. While holding down the left mouse button, drag the icons to the target. If the target is an open window, drag the icons to an open space in the window. If the target is an icon in an open window, drag until the cursor rests over the icon. The target icon changes colour when you have the cursor in the right place.
4. Drop by releasing the mouse button.

☞ *To copy the objects press and hold down the* Ctrl *key as you drag.*
To move objects press and hold down the Shift *key as you drag.*
To create a shortcut press and hold down Ctrl *and* Shift *keys as you drag.*

Deleting Files and Folders

➡ To delete file(s) and folder(s) do this:

1. Select the objects to be deleted in Folder or Windows Explorer window.

2. Click the Delete button on the toolbar.

3. Click **Yes** in the dialog box.

Alternatively, you can right click the objects and then choose **Delete** from the context menu. The dialog box as in step 2 above appears.

☞ *Under the default settings, objects deleted from your computer's hard drive go to the Recycle Bin, from which they can be recovered, if desired later.*

Using the Undo Button

The Standard Buttons toolbar in Folder windows or Windows Explorer windows has an Undo button—the button with the counterclockwise arrow on it. If you delete something you wanted to keep, or cut-and-paste the wrong files, just click Undo and you can say that the mistake never happened.

☞ *Clicking Undo multiple times steps you back through your recent actions only.*

1.16.6   Finding Files and Folders

Windows offers a number of ways to find files and folders. Search offers the most direct way to locate a file. Use Search if you are looking for common file types. If you remember all or part of the name of the file or folder you want to find, or if you know when you last changed a file. If you know only part of the name, you can use wildcard characters to locate all files or folders that include that part in the name.

Windows Explorer provides a quick way to see all the files and folders on your computer, and it is also a good way to copy or move files from one folder to another. Use Windows Explorer if you know where the file or folder is located.

By using Find, you can search for a file:

• By name or part of a name
• By date created, modified, or last accessed
• By file type
• By size
• By a string of text contained in the file
• By some combination of all the above

All searches that you do with Find allow the same basic.

Starting the Find Process

1. Select **Start** menu and choose **Files or Folder**. Or Choose the **Tools** menu and choose **Find** and then select **Files or Folders** command from a folder or Windows explorer window.

2. Type the information about the files or folder you want to find into the *Name & Location, Date* or *Advanced tabs* of the **Find** dialog box.

3. Click Find Now button to start searching for all files or folders that you given in the **Named:** text box.

   The magnifying glass icon moves in circles while the search continues. As matching files and folders are found, they appear in a window at the bottom of the Find dialog box.

4. If you are not satisfied with the files and folders that Find locates, change the information you entered and search again. When you are done, close the Find dialog box.

1.17 The Control Panel

The *Control Panel*, is a window that displays icons for a number of programs that let you control your computer. Windows 98, and the software you have installed. These programs help you see and change the properties of many parts of Windows 98.

➡ **To open Control Panel do this:**

1. Click the start button highlight <u>S</u>ettings and choose Control Panel. The Control Panel window appears. The various icons available in the control panel are as follows.

☞ *The icons in the Control Panel Window may include these programs, depending on what Windows 98 components and any other software you have installed on your computer.*

Accessibility Options

The Accessibility Properties dialog box lets you configure Windows 98's keyboard, sound, display, mouse, and other options, for people with disabilities. This icon appears only if you installed Accessibility options when you installed Windows 98.

Add New Hardware

The Add New Hardware Wizard configures Windows 98 when you add new hardware to your computer system. To add new hardware click this icon in Control Panel.

Add/Remove Programs

The Add/Remove Programs Properties dialog box helps you install new programs or uninstall programs you no longer use. To change Add/Remove Properties click this icon.

Date/Time

The Date/Time Properties dialog box lets you set the date, time, and time zone where you are located. To change Date/Time Properties, click the Date/Time icon in the Control Panel.

Display

The Display Properties dialog box controls the appearance, resolution, screen saver, and other settings for your display monitor. To change display properties click the display icon in Control Panel window.

Fonts

The Fonts window lets you install new screen and printer fonts. To change Fonts, click Fonts icon in Control Panel window.

Game Controllers

The Game Controllers dialog box lets you install games. To change Game controller Properties click Game controllers in Control Panel Window.

Internet

The Internet Properties dialog box contains settings for your web browser and Internet connection. To change Internet Properties click Internet icon in Control Panel.

Keyboard

The Keyboard Properties dialog box contains settings that control your keyboard and the cursor. To change keyboard properties click keyboard icon in Control Panel window.

Mouse

The Mouse Properties dialog box lets you define the buttons on your mouse. It lets you choose how fast you need to double-click, what your mouse pointer looks like on-screen, and whether moving the mouse leaves a trail. To change mouse properties click mouse icon in Control Panel window.

Multimedia

The Multimedia Properties dialog box contains settings for the audio, video, MIDI, and audio CD settings of your computer. To change multimedia properties click multimedia icon in Control Panel window.

Network

The Network dialog box contains settings, you use when configuring a local area network. It also contains settings for connecting to the Internet. To change Network properties click Network icon in Control Panel window.

Passwords

The Passwords Properties dialog box lets you set a password for using Windows on your computer, user profiles if more than one person will use the computer, and other security settings. To change Passwords properties click the password icon in Control Panel window.

Power Management

The Power Management Properties dialog box contains controls to be set when Windows 98 automatically turns off your monitor, hard disks, and other computer components to save electricity. To change Power Management Properties click Power Management icon in Control Panel.

Printers

The Printers dialog box includes icons for each printer to which you have access, as well as an icon for adding a new printer. To change Printer properties click printer icon in Control Panel window.

Regional Settings

The Regional Setting Properties dialog box lets you tell Windows 98 the time zone, currency, number format, and date format you prefer to use. To change Regional settings, click Regional settings icon in Control Panel window.

Sounds

The Sounds dialog box lets you assign a sound to each Windows event, or events in other programs. For example, you can set your computer to play a fanfare when your e-mail program receives new messages. To change Sounds Properties click sound icon in Control Panel window.

System

The System Properties dialog box lets you use the Device Manager to change advanced settings for each hardware component of your computer. You can also optimize the performance of your computer. To change system properties click the system icon in Control Panel window.

Telephony

The Dialing Properties dialog box contains settings that control how Widows 98 dials the phone using your modem. To change telephony properties click the Telephony icon in Control Panel window.

Users

The Enable Multi-user Settings Wizard helps you set up users names and passwords so your computer can be used by more than one person. Each person's user name can store that person's desktop settings. To change users properties click the users icon in Control Panel window.

☞ *You may see additional icons if you have installed additional hardware or software on your computer.*

1.18 WINDOWS EXPLORER

Windows Explorer is a file and folder manipulating program that you can launch by selecting **Start** menu highlight **Programs** and choose **Windows Explorer**. The folder tree is displayed in the left pane called the Explorer bar, with the open folder highlighted. The contents of the open folder appear in the right pane.

The rest of the Windows Explorer window is similar to the Folder window. The title bar gives the name of the open folder. Beneath the title bar are the same menu bar and toolbars as in the Folder window. At the bottom of the window lies the status bar. The toolbars and status bar appear or disappear by toggling the toolbar or status bar commands on the view menu.

➡ **To start Windows Explorer in Open view do the following:**

Double click a Folder icons or Shortcut. The Folder Window opens.

➡ **To start Windows Explorer in Explorer View do the following:**

1. Click the Start button.
2. Highlight the Programs menu item.
3. Now choose Windows Explorer. Windows Explorer open in Explorer view as in Figure 1.27. *Alternatively* Right click a folder or shortcut menu appears. From the Popup menu choose Explorer. Windows Explorer opens in Explorer view.

The different elements of the Windows Explorer in the explorer view are shown in Figure 1.27. The role played by various elements in these two views are given in Table 1.4

Table 1.4 Elements and their function in the two views of Windows Explorer

Element	Function
Explorer box	The left part of the Windows Explorer window is called the *Explorer bar*
Standard toolbar	The standard toolbar is displayed just below the menu bar and the different buttons and the tool bar are as marked in Figure 1.27.
Up button	It makes the window up the folder tree.
Editing tool buttons	The five buttons after the up button are *cut, copy, past, undo* and *delete*. These editing buttons provide short cut to the file/folder operation.
Back; Forward Buttons	The back buttons moves to the previous folder it displayed. The forward button does the opposite. If

(Contd...)

Element	Function
	the back button appears grayed, it means you are at the first folder in window. If the forward button appears grayed it means you are in the last folder window. The Back/Forward buttons have downward pointing arrows attached to them. Clicking the arrow produces a list of locations you can go back or forward.
Property button	The property button when checked (i.e x), it brings up the properties dialog box for the selected object.

(Contd...)

Element	Function
View button	The view button allows you to choose among the several options for representing the contents of a folder.
Address box	The address box on the Address box toolbar. It displays the name and address of the open folder.
List tool bar	The list tool bar appears to the right of the address bar and has the buttons that connects you to the various Microsoft web sites. This toolbar is required if you are connected to the Internet.
Status bar	The right side of the status bar displays the name of the folder.

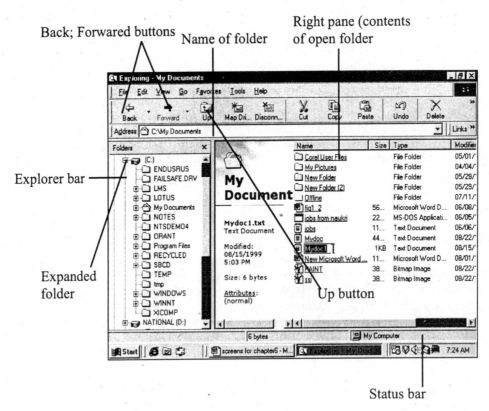

Figure 1.27 Windows Explorer in Open view

☞ *In the classic style open view of the Windows Explorer, the Back/Forward buttons do not perform any function.*

1.19 SHORTCUTS

A shortcut is a small file that is linked to a *program, document, folder,* or an *Internet address*. The file is represented by an icon with an arrow in its lower left corner, as in Figure 1.28.

If the shortcut is linked to a file or folder, that file or folder can be located anywhere—on a local hard disk or CD-ROM drive or on a floppy disk.

☞ *A shortcut is a pointer to an object, and not the object itself. This means that you can create and delete shortcuts without affecting any other objects.*

1.19.1 Creating a Shortcut

A shortcut can be created in the following three ways:
- by dragging and dropping or
- by using cut and paste or
- by using the Create Shortcut wizard.

➡ **To create a shortcut using drag and drop do this:**

1. If the item for which you want to create a shortcut is visible in a Windows Explorer window, right-drag that item to wherever you want the shortcut to appear. Then, from the context menu, choose **Create Shortcut(s)**.
2. You can also drag an item from the Start menu to create a shortcut on the desktop. Click the Start button to open the menu. Move your mouse pointer to the menu item for which you want to create a shortcut. Then drag the item on to your desktop.

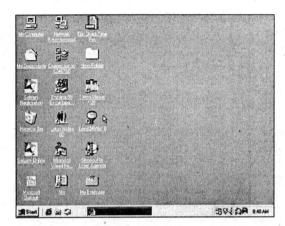

Figure 1.28 Shortcut on the Desk top for different application

3. You can turn any Web link into a dekstop shortcut by simply dragging the link (the underlined text) and dropping it on the desktop. Clicking or double-clicking that shortcut later will activate your browser, and it would connect you to the Internet, and take your browser to the appropriate URL.

➡ **To create a shortcut using copy and paste do this:**

1. Right click the items for which you want to create a shortcut.
2. From the context menu choose **C**opy.
3. Now right click on the desktop and choose paste from the context menu.

➡ **To create a shortcut using the create shortcut wizard do this:**

1. Right-click the desktop, from the Context menu, choose **N**ew, and then choose Shortcut.
2. Wizard for Create Shortcut appears, as seen in Figure 1.29.
3. Click the B**r**owse... button. The Browse dialog box appears. Locate the item for which you want to create a shortcut.

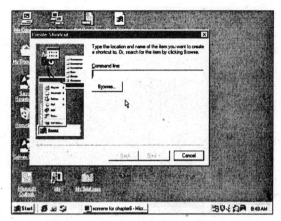

Figure 1.29 Create Shortcut Wizard

4. Click the Open button. After you click Open, the wizard returns you to its initial dialog box, with the command line filled in.

5. Click **N**ext, type a name for your shortcut, click **Finish**, and the shortcut will appear.

1.19.2 Renaming a Shortcut

When you create a shortcut, Windows gives it a default name based on the underlying object.

➡ **To change the shortcut name do this:**

1. Right-click the shortcut
2. From the context menu, choose R**e**name
3. Type the name you want to use.

☞ *You can also rename any object by selecting it, pressing* F2 *key and typing the new name.*

1.19.3 Deleting a Shortcut

➡ **To delete a shortcut do this:**

1. Select the icon and press the Del key. *Alternatively*, right click the shortcut to be deleted and choose **D**elete from the context menu.

2. Windows asks you for conformation before deletion.

☞ *Note that deleting a shortcut does not delete the program or document that the shortcut points to. In doing so it deletes only the shortcut itself.*

1.20 SCANDISK

The ScanDisk utility in Windows 98 diagnoses and repairs errors on hard disks, diskettes, and laptop memory cards. It also checks the physical surface of disk drive for bad sectors. Moreover, it checks the File Allocation Table (FAT), and directory structure.

➡ **To start ScanDisk do as follows:**

1. Click the Start button, highlight **P**rograms, highlight Accessories then highlight System Tools and click ScanDisk. The ScanDisk dialog box appears.

2. To select the dri**v**es you want to check for errors, select the drive you want to scan.

3. In the Type of test choose between stan**d**ard and **T**horough. If you select Thorough option you can further select the options by clicking the **O**ptions button.

4. To select the other options, click the **A**dvanced button.

5. After choosing the option select **S**tart.

1.21 DISK DEFRAGMENTATION

This utility in Windows 98 rearranges files so that they are contiguous and thus makes the access of the hard disk faster.

➡ **To run Disk Defragmentation do as follows:**

1. Click the Start button, highlight Programs, highlight Accessories then highlight System Tools and click Disk Defragmentation. Select the drive you want to clean up.

2. In the select drive dialog box select the drive you want to defragement. To change the setting click the settings tab to start the defragmentation and then click OK.

☞ *Defragmentation is a very time consuming process and you can stop it any time by clicking the stop button.*

1.22 IMPORTANCE OF DOS WITHIN WINDOWS

There are still some things that Windows can not do compared to DOS. The Windows Disk-copy and disk format are compared to the original DOS ones. And windows can not do multiple renaming which DOS can. And DOS batch files can be quite powerful, useful and easy to learn for automated tasks. But the most important one is-you will need to restore Windows in case Windows crashes.

In addition to its name, each file and folder in Windows 98 has an *MS-DOS name*. The MS-DOS name exists for the purpose of backward compatibility with programs written for MS-DOS or earlier versions of Windows. So, when dealing with pre-Windows 95 or Windows 98 application programs, Windows gives the application the MS-DOS name of a file rather than its real name.

➡ **To see a file or folder's MS-DOS name do the following:**

1. Select the file or folder in a Folder or Windows Explorer window.

2. Right click the file and choose Properties from the content menu. Alternatively, click the Properties button on the toolbar. The file or folder's Properties dialog box appears.

3. Click the General tab.

4. At the top of the third section of the page you will see the MS-DOS Name of a file.

1.22.1 Files and Folders Properties

Files and folders in Windows 98 have *properties*. It gives the information about a *file* or *folder* that can be accessed and changed without opening the file or folder.

The General Properties of a file are as follows:

- Name and icon
- File type
- Location in the folder tree
- Size
- MS-DOS name
- Date and time of creation, the recent modification, and the recent access
- The Attributes

1.22.2 File Attributes

The *attributes* are the markers to identify certain characteristics of *Files/Folders*. The various attributes of files are given in Table 1.5. The attributes of a file or folder appear at the bottom of the General tab of the Properties dialog box.

Table 1.5 File Attributes

Attribute	Explanation
Read-only	You can only read this file or folder, but can not delete or modify it. If you try to delete a read-only file or folder, Windows asks if you really want to delete it. First you will require to change its attribute and then only delete it.
Hidden	File or Folder that does not usually appear in Folder or Windows Explorer windows.

(Contd...)

Attribute	Explanation
Archive	Depending on Which backup program you use, this setting may means that the file or folder has been changed since the last time it was backed up.
System	This file or folder is part of Windows 98 itself, and may not appear in Folder or Windows Explorer windows.

1.23 DIFFERENCE BETWEEN SERVER AND WORKSTATION

1.23.1 Server

A server is a computer containing programs that provides services to other coputer programs in the same or other computers. The computer that runs server programs is frequently referred to as a server. In the client/server programming model, a server is a program that awaits and fulfills requests from client programs in the same or other computers.

☞ *A given application in a computer may function as a client with requests for services from other programs and also as a server of requests from other programs.*

1.23.2 Workstation

A workstation is a computer intended for individual use that is faster and more capable than a personal computer. Its purpose is for business or professional use. Workstations and applications designed for them are used by samll engineering companies, architects, graphic designers, and any organization, department, or individual that requires a faster microprocessor, a large amount of random access memory (RAM), and special features such as high-speed graphics adapters.

☞ *The workstation developed technologically for the same audience as the UNIX operating system, which is often used as the workstation operating system.*

1.24 INTRODUCTION TO CLIENT/SERVER

Client/server describes the relationship between two computer programs in which one program, the client, makes a service request from another program, the server, which fulfills the request. Although the client/server idea can be used by programs within a single computer, it is a more important idea in a network. In a network, the client/server model provides a convenient way to interconnect programs that are distributed efficiently across different locations. Computer transactions using the client/server model are very common. For example, to check your bank account from your computer, a client program in your computer forwards your request to a server program at the bank. That program may in turn forward the request to its own client program that sends a request to a database server at another bank computer to retrieve your account balance. The balance is returned back to the bank data client, which in turn serves it back to the client in your personal computer, which displays the information for you.

☞ *The client/server model has become one of the central ideas of network computing. Most business applications being written today use the client/server model.*

In the client/server model, one server, sometimes called a daemon, is activated and awaits client requests. Typically, multiple client programs share the services of a common server program. Both client programs and server programs are often part of a larger program or application. Relative to the Internet, your Web browser is a client program that requests services (the sending of Web pages or files) from a Web server (which technically is called a Hypertext Transport Protocol or HTTP server) in another computer somewhere on the Internet.

☞ *Similarly, your computer with TCP/IP installed allows you to make client requests for files from File Transfer Protocol (FTP) servers in other computers on the Internet.*

Summary

This chapter presents concepts of Operating System. It also explains different types of operating systems. Character User Interface commands are discussed. Working in command line are: view the contents of a directory by using the dir command. Change directories by using the cd command. Create directories by using the md command. Delete directories by using the rd command. Copy files by using the copy command. Rename files by using the ren command and Delete files by using the del command. And finally the concept of window and general features of window are discussed for working in GUI opearting systems such as Windows 98.

REVIEW QUESTIONS WITH ANSWERS

A. Multiple Choice

1. One of the following statements of Internal commands is not true.

    a. Internal commands are those that have builit into MS-DOS

    b. At the time of booting, Internal commands are automatically loaded into memory

    c. Internal commands are executed instantly without referring to the disk

    d. None of the above

2. One of the following on External commands is incorrect.

    a. External commands are stored onto disk in the form of a file

    b. For executing External commands they must be first loaded into memory

    c. For executing these commands path must be set to DOS directory

    d. None of the above

3. The purpose of the MOVE command is to

    a. move one or more files to the location you specify

    b. rename directories

    c. both a and b above

    d. None of the above

4. The _____ provides access to all active application by maintaining a row of open application title boxes.

    a. Title bar   c. Start menu

    b. Task bar   d. None

5. The appropriate application has to be selected from _____ in the Start menu to run the application.

    a. Programs   c. Documents

    b. Help   d. None

6. GUI is used as an interface between

    a. Hardware & Software

    b. Man & Machine

    c. Software and user

    d. None of the above

7. A file deleted from C: drive in Windows goes to _____.

    a. Recycle Bin   c. Windows Explorer

b. My Computer   d. Permanently deleted
8. An application can be opened through shortcut on desktop by
   a. Double clicking on its shortcut
   b. Right clicking and choosing "Open" option
   c. Selecting the icon and pressing Enter
   d. All of the above
9. Windows Explorer is a file management programs that you can use to:
   a. View and change the folder/file structures of your disks
   b. View and change the contents of your folder and files
   c. Move, copy, rename create and delete folder and files
   d. All of the above
10. A shortcut can be created
    a. by dragging and dropping
    b. by using cut and paste
    c. Both (a) and (b)
    d. None of the above

B. Descriptive Questions

1. What is a shortcut menu? How is it useful?
2. Differentiate between CUI and GUI? List the advantages of using GUI.
3. Differentiate between XCOPY *.* A: and COPY *.* A: commands.
4. List the areas of a disk that ScanDisk can check
5. How can you see defragmentation information for a drive?
6. Write Short Notes on the following:
   (a) My Computer system icon
   (b) Recycle bin
   (c) Shortcut menu

7. (a) Name any four operating systems commonly used in personal computers.
   (b) Explain the use of the DIR command to display a list of files.
      i. One page at a time
      ii. All files including files in sub directories
      iii. All files with extension name .doc
      iv. All files without displaying the file size for each file.

A. Answers to Multiple Choice

1. d   2. d   3. c   4. b   5. d   6. c
7. d   8. d   9. d   10. c

B. Answers to Descriptive Questions

1. [*Refer to Section 1.9*]
2. The CUI is an acronym for Character User Interface. It is a type of display format used with most of the DOS based application packages that enables a user to choose commands and see list of files and other option by pointing to drop down menus using mouse or keyboard keys. The familiar example is the CUI used with FoxPro package for DOS.

   GUI (pronounced "gooey") is an acronym for Graphical User Interface. It is a type of display format that enables the user to choose commands start programs, and see list of files and other options by pointing to pictorial representations (icons) and lists of menu items on the screen. Choices can generally be actived either with the keyboard or with a mouse. GUI offers an environment of what you see what you get.

For application developers, GUIs offer an environment that takes care of the direct interaction with the computer. This frees the developer to concentrate on the application without getting bogged down in the details of screen display or mouse and keyboard input. As the interface changes to support new input an output devices, such as a large-screen monitor or an optical storage device, the applications can also, without modification, use those devices.

3. The Xcopy command is an enhanced version of copy. **Xcopy *.* A:** will copy a group of files much more quickly then the **copy *.* A:** with a single floppy drive if you are copying more than one file, the best way to perform this operation is to use Xcopy. The COPY command copies only one file's contents at a time. As a result you must repeatedly exchange the floppy disks between drives A and B. Xcopy, on the other hand, reads as many files into memory as it can before prompting you to exchange disks. You can also use Xcopy to copy subdirectories and their contents; you cannot use copy to do so.

4. The areas of a disk that ScanDisk can check are the following:
   (a) File allocation table (FAT)
   (b) Long filenames
   (c) Directory tree
   (d) DriveSpace or DoubleSpace
   (e) Physical Surface test
   (f) File system structure

5, Right-click the drive's icon in My Computer, select Properties from the pop-up menu, and then select the Tools tab.

6. (a) My Computer system icon

The My Computer icon lets you browse through all the resources attached to your PC system. When you open My Computer, a Windows Explorer window appears. Windows Explorer, or Explorer, is the program that Windows uses to display folder contents. This window includes icons for each of the computer's disk drives (floppy, hard disk, CD-ROM,) and network directories if you have connected your PC to a network. It also shows additional *system folders*, providing access to the Windows Control Panel, printers, Dial-Up Net-working, and a folder that manages scheduled tasks.

(b) Files and folders deleted from your hard drirves are not actually deleted but transferred to the *Recycle Bin*. The Recycle bin icon appears on the desktop and looks like a waste paper basket. When you open the icon, a Recycle Bin window opens, display-ing the files and folders that have been deleted since the Recycle Bin was last emptied. In effect, the Recycle Bin works like a folder.

(c) A shortcut is a small file that is linked to a program, document, folder, or an Internet address. The file is repre-sented by an icon with an arrow in its lower left corner. Shortcut is linked to a file or folder, that file or folder can be located anywhere–on a local hard disk or CD-ROM drive or on a floppy disk.

7. (a) Four operating systems are: MS-DOS, Unix, Linux and MS-Windows XP

(b) i. DIR/P   iii. DIR *.DOC
    ii. DIR/S   iv. DIR/W

"Vision isn't forecasting the future, it is creating the future by taking action in the present to prepare for it."

– Edward I. Koch

CHAPTER 2

Word Processing Package

In this chapter, the reader will be able to understand
- What is Word Processor and why it is used?
- Creating and editing a document
- Different types of views, one can see of a document
- Document formatting
- Inserting Tables in a document
- Mail Merge
- Templates used for Word process package

2.1 INTRODUCTION

Word processor is a software package that helps you to enter text and manipulate words and phrases. You can change a typed letter, document and report easily and store them for further use. You can print these documents on a printer as and when desired. Thus, documents created on a word processor can be made accurate, giving better look, and prepared and printed in very short time. A word processor allows you to function more effectively and efficiently with minimum effort.

2.1.1 Why Word Processor?

You can use a word processor for printing letters, preparing mailing lists, creating documents and reports and the speed of these operations is much faster than what is possible on a typewriter. You can even check the spellings in the documents. You can get help to select appropriate words in a sentence. Moreover, you can add page numbers or change margins. You can emphasize the selected words by printing them in **bold-face**, *italics* or in ***bold italics***.

A word processor can store very long letters in computer's hard disk. You can then modify such letters or print copies just by pressing a few keys from the keyboard. In case you have to make some changes in a letter, you can do so without retyping the whole letter. In addition, a word processor can be used to send the same letter to several different addressees using the *Mail-Merge* facility or using electronic mail facility on the Internet. Thus, you do not have to type each individual letters for every person.

2.2 WORD PROCESSING TERMINOLOGIES

The terminologies used in Word processing are described here under.

2.2.1 Word Wrap

A word processor automatically moves the text to the next line when you type beyond the right margin. This is known as word wrap. Unlike a typewriter, you do not have to keep watch on the end of each line.

2.2.2 Editing of Text

On a typewriter, when you miss a word or a line, you need to type the whole letter again. But using a word processor, you can insert new words, new sentences or paragraphs anywhere in the text typed earlier. The new text will get adjusted automatically. Similarly, you can delete any portion of the text and the remaining part of the matter will get adjusted automatically.

2.2.3 Selection

A selection is a group of words that are put together. A word processor can perform various operations on a selection such as copying, moving or deleting. The selection appears highlight or in reverse. Then by giving the appropriate command, you can move or copy the selection to another place in the same document or to another document.

2.2.4 Search and Replace

A word processor can conduct a search for any specified word or character in a document and replace it with another word as desired. For example, suppose you have written DISC in a document and you wish to replace it with DISK throughout the document, then you can use search and replace feature of a word processor to do the same.

2.2.5 Dictionary/Grammar Check

You can check spellings and locate errors in your document using a word processor. Figure 2.1 shows the facilities available in most of the word processor packages.

You can use the dictionary available in a word processor to check every word in your document. The dictionary may contain words ranging from 10,000 to 100,000.

If a word in your document does not match with the word in the dictionary, it means that either that word is misspelled or that word is correctly spelled but not located in the dictionary. The dictionary feature will make a list of unmatched words for you to take appropriate action. If your document is a legal or technical one, you can even use a legal/technical dictionary for checking spellings.

2.2.6 Character Styles and Sizes

You can change the type and the size of characters so that a printed document

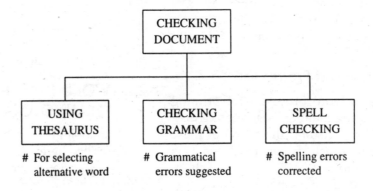

Figure 2.1   Facilities available for checking a document in a word processor

appears more attractive and professional. You can use bigger and bold letters for main headings. You can use italic characters to emphasize a word. Some examples of styles and sizes of characters are shown below:

Style	Size
Bold	10 Pt. Times
Italics	12 Pt. Helvetica
~~Strikeout~~	14 Pt. Avant Garde

UnderLine **16 Pt. Helvetica Bold**

2.2.7 Header, Footer and Page Numbering

A header is a special text which is printed at the top of each page above the normal text. Figure 2.2 shows the footer and page number printed by a word processor on a document.

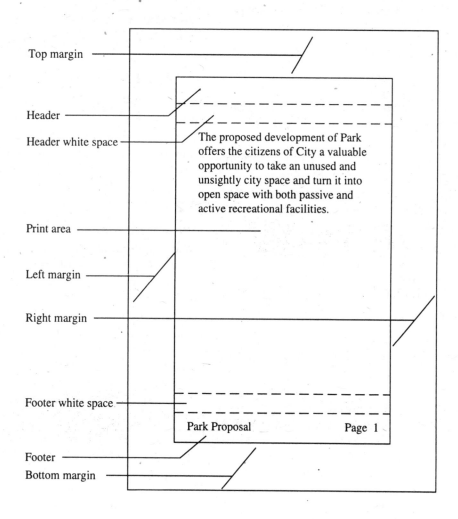

Figure 2.2 Header, footer and page number on a document

A footer is a special text which is printed at the bottom of each page. A word processor can generate page numbers automatically in a document and print headers and footers on each page.

2.2.8 Margins and Columns

The left and right margins are the distances between the text and the left and right edges of the paper. It is normally one inch but you can adjust it easily. You can also print text in two or more columns as in a newspaper. (See Figure 2.2)

2.2.9 Justification of the Text

Justification is the alignment of the text, typed within the given margins. The text can be *left*, *right*, *centre* or *even* justified. Following examples illustrate various types of text justification.

In left justification, the text has a straight left edge and an uneven right edge.

In right justification, the text has a straight right edge and an uneven left edge.

In center justification, the text will be printed between the right and left edges of the paper.

In even (full) justification, the text is aligned on both the left and right margins of the page.

2.2.10 Line Spacing

In a word processor, the spacing between the lines can be adjusted. You can leave one or more blank lines between every two typed lines but the default line spacing for a word processor is single line spacing. When one line is left blank between two typed lines, then it is known as double line spacing. Double line spacing is normally used for draft letters. Figure 2.3 shows a paragraph first typed in single line spacing and then typed in double line spacing.

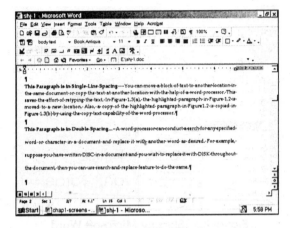

Figure 2.3 Single and double line spacing

2.2.11 Tab Setting

You can set tabs in a word processor for typing columns in a document as in the case of a typewriter. It saves you from pressing the space bar many times for moving the cursor to the specified position.

2.2.12 File Length

File length determines how large a document can be in the size. This is usually expressed in terms of kilobytes. One byte refers to one character. One kilobyte exactly means 1024 bytes. A double spaced typewritten 8.5 × 11 inch sheet with 1 inch left and right margins and 1 1/2 inch top and bottom margins takes roughly 2000 bytes or 2 kilobytes of memory. A file can be as long as one character in length or to the maximum length permitted by a word processor.

2.3 STARTING MS WORD

➡ **To start Word, do this:**

1. Click Start button, highlight Programs and click Microsoft Word (See Figure 2.4).

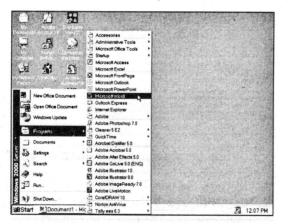

Figure 2.4 Starting Microsoft Word

2. The Word window opens and the Today's tip is: dialog box appears as seen in Figure 2.5.

Figure 2.5 Word with Tip of the Day Dialog Box

3. Click the MS Word icon. Figure 2.4 shows the Program menu with the MS Word item is selected.

The elements among the MS Word Window are described in Table 2.1 as marked in Figure 2.6.

Table 2.1 Parts of Word screen with Description

Part	Description
Application window	The window within which Word 2000 runs.

(Contd...)

Part	Description
Application icon	The taskbar button of a running application.
Application Control menu	The menu that enables you to manipulate the application window.
Document window	The window within which documents are displayed.
Document Control menu	The menu that enables you to manipulate the active (top) document window.
Active document window	When you have multiple documents open simultaneously the window that accepts entries and commands. This window is shown with a solid title bar and is normally the top window.
Mouse pointer	The on-screen arrow, I-beam, or drawing button indicates the current location affected by your mouse actions.
Inactive document window	The background window which does not accept commands unless it is activated. This window is shown with a light coloured title bar.
Insertion point	The point where text appears when you type.
Title bar	Title bar at the top of an application or document window.
Menu bar	A list of menu names displayed below the title bar of an application.
Toolbar	A bar containing buttons that gives quick access to commands and other features.
Minimize button	An underscore(_) at the right of a title bar which stores an application programme at the bottom of the screen.

(Contd...)

Part	Description
Maximize button	A box at the right of a title bar that fills available space with the document or application.
Close button	A box at the right of a title bar (X) that closes the window or dialog box.
Restore button	A double box at the right of a title bar that restores an application or document into a sizable window.
Scroll bar	A gray horizontal and vertical bar that enables the mouse to scroll the screen; a scroll box in the bar shows the current display's position relative to the entire document.
Status bar	A bar at the bottom of the screen that shows what Word is prepared to do next.
Select Browse Object	The toolbar that enables you to browse through an active document by field, endnote, footnote, comment, section, page, edits, heading, graphic, or by table; Go To and Find functions are also part of this toolbar.
Menu	A drop-down list of commands.
Command	A function or action chosen from a drop-down menu.
Ruler	A bar containing a scale that indicates *tabs, paragraph indents,* and margins in the paragraph where the insertion point (cursor) is located. The ruler can be used with the mouse to format paragraphs quickly.
End of document marker	The point beyond which no text is entered.
Split box	Light gray bar at the top of the vertical scroll bar that you can

(Contd...)

Part	Description
	drag down to split a window into two views of the same document.

In Word, you can work simultaneously with more than one document as seen in Figure 2.6.

2.4 CREATING A DOCUMENT

➡ **To create a new document, do this:**

1. Click the New button on the Standard toolbar or click the File menu and choose New....
2. The New dialog box appears as in Figure 2.7.
3. If you are creating a document such as a *memo, letter, report,* or *resume,* you can save time by using one of the wizards or templates that come with MS-Word. To start from scratch click the blank document. The preview box display the preview of the document type selected.

2.4.1 Typing and Editing a Document

You can start typing in a document without worrying about the end of the right margin. The words at the end of the line will automatically wrap text to the next line. You may correct the text by pressing [Backspace] key. The editing of documents is based on the windows principle, that is *select* and *do*.

2.4.2 Opening an Existing Document

➡ **To open an existing document, do this:**

1. Click the File menu and choose Open. *Alternatively,* click the Open button on the Standard toolbar. The open dialog box appears as in Figure 2.8.

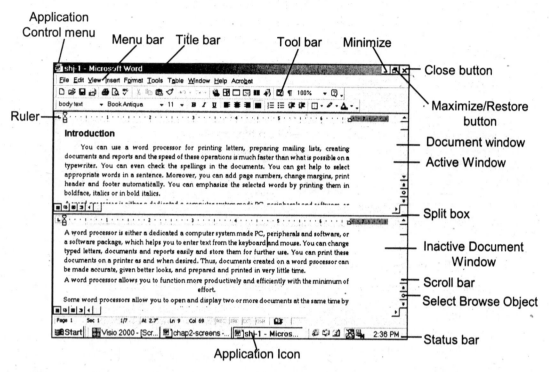

Figure 2.6 Elements of Microsoft Word Window

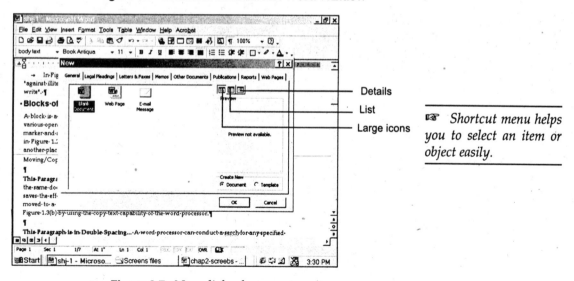

Figure 2.7 New dialog box

☞ *Shortcut menu helps you to select an item or object easily.*

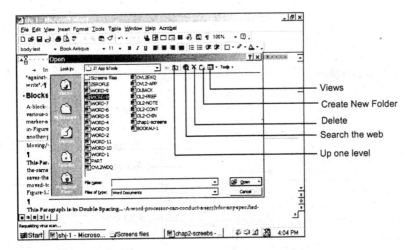

Figure 2.8 Open dialog box

2. In the Open dialog box choose the location of the file you want to open. *Alternatively*, click the open drop down list and choose the desired option.

   In the Look in: Choose the location of the file.

3. Click the drop-down triangle views button to change the way the folder and file list is displayed in the table form:

Button	Function
List	displays a list of command.
Details	displays the details the size type, last modifies, etc.
Properties	displays the properties of the file.
Preview	displays a preview of the file.
Arrange Icons	displays the icons by name, type, size and date.

4. To locate a file by the last modified date, click the Last **m**odified drop down list and choose the desired option.

☞ *The names of the last four files you have worked on appear at the bottom of the File menu.*

2.4.3 Navigating a Document

Navigate through a document

You can scroll through a document by using the mouse or the keyboard. If you split the document window, you can display two different parts of a document.

Navigate through a document using the mouse

To	Do this
Scroll up one line	Click the up scroll arrow
Scroll down one line	Click the down scroll arrow
Scroll up one screen	Click above the scroll box
Scroll down one screen	Click below the scroll box
Scroll to a specific page	Drag the scroll box
Scroll left	Click the left scroll arrow
Scroll right	Click the right scroll arrow
Scroll left, beyond the margin, in normal view	Hold down Shift key and click the left scroll arrow

For a quick way to scroll up or down one page, click Select Browse Object on the vertical scroll bar, and then click the desired option.

☞ *If you are working in a dialog box that contains tabs for different sets of options, press* (Ctrl)+(Tab) *keys together to move between tabs.*

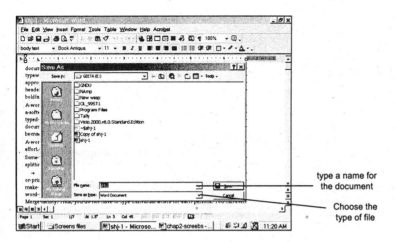

type a name for
the document

Choose the
type of file

Figure 2.9 Save As dialog box

2.4.4 Saving a Document

➡ **To save a document, do this:**

1. Click the Save button on the Standard toolbar or click the File menu and choose Save or press Ctrl+S keys together.

2. When you save a document for the first time, Word displays the Save As dialog box (see Figure 2.9) so that you can type a name for the document.

3. To save an existing document under a new name click the File menu and choose Save As... command.

Naming a document

In Windows, a filename can be from one to 255 characters long, followed by a period and upto three character filename extension. (In most cases, it is best to let Word supply the default extension for Word documents, which is .DOC). You can use any characters except the following characters for naming the files:

* ? : [] + = \ / : / < >

You cannot use a period except to separate the filename from the extension.

2.4.5 Printing a Document

Before you print a document, it is necessary to preview it to check page breaks and the overall appearance of the document.

➡ **To preview a document, do this:**

1. Click the File menu and choose Print Preview. The document preview appears as in Figure 2.10.

When you are ready to print, click the Print button on the Standard toolbar or click the File menu and choose Print. The

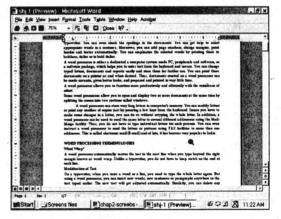

Figure 2.10 Previewing a document

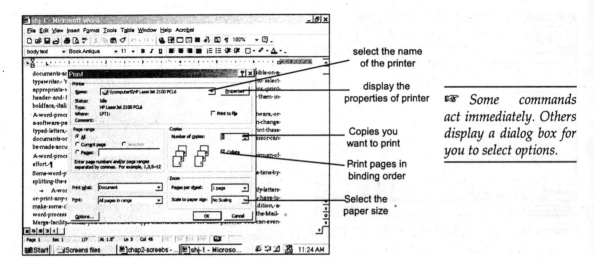

Figure 2.11   Print dialog box

Print dialog box appears as in Figure 2.11.

2. Complete the dialog box and click OK. Make sure that the printer is On-line and switched on.

2.4.6 Closing, Opening Document and Quitting Word

After finishing with a document, you should close the window to remove it from the screen and to free compute;s main memory.

➡ **To close a document and exit word, do this:**

1. If you have multiple documents open at the same time, click the **W**indow menu and choose the document you want to close.

2. Click the **F**ile menu and choose **C**lose.

3. To quit Word, click the **F**ile menu and choose E**x**it.

2.5 EDITING A DOCUMENT

Some of the most common editing actions in word processing are *inserting, moving, copying, deleting* the selected text. You will be able to find and replace text. You can also use Word's correction tools to assist you in checking spelling and grammar.

2.5.1 Inserting Text

If you notice that some text has been left out of the document, you can move the Insertion pointer to that position and type it in. This method is called *Inserting*.

2.5.2 Overwriting Text

In typeover mode, the character you type in from keyboard are inserted at the cursor position on the screen but the characters to the right are deleted i.e. when you start typing, the new words replace or overwrite the existing word. Make sure that OVR button on the status bar is highlighted (active). If OVR is not highlighted, double click the left mouse button on OVR button. It gets highlighted. (See Figure 2.12)

2.5.3 The Undo/Redo Feature

If you make an error in Word, you can correct it using "Undo" command. For example, if you accidentally delete a word, you can bring it back with the undo command. To reverse the action of undo use the "Redo"

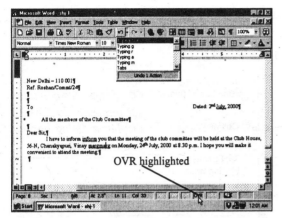

Figure 2.12 Selecting Undo list and OVR button highlighted

command. There are certain actions you cannot undo, such as saving a document or printing it.

➡ **To undo or redo changes in a Word document do this:**

1. To undo or redo the most recent action, click the Undo (press Ctrl + Z keys together) or Redo button (press Ctrl+Y keys together) on the Standard Toolbar.
2. To undo or redo multiple actions, click the down arrow next to either the Undo or the Redo button, and then select the actions you want to undo or redo. (See Figure 2.12)

☞ *Note that multiple actions must be undone or redone is sequence.*

Selecting Text

Before you can *move, format, delete,* or otherwise change text or a graphic picture, you must select the items. You can select the item using a mouse or keyboard. Note that the selected text or graphics are highlighted. To cancel the selection, click outside the selection, or use the arrow keys to move the insertion point.

➡ **To select text do this:**

1. Position the insertion point from where you want to select text.
2. Now press the left mouse button and select the text by moving mouse pointer. *Alternatively,* you can also select text and graphics by positioning the insertion point at the beginning of the text or graphic you want to select, holding down the Shift key, and then clicking where you want the selection to end. The selected text highlighted appears as seen in Figure 2.13.

Figure 2.13 The selected text highlighted

2.5.4 Copying Text

"Copying" means to make a copy of the selected text or graphic and insert it in another location, leaving the original document unchanged".

➡ **To copy text from one location to another in the same document do this:**

1. Select the text you want to copy by adopting the method given earlier.
2. Click the Edit menu and choose Copy or click the copy button on the Standard toolbar. The selected text will be placed on the clipboard which is an accessory in MS-Word.

3. Now position the insertion point at the location you want to place the text.

4. Click the <u>E</u>dit menu and choose <u>P</u>aste or click the paste button on the Standard toolbar. The selected text will be pasted. (See Figure 2.14)

Figure 2.14 Highlighted text in Figure 2.13 copied to new location

2.5.5 Moving Text

"*Moving*" means to remove (cut) the selected text or graphic from one location and insert it in another location in the same document.

➡ **To move text from one location to another in the same document do this:**

1. Select the text you want to move.
2. Click the <u>E</u>dit menu and choose Cu<u>t</u> or click the cut button on the Standard toolbar. The selected text will disappear from the screen and will be placed on the clipboard.
3. Now position the insertion point at the location you want to paste the text.
4. Click the <u>E</u>dit menu and choose <u>P</u>aste. The selected text will be moved. (See Figure 2.15)

2.5.6 Moving and Copying using Drag and Drop Technique

Drag-and-drop editing is an easy way to

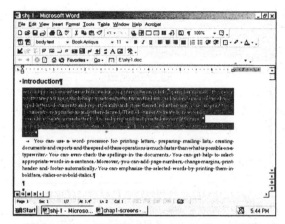

Figure 2.15 Highlighted text in Figure 2.13 moved to new location

move or copy a selection. You can *drag* and *drop* items between documents. However, to move or copy a selection to a longer distance in a document or to a different document, you should use the Cut, Copy, and Paste commands.

➡ **To move text using drag-and-drop editing, do this:**

1. Select the text you want to move.
2. Point to the selected text and then press and hold down the left mouse button. When the drag-and-drop pointer appears as in Figure 2.16, drag the dotted insertion point to the new location.

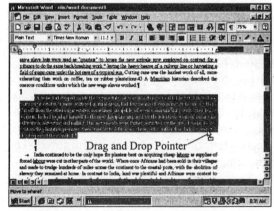

Figure 2.16 Drag and Drop Mouse Pointer

3. Release the mouse button to drop the text into place.

➡ To copy text using drag-and-drop editing, do this:

1. Select the text you want to copy.
2. Press and hold down Ctrl key, point to the selected text and then press and hold down the left mouse button while you drag the dotted insertion point to the new location.

2.5.7 Deleting Text

To Delete characters to the right of insertion point press Del key but to delete characters to left of insertion point use Backspace key. However, when you have to delete number of lines, deleting one letter at a time becomes a lengthy process. It would be better if you select or highlight all the lines to be deleted as a block.

➡ To delete text do this:

1. Select the text to be deleted by pressing the left mouse button.
2. Now press Del key from the keyboard. *Alternatively* click the Edit menu and choose Clear You will see that highlighted text (block) gets deleted.

2.6 DIFFERENT VIEWS

The type of work that you do will help to determine the best screen view as per your needs. If you are typing a document, you may desire as much on-screen typing space as possible and use *Normal view*. If on the other hand, you are formatting and constantly use various Word tools, you will need to work in *Page Layout* view and get those tools easily accessible at all times. When you switch from one view to another, the insertion point remains in the same location in the document. The different views available in Word are:

- Normal view
- Full screen view
- Web layout view
- Print layout view
- Outline view

There are three ways so that you can change the view. These are:

- Menu commands
- Shortcut keys
- View buttons that are found on the left of the horizontal scroll bar (See Figure 2.17).

2.6.1 Editing in Normal View

Normal view is the best view for most of your typing and editing work as can be seen in Figure 2.17. This is the Word's default view. In this view, you see character and paragraph formatting as they will be printed. Line and page breaks, tab stops, and alignments are accurate. The area outside the text body—the area containing *headers, footers, footnotes, page numbers, margin spacing,* etc. does not appear. Images are also not shown in Normal view. However, the cursor movement is very fast in Normal view.

Normal view has the following advantages:

- If you are working in normal view or outline layout view, you can rewrap the text by clicking Tools menu and choose Options... . You can "rewrap" the text (that is, readjust the line lengths) so that it fits within the document window. Click the View tab, and then selecting the Wrap to window check box.
- You can see style names for all paragraph. To make it visible, choose Tools menu and choose Options..., click the view tab and use the Style area width: spinner box to set a width greater than zero. If you are scanning a document, ensure that style standards are being observed.

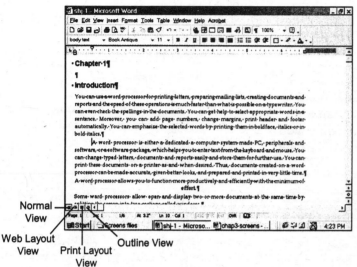

Normal View

Web Layout View

Print Layout View

Outline View

☞   The horizontal scroll bar at the bottom of the screen includes four button for changing the view. You can choose the first one to switch to Normal view, the second to switch to Online Layout view, the third to switch to Page Layout view, and the fourth to switch to Outline view.

Figure 2.17 Editing a document in Normal view

• Select the Draft font character to display the documents very fast with extensive formatting. It can not display character formatting such as bold, underline and graphics show empty boxes.

➡ **To switch to normal view, do this:**

1. Click the Normal view button on the horizontal scroll bar or click the View menu and choose Normal or press Alt + Ctrl + N keys together or click the Normal view button on the horizontal scroll bar.

2.6.2 Editing in Full Screen View

Full Screen view is very useful when you want to enlarge typing area on the monitor. It is comparable to Normal view in its display of character and paragraph formatting, line and page breaks, tab stops, and alignments. However, the *title bar*, *menu bar*, *toolbars*, the *ruler*, the *scroll bars*, and the *status bar* are all removed from the screen in Full Screen view. A special Full Screen toolbar appears on screen the to indicate that

Full Screen view is currently displayed. Figure 2.18 shows a document in Full screen view with the Full Screen toolbar displayed.

➡ **To switch to Full Screen view do this:**

1. Click the View menu and choose Full Screen. To close the Full Screen view click the Close Full screen button on the Full Screen toolbar.

2.6.3 Editing in Web Layout View

While creating a web page in Word, you should work in Web Layout view. In Web Layout view, you can see background, text is wrapped to fit the window, and graphics are positioned at proper places, so that the page will look just as it would look in a Web browser. The Document Map appears to the left of the screen in Web Layout view. This view enables you to quickly jump to any heading within a document (See Figure 2.19)

➡ **To switch to Web Layout view do this:**

1. Click the Web Layout view button on the horizontal scroll bar or click the View menu and choose Web Layout.

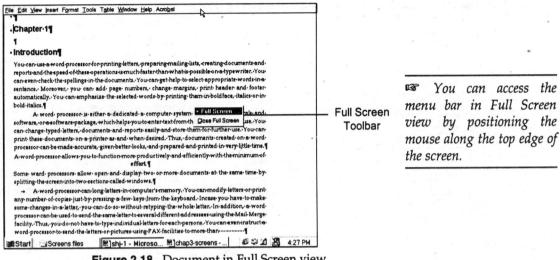

Figure 2.18 Document in Full Screen view

2.6.4 Editing in Print Layout View

Print Layout view is used to see how text, graphics, and other elements such as header, footer, etc. will look on the printed output. This view is useful for editing headers and footers, for adjusting margins, and for working with columns and drawing objects.

Figure 2.19 Document in Web Layout view

➡ To work in Print Layout view, do this:

1. Click the View menu and choose Print Layout, or click the print layout view button on the horizontal scroll bar or press Ctrl+P, keys together. (See Figure 2.20)

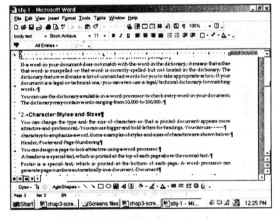

Figure 2.20 Print Layout view

2.6.5 Editing in Outline View

In the Outline View, you can collapse a document to see only the main headings or expand it to see the entire document. In this view it is easy to scroll or move text to a longer distance or to change the hierarchy of topics. (See Figure 2.21).

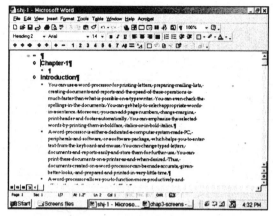

Figure 2.21   Document in outline view

➡ **To switch to Outline View, do this:**

1. Click the Outline View button on the horizontal scroll bar, or click the <u>V</u>iew menu and choose <u>O</u>utline or press (Alt)+(Ctrl)+(O) keys together.

In the outline view, the outline toolbar appears as seen in Figure 2.21. Word indents the formatting headings and body text paragraphs to different levels. Note that (+) or (–) sign appears to the left of each heading.

- A plus sign (+) indicates that sub-heading or paragraphs of the body text are associated with the heading.
- A minus sign (–) indicates that no headings or paragraphs are beneath the heading.

☞ *In the outline view you will also get the options of viewing headings at different levels or of viewing entire document, including the body text.*

2.6.6   Zooming In or Out a Document

The zoom command enables you to control the on-screen size of the contents of document, which are shown on the screen.

➡ **To use the Zoom command, do this:**

1. Click <u>V</u>iew menu and choose <u>Z</u>oom.

2. The Zoom dialog box as seen in Figure 2.22 appears. Select the desired magnification and click OK.

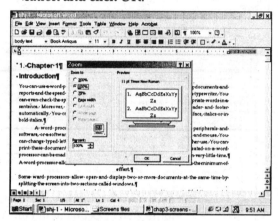

Figure 2.22   Zoom dialog box

The lower the magnification the more you will see of your document on-screen. The Whole Page and Many Pages options are only available if you are working in Print Layout view.

➡ **To change the screen magnification from the toolbar, do this:**

- Click the Zoom Control's down arrow, and then select a preset percentage or document size.
- Click within the Zoom Control's text box, and then type a new percentage between 10% and 500%. Press (Enter) key.

2.6.7   What is Bookmark?

A bookmark is an item or location in a document that you identify and name for future reference. You can use bookmarks to quickly jump to a specific location, mark page ranges for index entries and so on.

Adding bookmarks

To add a bookmark, just select an item or location and assign it a bookmark name.

➡ **To add a bookmark, do this:**

1. Select an item you want a bookmark

assigned to, or click where you want to insert a bookmark.

2. Click the **Insert** menu and choose **Book-mark...** . The **Bookmark** dialog box appears as shown in Figure 2.23.

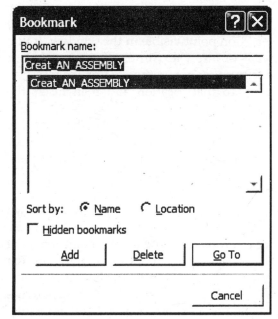

Figure 2.23 Bookmark dialog box

3. Type a name for the bookmark name: in the list box.
4. Click **Add** button.

Show bookmarks in a document

➡ **To show bookmarks in a document, do this:**

1. Click **Tools** menu and choose **Options**, and then click the **View** tab.
2. Select the Bookmarks check box. If you assigned a bookmark to a Name, the bookmark appears as an I-beam.

To Go to a Specific bookmark

➡ **To Go to a specific bookmark, do this:**

1. Click the **Insert** menu and choose **Book-marks**.

2. Choose the way you want to display bookmark names at **Sort by**: radio button either by **Name** or **Location**.
3. Under Bookmark name, you entered in the list, click the bookmark you want to go to.
4. Click the **Go To** button.

Delete a Bookmark

➡ **To delete a bookmark, do this:**

1. Click the **Insert** menu and choose **Book-marks**.
2. In the Bookmark name list box, click the name of the bookmark you want to delete.
3. Click the Delete button.
4. After finished, click the Close button.

2.6.8 Comment

Just as yo use sticky notes on a paper document, you can use comments on a Word document. The text you comment on is highlighted and when you point to it the comment appears.

Inserting Comment

Inserting comments can make annotations on the screen without changing the document text by typing comments by using Insert command. When a comment is added, Word numbers it and records it in a separate comment pane. Word then inserts a comment reference mark in the document and shades the text that is commented on with light yellow. Word tracks each reviewer's comment reference marks in a distinct color.

➡ **To insert comment, do this:**

1. Select the text you want to comment on.
2. Click **Insert** menu and choose **Comment** to open the comments pane.
3. Word opens the comments pane under the document.

4. Type your comment in the comments pane. (See Figure 2.24)

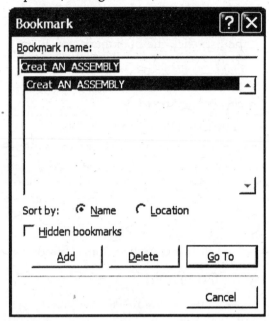

Figure 2.24 Word document opens comments pane

5. After finishing the entering of your comment, click close button to close the comment pane. Word highlights the text where you entered the comment.

6. You can view comments in Screen Tips whenever you position the cursor in the highligted text.

Edit a Comment

➡ **To edit a comment, do this:**

1. Right-click the highlighted text to display the shortcut menu.

2. Click **Edit Comment**. Again the Commnets pane appears. Make changes and close the button

Delete a Comment

➡ **To delete a comment, do this:**

1. Right-click the highlighted text to display the shortcut menu.

2. Click **Delete** Comment.

2.7 MOVING OR SCROLLING A DOCUMENT

The blinking insertion point indicates where the text you type will appear. As you type, Word scrolls the document to keep the insertion point visible in the window. If you want to insert text in another part of your document, you must move first the insertion point to that location and then insert the text.

You can use the scroll bars at the right side and bottom of the window to show another part of the document in the Word window.

☞ *Note that scrolling does not move the insertion point.*

When you are ready to type text in a new location in your document, point with the mouse and click to position the insertion point at the new location. Otherwise, as soon as you start typing, Word scrolls back to the location of the insertion point and inserts the new text there.

2.7.1 Moving or Scrolling with a Mouse

Directing the mouse pointer in the horizontal and vertical scroll bars allows you to scroll a document easily (See Figure 2.25). In this Figure, you can see the parts of the scroll bars, including the scroll box and page view buttons.

☞ *The location of the scroll box in the vertical scroll bar shows the screen's location relative to the entire document's length and width.*

If you use a mouse, and drag the scroll box down the vertical scroll bar, the page number will show to the left of the scroll bar (See Figure 2.25). Table 2.2 lists the scrolling methods you can use with the mouse and the scroll bars.

Table 2.2 Methods for Scrolling Text using a Mouse

To Move	Click
One line up or down	Click once up or down scroll arrow for one line up or down.
One screen up or down	Click gray area above or below the scroll box in the vertical scroll bar.
One page up or down	Click next or Previous Page buttons.
Large vertical moves	Click drag vertical scroll box to a new location in the vertical scroll bar.
Horizontally	Click right or left scroll arrow and drag.
Into left margin	Click left scroll arrow while holding (Shift) key if in Normal view. Otherwise, click left scroll arrow if in print Layout view.

➡ **To move the insertion point using the mouse, do this:**

1. Using the scroll bars, scroll until you reach the location you want the text to be inserted.

2. Click the location where you want to position the insertion point.

☞ *You must click the I-beam at the new typing location when you arrive at the text you want to edit. If you scroll to a new location and leave the insertion point at the old location, your typing or editing appears at the old location.*

2.8 USING FIND AND REPLACE

Word has a very powerful, *Find* and *Replace* feature which *greatly* simplifies editing of text. The <u>E</u>dit menu has a command for Finding and Replacing text. You can use this command to search for *text, footnotes, graphics*, etc. To replace these items, you can then use the Replace command.

2.8.1 Finding Text

With the Find feature in Word, you can locate a specific text or phrase of a maximum size up to 255 characters. You can also search for special characters, such as *tabs, page breaks, extra spaces, line numbers, footnotes*, etc. within a document.

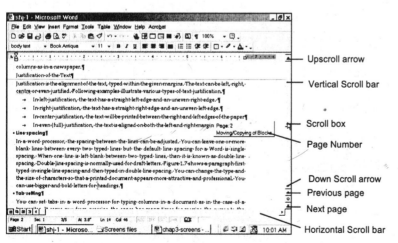

Figure 2.25 Scroll bar elements

— Upscroll arrow

— Vertical Scroll bar

— Scroll box

— Page Number

— Down Scroll arrow
— Previous page

— Next page

— Horizontal Scroll bar

☞ *Word enables you to zoom in up to 500%. You can accomplish this by typing any number between 10 and 500 in the Percent box while in the Zoom dialog box.*

☞ *If you want to search for or replace text in only a portion of a document, then select the portion of the text and then follow the general instructions for finding or replacing.*

➡ **To find specific text do this:**

1. Click the Edit menu and choose Find... or press Ctrl + F keys together. The Find and Replace dialog box appears with the Find tab selected (See Figure 2.26).
2. In the Find what: text box, type the text or special characters you want to search for.
3. Click the More button to display more search options (See Figure 2.27).
4. Select one or more of the options given in Table 2.3 in the Find and Replace dialog box.

Table 2.3   Find and Replace Options

Option	Function
Search	Determines the direction of the search.
Match case	Matches the text exactly as you have typed it.
Find whole words only	Finds complete words only.
Use Wildcards	Uses special search operators.
Sound like	Matches words that sound alike such as *seize* and *sees*.
Find all word forms	Finds all forms of a word, such as *entry* and *entries*.
Format	Displays the Format options, which include Font, Paragraph, Tabs, Language, Frame and Style.
Special	Allows search for special codes in the text, such as paragraph marks or a tab characters.
No Formatting	Removes any formatting codes displayed beneath the text box from a previous Find operation.

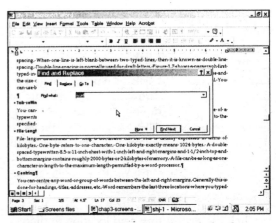

Figure 2.26   Find and Replace dialog box

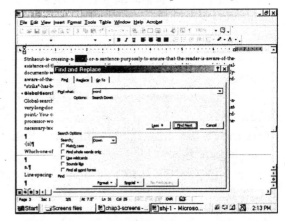

Figure 2.27   Find and Replace box with search options

5. Click the Find Next button to begin the search again or click the Replace tab to show the Replace With text box.

Word searches and selects the first occurrence of the text or special character. The dialog box remains open and you can continue search for other occurrences of the text or special character by clicking Find Next.

6. To close the Find and Replace dialog box, click Cancel or press Esc key.

2.8.2 Replacing Text

You can replace searched text automatically using replacing text facility in Word. You can use the Replace command to search for every occurrence of the incorrect spelling and replace it with the correct version. For example replacing incorrect word Rajeev by Rajiv.

☞ *If you want to search for or replace text in only a portion of your document, select that portion first and then follow the general instructions for finding and replacing.*

➡ **To replace text do this:**

1. Click the **E**dit menu and choose R**e**place... or press Ctrl+H keys together. The Find and Replace dialog box appears (See Figure 2.28). Click the Re**p**lace tab.

2. In the Fi**n**d what: text box, type the text that you want to replace.

3. In the Replace w**i**th: text box, type the new text.

4. Click the More button to choose from other option if need be.

5. Choose the **F**ind Next or Replace **A**ll button.

☞ *If you want to confirm each change, click* **F**ind Next. *When Word finds an occurrence of the text, click the* **R**eplace *button to change the text. To change all occurrences of the specified text without confirmation, click the* Replace **A**ll *button.*

6. Click Cancel or press Esc key to return to the document.

2.9 USING SPELLING CHECKER

The spelling checker is a very flexible and powerful tool that automatically checks spelling in a paragraph or the entire document. It finds and corrects the spelling errors but does not consider the context of words. For example, it cannot check the improper usage of various words, namely *farm* in place of *form* or *no* in place of *know*.

The spelling checker compares each word in the document with the correct spelling stored in its electronic dictionary. If it does not find a word, then it asks you to verify the spelling of the word.

When automatic spell checking is turned on, Word uses a *red wavy line* to underline

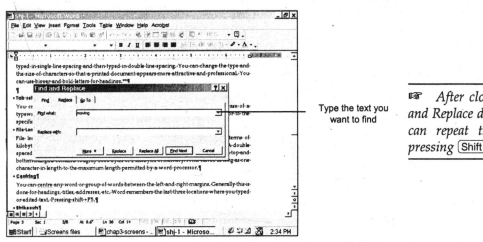

Type the text you want to find

☞ *After closing the Find and Replace dialog box, you can repeat the search by pressing* Shift+ F4 *keys.*

Figure 2.28 Find and Replace dialog box with Re**p**lace tab selected

words it thinks are misspelled. So that you can spot them on the screen. An icon of an open book with a red cross also appears at the right in the status bar to indicate that the current document has spelling mistakes.

The spelling checker also searches for several other problems namely, double words (the the), oddly capitalized words (mY), and words that should be all capitals (USA). If need be, you can also set some additional options.

☞ *You can add words not available in the dictionary to a separate dictionary known as the custom dictionary. You can also maintain several custom dictionaries specific to specialized types of documents, like legal, medical or computers.*

Spell checking begins at the insertion point in your document and works through out your document, checking its entire contents. You can check spelling in a smaller selection of text by first selecting that area and then checking the spelling.

2.9.1 Checking a Document's Spelling Automatically

Spell checking and underlining occur as you type the text in Word's document. However, automatic spell checking works only when this feature is enabled.

➡ **To switch on automatic spell checking, do this:**

1. Click the Tools menu and Choose Options... .
2. Select the Spelling & Grammar tab, and then select the Check spelling as you type check box (See Figure 2.29). Then click OK.

➡ **To check spelling of words with a wavy underline, do this:**

1. Right-click an underlined word. A popup menu appears. (See Figure 2.30) It displays a list of suggested words and additional options.

2. You have four choices for correcting the misspelled word. These are:

   - Select a word from the list shown in the popup menu.
   - Select Ignore All to ignore all occurrences of the word in your document.
   - Select Add to add the word to the selected dictionary displayed in the Custom Dictionary in the Spelling dialog box.
   - Select AutoCorrect and choose the correct spelling to automatically correct the misspelled word.

   To go to the next word double-click the open book icon in the Status bar at the bottom of the screen to find the next underlined word in the document.

3. Repeat step 2 for each word you want to check, spelling.

2.9.2 Spelling Command for Spelling checks

➡ **To check spelling with spelling command, do this:**

1. Select the word or select a document that you want to check for spelling. If you select nothing, Word checks the entire document.

2. Click the Tools menu and choose Spelling and Grammar... . *Alternatively*, click the Spelling button on the Standard toolbar or press F7 key. Word scrolls through your document, and selects words that it does not recognize. The misspelled word is highlighted in the text and displayed in the Not in Dictionary: box (See Figure 2.31).

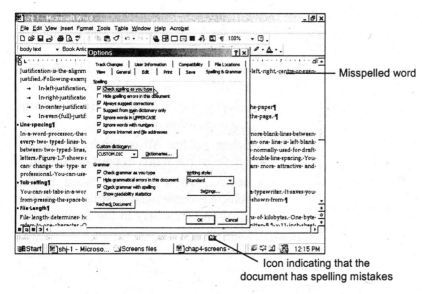

— Misspelled word

☞ *A spelling checker is an important tool but cannot replace thorough proof reading.*

Icon indicating that the document has spelling mistakes

Figure 2.29 Spelling & Grammar tab of options dialog box

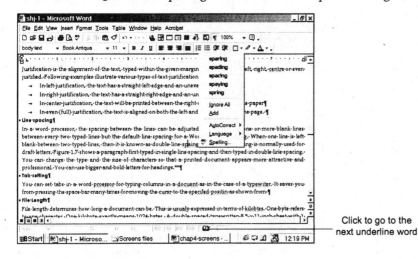

☞ *Suggestions are displayed by Word only if the Always suggest corrections options is switched ON in the Spelling options.*

Click to go to the next underline word

Figure 2.30 Popup Menu showing a list of suggests words

3. Select the correct word from the Suggestions: list and then choose any one from the following list:
   - Click the **C**hange button to change the word.
   - Click Change A**l**l to change all occurrences of the misspelled word in the document.

   - Click **I**gnore to leave the word as it is.
   - Click **I**gnore All to ignore all occurrences of the word in the document.
   - Click the **A**dd button to add this word to the Word dictionary. The word will be added to the dictionary.

4. If none of the words in the Suggestions: list are correct, you can edit the word

from within the Not in Dictionary: box.

5. After editing the word do one of the following:

   • Click the Change button to update the document window.

   • Click the Undo Edit button to undo the spelling change.

6. Word will now continue searching. Click Cancel to stop the spell checking if so desired.

7. If you are checking a selected portion of a document, then after reaching the end of the selection, a dialog box asks whether you want to check the remaining portion of the

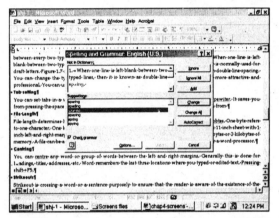

Figure 2.31 Spelling and Grammar dialog box

document. Click Yes to check the remaining document or No to exit the spell checker.

➡ **To edit your document without closing the spelling and grammar dialog box, do the this:**

1. Drag the Spelling and Grammar dialog box away from the area that you want to edit.

2. Click in the document or press Ctrl + Tab keys to activate the document window.

3. After editing your document, click the Resume button in the Spelling and Grammar dialog box or press Ctrl + Tab keys to resume spell checking where you had stopped.

2.11 WORKING WITH GRAMMAR CHECKER

The grammar checker evaluates a document for grammatical errors. Word uses collections of rules while reading a document. It also gives you the flexibility of deciding which rule you want to use.

➡ **To check a document's grammar, do this:**

1. Click the Tools menu and choose Spelling and Grammar... or press F7 key.

   The Spelling and Grammar dialog box appears on the screen as soon as Word finds a sentence with a grammatical error or questionable style (See Figure 2.32). The mistaken words are highlighted in the upper text box.

   Word lists the suggestions in the Suggestions: text box if it finds error. An explanation of the error or questionable style appears just above the upper text box as in Figure 2.32).

Figure 2.32 Spelling and Grammar dialog box

2. Correct the sentence by selecting a suggestion in the Suggestions: box and then clicking the Change button. Or

Correct the sentence by editing it in the upper text box and then click the Change button.

The option of the spelling and Grammar box are given below:

Option	Function
Ignore	Ignores the questioned word or phrase.
Ignore All	Skips other similar occurrences that break the same grammar or style rule.
Undo Edit	Undoes all edits made in the upper text box. Appears when you edit the sentence.
Next Sentence	Leaves the sentence unchanged and moves to the next sentence.
Question Mark	Provides more information about the error. A window appears describing the relevant grammar or style rule. After you read the information, click the window's X button to clear the window and return to the Spelling and Grammar dialog box.
Options	Selects different rules of grammar and style. The Spelling & Grammar Options tab that appears enables you to select an option button for the rule group that you want to observer for the remainder of the check.

2.11.1 Selecting Styles and Grammar Rules

You can select style and rules for grammar that Word would use during grammar checks.

➡ **To choose the grammar rules, do this:**

1. Click the Tools menu and choose Options... and then select Spelling &

Grammar tab property sheet as seen in Figure 2.33.

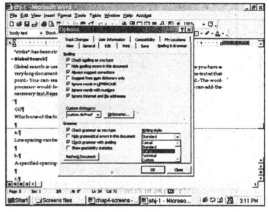

Figure 2.33 Spelling & Grammar tab property sheet with options

2. In the Writing style: drop down list choose from the undermentioned styles.
   - Casual—Rules for informal written communication. Minimum number of rules are applied in this case.
   - Standard—Rules appropriate for business letters and documents.
   - Formal—All grammar and style rules are applied.
   - Technical—Rules as applicable for technical writing.
   - Custom—Rules that you wish to apply.

2.12 USING THESAURUS

Thesaurus is a Word's electronic database, that contains words with similar meaning. It defines selected words and offers alternative terms. When you are not sure of a particular word's meaning, or you think you are using a particular word too often, or when you cannot come up with the right word, use Word's thesaurus.

➡ **To use the thesaurus, do this:**

1. Select the word for which you want to locate a synonym (similar meaning word).

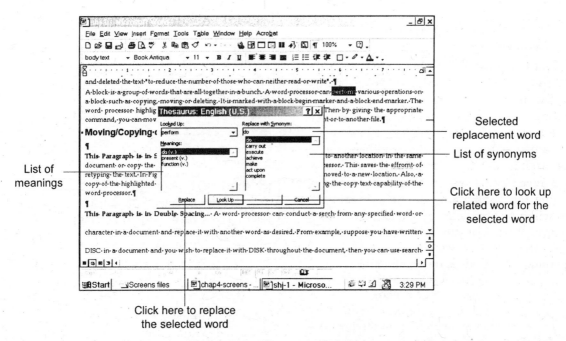

List of meanings

Selected replacement word

List of synonyms

Click here to look up related word for the selected word

Click here to replace the selected word

Figure 2.34 Thesaurus dialog box

2. Click the Tools menu and choose Language, and then select Thesaurus... or press [Shift]+[F7] keys. The Thesaurus dialog box appears as in Figure 2.34.

Note that the Looked Up text box displays the selected word.

Also, the Replace with Synonym: text box shows the first synonym, followed by a list of other synonyms.

The Meanings: box shows the word's definition.

3. Thesaurus dialog box option are given below:

Action	Result
Select a synonym in the Replace with Synonym: list.	The selected synonym word moves into the Replace with Synonym box.

(Contd...)

Action	Result
Select a different meaning from the Meanings: list	A new list of synonym words appears in the Replace With Synonym list. Now you can select a word from the new list.
Select related words or antonyms in the Meanings: list	The Replace with Synonym list displays related words or antonyms.
Type a word and click Look Up.	Meanings of the new words appear.
Click Previous	The word that the thesaurus previously looked up appears.

4. Click the Replace button to replace the selected word in a document with the word in the Replace with Synonym or Replace with Antonym, or Replace with Related Word box, or click the Cancel button.

2.13 AUTOTEXT FEATURE IN MS WORD

AutoText feature is a shorthand method for word processing. You will save time and effort by storing selected text and graphics including formatting that you use repeatedly. For example, if you have a long company name that you frequently use then you can shorten it as AutoText and insert it with only a few keystrokes. In this way, when you type the short name of the company, Word will type out the complete name of the company automatically. AutoText also ensures that repetitive material is consistently typed correctly.

AutoText can also contain pictures and graphics or digitized signatures, graphic letterheads, logos, or symbols. If you frequently use a table with special formatting, you should make it an AutoText entry.

Word also contains over 40 predefined AutoText entries that are used frequently by most users. These entries like *Sincerely* or *Best regards, Confidential*, etc. can also be used for automatically placing them in a document without typing.

Figure 2.35 Displaying AutoText entries

➡ **To display the autotext entries, do this:**

1. Click the Insert menu and highlight

AutoText menu. Now highlight the menu to display the entries under the menu (See Figure 2.35).

2.13.1 Creating an AutoText Entry

➡ **To create an autotext entry, do this:**

1. Select the *text, graphic table*, or combination of items that you want to add as an AutoText entry.

2. Click the Insert menu and choose Auto-Text, and then select New... or press [Alt]+[F3]. The Create AutoText dialog box appears as seen in Figure 2.36. Word suggests a name for entry based on the selected text in the Please name your AutoText entry: box.

3. Change the suggested name or accept the same, as shown by Word.

4. Click OK.

Figure 2.36 Create AutoText dialog box

2.13.2 Inserting AutoText

Once you have created an AutoText entry, it is easy to use it in your document, again and again.

➡ **To insert an autotext entry, do this:**

1. Position the insertion point where you want the AutoText entry to appear.

2. Type the abbreviation you gave the AutoText entry and press F3. Word replaces the AutoText abbreviation with the AutoText.

☞ *The AutoText abbreviation you type in your document must be at the beginning of a line or preceded by a space. Otherwise, the Auto-Text abbreviation will not be replaced with the AutoText.*

3. In case you forget Autotext abbreviation or you want to insert a predefined entry, then Select the AutoText entry from the AutoText menu (See Figure 2.35). The entry is inserted.

2.13.3 Deleting AutoText

You may want to delete an AutoText entry when you do not need it anymore.

➡ **To delete an autotext entry, do this:**

1. Click Insert menu and choose AutoText and select AutoText from the AutoText menu. *Alternatively*, click the AutoText icon on the AutoText toolbar.

2. Type the name of the AutoText entry you want to delete in the Enter AutoText entries here: text box, or select the name from the list (see Figure 2.37).

3. Click the Delete button.

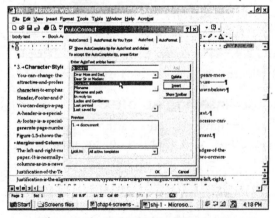

Figure 2.37 Deleting AutoText entry

2.14 USING AUTOCORRECT FEATURE

The AutoCorrect feature in Word recognizes typing mistakes and automatically corrects them. AutoCorrect can also be used to automatically type long words from an abbreviation. For example, to automatically type the phrase *not applicable,* when you type the abbreviation *na.*

2.14.1 Creating AutoCorrect Entries

You can create AutoCorrect entries in any two ways:

• Manually add entries using menu commands.

• Add an AutoCorrect entry while performing spelling check.

➡ **To add an autocorrect entry with the menu commands, do this:**

1. Click Tools menu and choose AutoCorrect... . Word shows the AutoCorrect dialog box with the AutoCorrect tab selected (See Figure 2.38).

Figure 2.38 The AutoCorrect dialog box

2. In the Replace: text box, type misspelled words or abbreviations that you wish to get corrected by Word automatically.

3. In the With: text box, type the correct spelling of the word or phrase.

4. Click **A**dd to add these selected entries to the list of AutoCorrect list.

5. Click OK.

Word will insert the phrase and then return(s) into the **W**ith text box.

2.14.2 Customizing AutoCorrect

The AutoCorrect feature works automatically as you type, but offers several options that you can change to suite your working style and preferences.

➡ **To change the autocorrect options, do this:**

1. Click the **T**ools menu and choose **A**uto-Correct... . The AutoCorrect dialog box appears (refer to Figure 2.38).

2. The various available option are as discussed in the following table.

Option	Result	Example
Correct TWo INitial CApitals	Changes the second of two capital letters at the beginning of a word to lower-case	"THe" becomes "The".
Capitalize first letter of sentences	Changes the first letter of a word beginning a sentence to upper-case	"now is the time..." becomes "Now is the time...".
Capitalize names of days	Capitalizes the first letter of names of days of the week	"monday" becomes "Monday".
Correct accidental usage of cAPS LOCK key	Corrects the case of text accidentally typed while the Caps Lock key is on (automatically turns	"wORD FOR wINDOWS" becomes "Word for Windows".

(Contd...)

Option	Result	Example
	off the Caps Lock key after the first correction)	
Replace **t**ext as you type	Replaces misspelled words with correct spellings, based on the list of entries maintained by AutoCorrect	"teh" becomes "the".

2.14.3 AutoCorrect Exceptions

Sometimes you will use words that should not be capitalized, even if they appear at the beginning of a sentence. For example, you will often have abbreviations that end in periods that you do not want capitalized. You may also have exceptions for "Correct TWo INitial Capitals," such as trademarked names that may use nonstandard capitalization. To accommodate these, you can set up exceptions in the AutoCorrect Exceptions dialog box.

➡ **To set up autocorrect exceptions, do this:**

1. Click the **T**ools menu and choose **A**uto-Correct. The AutoCorrect dialog box appears (See Figure 2.38).

2. Click **E**xceptions... . The AutoCorrect Exceptions dialog box appears as in Figure 2.39.

3. To prevent Word from capitalizing a first letter, select the **F**irst Letter tab.

4. Type the exception into the D**o**n't capitalize after: box and click **A**dd button.

If you want to set up an exception for initial caps, select the **IN**itial CAps tab. Type the exception into the do not Correct text box and choose **A**dd.

5. Select Automatically add words to list if you want Word to automatically add words to the exceptions list.

Words are added to the exception list if you use Backspace to erase the word immediately after a correction is made by AutoCorrect, and then you retype the original word into the document.

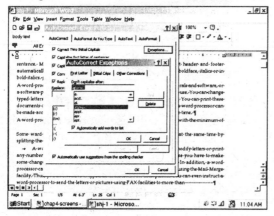

Figure 2.39 AutoCorrect exceptions dialog box

☞ *If you use Edit, Undo (or press Ctrl+Z), Word will restore the original word, but will not add it to the exceptions list.*

6. Click the Other Corrections tab, and then type the misspelled word in the Don't correct box.

7. In the Other Corrections tab, you can enter exceptions for spelling corrections that are generated by the spelling checker. If you enter an exception that is already included in the list of built-in AutoCorrect entries, AutoCorrect will ignore this exception. For example, if the "recieve/receive" is included in the Auto-Correct list, and you type recieve in the Don't correct box, in the Other corrections tab. AutoCorrect will still change "recieve" to "receive". However, you can delete the spelling correction from the AutoCorrect list.

8. Click Add, and then click Close.

2.14.4 Deleting AutoCorrect Entry or Exception

➡ **To delete an autocorrect entry, do this:**

1. Click the Tools menu and choose Auto-Correct... to display the AutoCorrect dialog box.

2. Select the entry you want to delete in the list at the bottom of the dialog box (See Figure 2.38).

3. Click the Delete button.

4. Click OK.

When you choose Delete, Word leaves the deleted entry in the Replace and With text boxes. If you decide not to delete this entry, click Add to once again add this item to the list.

➡ **To delete an autocorrect exception, do this:**

1. Click the Tools menu and choose Auto-Correct... to display the AutoCorrect dialog box.

2. Click Exceptions... to display the Auto-Correct Exceptions dialog box (See Figure 2.39).

3. Select either the First Letter or INitial CAps tab.

4. Select the entry you want to delete in the list at the bottom of the dialog box.

5. Click the Delete button.

6. Click OK.

2.15 FORMATTING A DOCUMENT IN WORD

The feature that control the appearance of the document is referred to as formatting. The formatting can be categorized as *character*, *paragraph* and *page formatting*.

2.15.1 Character Formatting

Word enables the under mentioned character formatting options:

- Font, font style and font size changes
- Underline options, and color applications
- Applying font effects namely italics, bold, etc.
- Changing inter character spacing

2.15.2 Character Formatting using the Font Command

Word can use any font installed in a PC system. Theoretically, you can print any font in any size from 1 point to 1637 points. This corresponds to character heights ranging from approximately 1/72 of an inch to about 22 inches. In actual work you will probably work with type sizes ranging from about 7 to 72 points most of the time. Some of the character formatting options discussed later in the section vary depending on the font you select.

➡ To change the font of an existing text, do this:

1. Select the text you want to format.
2. Click the Format menu and choose Font... command. The Font dialog box as in the Figure 2.40 appears.
3. Click on the Font Tab of the Font dialog box.
4. The Font Tab property sheet appears as in Figure 2.40. It offers the options for changing the font style and size.

- To change the font, enter the name of the font in the Font: text box. *Alternatively*, use the scroll box on the right of the Font list to see all the fonts available.
- To change the Font Style options, type the desired option in the Font style: option box *Alternatively*, select from the list box below the Font style: box.

Figure 2.40 Font dialog box with font property sheet

- The Size: text box displays the current font size. To change the size enter the new size in the Size: text box. *Alternatively*, select the font size from the list box just below the Size: text box.
- Underline: drop down list offers different underlining options as explained in Table 2.4 and shown in Figure 2.41. Click the down arrow to see the various underlining options.

Table 2.4 Underline: text box Options

Option	Effect
None	Characters are not underlined.
Single	Both words and spaces are underlined.
Words only	Words are underlined but the spaces are not underlined.
Double	Both words and spaces have a double underline.
Dotted	Both words and spaces have a dotted underline.
Thick	The words are underlined with a thick line.
Dash	The words are underlined with a dashed underline.
Dot Dot Dash	The words are underlined with a dot dot and dashed line.
Wave	The words are underlined with a wavy line.

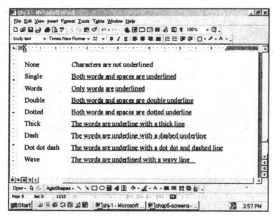

Figure 2.41 Different types of Underline

- **C**olor: drop down left offers different colours option to the text. You would see the displays of the text in colour if you have a colour monitor. You can also print it on a colour printer.

- The Effects box of the Fo**n**t tab enables you to give various font effect as given in Table 2.5.

Table 2.5 Effects box options

Effect	Appearance
Stri**k**ethrough	Characters appear with a straight line through them, as ~~strike~~.
Doub**l**e strike-through	Characters appear with double line through them.
Su**p**erscript	Characters are raised above the regular line of type and in a smaller point size. For example 10^2. 2 is superscript.
Su**b**script	Characters are lowered below the regular line of type in a smaller point size. For example, H_2.
Shado**w**	The text appears with a shadow.
Outline	The text appears with an outline.
Emboss	The text appears as embossed.

(Contd...)

Engrave	The text appears, engraved or imprinted on a page.
S**m**all caps	Characters are all uppercase, but initial caps are in the assigned point size and rest of the characters are in a slightly smaller point size. For example, SMALL CAPS.
All caps	This option changes only the appearance of the characters without actually changing the characters themselves.
Hidden	Characters or text in a document which you do not want to be printed. The hidden text is displayed with a dotted underline.

The preview box at the bottom of the Font dialog box shows the effect of selected options. (See Figure 2.42)

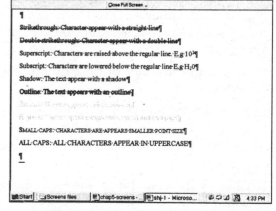

Figure 2.42 The Font effects options

2.15.3 Paragraph Formatting

The traditional definition of the term paragraph in English language is "a series of related sentences". In Word, a paragraph can be — *single text character, a graphic,* or *even a blank text consisting of only the paragraph marker.* Each paragraph in a Word document can be formatted. You can see the paragraph marker if the paragraph display option is turned on.

A Paragraph can have the following characteristics:

- Alignment
- Indents
- Line spacing
- Space before and after the paragraph

Text Effects

The attribute Alignment of a paragraph refers to the position of the main document text on the page. Different alignment options in Word are given in Table 2.6 and shown in Figure 2.43.

Table 2.6 Different Alignment Option for a Paragraph

Left Alignment	Aligns the text at the left margin and makes a zigzag right margin.
Right Alignment	Aligns the text to the right margin and makes a zigzag left margin.
Centre Alignment	Centers text between the left and right margins on the centre line. In this case both the margins are zigzag.
Justify	Aligns the text at both the margins by increasing the spacing between the words.

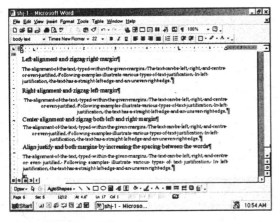

Figure 2.43 Different alignment options in paragraphs

Indents

Indents are the white space added to the margins, and thus decreasing the text area for paragraphs. So, when you have a "right margin and you want to add a right indent of 1.0", your text will be printed 2.0" from the right edge of the paper.

> ☞ *The first line of each paragraph can be indented differently from other lines in the paragraph. The first line can be shorter than the others, creating a regular indent, or longer than the others creating a hanging indent.*

Once you change the indent, each new paragraph you start by pressing the (Enter) key will maintain the same indentation setting until you change it.

Line Spacing

Line spacing in a paragraph means the amount of space between the lines. Word offers the line spacing options as given in Table 2.7.

Table 2.7 Different Options of Line Spacing

Option	Description
Single spacing	No blank line space appears between the lines of text.
Double spacing	A blank line space appears between the lines of text.
1 1/2 spacing	Half the height of one line space of text appears between the lines of text.
Exact line height	Specify the space you want between the lines.

Space before and after Paragraphs

There is a spacing box in the Paragraph dialog box which lets you define the amount of white space that Word must place before and after paragraphs. Space settings can be entered in *points* (pts), *inches* (in), *centimetres* (cm), or *lines* (li). Thus, 12 points would be entered as **12 pt**, 2 lines as **2 li**, etc.

2.15.4 Formatting Paragraph using Format Menu

➡ **To format paragraphs using the format menu, do this:**

1. Position the insertion point anywhere in the paragraph to be formatted or select multiple paragraphs.

2. Click the **F**ormat menu and choose the **P**aragraph... command. The Paragraph dialog box as in Figure 2.44 appears.

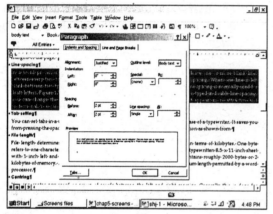

Figure 2.44 Paragraph dialog box with **I**ndents and Spacing Property sheet

3. Click the **I**ndents and Spacing tab, the property sheet as in Figure 9.14 appears.

Alignment Options:

4. The Alignment list box show the current alignment.

5. Change the current alignment, if need be. For this, click the down arrow next to the list box, open it to show the list. From the list, click alignment option as required.

Paragraph Indent Options:

6. The **I**ndents and Spacing tab (See Figure 2.45) to displays line spacing/indentation options.

7. The **L**eft text box shows the current left indentation. Enter the new value for indentation or use the up and down arrow keys to change the indentation.

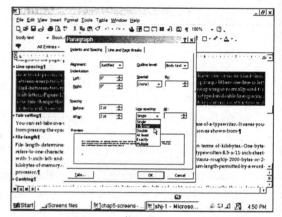

Figure 2.45 Indents and Spacing tab with li**ne** spacing options

8. The **R**ight text box displays the current right indentation. Enter the new value for indentation or use the up and down arrow keys to change the indentation.

9. To apply the first line indent or the hanging indent use the **S**pecial: list box. Click the down arrow key of the **S**pecial: list box to display the options given below:

Option	Effect
First line	This indents only the first line of the paragraph.
Hanging indent	This indents all except the first line of the paragraph.

Click the option as needed to select it.

10. In the **B**y: text box, enter the indention or use the up and down arrow to give the required indentation. The Preview box displays the effect of the selected indentation.

Line Spacing Options:

11. Li**ne** spacing text box in the spacing box that has the option for controlling the line spacing. Click the down arrow in the spacing box. The options are give below:

Option	Explanation
Single	Default value.
Double	Places a blank line between successive lines.
1.5 Lines	Leaves half the line space between the lines.
At Least	Indicate the minimum space between lines.
Exactly	Give the exact space between lines.

Space Before/After Paragraphs Options:

12. Type the space or select the space required in the **B**efore: text box for adding space before the paragraph.

13. Type the space or select the space required in the Aft**e**r: text box for adding space after the paragraph.

14. Click OK or press the (Enter) key to close the paragraph dialog box.

2.16 PAGE FORMATTING

Setting a page design and layout is known as page formatting. Page layout options include:
- Margins
- Vertical alignment on the page
- Page numbers
- Headers and footers
- Paper size
- Orientation and the paper source

By default, margins, headers and footers and page numbers apply to the entire document. However, you can also apply these options to a particular section of text or from the position of the insertion point forward in your document.

2.16.1 Document Margins and Indents

Word's default margins are 1 inch at the *top* and *bottom* and 1.25 inches on the *left* and *right*. You can change the margins for the entire document or for different parts of the

document (if you divide the document into sections).

Note that in Normal and Outline view, you do not see the margins. However, you can see the space between them. In Print Layout view, you see the page as it will print. Always select the Print Layout view if you want to see *headers, footers, page numbers, footnotes*, etc.

A *page* can have only one user-defined left margins setting and only one user-defined right margin setting, but each *paragraph* on the page can have different left and right indentation.

Setting Document Margins

There are three methods to set margins. These are:
- Page Set**u**p command from the **F**ile menu.
- Adjust the margin using the rulers in the Print Preview.
- Adjust the margin using the rulers in the Print Layout View.

➡ **To set margins with the page setup command, do this:**

1. Select the sections for which you want to change margins. *Alternatively*, position the insertion point in the section whose margins you want to change.

2. Click the **F**ile menu, choose Page Set**u**p.... . The Page Setup dialog box appears. Click the **M**argins tab property sheet as in Figure 2.46 appears.

3. **M**argins Property sheet has the following options:

Option	Description
Top:	Select or type out the desired margin from the top of the page.
Bottom:	Select or type out the desired margins from the bottom of the page.
Le**f**t:	Select or type out the desired margin from the left edge of the page.

(Contd...)

Option	Description
Right:	Select or type out the desired margin from the right edge of the page.
Gutter:	Select or type out the gutter space as required. Gutter is the extra space added to the margins to leave the space for binding the documents.

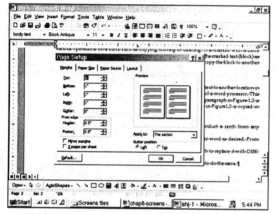

Figure 2.46   Margins property sheet of page setup dialog box

4. In the Apply to: choose the portion of the document from where you want to apply the new settings.

Mirror margins—This option adjusts left and right margins so that when you print on both sides of the page the inside and outside margins of the facing pages are of the same width.

The Preview box displays the effect of the settings you select.

5. Click OK.

2.16.2 Paper Size and Page Orientation

Page margins are usually set in according to paper size you use. You can also select one of the two types of page orientations namely, portrait (*vertical*) and landscape (*horizontal*). You can change the paper size and page orientation for a section or for the entire document.

➡ **To select paper size and page orientation, do this:**

1. Select the text, in the section you want to change.
2. Click the File menu, choose Page Setup... . In the Page Setup dialog box click Paper Size tab. The property sheet as in Figure 2.47 appears.
3. The options are as follows:

Option	Function
Paper size:	The list in the form of drop down offers different standard paper size. Select from the standard sizes or specify the width and height as the case may be. The commonly used paper size is A4 and legal.
Width:	Type or select the width of the paper you are using.
Height:	Type or select the height of the paper you are using.
Orientation :	Select between Portrait (vertical) or Landscape (horizontal) page setting.

5. In the Apply to: select the portion of the document you want to print on the selected paper size or in the selected orientation.

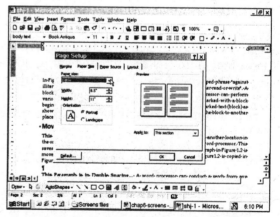

Figure 2.47   Page size property sheet of page setup dialog box

6. Click the Default... buttons if you want to save these settings as default settings, so that they can apply to all pages printed hereafter.

7. Click OK.

2.17 PAGE BREAKS

Page breaks are the places in your document where one page would end and a new page would begin. The size of the *paper, margin settings, paragraph formats* and *section breaks* affect the page breaks. Note that Word automatically computes and displays page breaks as you type new data or delete information. You can see page breaks in all views prior to printing. Page Breaks appear as dotted lines in *Normal* and *Print layout* views.

There are two types of page breaks. Soft page break and Hard page break. When word automatically starts a new page, this page break is called the soft page break where as when user manually inserts a page break at a particular position in the document, this page break is called the hard page break.

2.17.1 Inserting Page Breaks

When you want to force a page break, you can also insert manual page breaks. In Normal and Print views they look thicker than the Word's automatic page breaks and contain the Word's *Page Break.*

➡ **To insert a manual page break, do this:**

1. Move the insertion point to where you want to place the break.

2. Click the Insert menu and choose Break... . The dialog box as in Figure 2.48 appears.

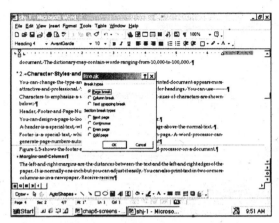

Figure 2.48 Page break dialog box

2.18 HEADERS AND FOOTERS

Header or *footer* is the text or graphics which is printed at the top and bottom of every page in a document. A header is printed in the top margin whereas a footer is printed in the bottom margin.

☞ *Headers and footers contain information repeated at the top or bottom of the pages of a document. Word has the option of printing a different header or footer on the first page of a document or section.*

2.18.1 Creating Headers or Footers

When you add headers and footers, Word switches you to Print Layout view. It activates a separate pane where you can create a header/footer for the document. It also displays a special Header and Footer toolbar, and dims the text of your document so that you cannot edit it (See Figure 2.49).

2.18.2 Inserting Headers/Footers

The procedure for inserting a header or a footer in a document is the same, and it is detailed below.

➡ **To add a header/footer, do this:**

1. Click the View menu and choose Header and Footer.

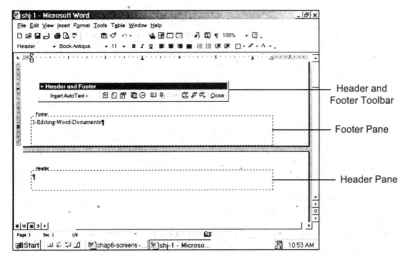

Header and
Footer Toolbar

Footer Pane

Header Pane

☞ *For printing head-ers/footers in the margins, you set negative indents by using the Paragraph command on the Format menu. To create a negative indent of 1 inch to run a header or footer into the left margin, type -1 in the Left box under Indentation on the Indents and Spacing tab in the Paragraph dialog box.*

Figure 2.49 Header and Footer pane and toolbar

2. Word switches to Print Layout view and displays the Header and Footer Toolbar. The Header box appears at the top of the page and the Footer box appears at the bottom of the page. The buttons on the Header and Footer toolbar are explained in Table 2.8.

3. Now type and format Header/Footer text as you would do with text. You can paste graphics, or apply styles.

4. Click the Page number, Number of Pages, Date, and/or Time buttons to be inserted in Header/Footer.

5. Double click in the main document.

☞ *While working in Header/Footer box, the main document appears grayed. To work in the main document double click the main document.*

Table 2.8 Functions of the buttons in Toolbar for Header and Footer

Icon	Button	Function
⊞	Insert page number	It inserts page number which is automatically updated when you add or delete pages in a document.
⊞	Insert Number of Pages	Prints the total number of pages in the document.
⊞	Format Page Number	Adds special appearance to the page number in the current section.
⊞	Insert Date	Inserts the date, which is automatically updated so that the current date is shown whenever you open or print the file.

(Contd...)

Icon	Button	Function
	Insert Time	Inserts the time which is automatically updated so that the current time is shown whenever you open or print the file.
	Page Setup	Opens the page Setup dialog box.
	Show/Hide Document text	Shows or hides the document text as you type in the header/footer area.
	Same as previous	Inserts the header or footer from the previous section in the current section. It can also create a different header or footer by changing the header or footer connection between the two sections.
	Switch between Header and Footer	Moves the insertion point between the areas in which you type or change header or footer.
	Show Previous	Moves the insertion point to the previous header or footer.
	Show Next	Moves the insertion point to the next header or footer.

2.18.3 Deleting Header or Footer

➡ **To delete header/footer, do this:**

1. Position the insertion point in the section with the header or footer you want to delete.

2. Click the **V**iew menu, choose **H**eader.

3. Select the *Header/Footer* you want to delete, and then press (Backspace) or (Del) key.

   If you have different headers or footers in other sections of the document, click the Show Next or Show Previous button on the Header and Footer toolbar to find the next header or footer you want to delete.

4. To return to the document, click the **C**lose button on the Header and Footer toolbar, or double click in the main text area.

2.18.4 Formatting Page Numbers

You can easily customize page numbers and print page numbers in the following format. You can add the chapter number as part of the page number.

➡ **To change the page number format, do this:**

1. Position the insertion point in the section whose page number format you want to change.

2. Click the **I**nsert menu, choose the Page **N**umbers... command.

3. Click the **F**ormat... button Page Number Format dialog box as in Figure 2.50 appears.

4. In the Number **f**ormat: box select the format you want, from the drop down list.
   • Standard Arabic numbers (1, 2, 3...), which is the default option.

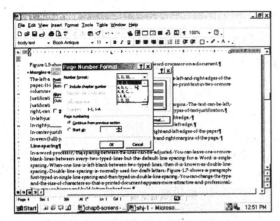

Figure 2.50 Page numbers format box

- Captial/Roman numerals (I, II, III,..)/lower case (i, ii, iii,...)
- Capital/Lowercase letters (A, B, C,...)/(a, b, c,...)

5. Click OK.

6. You can change the appearance of a page number by selecting the page number and then clicking the buttons on the Formatting toolbar or by choosing the Font command from the Format menu.

If you want all sections to have the same format, then select a format before you break up the document.

2.19 INSERTING FOOTNOTES AND ENDNOTES

Word's footnote features enable you to *enter*, *edit*, and *view* footnotes/endnotes in a variety of formats. The only difference between footnotes and endnotes is that, the *footnotes appear at the bottom of the page* and *endnotes appear at the end of the section or document.*

Creating footnotes and endnotes involves two steps:

1. Insert the note reference to mark the location in the document where a footnote or endnote is referred to. The note reference is usually a number.

2. After Word inserts the note reference, type the note entry. The note entry is the text information that appears in the footnote or endnote.

Several options are available for specifying where footnotes and endnotes appear, the type of separator line that is used, and the style of numbering used for the reference numbers. All these are discussed in the following sections.

2.19.1 Entering Footnotes/Endnotes

When you insert a footnote or endnote, Word inserts a reference mark in the text at the current insertion point. The reference mark is usually a sequential number that identifies the note you are adding. You are then given the opportunity to type the text to which the reference mark would refer.

In the Normal view, a pane opens at the bottom of the window. In that pane, you can type either a footnote/endnote, depending on the type of note you select. If you are in Page Layout view, Word moves the insertion point to the bottom of the page for footnotes, or to the end of the document for endnotes.

➡ **To enter a footnote/endnote, do this:**

1. Position the insertion point after the text where you want to insert a reference mark. Word inserts the reference mark at the insertion point, unless you have selected text, in which case it positions the mark after the selection.

2. Click Insert menu and choose Footnote.... The Footnote and Endnote dialog box appears (See Figure 2.51). *Alternatively,* press Alt+Ctrl+F for footnote; Alt+Ctrl+D for endnote.

3. Select either the Footnote or the Endnote option.

4. The default numbering selected in Auto-Number.

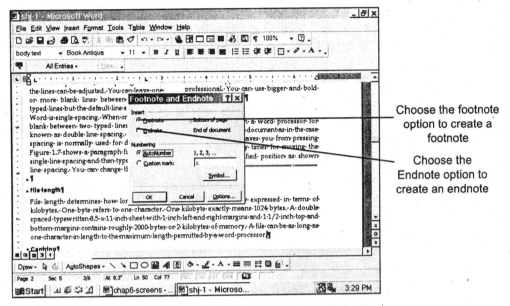

Choose the footnote option to create a footnote

Choose the Endnote option to create an endnote

Figure 2.51 Footnote and Endnote dialog box

5. To customize the numbering click <u>C</u>ustom mark: now click the <u>S</u>ymbol... button, the symbol opens. In the symbol box select the symbol you want to use for numbering and then click Ok. The selected character appears in the <u>C</u>ustom mark: text box.

6. Click OK. Word displays the note pane in the Normal view (See Figure 2.52). Or the bottom margin in Print Layout view, so that you can type your footnote. (See Figure 2.53)

7. Type the text of your footnote or endnote.

8. If you are in Normal view, leave the note pane visible and press F6 key. Click the document to move back to the document window.

   If you are in Page Layout View, you can use Shift + F5 (the Go Back key to return to where you inserted the reference. You can use the mouse to click at any location in the document.

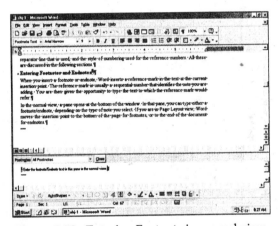

Figure 2.52 Entering Footnote in normal view

2.20 WORKING WITH TEMPLATES

Word comes with a set of predefined templates that you can use to create documents. Many of the templates contain special tools, formatting styles, custom menus, macros, and AutoText for often used procedures. The template layouts are of three categories namely, *contemporary*, *elegant*, and

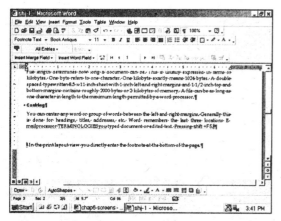

Figure 2.53   Entering footnote in layout view

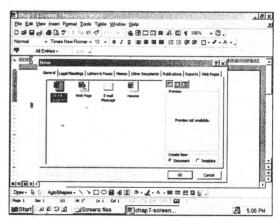

Figure 2.54   New dialog box

professional. You can select a style that would meet your needs.

The predefined templates are organized on different tabs in the New dialog box (See Figure 2.54) and are discussed in Table 2.9.

Table 2.9   Predefined Templated Description

Category	Template
General	Normal (default document).
Legal pleadings	Pleading wizard.
Letters & Faxes	Contemporary letter and fax; Elegant Letter and fax; Professional Letter.
Memos	Various types of Memos.
Other documents	Different types of Resume etc.
Publications	Newsletter, brochure, directory, thesis, etc.
Reports	Variety of Reports.
Web Pages	Blank Web Page of various designs.

You can make use of templates in one of the following four ways:

- Start a new document based on a template supplied with MS-Word
- Modify an existing document by choosing a template and reformatting document in the template's style.

- Copy selected styles from templates for use in a document.
- Create and save new template meeting your needs.

2.20.1   Basis of Templates

Word normally saves templates as files with a **.DOT** file extension in the Templates subfolder. Word looks in the Templates folder when it searches for the templates used in the New dialog box. The tabs that appear in the New dialog box are determined by the structure of the folder that contains all such template files.

All documents created in Word are based on a template. Even the default new document is based on a template, **NORMAL.DOT**. **NORMAL.DOT** template file contains the formatting and default settings for a new document, when you click the File menu and choose New... .

☞ *Styles, macros, AutoText and other items stored in the **NORMAL.DOT** template are available to all documents at all times.*

All Templates contain the following predefined values.

- Body text, headers, footers, footnotes, and graphics with formatting information
- Page and paper layouts

- Styles
- AutoText entries
- Bookmarks
- Custom menus and commands
- Tools
- Shortcut keys

When you create a document based on a template, the document opens to show the body text, graphics and formatting contained in the template. All the styles, macros, tools, etc. in the template are available for use with the document.

2.20.2 Opening a New Document Based on a Template

➡ **To open a new document, do this:**

1. Click the File menu and choose New... . The New dialog box opens. (See Figure 2.54).
2. Select a tab depending on the type of document you want to create, then click the name or icon of the template you want to use. The Preview box shows a sample document for which the template is designed.
3. Click OK.

2.20.3 Creating a New Template

Word comes with many predesigned templates, but you will find many documents or forms that do not fit in any of the templates. You can create a completely new template based on an existing template or document depending on your requirement.

Creating a New Template Based on an Existing Template

You can create a template in almost the same way as you create any document. If you have a template that already has most of the features you want, you can save time by

creating a new template based on that existing template.

➡ **To create a template based on existing template, do this:**

1. Click the File menu and choose New... . The new dialog box appears as in Figure 2.55.
2. Click the Template radio button under the Create New.
3. Click the tab that contains the template on which you want to base the new template.
4. Select the template you want. Select the Normal template if you want to start with a blank template and the default settings.
5. Click OK.
6. Layout and format the template as you would do to a document.

➡ **To save a template, do this:**

1. Click the File menu and choose Save As... .
2. Select the folder in which you want to save the template. The folder you select determines the tab on which the template appears when you create a new file.
3. Enter a name for the template in the File name box. The extension .DOT is assigned to templates.
4. In the Save as type: select document template as seen in Figure 2.56. This file type will already be selected if you are saving a file that you created as a template.
5. Click OK.

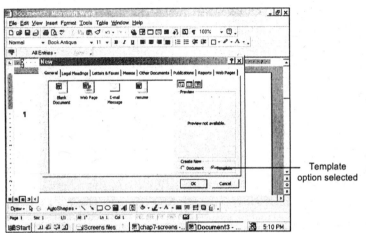

☞ *If you select the Blank Document icon in the New dialog box, you are actually selecting the* NORMAL.DOT *template. In this case, because the document is blank, Word does not offer a preview. (See Figure 2.54).*

Figure 2.55 New dialog box with Template option

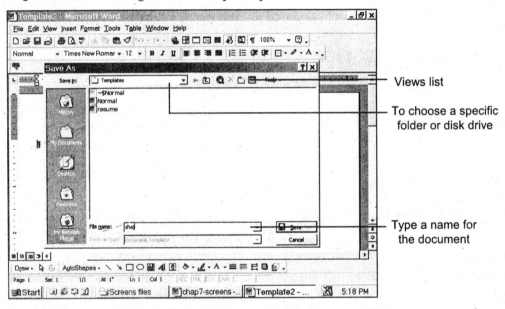

Figure 2.56 Save as document Template

2.21 WORKING WITH TABLES

You should use tables to create documents such as *forms*, *financial reports*, *catalogs* and *biodata*. Word tables consist of horizontal *rows* and vertical *columns*. You type in the areas called cells formed by intersection of rows and columns. Cells can contain *text*, *numbers*, or *graphics*.

You can even control the size, shape, and appearance of the cells, and use border and shading features. You can insert and delete rows and columns in a table.

☞ *A new feature called the Table Wizard helps you to automate table creation.*

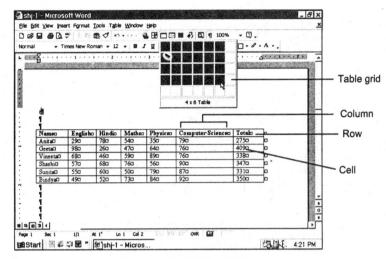

Figure 2.57 Table Grid

> ☞ *Unless you specify column width in the Column width box, Word automatically calculates the column width, taking into account the available text area in the document and the number of columns you have specified. Initially, all the columns are of the same width.*

2.21.1 Creating a Table

Word allows you to create a table using the Table button on the Standard toolbar or insert a table using the Table menu.

➡ **To create a table using the toolbar, do this:**

1. Position the insertion point where you want to insert a table.

2. On the Standard toolbar click the Insert Table button. The grid as in Figure 2.57 appears. Drag while holding down the mouse button to highlight the desired number of *rows* and *columns.*

3. The displayed grid represents the required number of rows and columns. Release the mouse button after getting the right number in the grid.

4. Word inserts an empty table when you release the mouse button.

➡ **To create a table using the table menu, do this:**

1. Position the insertion point where you want to insert the table.

2. Click the Table menu highlight Insert and choose Table... . The Table dialog box as in Figure 2.58 appears.

3. Enter the desired number of rows and columns as required in the table.

4. Click OK.

2.21.2 Entering and Editing Text in a Table

You can move, enter and edit text in a table just as you do with other type of text matter. Use mouse or arrow keys to position the insertion point, then type the text. The cell borders work as margins. Word automatically wraps text within the cell as you reach the right edge.

➡ **To move within a table using the mouse, do this:**

1. Position the pointer in the cell you want to move and click.

➡ **To move within a table using the keyboard, do this:**

1. The insertion point will move *left* and *down* to the next row when you press (Tab) key in the last column on the right side of a table.

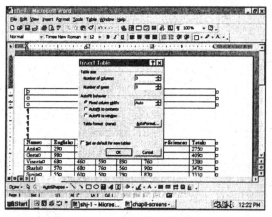

Figure 2.58   Insert table dialog box

2. It will move right and up one row when you press (Shift)+(Tab) past the last column on the left.

You can apply all of Word's paragraph and characters formats to the text in cells as explained earlier. Cells can contain multiple paragraphs, as well as multiple paragraph formats.

2.22   WORKING WITH TABS

Tabs are used for creating relatively simple lists of items. Each paragraph in a Word document can have several different tab settings. Word offers five types of tab settings (See Figure 2.59). Each tab is meant to align text. Tabs are particularly useful for making columnar lists. The different tabs and their functions are as given below:

Tab	Function
Left Tab	Text typed at these tabs aligns against the left edge of the stop.
Centre Tab	A centre tab stop, centres your text around the tab stop.
Right Tab	Right tab stop, positions whatever you type to the left of the tab.
Decimal Tab	Decimal tab stops, align columns of numbers on the decimal point. This is mainly used for financial reports.

2.22.1   Difference between Tables and Tabs

Simple tabular columns are typed if you have items that always fit with in one line. But if any item is longer than one line, in such a case, if you use tabs, the title would not automatically wrap to fit the format. You would need to redesign the tab layout, or move text by pressing (Enter). Long items

Tab selection box

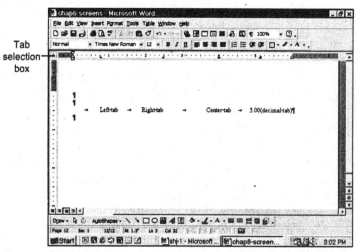

☞ *Measurements in the Tabs dialog box are in inches as default, unless you type another one (cm for centimeter, pt for point, or pi for pica). As an example, 5 cm would position the left tab stop five centimetres from the left margin.*

Figure 2.59   Different tabs available in Word

create problems for typists. Table format makes it easy to deal with this and may other problems.

You would prefer table feature over tabs for most of the text. Word's table features can be slow at times and may require an understanding of tabs as well.

2.22.2 Setting Tab Stops with the Tabs Dialog Box

➡ **To set tabs using the tabs dialog box, do this:**

1. Position the insertion point in paragraph for which you want to insert tab.

2. Click the Format menu and choose Tabs... .

3. The **Tabs...** dialog box appears as in Figure 2.60.

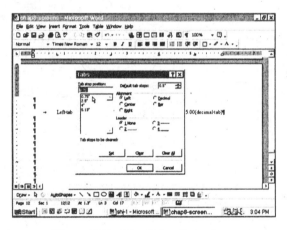

Figure 2.60 The Tabs dialog box

4. In the Tab stop position box, enter the position where you want to insert the tab stop.

5. In the alignment area select the type of tab you want to insert.

2.23 CREATING GRAPHS AND CHARTS

Word uses Microsoft Graph program for creating charts. It enables you to create 14 standard types of charts. Text and numbers for drawing the chart can be entered into a datasheet in any of the following ways:

1. You can create a chart using data entered in Word document.

2. You can create a chart entering the data for the chart in Microsoft Graph datasheet.

➡ **To insert a chart using data in Word document, do this:**

1. Select the cells of the table for which you want to draw a graph.

2. Click the Insert menu highlight Pictures and choose Chart. (See Figure 2.61).

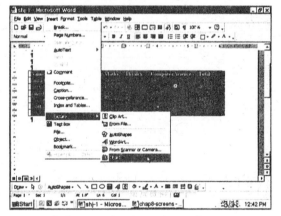

Figure 2.61 Inserting a chart

3. Microsoft Graph opens as in Figure 2.62 with the graph plotted for the selected data.

4. The selected data appears in the data sheet and the corresponding graph appears. Data and Chart menus appear on the menu bar.

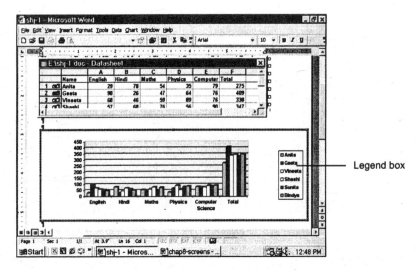

Legend box

☞ *If your data uses the reverse orientation on the datasheet, so that each data series goes down a column, you must click the Data, menu and choose Series in Columns. When you use the command, Microsoft Graph takes the category names (x-axis labels) from the left column of the datasheet and the series names (legend labels) from the top row (See Figure 2.64).*

Figure 2.62   Graph plotted for selected data

➡ **To insert the chart by entering data in Microsoft graph, do this:**

1. Position the insertion point where you want to insert the chart.

2. Click the Insert menu highlight Picture and choose Chart. The Microsoft graph opens as in Figure 2.63 with the sample datasheet.

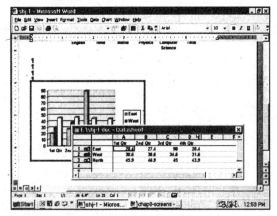

Figure 2.63   Microsoft chart with sample data

3. Now enter the data you want to plot in the datasheet.

When you are finished making changes, click outside the border surrounding the chart to return to your document. Microsoft Graph closes and the Word toolbar reappears.

2.23.1 Using the Microsoft Graph Datasheet

Microsoft Graph plots data point as markers that can be *lines, bars, columns, data points* in X-Y charts, or *slices* in a pie chart. The default orientation, known as Series in Rows where in:

• The text in the first row of the datasheet becomes the *category names* that appear below the *category (X) axis* (the horizontal axis) See Figure 2.62.

• The text in the left column becomes the *series names*, which Microsoft Graph uses as labels for the legend (See Figure 2.62).

• The *legend* is the box that labels the colors or patterns used by each series of markers.

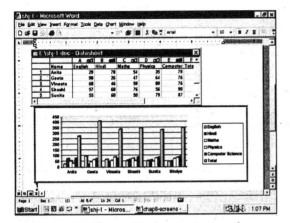

Figure 2.64 Chart with data series in columns

2.24 PRINTING IN MS WORD

Word uses the printer installed by you in Windows. Word prints on the printer you have currently selected as the default printer.

➡ **To print a document do this:**

1. Open the document you want to print.
2. Click File menu and choose Print. The Print dialog box appears (See Figure 2.65).

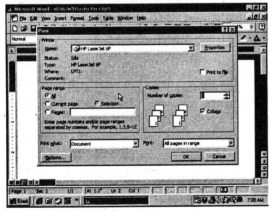

Figure 2.65 Print Dialog Box

3. Select a printer from the Name: list in the Printer group.
4. Click Properties to set the properties of the printer your are using. The Properties differ from printer to printer.

5. In the print Range section, select the part of the document you want to print.
6. Click OK to print the document.

2.25 USING MAILMERGE

Mail Merge is a mass-mailing facility that takes names, addresses, and pertinent facts about recipients and merges the information into a form letter or other such basic document. Mail Merge printing (merge printing in short) uses two files: a data file that contains a listing of data items (or fields) arranged in some specific order and a master file that contains the standard text as well as the data variables which are replaced with specific data items from the data file during the merge operation by MS-Word.

For example, if you want to send greeting message to your friends, then you can get the addresses of your friends from data file and the message typed in another master file. You can then merge these two files and print each letter without preparing separate files for all the letters. In this case, the names and addresses from one file (the *data file*) with the greeting message in another file (*main document*) will be taken by Word to produce the combined document. This process is known as the process of Merging the two files in Word Processing.

2.25.1 Data Source and Main Documents

Data sources are the organized collections of *information—databases—*stored as tables in MS-Word. Word can also use data from other applications, such as Microsoft Excel or Microsoft Access. All such data sources contain *records* and *fields*. For example, in the above discussed case, the data source would contain one record for each friend's details. This record again would have multiple fields — say one for the *name;* one field each part of the *address;* one field for the *city* and one field for the *pincode*.

The *main document*, in such a case, would contain the text of the greeting message field, and the merge instructions.

☞ *When you open the main document in Word, it brings with it the associated data source with which it was saved last. If you use a different main document, then remember to attach it with a new data source that you may want to use.*

2.25.2 Creating a Mail Merge Letter

The best way to learn how to create and print a merged document is to consider a practical example. This is described in the following sections.

How to Create a Document for Mail-Merge?

For mail-merge, you need to do the following:
- Create a data source
- Create main document
- Insert fields into the main document
- Check for design and data entry errors
- Merge the data source document and the main document and finally, print merged documents.

Planning Data Source

Designing a data source document is one of the most important parts of using the mail-merge feature. To begin with, you may want to create a data source document which has one field for the *name of your friend; one field for the address* and *one field each for the city and pincode*. It is always good if you read data into multiple fields. That is you should have two fields namely, *Last name* and *First name* for name field. Similarly, keep separate fields for *house number, colony, city* and *pin*.

For example, if you want to deliver an invitation through a messenger, you may need to sort the addresses on the basis of *colony* field in the address, so that invitations belonging to one colony can be sent together.

2.25.3 Using the Mail Merge Helper

MS-Word has a Mail Merge Helper that guides you through the steps for creating merged documents.

➡ **To use the mail merge helper, do this:**

1. Click the Tools menu and choose Mail Merge... . The Mail Merge Helper dialog box appears (See Figure 2.66).

   The first step in the mail merge process is to Create the Main document, because the type of main document governs the subsequent choices you can make in the Mail Merge Helper. *Form Letters, Mailing Labels, Envelopes*, and *Catalogues* are various types of documents you can produce using Mail Merge. Hence, the Helper offers you different choices of data source.

Creating Main Document

➡ **To create main document, do this:**

1. In the Mail Merge Helper dialog box, click the Create button to start creating the main document. Drop down list appears as in Figure 2.67 offering four choices—*Form Letters, Mailing Labels, Envelopes* and *Catalogues*.

2. From the Create drop down list (See Figure 2.67). Click Form Letters. A dialog box appears offering you the choice of the Active Window or a New Main Document (See Figure 2.68).

   Select the window you want to use.

3. If you are starting from a new document, click New Main Document button.

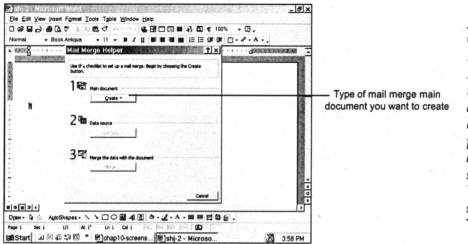

Type of mail merge main
document you want to create

☞ *If you click
the New Main
Document but-
ton, Word opens
a new
document. The
previously
active document
stays open —
Word does not
save or close it.*

Figure 2.66 The Mail Merge Helper dialog box

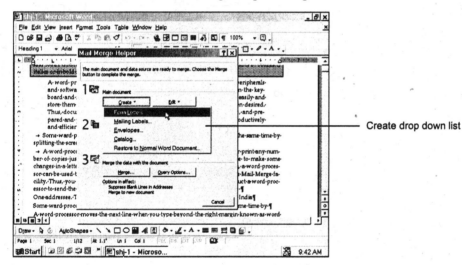

Create drop down list

☞ *Mail Merge
facility in Word
2000 guides you
to design main
document and
data source doc-
ument very eas-
ily.*

Figure 2.67 Create data source drop down list

If the active window contains information for your main document, click the **A**ctive Window button in the dialog box; for this example click the **A**ctive Window button.

Word returns you to the Mail Merge Helper dialog box for the next stage of the mail merge, arranging the data source. You will see that the space below the **C**reate button now lists the information you have entered that is:

- the type of merge
- the main document to use

The information box at the top of the Mail Merge Helper dialog box tells you that the next step is to specify data source.

Specifying Data Source

The information box at the top of the Mail Merge Helper dialog box tells you that the

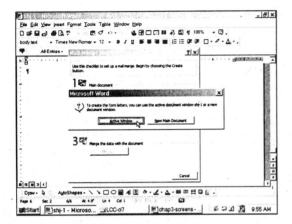

Figure 2.68 Forms Letter Dialog Box

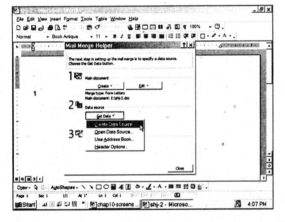

Figure 2.69 Selecting Create Data Source

next step is to specify the data source. So, you need to specify the data source and create in it the *fields* that will be available to your main document for the merging.

➡ To specify the data source, do this:

1. After step 2 in the previous section click the Get Data button to display a list of options for your data source (See Figure 2.69).

2. Select Create Data Source... .

A list of commonly used field names for the type of mail merge you perform will appear. Figure 2.70 shows the Create Data Source dialog box for form letters.

Adding and Removing Field Names

Since you will not require all the field names in the Field names in header row: you can remove the ones you do not want. For each of the following field names, first select the field and then click the Remove Field Name button to remove it from the list.

1. Delete the following fields from the Field names in the header row: box. To delete the field, highlight the field and click Remove Filed Name button.

   ```
   JobTitle
   Company
   Address2
   State
   PostalCode
   Country
   HomePhone
   WorkPhone
   ```

2. Now add the *pin* field, type Pin in Field name: box and click Add Field Name button. It displays *Pin* field in Field names in the header row: list the field is added at the bottom of the list. To position the field–highlight the field in the Field names in header row: box and click move button. (See Figure 2.71)

3. Click OK.

Saving Data Source

When you have finished adding, removing and arranging fields, click OK to save your data source. The Save As dialog box appears as in Figure 2.72, enter a name and location for your data source file, say, **Data.doc** and click OK to save the file.

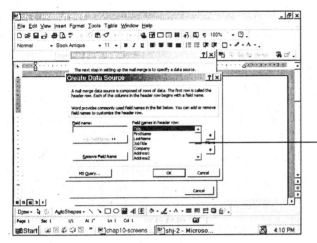

Use the data fields provided by word in this list box, add your own fields, or delete unnecessary fields

☞ *Ensure that no important part of the address is left out because of the non-availability of an appropriate field. If need be, add an extra field.*

Figure 2.70 Create Data Source dialog box

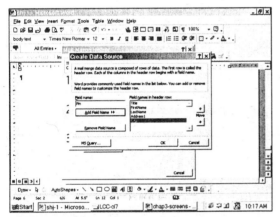

Figure 2.71 Create Data Source dialog box with selected fields

Word saves the data source file under the name you give and the dialog box appears as in Figure 2.72.

1. Click the Edit **D**ata Source button, from the dialog box that appears as in Figure 2.73.

2. The Data Form dialog box appears. (See Figure 2.74)

Entering Data Records

The Data Form dialog box essentially resembles a form on paper. Just as you fill a paper form with a pen or pencil, same way you will fill this form on your computer screen. It contains the fields you specified in the data source. You can enter as many data records as are required.

➡ **To enter the data record, do this:**

1. Type the under mentioned information in the form (see Figure 2.75). As you complete each field, you press the (Enter) key to move to the next field. To move to a previous field, press (Shift)+(Tab) keys together:

Title:	**Mr.**
FirstName:	**Rahul**
LastName:	**Verma**
Address1:	**120-A, Vikaspuri**
City:	**New Delhi**
Pin:	**110 018**

2. Click the **A**dd New button to enter another data record. *Alternatively*, you can also press the (Enter) key at the last field to enter a new record.

3. To move between different records, click the Forward/Backward arrow at the **R**ecord: text box. Add new data records for the following individuals.

   Click the **A**dd New button when you move to a new data record.

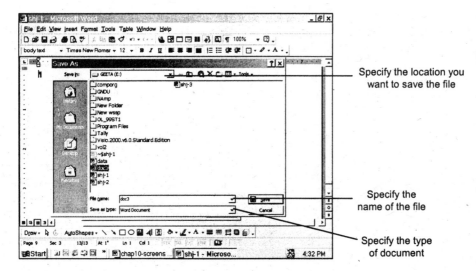

☞ *Data source field name should be chosen so that it would identify the list of the address-ees. For exam-ple, business_associated.doc for your friends associated with the business, etc.*

Figure 2.72 Save As dialog box

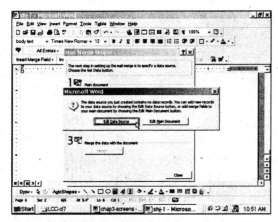

Figure 2.73 Edit Data Source button

Title:	Ms.
FirstName:	Urvashi
LastName:	Batra
Address1:	A-3, Janakpuri
City:	New Delhi
Pin:	110 049

Title:	Mr.
FirstName:	Ravi
LastName:	Kumar

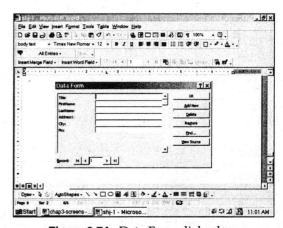

Figure 2.74 Data Form dialog box

Address1:	D2/4, Model Town
City:	New Delhi
Pin:	110 009

3. Click the OK button to return to the master document. (See Figure 2.76)

Note that the New Mail Merge toolbar is shown. Each new tool is also labeled in Figure 2.76. The buttons on this toolbar will be used while working with merged documents.

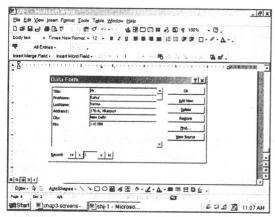

Figure 2.75 First Data Form filled with values in data fields

2.25.4 Saving the Master Document

➡ **To save the master document, do this:**

1. Click the File menu and choose Save.
2. Give a filename along with the path such as, **Letter.doc** and press the (Enter) key or click OK.

After saving, your data source document will be attached to the master document.

2.25.5 Typing Letter

Now type the following letter.

```
Pitampura
New Delhi-110 034
Ref.Rahul/Comm/20
                Dated: 3ʳᵈ June, 2002
To
    <<Title>> <<FirstName>>
    <<LastName>>
    <<Address1>>
    <<City>>-<<Pin>>

Dear <<Title>> <<LastName>>
    I have to inform you that the
meeting of the club committee will
be held at the Club House, 36-N,
Chanakapuri, Vinay Marg on Tuesday
```

25ᵗʰ June, 2002 at 8.30 p.m. I hope you will make it convenient to attend the conference.

The agenda for the conference is as under:

1. Confirmation of the minutes of the last meeting (enclosed).
2. Accounts and Internal Auditors Report for the months of Feb and March 2002 (enclosed).
3. Election of new members.
4. List of outstanding.
5. Any other matter with the permission of the Chairman.

Yours faithfully,

P.K. Verma
(Secretary)

Inserting Fields Names in the Master Document

When you place the merge field names into a master document, you are essentially telling Word where you desire the variable information from the *data source* file to appear. You will see that Word encloses each *field name* in chevrons i.e the marks represented as << >>.

➡ **To insert a field, do this:**

1. On the Mail Merge toolbar, click the Insert Merge Field button. When you click this button, a list of field names that you can insert in your master document appears. You select field names from this list. (See Figure 2.77)
2. Click the Title from merge field name to insert it into the document.
3. Press the (Spacebar) key to insert a blank space between the Title and the First-Name.
4. Click the Insert Merge Field button to insert the next field name and select FirstName.

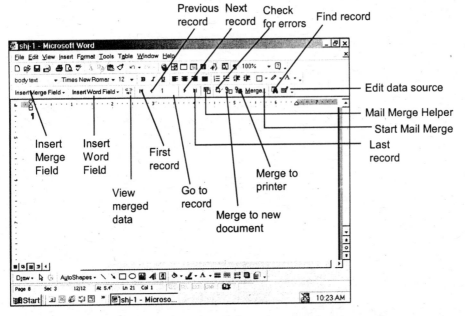

Figure 2.76 Master document with New Mail Merge toolbar

☞ *Before entering a new record, ensure that the data filled in the data form is correct. Pay special attention to the First Name and Pincode.*

5. Press the (Spacebar) key to insert a blank space between the fields FirstName and LastName.
6. Click the Insert Merge Field button and select LastName.
7. Press the (Enter) key to move to the next line.
8. Place the cursor below the **<<Title>>**. Click the Insert Merge Field button. Select **<<Address1>>** and press the (Enter) key.
9. Again place the cursor below **<<Address1>>**. Click the Insert Merge Field button. Select **<<City>>** type a hyphen and select **<<Pin>>** from the merge field button and press (Enter) key.
10. Press the (Enter) key twice to leave a blank line.
11. Type *Dear* and press the (Spacebar) key.
12. Click the Insert Merge Field button and select **<<Title>>**.

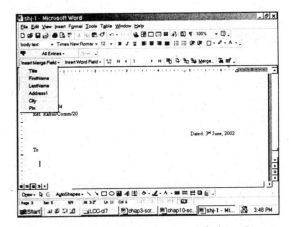

Figure 2.77 Pull down menu on clicking Insert Merge Field on the toolbar

13. Press the (Spacebar) to leave a space between the Title and the LastName.
14. Click the Insert Merge Field button and select **<<LastName>>**.
15. Type a comma, and then press the (Enter) key twice to leave a blank line.

16. After completing the above steps, your screen will be as in Figure 2.78.

17. Now type the remaining part of the letter.

Figure 2.78 Partially completed screen

Merge Documents

➡ **To Merge letter, do this:**

1. To merge the master document and values of different fields from the data source as well as to store the results in a new file, click the *Merge To New* Document button on the Mail Merge toolbar (See Figure 2.76).

2. Word will now quickly merge the data with master document and put it on display. Figure 2.79 and Figure 2.80 show the first and the second merged letters respectively.

3. Each form letter is separated with a double dotted line on the screen which indicates a section break. Each section is automatically formatted to begin on a new page.

   View all the letters one by one, as you scroll through the letters. You would find in the preview that the same letter is printed but with different person's addresses.

2.25.6 Printing the Merged Letters

If you want to print the letters, make sure that the printer is

Figure 2.79 The letter after mail merging

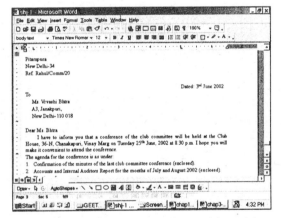

Figure 2.80 Another letter taking address from *data.doc* file

switched on and is in *ready* mode. Then click the Print button on the Standard toolbar.

2.25.7 Closing the Merged Document File

➡ **To close the Merged Document File, do this:**

1. Click the File menu and choose select Close.

2. When a message appears asking whether you want to save this document, click the No button.

You do not require to save this file as, you can quickly generate another merged document, whenever required.

2.26 WORKING WITH GRAPHICS

Word lets you *draw, place, resize, reposition* and format graphics. You can work with your own drawings, charts from spreadsheet packages, take photos using scanners, or any other computer-compatible art form. Word comes with some clipart that you can use to create your own graphics library.

2.26.1 Importing Graphics

Like text, art work can also be stored as disk files. Different drawing packages, scanners and other graphic tools create files in their own unique formats. Word can use some graphic formats. The program comes with a number of built-in translation utilities (called filters) that can convert graphics from many sources, allowing you to insert them into Word documents.

You can work with the following graphic formats.

Graphic Format	Extension
AutoCAD 2-D	.DXF
Computer Graphics Metafile	.CGM
CompuServe GIF	.GIF
DrawPerfect	.WPG
Encapsulated PostScript	.EPS
HP Graphic Language	.HGL
Kodak Photo CD	.PCD
Lotus 1-2-3	.PIC
Macintosh PICT	.PCT
Micrografx Designer 3/Draw Plus	.DRW
PC Paintbrush	.PCX

(Contd...)

Graphic Format	Extension
Targa	.TGA
TIFF (Tagged Image File Format)	.TIF
Windows Bitmap	.BMP
Windows Metafile	.WMF

2.26.2 Using the Insert Picture Command

The easiest way to add graphics is to import a picture from the clipart gallery.

➡ Το ινσερτ α πιχτυρε φρομ Χλιπαρτ, δο τηισ:

1. Open the document in which you want to insert the graphic.

2. Position the insertion point where you want the graphic to appear.

3. Click the Insert menu and highlight Picture and choose ClipArt... (See Figure 2.81). Click the type of picture you want to insert. To insert Clipart choose ClipArt... dialog box as shown in Figure 2.82 appears.

Figure 2.81 Insert Picture command

4. Click the category from which you want to insert from the list. From category list, click the clips you want to insert and choose insert clip (See Figure 2.83). The image is inserted.

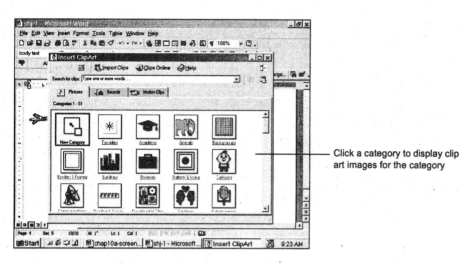

Click a category to display clip art images for the category

☞ *Putting an appropriate art work in your documents enhances its readability and comprehension.*

Figure 2.82 Insert ClipArt gallery dialog box

2.26.3 Customizing Graphics

Resizing Graphics

➡ **To resize the graphics, do this:**

1. Click the graphic you want to select. The picture is surrounded by a box containing eight handles (See Figure 2.84). You will find one in each corner and one on each side of the outline box.

   When you position the mouse pointer on a handle, it turns into a two-headed arrow.

2. To increase or decrease the size of the entire graphic proportionally (*height* and *width* increases proportionaly), drag a *corner* handle diagonally, releasing it when the image is of proposed size.

3. To distort a dimension, use the handles on the edges of the graphic.

2.26.4 Creating a Drawing in Word

➡ **To create a new drawing using the Word's drawing features, do this:**

1. Open a new or existing Word document.
2. Position the insertion point where you want the new art to be inserted.

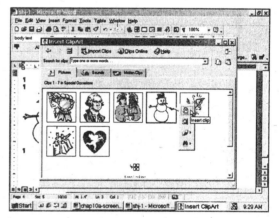

Figure 2.83 Clips menu

3. Click on the Standard toolbar's Draw button.
4. You will see the Drawing toolbar (See Figure 2.85).

➡ **To draw an object, do this:**

1. Click a shape button or a line button (*line, oval, rectangle,* etc) on the Drawing toolbar; then use your mouse to create lines or shapes.

   • To create a *rectangle* click on the rectangle button, click on the page to set the rectangle's upper left corner, and

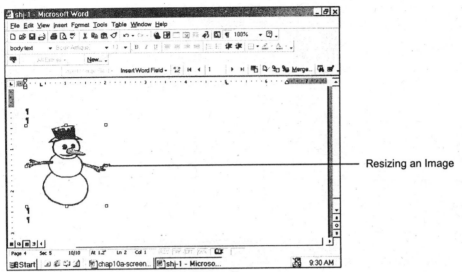

☞ *Drawing a diagram using Word's drawing toolbar is very simple to use. Moreover, you need not buy a separate graphic package for this purpose.*

Figure 2.84   Resizing an Image

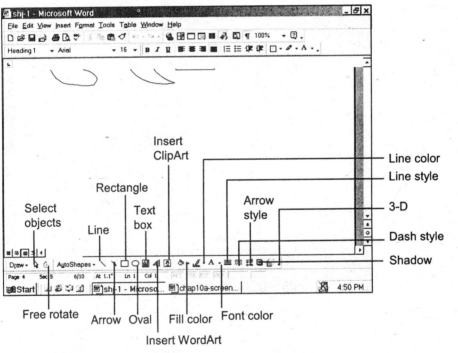

☞ *Drawing a diagram using Word's drawing toolbar is very simple to use. Moreover, you need not buy a separate graphic package for this purpose.*

Figure 2.85   Drawing Toolbar

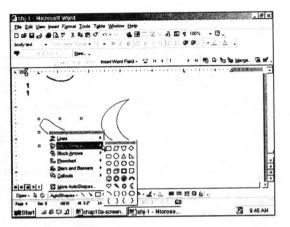

Figure 2.86 Selected Object and AutoShapes

drag with your mouse to create a rect-angle of the desired shape and size. (Holding down the (Shift) key while you do this creates squares.)

- To create ovals click the oval button, click on the page to set the oval's upper left corner, and drag with your mouse to create the oval of desired shape and size. Holding down the (Shift) key creates circles.)

2. Use the AutoShapes menu on the toolbar to create more sophisticated shapes. To use Autoshapes Click Autoshapes and choose from the various categories. (See Figure 2.86)

Selecting Objects

➡ **To select objects, do this:**

1. Click the Objects button on the left side of the Drawing toolbar, and then click on the item you want to modify. This selects it, hold down the (Shift) key to select mul-tiple objects.

2. Selected objects are surrounded by small handles. Click outside any selected object to deselect objects.

Text in Drawings

You can create text for drawings in *text boxes*.

➡ **To insert text in drawing position, do this:**

1. Click on the Text Box button.
2. Drag the text box to its desired size and shape. Text box is inserted as in Figure 2.87.
3. Type the text.
4. If necessary, you can increase the size of the text box by dragging, just as if it were any other graphic object.

Customizing Text Box

➡ **To increase/decrease the white space between the text and text box lines, do this:**

1. Select the text box to be modified.
2. Click the Format menu and choose Text Box... the Format Text Box dialog box appears as in Figure 2.88.
3. In the Format Text Box, click Text Box tab, specify *internal margins* i.e. *left, right, top,* and *bottom margins* by typing new set-tings in the appropriate boxes or using the up and down arrow buttons.

➡ **To remove the lines surrounding the text box, do this:**

1. Select the text box.
2. Click on the Drawing toolbar's Line Color button to display the line color palette.
3. Click on the No Line choice.

Moving Objects

➡ **To move objects, do this:**

1. Select the item or items to be moved.
2. Point to one of the selected items with your mouse pointer, avoiding the object's handles.
3. The pointer will change, to an arrow with four heads.

4. While the pointer has this shape, drag it with your mouse and watch as an outline of the object(s) proposed a new location.

5. Releasing the mouse button completes the move.

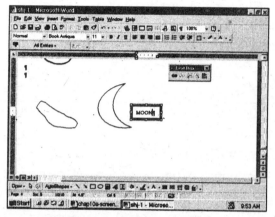

Figure 2.87   Text Box is inserted

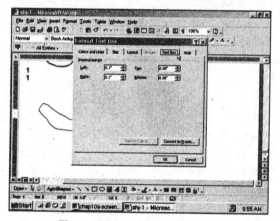

Figure 2.88   Format Text box

2.26.5 Inserting Hyperlinks

Insert a hyperlink that goes to another document, file, or Web page. You can create a hyperlink that goes to an existing file or to a new file. After you have specified a name for the new file, you can choose to open the file for editing immediately or come back to it later.

➡ **To insert hyperlink in a document, do this:**

1. Select the text you want to display as the hyperlink, and then click **Insert Hyperlink**. (See Figure 2.89)

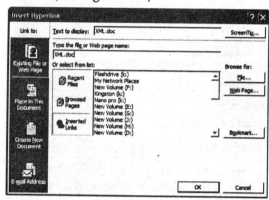

Figure 2.89   Insert Hyperlink dialog box

2. Do one of the following:

   • To link to an **existing file** or **Web page**, click **Existing File** or **Web Page** under **Link to**.

   • To link to a file that you have not created yet, click **Create New Document** under **Link to**.

3. After you clicked **Existing file** or **Web page**, choose **File...** button. The **Link to file** dialog box appears as shown in Figure 2.90.

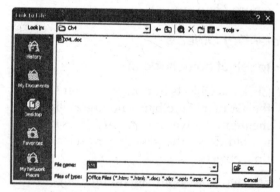

Figure 2.90   Insert Hyperlink dialog box

4. Choose the desired file in the Look in: drop down list, and then select the file you want to link the file. Click OK button.

5. Position the cursor over the selected text the mouse shown screen tips with hyperlink as shown in Figure 2.91.

6. Click the hyperlink selected text, the linked file get opend as shown in Figure 2.92.

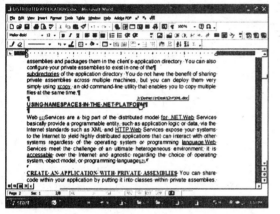

Figure 2.91 The selected text gets hyperlink

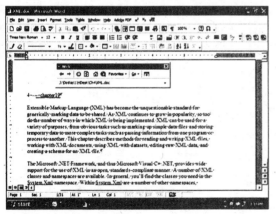

Figure 2.92 The selected hyperlinked file opened

Summary

This chapter presents concepts of *Word Processing*. MS-Word is a program that helps you create documents easily and quickly compared to a typewriter. You can store documents in your computer and reuse them easily whenever you need them. Features like spell check, grammar check, navigating documents and different views of documents are also discussed. It also allows you to change the appearance of text and organize the information in a document in a systematic manner. The appearance of the text can be changed by changing the font sizes, styles and colours. A document looks organized if you align the text, add page numbers, page headers and footers at the top and bottom of a page to display useful information. MS Word allows you to present the information in your document in a tabular form, i.e. within Tables. Mail Merge facility is a very useful feature of Word. It helps you to quickly produce a personalized letter for each and every person in your mailing list. Wizard and templates are two very powerful features in MS-Word which will help you in designing a document easily.

REVIEW QUESTIONS WITH ANSWERS

A. Multiple Choice

1. Word wrap means
   a. inserting spaces between words
   b. aligning text with the right margin
   c. moving text automatically to the next line
   d. None of the above

2. MS-Word offers certain ways by which you can move around in a document
   a. by scrolling
   b. by moving to a specific page
   c. both a and b above
   d. None of the above

3. To insert a picture from a file, select
   a. Insert >> Picture

b. Insert >> Picture >> File

c. Both (a) and (b)

d. None of the above

4. Using MS-Word's Find and Replace feature, you can

a. replace both text and formatting

b. replace text of a document only

c. replace formatting only

d. replace document's name with a new name

5. When you activate the Spelling and Grammar checker,

a. it displays the misspelled words in a dialog box

b. it highlights to misspelled words in the document

c. it allows you to either correct the misspelled word manually

d. all of the above

6. The difference in AutoText and Auto-Correct is

a. the way they are created and put to use.

b. to insert an AutoText entry, you have to type first four letters and then press Enter key whereas in case of AutoCorrect entry, you type the abbreviated name and the moment you press the spacebar to move to the next word, Microsoft automatically replaces the name with its entry.

c. both a and b above are correct

d. None of the above is correct

7. By default MS-Words format your text as

a. 14 point Times New Roman

b. 12 point Times New Roman

c. 11 point Times New Roman

d. None of the above

8. In header and footer options, one of the following options is not available:

a. Similar header and footer on every page

b. A missing header on first pages but subsequent pages to have a header

c. Different headers and footers for odd and even pages

d. Varying headers and footers for each paragraph of a document

9. In Word, if you will press a tab within a table the cell moves you to

a. Next row

b. Next column

c. Next cell

d. Next table

10. Which of the following is not one of the four basic steps in creating a document that merges data from a database?

a. open a new document in Word and start the Mail Merge procedure

b. Link the document to a data source

c. Select AutoField Fill to place the fields in the Word document

d. Preview and print the form letters

B. Descriptive Questions

1. What do you mean by Word Processor?

2. MS-Word provides eight view: Normal, Outline, Print layout, Web Layout, Print Preview, Web Page Preview, Document Map and full Screen. Explain any four of them.

3. Describe the AutoCorrect feature of Word for Windows.

4. Define and explain how to adjust "Line spacing" and "Paragraph spacing" in the MS-Word document.

5. Explain the Setting up headers and footers in Word document.

6. Differentiate between Tables and Tabs in MS-Word.

A. Answers to Multiple Choice

1. a 2. c 3. c 4. a 5. d 6. c
7. b 8. a 9. c 10. c

B. Answers to Descriptive Questions

1. A word processor can store very long letters in computer's hard disk. You can then modify such letters or print copies just by pressing a few keys from the keyboard. In case you have to make some changes in a letter, you can do so without retyping the whole letter. In addition, a word processor can be used to send the same letter to several different addressees using the *Mail-Merge* facility or using electronic mail facility on the Internet. Thus, you do not have to type each individual letters for every person. You can even instruct a word processor to send the letters or pictures using FAX facilities.

2. Word provides eight view these are: Normal, Outline, Print layout, Web Layout, Print Preview, Web Page Preview, Document Map and full Screen.

Normal view: Normal view is the best view for most of your *typing, editing*, and *formatting* of text. Normal view shows text formatting but simplifies the layout of the page, so that you can type and edit quickly. In normal view line and page breaks, tab stops, and alignments are accurate but the area outside the text body i.e., the area containing headers, footers page numbers etc. does not appear.

Outline view: Work in outline view to look at the structure of a document and to move, copy and reorganize the text by dragging the headings. In the outline view, you can collapse a document to see only the main headings or expand it to see the entire document. In this view it is easy to scroll or move text to a longer distance or to change the hierarchy of topics. In outline view, page boundaries, graphics, headers and footers do not appear.

Print Layout view: Print Layout view is used to see how text, graphics, and other elements such as header, footer, etc. will look on the printed page. This view is useful for editing headers and footers, for adjusting margins, and for working with columns and drawing objects.

Web Layout view: Work in Web layout view when you are creating a web page or document that is viewed on the screen. In Web layout view, you can see background, text is wrapped to fit the window, and graphics are positioned at proper places, so that the page will look just as it would look in a Web browser.

Print Preview: In print preview, you can display multiple pages of a document in a reduced size. In this view, you can see page break, hidden text, watermarks etc. In Print preview, you can access to the normal, page layout, and outline icons at the left corner of the horizontal scroll bar. Clicking any of these buttons closes the preview screen and displays the document in the view mode you selected.

Web Page Preview: In a Web page preview, you can see how your document will look in a Web browser. Word saves a copy of your document and then opens it in the default browser. After you close the Web page preview you can return to your document in Word at any time.

Document Map: The Document Map is a separate window pane that displays a list of headings in the document. Use the Document Map to quickly navigate through the document and keep track of your location in it. When you click a heading in the document map, Word jumps to the corresponding heading in the document. It displays at the top of the window, and highlight the headings in the Document map.

Full Screen: Full Screen view is very useful when you want to enlarge typing area on the monitor. It is comparable to Normal view in its display of character and paragraph formatting, line and page breaks, tab stops, and alignments. However, the *title bar*, *menu bar*, *toolbars*, the *ruler*, the *scroll bars*, and the *status bar* are all removed from the screen in Full Screen view. A special Full Screen toolbar appears on-screen to indicate that Full Screen view is currently displayed.

3. [*Refer section 2.14*]

4. **Line spacing:** The amount of space from the bottom of one line of text to the bottom of the next line. Line spacing determines the amount of vertical space between lines of text. Microsoft word uses single line spacing by default. The line spacing you select will affect all lines of text in the selected paragraph.

   1. Select the paragraphs in which you want to change the line spacing.

   2. On the Format menu, click paragraph and then click the Indents and spacing tab.

   3. Under spacing do one of the following:

4. To change line spacing, select the options you want in the line spacing box.

   Single spacing: No blank line space between the lines of text.

   Double spacing: A blank line space between the lines of text.

   1 1/2 spacing: Half the height of one line space of text between the lines of text.

   Exactly: Give fixed line space between lines.

   Multiple: Line spacing that is increased or decreased by a percentage that you specified. In the At box, enter or select the line spacing you want. The default is three lines.

Paragraph spacing: The definition of the term paragraph in English language is "a series of related sentences". In Microsoft word, a paragraph is a distinct unit of information that has its own formatting characteristics, such as alignment, spacing and styles. A paragraph is always followed by a paragraph mark. The way you format paragraphs in a document depends on how you intend to use the document and how you want it to look.

1. Select the paragraph(s) in which you want to change paragraph spacing.

2. On the Format menu, click paragraph and choose Indents and Spacing tab.

3. There is a spacing box, in Indents and spacing tab, which lets you define the amount of white space that word must place before and after paragraphs.

4. Select the space required in the Before: text box for adding space before the paragraph.

5. Select the space required in the After: text box, for adding space after the paragraph.

6. Click OK.

5. Headers and footers are normally used in printed documents. You can create headers and footers that include text or graphic. For example, page numbers, the date, or a company logo, the document's title or file name, or the authors name that are usually printed at the top or bottom of each page in a document. A header is printed in the top margin, whereas footer is printed in the bottom margin. You can use the same header and footer throughout a document or change the header and footer for part of the document. For example, use a unique header or footer *on* the first page, or leave the header or footer *off* the first page. You can also use different headers and footers on odd and even pages or for part of a document.

6. [*Refer section 2.22.1*]

CHAPTER 3

Presentation Package

The reader will be able to understand in this chapter
- Create and edit a chart on a slide.
- Different views of slides.
- Customize the object drawn or shape the object by rotating, filing, scaling or shaping it.
- Insert and edit a table in the slide.
- Add transition and animation effects to a presentation.
- Add Rehearse timing. Add Speacker notes.
- Customize and Preset Animations.

3.1 INTRODUCTION

PowerPoint is the largest selling presentation graphics software package that is designed by Microsoft Corporation of USA. Since its introduction in 1987, PowerPoint has set new standards for the working of presentation graphics.

PowerPoint helps you bringing *ideas* and *information* that you want to convey to your audience with no difficulty. With Power-Point you can:
- Quickly create *paper for overhead projector (OHP), 35mm slide,* or *on-screen* presentations.
- Supplement your presentations with *speaker's notes.*
- Use material you have created in other application packages such as *Microsoft Word* and *Microsoft Excel.*

3.1.1 Uses of PowerPoint

Presentations

You can make presentation in the form of *slides, handouts* or *speaker's notes.*

Slides

Slides are individual "*pages*" of a presentation. It may contain *text, graphs, clipart,* etc. You can even print slides for overhead projector transparencies.

Handouts

Handouts consist of printed versions of your slides – either two, three, or six slides per page.

3.2 STARTING POWERPOINT

➡ **To start PowerPoint, do this:**

1. Click the Start button on the Taskbar.
2. Highlight the Programs menu item and click Microsoft PowerPoint (See Figure 3.1).

When you start PowerPoint for the first time, you will see the Office Assistant, an animated little figure ready to help you work. For now close the Office Assistant by clicking the close button at the upper right corner of the Assistant window. (See Figure 3.2)

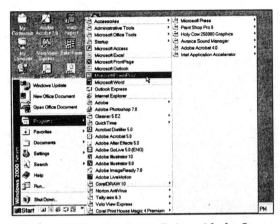

Figure 3.1 Starting PowerPoint with the Start Button

3.2.1 The PowerPoint Window

You will notice a close resemblance of the PowerPoint opening screen with the opening screens of Word and Excel. The main elements of the PowerPoint window are as seen in Figure 3.3.

Title Bar

The *Title bar* is at the top of the screen (See Figure 3.3). It shows the title Microsoft PowerPoint and the name of presentation. If you have not yet saved any presentation then it displays the default name for the presentation which is *Presentation1*. On the right of the title bar are the *Minimize, Restore/Maximize* and *Close* buttons.

Menu Bar

Just below the Title bar is the *Menu bar*. On the right of the menu bar are the *Minimize, Restore/Maximize* and *Close* buttons. In the middle of this bar are the menus such as File, Edit, etc. These menus contain various commands for doing a job in PowerPoint. The menus that expand when clicked, are briefly explained in Table 3.1

Table 3.1 PowerPoint Pull down Menu Commands

Menu	Types of Commands
File	File menu has commands for opening printing or saving files.
Edit	Edit menu has commands for cutting, copying and pasting text.
View	View menu has commands that control how you see a presentation.
Insert	Insert menu has commands for including a file, slide, or any other information in the presentation.
Format	Format menu has commands for changing the shape or size of characters. You can also modify drawings.
Tools	Tools menu besides others, has the commands to check spellings, etc. for typed text.
Slide Show	Slide Show menu has commands for managing animation.
Window	Window menu has the commands to arrange different windows seen on the screen.
Help	Help menu has the command to get immediate help on PowerPoint.

Toolbars

Toolbars as seen in Figure 3.3 contains buttons or shortcuts for the PowerPoint commands PowerPoint window shows two toolbars: the *Standard* toolbar and *Formatting* toolbar.

The Standard Toolbar

The buttons on the Standard toolbar and what each one does is given in Table 3.2. If you move the mouse pointer on any button, then you will get the name of the button shown on the screen.

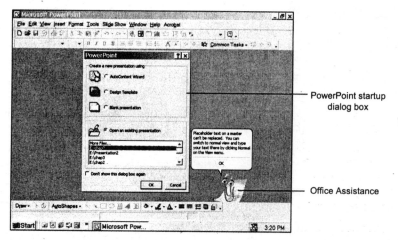

☞ A presentation package can be defined as a software that is used for presenting information using PC display in a simple and effective manner.

Figure 3.2 PowerPoint dialog box

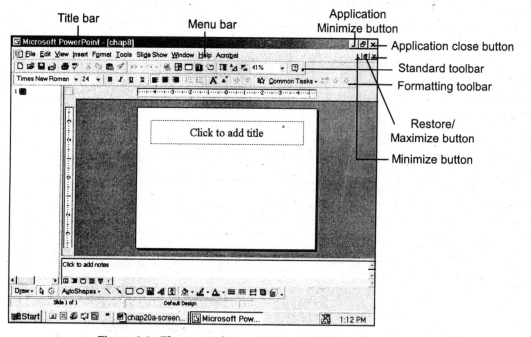

Figure 3.3 Elements of PowerPoint window

The Formatting Toolbar

The Toolbar just below the Standard toolbar is the Formatting toolbar (See Figure 3.3).

The menu and function of buttons of formatting toolbar are given in Table 3.3.

Table 3.2 The Jobs done by Standard Toolbar Buttons

Name	Function
New	Opens a new PowerPoint file.
Open	Opens a previously saved PowerPoint file.
Save	Saves the current file.
E-mail	It sends the current slide as the body of e-mail message.
Print	Opens the print dialog box to print a file.
Spelling	Helps in spelling check.
Cut	Cuts the selected text or objects and places them on the Windows Clipboard.
Copy	Places a copy of selected text or objects on the Windows Clipboard.
Paste	Pastes the contents of the Clipboard on the slide.
Format Painter	Enables you to copy formatting from one object to another.
Undo	Undoes the last action.
Redo	Redoes the last undone action.
Insert Hyperlink	Inserts a link to a World Wide Web site on the slide.
Tables and borders	Displays the tables and borders toolbar, which contain tools for creating, editing, and sorting a table.
Insert Table	It inserts a Word table with Word tools available for editing.
Insert Chart	It inserts a Microsoft Graph Chart.
New Slide	Opens the New Slide dialog box.
Expand all	Displays the titles and all the body of text for each slide.
Show Fromatting	It allows you to display the formatting of your presentation.
Gray scale preview	It allows you to have a preview of the presentation in gray scale rather than color.
Zoom	Allows you to zoom *in* or *out* to view the slide larger or smaller.
Microsoft PowerPoint help (F1)	Opens the Office Assistant or Help.

Table 3.3 The Jobs done by the Formatting Toolbar Buttons

Name	Function
Font	Opens a drop-down list so you can select another font.
Font Size	Allows you to enter a new size for selected font.
Bold	converts text from bold to normal form such as **B** to B.
Italic	converts text from italic to non-italic such as *B* to B.
Underline	converts text from underlined to non-underlined such as B to B.
Shadow	Applies a shadow effect to selected text.
Left Alignment	Aligns the selected text to the left.
Center Alignment	Aligns the selected text in the center.
Right Alignment	Aligns the selected text to the right right.

(Contd...)

Name	Function
Numbering	It automatically numbers the points in your slide.
Bullets	Applies a bullet list format to the selected text.
Increase Font Size	Increases the size for selected text.
Decrease Font Size	Decreases the size for selected text.
Increase Paragraph Spacing	It increases spacing between the selected lines of text.
Decrease Paragraph Spacing	It decreases spacing between the selected lines of text.
Promote	It moves selected text one level up in the outline hierarchy.
Demote	It moves selected text one level down in the outline hierarchy.

Screen Tips

Screen Tips show you the description of any buttons on the screen. Position the mouse pointer on the button and a small screen tip popup box opens near the mouse pointer, showing the buttons name.

Scroll Bars

There are two *scroll bars*. The vertical scroll bar is located on the right. The horizontal scroll bar is located at the bottom of the screen (See Figure 3.4). When you drag the scroll button on the vertical scroll bar, PowerPoint displays a Screen Tip which indicates the slide you are going to display (See Figure 3.4).

Status Bar

At the bottom of the PowerPoint window in Figure 3.4 is the *Status Bar*. The status bar has the following items.

- The first item on the Status bar in the Slides view or Notes view tells you which

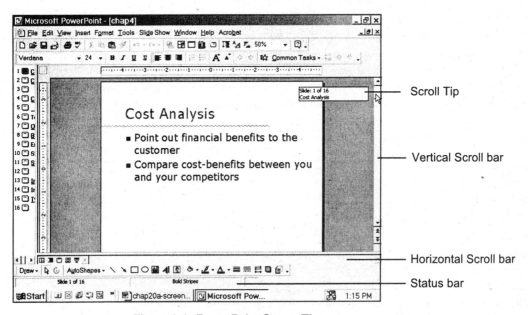

Figure 3.4 PowerPoint Screen Tips

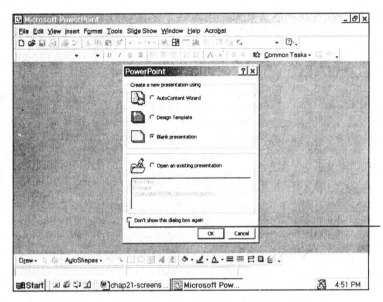

Click the check box if you don't want the dialog box to appear when you start PowerPoint

Figure 3.5 The PowerPoint dialog box

slide is currently on the screen and how many slides are there in the presentation.

- The middle item on the Status bar provides the name of the template that the presentation is based on.

3.3 CREATING A POWERPOINT PRESENTATION

3.3.1 Starting Presentation

After you start PowerPoint, firstly the PowerPoint banner is displayed and then the PowerPoint dialog box as shown in Figure 3.5 appears.

The PowerPoint dialog box offers the following three ways to start a presentation.

Auto contents wizard Template	When you select this option, PowerPoint asks you select a type of presentation from a list of predefined list of presenta-

(Contd...)

tions. It then loads the set of slides for this selected presentation. When you select this option, PowerPoint displays a list of templates. These templates automatically format the presentation. As you get more experienced in using Power-Point you will use this option often.

Blank presentation	On selecting this option, Power-Point starts a blank presentation without any design or sample text.
Open an existing presentation	You select this option to work on an existing PowerPoint presentation.

3.3.2 Selecting the Design

In this *Step* you decide the design of the presentation and also type the contents of the presentation. For beginners, the easiest way is to use the **A**utoContent *wizard* option. This wizard lets you select sample content for a set of presentation slides and also decides the design for the presentation. You can always change the design of the presentation as discussed in *Step 3*. Another way to choose a design for a new presentation is to select a Template option from the PowerPoint dialog box. This option is helpful for experienced users of PowerPoint.

3.3.3 Improving Presentation

After you have completed the initial draft of a presentation you may like to improve upon the initial draft. This step helps you to refine presentation. In this step you would do the following tasks:

Entering and Editing the text

Even if you had used the AutoContents Wizard, still you have to replace the wizard's default text with your own. You can work either side by side and enter or edit the text or you can work in *outline view*. The outline view is the easiest to work in while *entering, editing* or *rearranging* text.

Adding charts and Tables to a Presentation

Charts — Charts and pictures are the most effective way to get your point across to the audience. PowerPoint offers *eighteen* different type of charts, that you can add to a presentation.

Organization Charts — The types of charts show the hierarchy of an organization using a series of boxes and connecting lines. You may also use them to represent information other than an organization of an organization. (See Figure 3.7)

Tables — Tables are used as back up for charts or if you want to bring out a comparison of an issue. Table slides can hold text as well as numbers. (See Figure 3.6)

3.3.4 Adding Annotation and Graphics

In *Step 3* you refined the presentation and in *Step 4* you give the finishing touches. You may review each slide separately and like to add explanation on some slides. You may also use the Text Box tool to add text as annotation that highlight or explain special features if needed.

You may use the Drawing Toolbar to add graphics to accompany the text or image on a slide. PowerPoint comes with a library of

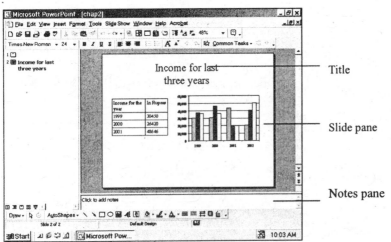

☞ *Charts when added cwith tables give easy assimilation of information to the audience.*

Figure 3.6 Slide with Chart and Table

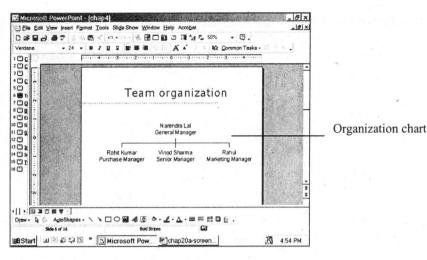

Organization chart

Figure 3.7 Slide with organization chart

ready made images which can be used for the slides using the Auto ClipArt command.

3.3.5 Previewing the Presentation

You can change the style and compare the different styles to select the best suited style in the final stage.

Slide sorter view is the best view to organize your slides as you will see the entire segment of the presentation at one go. In this view, you can see the effect of different styles in all the slides at one time and adjust the order of slides or delete the unwanted slides for better effects.

Finally, using the slide show view, you can watch and rehearse the presentation before putting it across to your audience.

3.3.6 Saving and Printing the Presentation

Make it a practice to save your presentation file at regular intervals so that you do not lose your work in case of the power or system failure.

PowerPoint can give you the output in three formats. These are:

- Print your slides on paper with any of the printers supported by Windows 9x or 2000.
- Generate 35 mm slides provided your computer is connected to a film recorder, which records your slides on a slide film.
- The third form of output which is fast becoming popular is the electronic presentation. An electronic presentation displays your presentation on the computer screen or on a large screen with the help of a (LCD) projector. Thus electronic presentations retains all the visual and sound effect of your presentation as is in the original display.

3.4 POWERPOINT VIEWS

PowerPoint offers five ways (*views*) to look at your presentation. Each view enables you to work on a different aspect of the presentation. The changes made in one view are also reflected in all other views.

To understand the function of views, consider that you are looking at a house. Now assume you are standing in front of a house. You see one view. Now you move to one of

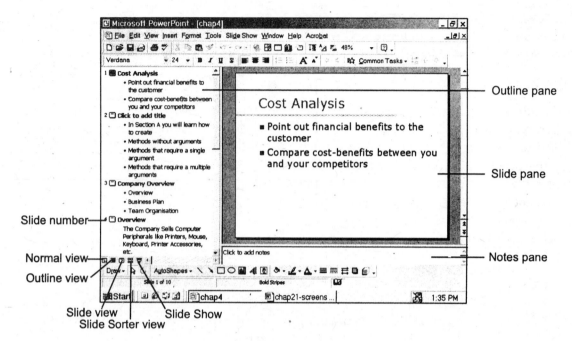

Figure 3.8 Normal View

the sides and you see a different view of the same house. PowerPoint views also allow you to see a presentation in various ways.

The buttons located at the lower left corner of the PowerPoint window just above the status bar as shown in Figure 3.8 help you to switch to different views.

In the following section, you will conceptually learn about the view.

3.4.1 Normal View

Normal view contains three panes:
- the outline pane
- the slide pane
- the notes pane

These panes let you work on all aspects of your presentation in one place. You can adjust the size of different panes by dragging the pane borders.
- Outline pane: Use the outline pane to organize and develop the contents of

your presentation. You can type all of the text of your presentation and rearrange bullet points, paragraphs and slides.
- Slide pane: In the slide pane, you can see how your text looks on each slide. You can add graphics, movie and sound clipping, create hyperlink and add animations to individual slides.
- Notes pane: The notes pane lets you add speaker notes or information you want to share with the audience. If you want to have graphic in your notes, you must add the notes in notes page view.

These three pane are also shown when you save a presentation as a Web page. The only difference is that the outline pane displays a table of contents so that you can navigate through the complete presentation.

You work with one slide at a time in Normal view. When you change to one of the other views, you can return to Normal view by clicking <u>V</u>iew menu and choose <u>N</u>ormal view or by clicking the leftmost button in the View buttons row in the lower-left corner of the work area. (See Figure 3.8)

3.4.2 Outline View

In Outline view, you see only the presentation text but you do not see graphs, tables or the design elements of the presentation such as the background design. You can easily enter the list of main topics of a presentation. Entering the main topics generates all the presentation slides you need, because each main topic becomes the title of a new slide. (See Figure 3.9)

3.4.3 Slide View

In slide view, you see and work on one slide at a time. You can type text, change the slide layout, add graphics, draw shapes and import graphics from other applications in the slide view.

3.4.4 Slide Sorter View

The slide sorter view displays a miniature of each slide in your presentation (See Figure 3.10). Working in this view is like laying out the pages of your presentation or report on the table so that you can see them all at once. In this view, you can see the design consistency and the flow of your presentation. If need be, you can easily reorder the slides, copy or delete the slides.

3.4.5 Notes Page View

This view helps you to prepare the speaker notes used while you are making the presentation to your audience. Notes pages view produces a smaller version of the slide on the top part of a page and leaves the lower part free for notes or keypoints (See Figure 3.11).

3.4.6 Slide Show View

This view of PowerPoint shows the progress of the presentation form slide to slide just

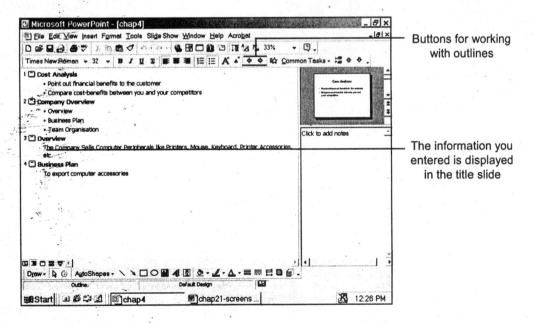

Figure 3.9 PowerPoint's Outline View

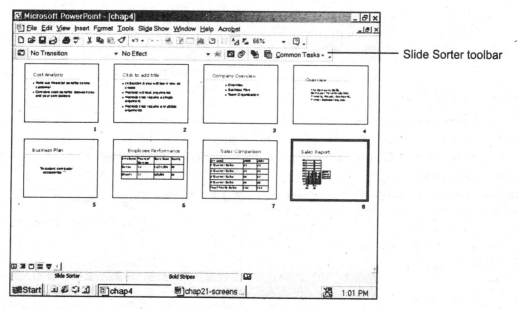

Slide Sorter toolbar

Figure 3.10 PowerPoint's Slide Sorter View

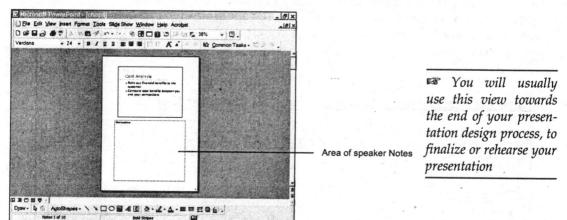

Area of speaker Notes

☞ *You will usually use this view towards the end of your presentation design process, to finalize or rehearse your presentation*

Figure 3.11 PowerPoint's Notes Pages View

like a real slide show. In this view, all *menus, toolbars, rulers,* the *status bar, scrollbars,* and the Windows *taskbar* are removed from the screen (See Figure 3.12).

3.5 HOW TO CREATE A NEW PRESENTATION

As seen in Figure 3.5, PowerPoint dialog box

has four options of which the first three are for creating a new presentation. These three options are placed in the *Create a new presentation using box.* The fourth option is for opening an existing presentation. The options are discussed below.

• <u>A</u>utoContents Wizard—This option starts the AutoContents Wizard which

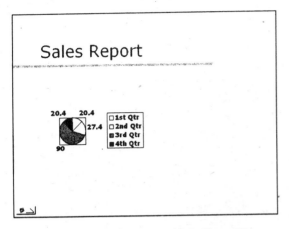

Figure 3.12 PowerPoint's Slide Show View

takes you step by step through the process of creating a presentation. This is also the best choice for the beginners.

- **T**emplate—When you select this option PowerPoint comes up with another dialog box which offers you a choice of built in design templates on which you can base you presentation.

- **B**lank presentation—When you select this option, PowerPoint gives maximum flexibility in creating a presentation. You start your presentation from scratch as there are no *elements* or *design backgrounds*.

- **O**pen an existing presentation — This option lets you open a presentation you have already created in PowerPoint.

3.5.1 Using AutoContent Wizard

If you select AutoContents Wizard, the dialog box as in Figure 3.13 appears. The *left portion* of the AutoContent Wizard dialog box shows the steps the wizard will take you through. The steps are as follows:

1. You see the AutoContents Wizard in the left half of window. Click the **N**ext > button at the bottom of the dialog box or press Ⓝ.

2. When you press **N**ext >, the Presentation type item is highlighted and the screen changes to the one shown in Figure 3.14.

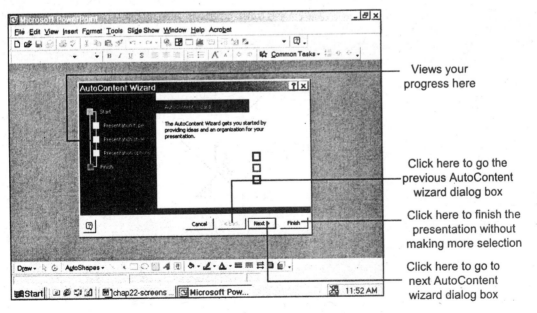

Figure 3.13 AutoContent Wizard dialog box

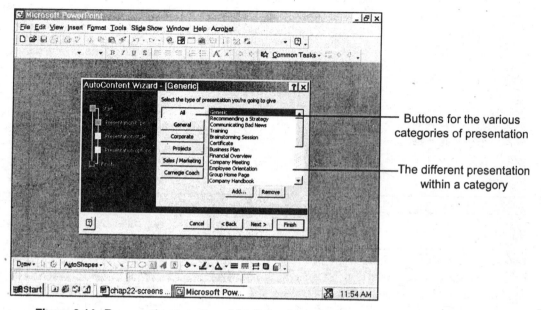

Figure 3.14 Presentation type item highlighted in AutoContent Wizard screen

The buttons in the middle of this box display the various categories of presentations. If you click the category buttons the scroll list on the right, you will get lists of different presentation types within the category. To see all the presentation types, click the **A**ll button. After you have selected the presentation type click **N**ext > to move to the next step.

3. Make the appropriate choice and click **N**ext button.

4. This takes you to the Presentation style item and the dialog box as shown in Figure 3.15 appears.

I. What type of output you will use? This offers five options that are as follows:

- On-**s**creen presentation: Choose this option if you want to give presentations on your computer screen or using LCD projector for wider screen.

- W**e**b presentation: Choose this option if you want to give presentations on the Web.

- Black and **w**hite overheads: Choose this option if you will make your presentation on OHP (over head projector) using black and white transparencies.

- **C**olor overheads: Choose this option if you want to make your presentation on OHP using colour transparences.

- **3**5 mm slides: Choose this option if you want to make your presentation using 35 mm slides.

After you select the appropriate choice click the **N**ext > button. This takes you to Presentation options item screen as shown in Figure 3.16.

5. Presentation options item asks you for the presentation title and any information to be included as a footer on each slide.

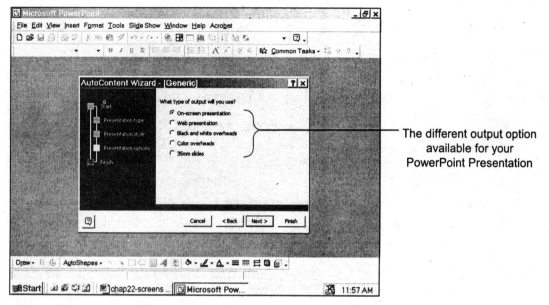

The different output option available for your PowerPoint Presentation

Figure 3.15 Presentation Style Item Highlighted in AutoContent Wizard screen

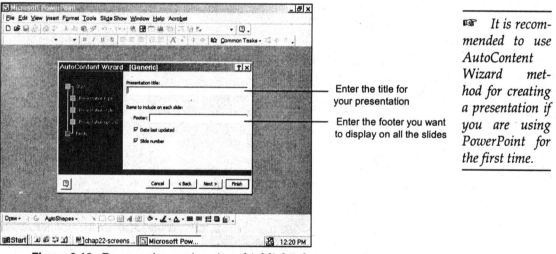

Enter the title for your presentation

Enter the footer you want to display on all the slides

☞ *It is recommended to use AutoContent Wizard method for creating a presentation if you are using PowerPoint for the first time.*

Figure 3.16 Presentation options item highlighted

You can also select whether you want the date for the presentation and the slide number to be included on each slide. Specify the information you want and then click <u>N</u>ext >. Complete the text boxes and click Next button. The Finish Screen is displayed as seen in Figure 3.17.

6. If you wish to make any changes to the selection in the first five steps, then click the <u>B</u>ack > button and make the changes. If no more changes are required then finally, click the <u>F</u>inish button.

After you click the <u>F</u>inish button, the new presentation appears in Normal view, which

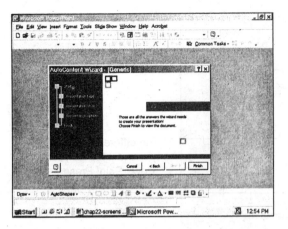

Figure 3.17 Finish Screen of the AutoContents Wizard

shows the outline on the left and the slides on the right.

3.5.2 Using PowerPoint Template

If you select the Design Template option from the opening PowerPoint screen (refer to Figure 3.5) then New Presentation dialog box appears. In the New Presentation dialog box click the presentation design tab and select the desired template (See Figure 3.18).

The three buttons on the right of this dialog box control the way the templates are displayed i.e. *as icons, in a list* or *as a list with details about the template files.* The preview box displays a sample of the template highlighted in the scroll list.

After selecting the desired template click OK, the new presentation appears on the screen.

3.5.3 Starting a Blank Presentation

When you select the Blank presentation option you begin with a blank presentation. This method is better till you get experienced and want to create a customized presentation.

➡ **To start a blank presentation, do this:**

1. Click the File menu and choose New or click the New button on the Standard toolbar or press Ctrl+N keys.

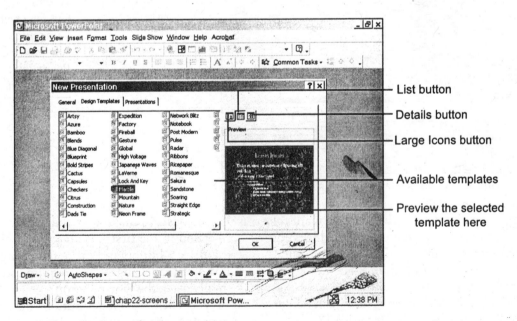

Figure 3.18 New Presentation dialog box with Presentation Designs tab active

2. Click the General tab in the New presentation dialog box. The screen as in Figure 3.19 appears.

3. Double click the Blank Presentation icon.

4. In the New slide dialog box, select an Autolayout Format for the first slide and click OK.

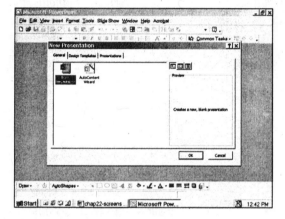

Figure 3.19 New Presentation dialog box with Presentation general tab

3.5.4 Opening an Existing Presentation

To open an existing presentation choose the Open an existing presentation option in the PowerPoint box (refer to Figure 3.20).

➡ **To open an existing presentation, do this:**

1. Open the File menu and choose Open or click the open button on the standard toolbar or press ⌃Ctrl+O. The open dialog box appears (See Figure 3.20).

2. Select the drive or folder in the list box.

3. Click the file you want to open. To see a preview of the presentation click the preview button.

4. Click Open button to open the presentation.

Figure 3.20 PowerPoint's Open dialog box

3.6 SAVING THE PRESENTATION

When working on a presentation, it is very important that you save it at regular intervals so that in case there is system failure you do not loose much of your work.

PowerPoint has two commands to save your file – Save and Save As command.

• The Save command is used to save the presentation.

• The Save As command is used when you want to save an existing presentation under a new name or you are saving your presentation for the first time.

➡ **To save a presentation, do this:**

1. Click the File menu and choose Save or click the Save button on the Standard toolbar or from the keyboard press ⌃Ctrl+S.

2. If you have already saved the file then PowerPoint updates the earlier saved file. If you have not saved the file before, the Save As dialog box as in Figure 24.21 appears.

3. In the Save As list box specify the location of your file.

4. In the File Name list box enter the name for your file.

5. Click Save after completing the details.

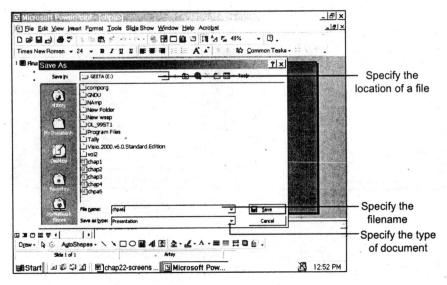

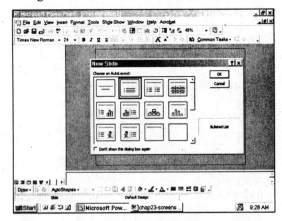

☞ *The Save As option gives you various file formats so that the presentation can be given without the presence of Power-Point software package on your machine.*

Figure 3.21 PowerPoint's Save As dialog box

➡ **To save a presentation using Save As command, do this:**

1. Click the File menu and choose Save As... . The **Save As** dialog box in Figure 3.21 appears. Now follow step 2 through 4 in the save procedure.

3.7 Working with Text

PowerPoint slide always contains text of some kind, even if it is just a title. Entering and editing text in PowerPoint is similar to entering and editing text in Word or Excel.

3.7.1 Adding Text To Slides

You can enter text in a presentation in two ways:

• Inserting a new slide with text place holder.
• Inserting text in an existing slide.

3.7.2 Adding Text in a Placeholder

PowerPoint comes with Autolayouts slides numbering 1 to 24. Many of these layouts contain text placeholders for title, body and

bulleted list.

➡ **To insert a new slide with text, do this:**

1. Click the Insert menu and choose New slide... or press Ctrl+M. From the New slide dialog box choose text layout (See Figure 3.22).

Figure 3.22 New Slide dialog box with text Layout Selected

2. Click anywhere within a placeholder to select it. The faint outline is replaced by a

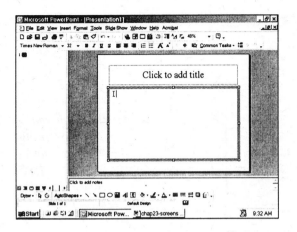

Figure 3.23 The Slide Layout with Placeholder for Text

wide hashed border (See Figure 3.23). This border indicates that the current placeholder is selected.

3. The sample text disappears and an insertion point appears inside the placeholder, indicating that you can enter text.

4. In a title or subtitle placeholder, the insertion point may be centered or left-aligned.

5. In a bulleted-list placeholder, the sample text disappears and the bullet remains, with the insertion point positioned where the text will begin.

6. Type the text for the slide inside the selected placeholder and press (Enter) key.

7. In the case of bullets, press (Enter) when you want to begin a new bulleted item. If the bulleted text is too long to fit on one line, PowerPoint automatically wraps the text to the next line and aligns the text.

8. When you finish entering text, deselect the object by clicking a blank area of the slide or the gray border around the slide.

3.7.3 Creating Text Outside a Placeholder

You can place text anywhere on a slide without being restricted to using a text placeholder.

➡ **To create a text object, do this:**

1. On the Drawing toolbar, click Text box.
2. Position mouse pointer at the place where you want to add text and then click it. A new text box appears (see Figure 3.24).
3. Enter the text you want to add. The text box expands to accomodate the new text.

3.8 EDITING TEXT ON A SLIDE

You can make changes to the text in any text object simply by clicking the object. An insertion point appears, indicating that the text is ready for editing. Then you can start making changes to the text.

3.8.1 Copying Text

You can copy text that appears in one place to another place. Copying of text occurs with the assistance of the Windows Clipboard. The *Clipboard* is an area of your computer's memory that is used for holding data. As long as the data is on the Clipboard, you can place it anywhere in any Windows software application. The data stays on the Clipboard until you replace it with new data, or until you exit Windows.

➡ **To copy text using menu command, do this:**

1. Select the text you want to copy.
2. Click the Edit menu and choose Copy, or click the Copy button on the toolbar or (press (Ctrl)+(C) keys together).
3. Move to the place in your presentation where you want to insert this text.
4. Click the Paste button on the toolbar (or press (Ctrl)+(V)).

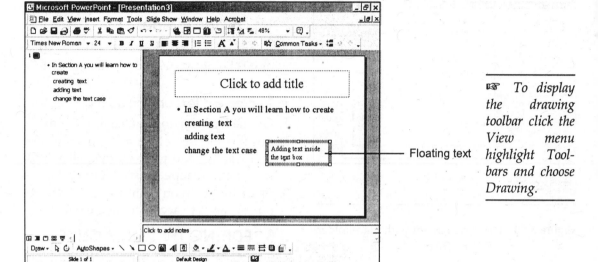

Figure 3.24 Slide with a Text Box

➡ To copy the text using drag and drop, do this:

1. Click the text to put the text box into edit mode.
2. Select the text you want to copy.
3. Position the mouse pointer anywhere within the highlighted text.
4. To copy the text hold down (Ctrl) key and drag to copy at the new location.

Because the text is still on the Clipboard, you can move to another slide and paste it again.

3.8.2 Moving Text

The move operation is similar to the copy operation except that text is moved i.e. it is deleted from the original location and copied to a new place.

➡ To move the text using drag and drop, do this:

1. Click the text to put the text box into edit mode.
2. Select the text you want to move.

3. Position the mouse pointer anywhere within the highlighted text.

4. Press and hold the left mouse button down while you drag the text to its new location. Then release the mouse button.

➡ To move the text using menu command, do this:

1. Click the text to put the text box in edit mode.

2. Select the text you want to move

3. Right-click and choose Cut from the shortcut menu or click the Cut button on the toolbar (or press (Ctrl)+(X)). Move to the new location, right-click, and choose Paste or click the Paste button (or press (Ctrl)+(V)).

☞ *Using Cut and Paste is another way to move text around between slides. Just select and cut the text, move to the appropriate slide, and paste it where you want it.*

Turn drag and drop editing on or off

1. Click the <u>T</u>ools menu and choose <u>O</u>ptions.... . The Options dialog box appears as in Figure 3.25.

Figure 3.25 Options dialog box

2. In the Options dialog box, click the Edit tab.

3. Select the Drag-and-drop text editing check box to turn the option on. To turn it off, clear the check box.

3.8.3 Deleting Text

You can delete characters, words, or all the text in a text box. Using one of these methods:

- The ⌈Delete⌋ key erases the character to the right of the cursor.

- The ⌈Backspace⌋ key erases the character to the left of the cursor.

If you delete text accidentally, you can undo your action by clicking the Undo button on the toolbar (You can also press ⌈Ctrl⌋+⌈Z⌋ or click the <u>E</u>dit menu and choose Undo).

Copy and Paste the multiple items

1. Select the items you want to copy.

2. On the Clipboard toolbar, click copy

3. To display the Clipboard toolbar, click the <u>V</u>iew menu highlight <u>T</u>oolbars and choose Clipboard.

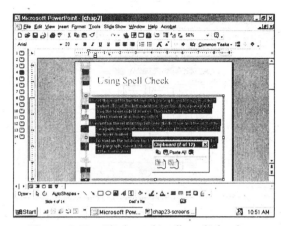

Figure 3.26 Clipboard toolbar dialog box

4. The Clipboard toolbar appears as in Figure 3.26.

5. If the next item you want to copy is in another program, switch to that program.

6. Select the next item you want to copy.

7. Repeat steps 3 to 5 until you have copied all the items (up to 12) you want to copy.

8. Click where you want the items to be pasted.

9. To paste all the items you copied, click Paste All on the Clipboard toolbar.

10. If you do not want to paste all of the items you copied, or if Paste All is not available, you can paste specific items.

3.9 INSERTING A TABLE SLIDE

You can insert a Table in a slide in two different ways. These are:

- Create a new slide which is specifically made to contain a table.

- Insert a table in the existing slide.

➡ **To create a new slide with table, do this:**

1. In the slide view, display the slide after which you want to insert the table.

2. Click the <u>I</u>nsert menu and choose <u>N</u>ew Slide... or click the New slide button on the standard toolbar. The New slide dialog box appears as in Figure 3.27.

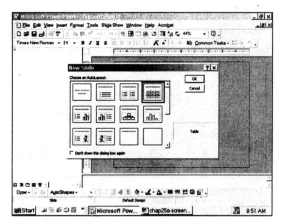

Figure 3.27 New Slide dialog box

3. In the New Slide dialog box, double click the Table button. A new slide appears.

4. Double click the table place holder. Insert Table dialog box appears as seen in Figure 3.28.

5. In the Insert Table dialog box, enter the number of *columns* and the number of *rows* you want to insert in the table. You can type the number of rows and the number of columns or click the up or down arrow on the right of the edit boxes to specify these numbers.

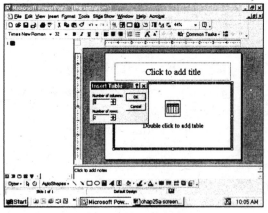

Figure 3.28 Insert Table dialog box

6. After you specify the number of rows and columns, click OK to create the table.

7. A table appears on the slide as seen in Figure 3.29.

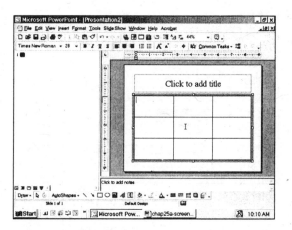

Figure 3.29 Slide with a Table

3.9.1 Entering Text in a Table

When you create a new table, an empty table appears within a gray frame on the slide as seen in Figure 3.29. When you insert a table, the insertion point flashes in the first cell in the upper left corner of the table. The text you type appears at the insertion point. After entering the text in the table and to exit the editing mode, click anywhere outside the table.

3.9.2 Editing a Table

Once you have created a table and entered text or numbers, you can modify its structure by *adding, deleting, moving* and *copying* cells, columns and rows. You can also change the width of columns, height of rows and merge or split cells to accommodate typed text in the cells.

Selecting Cells, Columns and Rows

➡ **To select cells, do this:**

1. For selecting a single cell, position the mouse pointer near the left inside edge of the cell. Once the pointer changes to a right arrow, click the cell.

2. To select adjacent cells in the same column, click any where in the first cell and drag the mouse pointer down the column.

3. To select adjacent cells in the same row, click anywhere in the first cell, and drag the mouse pointer across the row.

4. To select multiple cells click the first cell, press and hold down the (Shift) key, and click the other cell. Both the cells and any cell in between these two cells are selected.

➡ **To select column or columns of cells, do this:**

1. Position the mouse pointer on the top border of the column or columns. The pointer changes to a down arrow, click the left mouse button to select the entire column or columns (See Figure 3.30). *Alternatively*, position the cursor in a cell of the column to be selected.

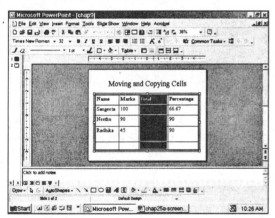

Figure 3.30 Selecting a Column

➡ **To select a row of cells, do this:**

1. Position the cursor in a cell of the row to be selected. In the Table and Borders toolbar click the Table menu and choose Select row. (See Figure 3.31)

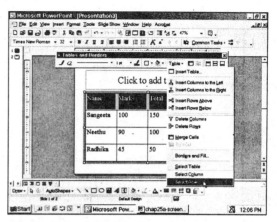

Figure 3.31 Selecting the entire row in a table

Adding Cells, Columns and Rows

➡ **To insert a column, do this:**

1. Click anywhere in the column next to where you want the new column to appear.

2. On the Tables and Border toolbar, click Table, and then choose Insert Columns to the Left or Insert Columns to the Right. A column is inserted to the left or right of the selected column.

➡ **To insert a row, do this:**

1. Click anywhere in the row next to where you want the new row to appear.

2. On the Tables and Border toolbar, click Table, and then choose Insert Rows Above or Insert Rows Below. A row is inserted above or below of the selected row.

Deleting Columns and Rows

➡ **To delete columns/rows, do this:**

1. Select the columns/rows you want to delete.

2. On the Table and Borders toolbar, click Table, and then choose Delete Columns or Rows. Or right click the mouse, choose Delete Rows or Columns.

Copying and Moving Cells

Once you select the contents of a cell, you can *copy* or *move* these to another location using drag and drop. *Alternatively*, use the Cut, Copy and Paste commands from the Edit menu on the standard toolbar or from the shortcut menu that appears when you select a cell and click the right mouse button.

➡ **To move or copy cell contents using drag and drop, do this:**

1. Select the text you want to move or copy.
2. From the Edit menu or the shortcut menu, choose Cut (to move) or Copy. Alternately, on the Standard toolbar, click the Cut or Copy button.
3. Click in the table, to position the insertion point where you want to insert the cut or copied text.
4. From the Edit menu or the Shortcut menu, choose Paste. *Alternatively*, on the Standard toolbar, click the Paste button. The cut or copied selected text is moved or copied at the insertion point.
5. *To move the selected text* — Position the mouse pointer over the selected text, press and hold down the left mouse button and drag the text to the destination cell.
6. *To copy the selected text* — Position the mouse pointer over the selected text, press and hold the (Ctrl) key, press and hold down the left mouse button and drag the text to the destination cell.

   A *plus* sign appears next to the pointer to indicate that you are copying instead of moving. (See Figure 3.32)

Changing Column Width and Rows Height

You can change the size of *rows* of a table by adjusting the height of the rows. Similarly, you can also change the size of the *columns* by adjusting the width of the columns.

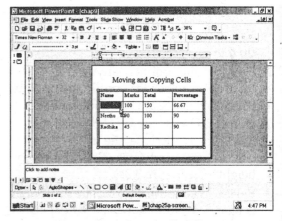

Figure 3.32 Copying a cell with contents

Changing Column Width

➡ **To change the width of a column in a table, do this:**

1. Position the pointer anywhere on the column's right border until the pointer changes to a double line and arrow. (See Figure 3.33)
2. Drag the column border to the left or right to decrease or increase the column width. A dashed line indicates the target column width.
3. Release the mouse button. The column width is changed to the new size you specified by dragging.

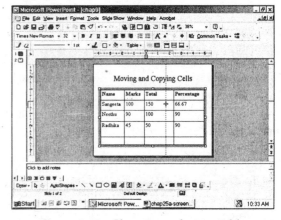

Figure 3.33 Changing column width

Changing Row Height

➡ **To change the height of a row in a table, do this:**

1. Position the pointer anywhere on the row's right border until the pointer changes to a double line and arrow.

2. Drag the row border up or down to decrease or increase the row height. A dashed line indicates the target row height. (See Figure 3.34)

3. Release the mouse button. The row height is changed to the new size you specified by dragging.

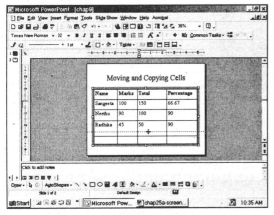

Figure 3.34 Changing row height

3.10 CREATING CHARTS

PowerPoint creates or modifies a chart using Microsoft Graph. Microsoft Graph is a graphing program shared by all MS-OFFICE components like *Word, Excel, PowerPoint*. So if you know how to create graphics in one of the MS-Office components, you can use the same technique in other MS-Office components also.

3.10.1 Creating a Chart Slide

➡ **To create a chart slide, do this:**

1. In the slide view, display the slide after which you want to add the chart slide.

2. Click the Insert menu and choose New slide or click the New slide button on the Standard Toolbar or press Ctrl+N. The New slide dialog box appears as in Figure 3.35 with Autolayout for chart slide selected.

3. Click the Autolayout for a chart slide.

4. Click OK.

5. Double click the chart place holder to start graph.

A sample chart appears within the place holder, and the data sheet window containing the sample data for the chart overlays as seen in Figure 3.36.

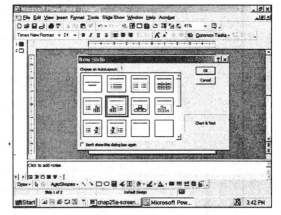

Figure 3.35 New Slide dialog box

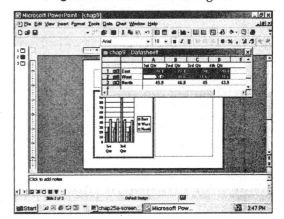

Figure 3.36 PowerPoint's Sample Data graphically displayed

⇒ **To add a chart to an existing slide, do this:**

1. Click the <u>I</u>nsert menu and choose <u>C</u>hart or click the Chart button.
2. Microsoft Graph starts and shows a sample chart along with the data sheet.
3. Enter the data for the chart and adjust size and position of the chart.

3.10.2 Entering Data for the Chart

When you start a new chart, PowerPoint shows a datasheet overlaying a graph. The Datasheet contains PowerPoint's sample data. PowerPoint also draws the chart and displays it. Both are visible together (See Figure 3.36)

3.10.3 What is a Datasheet?

A Datasheet looks like a miniature spread sheet. It contains *cells* formed by the intersection of rows and columns.

The left most column and the top most row contain the text labels. The data to be graphed occupies the cells below and to the right of the labels. Each cell is identified by an *address* that consists of a column letter and a row number.

For most of the chart types, each column represents a category of data and each row is a data series and is marked with a marker indicating the type of chart you are creating.

3.10.4 Entering Data in the Datasheet

Entering data in the Datasheet consists of 2 steps. These are:

• Entering the labels in the left most column and top most row.
• Entering the data to be graphed in the remaining cells.

⇒ **To enter data in a datasheet, do this:**

1. Click the top cell in column A and enter the category labels across the top row. (The categories along the rows appear along the *x-axis* in the graph).
2. Enter the name of the data series along the column, starting from the first cell labeled. Each row represents the data series for each category.
3. Enter the values for each category in the cell. (See Figure 3.37)

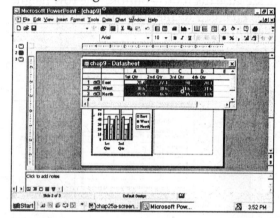

Figure 3.37 Entering Data in the cell A1 of the datasheet

Now type the numbers for each cell along the column and press (Enter). For practice, enter the numbers given below.

20.4 27.4 90   20.4
30.6 38.6 34.6 31.6
45.9 46.9 45   43.9

3.11 ORGANIZATION CHART

An *organization chart* is a graphical representation of the structure of an organization. The application of organization chart is not restricted only to represent the structure of an organization, but also can be used to show various other categories such as books published by a publishing company, etc.

3.11.1 Creating an Organizational (Org) Chart

There are two ways to add an organization (org) chart to a presentation:

- insert a new slide for an organizational chart.

- add an organizational chart to an existing slide.

➡ **To create an organizational chart slide, do this:**

1. In the slide view, display the slide after which you want to insert the chart slide.

2. Click the Insert menu and choose New Slide or click the New slide... or press Ctrl+M keys together. The New slide dialog box as in Figure 3.38 appears.

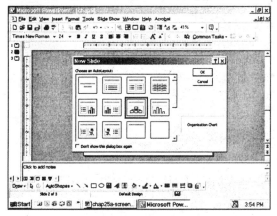

Figure 3.38 New Slide dialog box with Org Chart slide selected

3. Double click the org chart Autolayout. The new slide appears as in Figure 3.39.

4. Double click the org chart place holder to start a new organization chart. The *org chart* window opens as seen in Figure 3.39.

➡ **To add an org chart to an existing slide, do this:**

1. In the Slide view, display the slide to which you want to add the chart.

Figure 3.39 Org Chart window opens

2. Click the Insert menu and choose Object... .
The Insert Object dialog box as in Figure 3.40 appears.

3. Click the Create new radio button so that a dot appears in the button.

4. In the object type scroll list, double click MS-Organizational Chart 2.0. The Organizational Chart window appears. (See Figure 3.41)

3.11.2 Formatting the Org Chart

Different components of an Org chart which can be formatted are:

- The text in an org chart

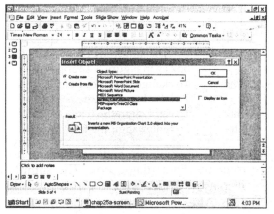

Figure 3.40 Insert Object dialog box with MS-Organization Chart selected

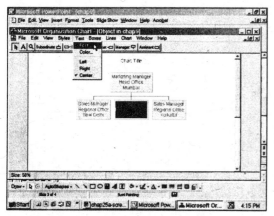

Figure 3.41 Format Text options of the organization chart window

- The position boxes
- The connecting lines

Formatting the Text

While formatting the text, you can change *font, colour* and *alignment* of the text in the organization chart box.

➡ To format the text, do this:

1. Select the text you want to format.
2. Click the Text menu and select from the available options (See Figure 3.41).
3. To change the alignment of the text choose from the options given in Table 3.1.

Table 3.1 Options for Text Formatting

Option	Purpose
Font...	On selecting font the font dialog box as in Figure 3.42 appears.
Colour...	To change the colour of the text
Left	To left align the text
Right	To right align the text
Center	To center align the text

Choose the options for *Font, Fontstyle* and *size* from the Font dialog box. The sample box displays a preview of the this options selected. After selecting the options click OK.

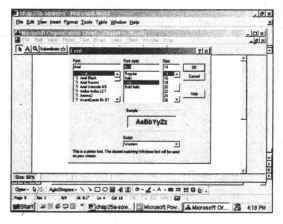

Figure 3.42 Font dialog box

Formatting Boxes

You can format the boxes by changing the following characteristics.

- Color
- Shadow
- Border style
- Border colour
- Border line style

➡ To format the position boxes, do this:

1. Select the position boxes you want to format.

2. To change the colour of the box, click the Box menu and choose Colour... . The colour dialog box as in Figure 3.43 appears. Select the desired colour and click OK. The chart changes to the desired colour.

3. To apply the shadows, click the Box menu and choose Shadow. The shadow options appear as in Figure 3.44. Click the desired shadow option.

4. To change border style click the Box menu and choose Border style. The Border style options appear as in Figure 3.45. Click the desired border style.

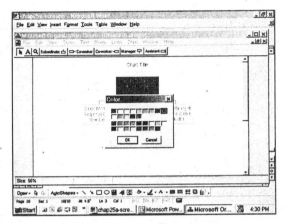

Figure 3.43 Colour dialog box

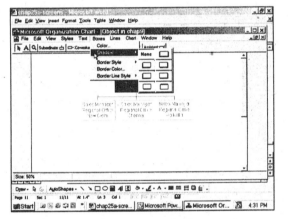

Figure 3.44 Boxes menu shadow options

5. To change the border colour, click the Box menu and choose Border color. The color dialog box as in Figure 3.43 appears. Click the desired colour.

6. To change the border line style, click the Box menu and choose Border Line Style. The border line style options appear as in Figure 3.46. Click the desired border line style.

Formatting the Lines

For the lines connecting the boxes you can change *thickness, style,* and *color.* To format a line first select it by clicking it. For selecting

multiple lines press and hold the (Shift) key while you click the lines. The selected lines appear dimmed and dashed.

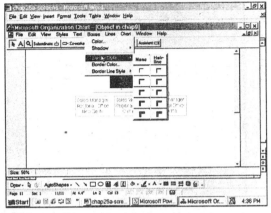

Figure 3.45 Boxes menu with border style options

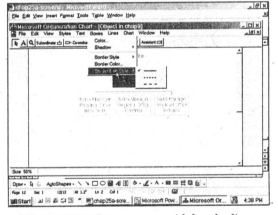

Figure 3.46 Boxes menu with border line style option

➡ **To format the connecting lines, do this:**

1. Select the connecting lines to be formatted.

2. To change the line thickness click the Line menu and choose Thickness, from the options shown in Figure 3.47.

3. To change the line style, click the line menu and choose Style and choose from the options (See Figure 3.46).

4. To change the line colour, click the line menu and choose Color.... The dialog box as in Figure 3.43 appears. Select the colour options.

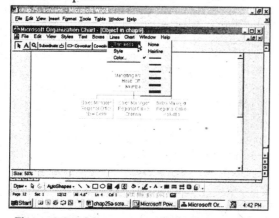

Figure 3.47   Line menu with thickness option

3.12   USING CLIP ART GALLERY

ClipArt gallery is a collection of graphic files in PowerPoint that you can insert in presentations. Microsoft has built a gallery of clipart images into the ClipArt gallery, so that you have your own collection of artwork available.

PowerPoint can help you select an appropriate piece of art for your slides by looking at key words in your presentation and trying to find pictures to match.

3.12.1   Adding Clipart

The easiest way to add graphics is to import a picture from the clip art gallery.

3.12.2   Inserting a picture from the ClipArt Gallery

1. Select the slide where you want to add a picture.
2. On the Drawing toolbar, click Insert Clip Art. The Insert Clip Art dialog box appears as in Figure 3.48.
3. Click the Pictures tab and then from the category choose the desired list.

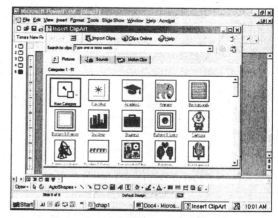

Figure 3.48   Insert ClipArt dialog box

4. After selecting the picture, click the picture and then choose Insert clip. *Alternatively* right click the mouse and choose Insert.
5. When you are finished using the Clip Gallery, click the Close button on the Clip Gallery title bar.

3.12.3   Adding a clip to the Clip Gallery

The clip gallery is full of files you can use in a presentation. However, all those images are common to all users of PowerPoint.

➡ **To add a clip art image to the Clip gallery, do this:**

1. Click Insert ClipArt on the Drawing toolbar. The Insert Clip Art dialog box appears.
2. Click Import Clips button in the Insert ClipArt dialog box. The Add Clip to Clip Gallery dialog box appears as shown in Figure 3.49.
3. Use the Look in: field to locate the file you want to import.
4. Select the clip file to add and click Import.

3.13   USING DRAWING TOOLBAR

The basic set of *drawing* and *editing* tools are located on the Drawing toolbar. You can draw and revise shapes, lines, text and pictures to create a professional looking presentation. Each of the objects you draw for your slide can be designed as per your need.

➡ **To display the drawing toolbar, do this:**

1. Click the Vjew menu and choose Toolbars. From the list of toolbars, click the drawing toolbar and click OK.

2. The drawing toolbar is displayed at the bottom of the window just above the status bar as seen in Figure 3.50.

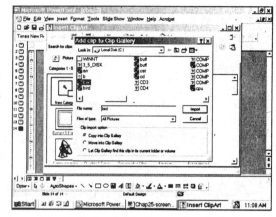

Figure 3.49 Add clip to Clip Gallery

Figure 3.50 Drawing Toolbar

☞ *You can rotate a single object or a group of objects around its own centre. You can also rotate the Autoshapes to make your slide attractive.*

3.13.1 Drawing with Autoshapes

PowerPoint Autoshapes are familiar shapes that you are likely to use very often. These shapes are fully adjustable in size. Many shapes include additional adjusting handle, which allows you to adjust many characteristic features. Autoshapes provides the following categories of tools:

- Lines
- Block arrows
- Connectors
- Stars and Banners
- Basic shapes
- Action buttons

➡ **To draw a shape with Autoshape lines, do this:**

1. Click the Autoshapes button on the Drawing toolbar.

2. Click at lines in the pop-up menu, as seen in Figure 3.51.

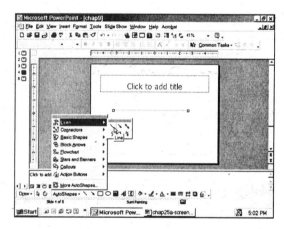

Figure 3.51 Selecting Autoshapes on the toolbar

3. *Alternatively*, click the Drawing toolbar and select the line button.

4. Select an Autoshape from the lines pop-up menu, that has six options. (See Figure 3.51)

5. Position the pointer on the slide, where you want the beginning of the line.

6. Click the first point, that is the starting point of the line.

7. Move the pointer to the next point for the line and click.

- To draw a straight line between two points, press and hold down the (Ctrl) key when you click the second point.
- To draw a straight line segment that is *horizontal*, *vertical*, or *diagonal*, press and hold down the (Shift) key as you move the pointer.

3.13.2 Rotating and Flipping Objects

If you want to change the angle at which an object is placed on your slide, rotating tool can be used to create new shapes. For example, a square can be rotated to form a diamond. You can rotate a single object or a group of objects around its own centre. You can also rotate the Autoshapes to make your slide attractive.

➡ To rotate a drawing object, do this:

1. Select the drawing object, by clicking mouse pointer on it.
2. Choose the Free Rotate tool from the drawing toolbar.
3. Four round green handles appear. Position the mouse pointer on any one of the handles of the drawing object or group, and then drag to spin the object around its centre.
4. When the object is in the desired angle position, release the mouse button. The object appears in its new rotated position as seen in Figure 3.52.

Flipping an Object

The flip tool on the drawing toolbar lets you flip an object. Flipping means to turn an object by 180°, either horizontally or vertically (leading to a *lateral/vertical* inversion respectively).

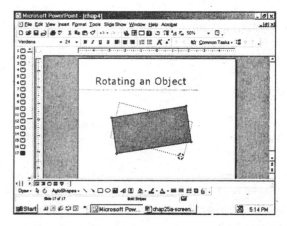

Figure 3.52 Effect created by rotating an object

The Drawing menu on the drawing toolbar offers you the option of Rotate or Flip. Moreover, the Rotate or Flip submenu further offers the following options:

- Free Rotate — The equivalent of selecting the Free Rotate button on the drawing toolbar.
- Rotate Left — Rotates the selected object 90 degrees to the left.
- Rotate Right — Rotates the selected object 90 degrees to the right.
- Flip Horizontal — Mirrors the object left to right (lateral inversion)
- Flip Vertical — Rotates the object 180 degrees top to bottom (vertical inversion).

➡ To Flip an object, do this:

1. Select the object(s) to be flipped.
2. Click the Draw menu on the Drawing toolbar. From the draw menu, choose Rotate or Flip as in Figure 3.53.
3. Click Flip Horizontal or Flip Vertical. The object is turned accordingly.

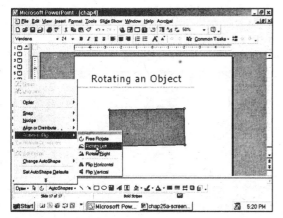

Figure 3.53 Showing a flipped object and menu

3.13.3 Cutting, Copying, Pasting and Deleting Objects

You can *cut, copy* and *paste* drawing objects as you would do with any object on a PowerPoint slide by using Cut, Copy and Paste buttons on the Standard toolbar or, the Cut, Copy and Paste commands on the Edit menu or the shortcut menu options.

➡ **To cut/copy and paste an object, do this:**

1. Select the object you want to cut/copy.
2. To cut an object click the Edit menu and choose Cut or click on the cut button, on the standard toolbar or press Ctrl+X keys together.
3. To copy an object click the Edit menu and choose Copy or click the copy button, on the standard toolbar or press Ctrl+C keys together.

   The object you cut/copy is placed on the Windows clipboard. In case the object is cut, the object is removed from the initial position. In case of copy, the copy of the original is placed on the clipboard.
4. To paste from the clipboard, position the insertion point where you want to paste.

5. Click the Edit menu and choose Paste or click the Paste button on the Standard toolbar or press Ctrl+V keys together.

3.13.4 Duplicating and Deleting Slides

You can duplicate i.e. copy or delete selected slides in slide sorter view.

➡ **To duplicate the slides, do this:**

1. Select the slide or slides you want to duplicate.
2. Click the Edit menu and choose Duplicate or press Ctrl+D.
3. Figure 3.54 shows you Slides (i.e 2 and 5) that are duplicated.

➡ **To delete the slides, do this:**

1. Select the slide or slides you want to be delete.
2. Click the Edit menu and choose Delete Slide or press Ctrl+X keys together.
3. Figure 3.55 shows you the view after deleting the duplicate selected slides i.e. slides 5 and 6 are deleted.

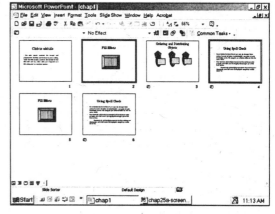

Figure 3.54 The selected slides (2 and 4) have been copied

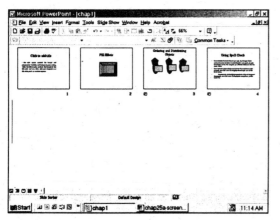

Figure 3.55 The Selected slides (5 and 6) have been deleted

3.13.5 Using AutoShapes Action Buttons

PowerPoint contains Action buttons and Action settings. These buttons or settings enable you to add buttons to your slides. In this way, viewers can click to jump to any slide in the slide show. Viewers can even play a video, jump to an Internet web page or start another software application.

➡ **To add an action button to a slide show, do this:**

1. Click Slide Show menu and choose Action Buttons. The Action Button submenu appears as in Figure 3.56. Select the button you want to add.
2. Now add the button to show in the slide. After you add the button, the Action Setting dialog box appears as in Figure 3.57. In the Action Settings tabs define the actions you want to associate with the button.
3. Click the Mouse Click tab.
4. Select the Hyperlink to: option, and select the desired option from drop-down list.
5. In the Hyperlink to: Other PowerPoint Presentation dialog box, select the folder of file you want to link to.

6. If there is more than one slide, Power-Point shows the Hyperlink to Slide dialog box.
7. Click the OK button.

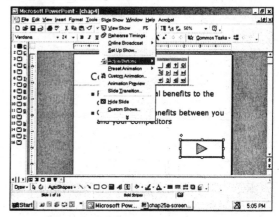

Figure 3.56 Action button sub menu

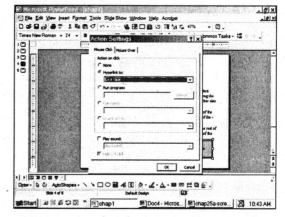

Figure 3.57 Action setting dialog box with mouse click tab

8. Click Run program: option if you want to open a different application from within the presentation. Specify the program you want to open.
9. Click OK.

3.14 Printing Presentation

To start printing, make sure the presentation you want to print is open on the screen.

➡ To print a presentation, do this:

1. Click the <u>F</u>ile menu and choose <u>P</u>rint... or press Ctrl+P, or click print button from the standard toolbar. The print dialog box appears as in Figure 3.58.

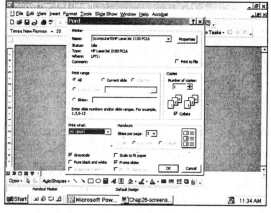

Figure 3.58 Print dialog box

2. The name of the currently selected printer is shown at the top of the Print dialog box in the Name: text box. To print the presentation on a different printer, select the desired printer from the Name: drop-down list.

3. If you want to take presentation file to another system for printing, click the Print to file check box. This will print the presentation output file on disk, which can than be downloaded on the printer without needing PowerPoint on your PC.

4. The Print range option has the following variations:

All	Choose All option to print the entire presentation at one time.
Current slide	Choose the Current slide option, to print the slide shown on the monitor.
Slides:	Choose to print the selected slides, and enter the corresponding slide numbers in the Slides: edit box. e.g., to print slide 3 and 6 through 8, enter 3,6-8 in the Slides edit box.

5. The Copies area has the following option:

Number of copies:	Specify the number of copies you want to print, for each slide.
Collate	Specify if you want to arrange while printing multiple copies. When you choose collate option, each set is printed completely from first page to the last page. Then the next set is printed.

6. In the Print what: drop-down list select the part of the presentation you want to print. Choose from, *Slides, Handouts, Notes, Pages,* or *Outline View.*

☞ *Another way to select the slides to print is to switch to Slide Sorter or Outline view. For this, press and hold down the* Shift *key as you click each slide or slide icon. When you open the Print dialog box, click the Selection option in the Print Range section.*

7. The Special Print Options are:

* Grayscale—To print in grayscale, select the grayscale check box.

* The P<u>u</u>re black & white option—converts all colours in the presentation to either black or white. Prefer this option if you need to print on a printer that cannot print gray shades.

* The Scale to fit paper option—scales the slides to fit the printed page even if the slides have been set up for a different page size.

* The Frame slides option—prints a narrow frame around each slide. Use it if you want to show slides on a overhead projector.

* The Print hidden slides option—prints slides that you have hidden using the <u>H</u>ide Slide command on the Sli<u>d</u>e Show menu. If your presentation has no hidden slides, the option is unavailable.

3.15 HOW TO DEVELOP A SLIDE SHOW?

The slide show displays each of the slides in the desired sequence. To start a slide show, you select one out of the following four choices:

1. Click <u>V</u>iew menu and choose Slide Sho<u>w</u>
2. Click the Sli<u>d</u>e Show menu and choose <u>V</u>iew Show.
3. Click the Sli<u>d</u>e Show menu and choose <u>R</u>ehearse Timings.
4. Click the Slide Show View button at the bottom of the PowerPoint.

☞ *To create a graceful ending to a slide show you can add a black slide to the end of presentation by clicking the <u>T</u>ools menu highlighting <u>O</u>ptions... and selecting the <u>E</u>nd with black slide option on the View tab of the Options dialog box.*

3.15.1 Assigning Slide Transitions

Transition is a term PowerPoint uses to describe the way that slide arrives on the screen.

As you progress from one slide to another during a presentation, a transition "draws" the next slide on the screen using a pre-recorded sound played.

Think about a cartoon film. When one scene ends and another scene begins, you must have noticed the transitions between them. For example, the picture can fade out and then fade in to new scene or the first scene slides off the screen as the second scene slides onto the screen. Such transitions are also available in PowerPoint.

➡ **To assign the transitions, do this:**

1. Click Slide Sorter view button or Click the <u>V</u>iew menu and choose Sli<u>d</u>e Sorter.
2. Select the slide(s) you want to add a transition effect.
3. Click Sli<u>d</u>e Show menu and choose Slide <u>T</u>ransition... . *Alternately*, click the Slide Transition button on the Slide Sorter toolbar if the Slide Sorter toolbar is displayed. (See Figure 3.59)

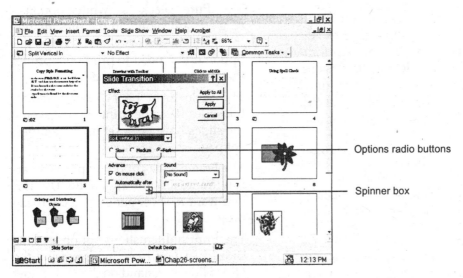

☞ *The slide show displays each of the slides in the desired sequence.*

— Options radio buttons

— Spinner box

Figure 3.59 Slide Transition dialog Box

4. In the Slide Transition dialog box, select a transition in the drop-down list in the Effect section. Choose the speed of transition from Slow, Medium, Fast.

5. The Advance section has two options for transition:
   - On mouse click check box–if you want the transition to take place on clicking the mouse.
   - Automatically after–in this case the transition takes place automatically after the time you specify in the *seconds* box.

6. Select the Sound option to give sound transitions to your slide show from the Sound drop-down list.

7. Click Apply

8. To apply the same transition effect to every slide in a presentation click Apply to All button. *Alternately*, to apply a single effect to all the slides, click Edit menu and choose Select All or press Ctrl+A keys together.

3.16 HOW TO ANIMATE TEXT AND GRAPHIC OBJECTS?

A movement given to an object is known as animation. You can give animation effect to each object on the slide such as text, graphics, charts etc. This is done to focus on important points, control the flow of information and give life to the presentation. You can set up the way you want an object or the text to appear. You can also set whether the text will appear by letter, word or paragraph. You can also choose whether you want the text or object to dim or change colour when you add a new element. You can change the order and timing of the animation and can also set them to occur automatically without having to click the mouse.

3.17 CREATING AND PRESENTING A CUSTOM SHOW

By creating custom shows in PowerPoint, there are two kinds of custom shows: basic and hyperlinked. A basic custom show is a separate presentation or a presentation that includes some of the slides of the original. A hyperlinked custom show is a quick way to navigate to one or more separate presentations.

3.17.1 Basic Custom Shows

Use a basic custom show to give separate presentations to different groups in your organization. For example, if your presentation contains a total of five slides, you can create a custom show named "Custom 1" that includes just slides 1, 3 and 5. You can create a second custom show named "Custom 2" that includes slides 1, 2, 4 and 5. When you create a custom show from a presentation, you can always run the entire presentation in its original sequential order.

3.17.2 Creating a Basic Custom Show

➡ **To create a basic custom show, do this:**

1. Click the **Slide Show** menu, and choose Custom Shows... .

2. **Custom Shows** dialog box appears as in Figure 3.60. Click **New...** button. The **Define Custom Show** dialog box appears as in Figure 3.61.

3. Under Slides in presentation: click the slides that you want to include in the custom show and then click Add >>

☞ *To select multiple sequential slides, click the first slide, and then hold down* Ctrl *key while you click the last slide that you want to select.*

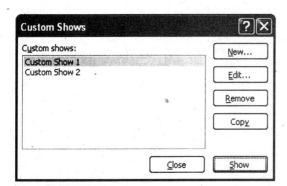

Figure 3.60 Custom Shows dialog box

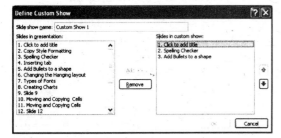

Figure 3.61 Define Custom Shows dialog box

4. To change the order in which slides appear, under Slides in custom show: click a slide, and then click one of the arrow to move the slide up or down in the list.

5. Type a name in the Slide show name box: and then click OK. To create additional custom shows with any slides in your presentation, repeat steps 1 through 5.

6. To Preview a custom show, click the name of the show in the Custom shows dialog box, and then click Show button.

3.17.3 Using Preset Animations

➡ **To use preset animations to text slides, do this:**

1. Select the object you want to animate.

2. Click Slide Show menu and choose Preset Animation as seen in Figure 3.62.

3. Click the animation setting as desired.

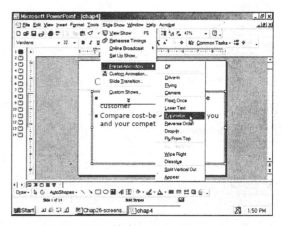

Figure 3.62 Slide Animation options

3.17.4 Animating Charts

➡ **To set the animation effects on charts, do this:**

1. Select the chart you want to animate.

2. Click Slide Show and choose Custom Animation... . The Custom Animation dialog box appears as in Figure 3.63.

3. In Introduce chart elements option, select the desired option from drop-down list.

4. Ensure Animate grid and legend option is *on*, in case you want to animate the chart's background.

5. Click Preview button to see a preview of the animation.

6. Click OK.

3.18 MAKING A SLIDE SHOW INTERACTIVE

PowerPoint contains Action buttons and Action settings. These buttons or settings enable you to add buttons to your slides. In this way, viewers can click to jump to any slide in the slide show. Viewers can even play a video, jump to an Internet Web page or start another software application.

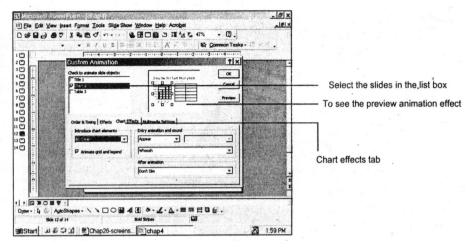

Figure 3.63 Custom Animation with Chart Effects tab Property Sheet

☞ *When you select the Custom option, the default settings for the width and Height are set to the printable area of the page for the current printer.*

➡ **To add an action button to a slide show, do this:**

1. Click Slide Show menu and choose Action Buttons. The Action Button dialog box appears as in Figure 3.64.
2. Select the button you want to add (See in Figure 3.65). Now add the button to show in the slide. After you add the button, the Action Setting dialog box appears as in Figure 3.66. The Action Settings tabs define the actions you want to associate with the button.
3. Click the Mouse Click tab.
4. Select the Hyperlink to: option, and select the desired option from drop-down list.
5. In the Hyperlink to: Other PowerPoint Presentation dialog box, select the folder of file you want to link to.
6. If there is more than one slide, Power-Point shows the Hyperlink to Slide dialog box.
7. Click the OK button.
8. Click Run program: option if you want to open a different application from within the presentation. Specify the program you want to open.
9. Click OK.

Figure 3.64 Action button menu

3.19 RUNNING A SLIDE SHOW

When you develop a slide show in Slide Sorter view, you can get a preview of transition effects for all slides. But to see the transitions full-screen and to see animated or bulleted text slides, you must select the presentation as a slide show.

3.19.1 Starting the Slide Show

When you view a slide show, you have following options:

1. Click **V**iew menu and choose Slide Sho**w**.

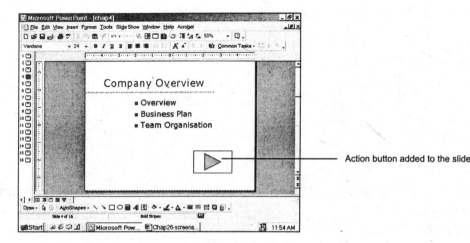

Figure 3.65   Action button added

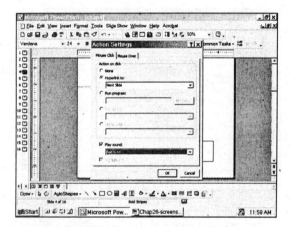

Figure 3.66   Action Setting dialog box with
Mouse Click Tab

2. Click Slide Show menu and choose **V**iew
   Show.

3. Click Slide Show View button.

4. In the Slide show, you go to next slide,
   press N or click the (Backspace) key to go
   to the previous slide.

➡ **To set a slide show option, do this:**

1. Click Slide Show menu and choose **S**et
   Up Show... . The Set Up show dialog box
   appears as in Figure 3.67.

☞ *The Action
Settings tabs
define the
actions you
want to associ-
ate with the but-
ton.*

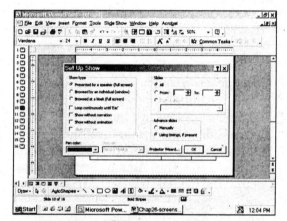

Figure 3.67   The Set Up Show dialog box

2. In the Slides section, click All to run the
   entire show. And also enter a starting and
   ending slide in From: and To: edit boxes.

3.19.2 Giving Special Show

PowerPoint offers three special slide show
types. These are available on the Set Up
Show dialog box (See Figure 3.67).

1. Click Presented by a speaker (full screen):
   Is the traditional, full-screen slide show.

2. Click Browsed by an individual (window): Runs the slide show in a standard
   window.

3. Click Browsed at a kiosk (full screen): It displays a full screen as a self running show which restarts after 5 minutes.

3.20 CONTROLLING THE SLIDE SHOW WITH A MOUSE

During a slide Show, you can use the popup menu button and popup menu appear. As mentioned earlier, the button appears in the lower left corner of the current slide as soon as you move the mouse pointer. You can then click the button to display the slide show popup menu.

The **N**ext and **P**revious commands on the popup menu let you move forward or backward through the slides in your slide show.

To move to a specific slide, highlight **G**o and then choose Slide **N**avigator from the menu, and then in the Slide Navigator dialog box, select the slide you want to go to slide and click Go To. (See Figure 3.68)

To stop a slide show at any time during a presentation, simply choose End Show from the popup menu.

3.20.1 Controlling the Slide Show with a Keyboard

In addition to the slide show pop-up menu, you can use the keys listed in Table 28.1 to control various aspects of the show.

Table 28.1 The Slide Show keyboard controls

Press This	To Perform This Action
Spacebar, →, ↓, PgDn, N	Advance to next slide.
Backspace, ←, ↑, PgUp, or P	Return to previous slide
Slide number + Enter	Go to slide number
B or period	Black screen/resume
W or comma	White screen/resume
Ctrl+A	Show mouse pointer as arrow
Ctrl+P	Show mouse pointer as pen

(Contd...)

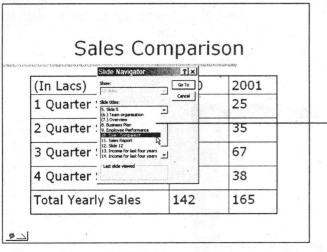

Figure 3.68 Slide Navigator dialog box

Select the slide in the Slide Navigator list box

☞ *PowerPoint offers three special slide show types. These are available on the Set Up Show dialog box.*

Press This	To Perform This Action
S or + (numeric keypad)	Pause/resume automatic show
H	Show/hide hidden slide
Esc	End Show

3.21 SETTING TIMINGS AND TRANSITIONS

If you do not want to move through a slide show manually, there are two ways you can set the length of time a slide appears on the screen. One way is to set a time manually for each slide, and then run the slide show and view the timings you set. The other way is to use the rehearsal feature, where you can record timings automatically as you rehearse. You can also adjust the timings you have already set and then rehearse the new ones.

3.21.1 Setting Slide Show timings Manually

1. In normal or slide sorter view, select the slide or slides you want to set the timing for.

2. Click the Slide show menu and choose Slide Transition... . The Slide Transition dialog box appears as in Figure 3.69.

3. Under Advance click Automatically after, check box, and then enter the number of seconds you want the slide to appear on the screen.

4. To apply the timings to the selected slides, click Apply. Or To apply the timing to all the slides, click Apply to All.

5. Repeat the process for each slide you want to set the timing for.

6. To view the timings, click Slide Show icon at the lower left of the PowerPoint window.

3.21.2 Set Slide timings Automatically while Rehearsing

1. On the slide show menu, click Rehearse Timings to start the show in rehearsal mode.

2. Click the advance button when you are ready to go to the next slide.

3. When you reach the end of the slide show, click Yes to accept the timings or No to try again.

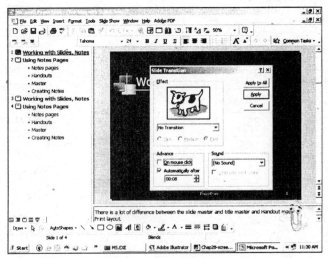

☞ *If you know the timings you want for a slide, you can enter it directly in the Rehearsal dialog box.*

Figure 3.69 Slide Transition dialog box showing timings setting

3.21.3 Add Transitions to a Slide Show

1. Select the slide(s) you want to add a transition.
2. Click the Slide Show menu and choose Slide Transition. (See Figure 3.69)
3. In the Slide Transition, click the Effect box, click the transition you want, and then select any other options you want.
4. To apply the transition to the selected slide, click Apply. Or to apply the transition to all the slides, click Apply to all.
5. To view the transition, click the Slide Show menu and choose Animation Preview as seen in Figure 3.70.

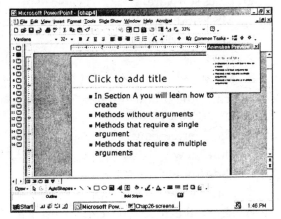

Figure 3.70 Animation Preview in the Slide Show view

3.21.4 Pack and GO

If you want to package your presentation and then use it on another computer, use the **Pack and Go Wizard**. With the Pack and Go Wizard, you can package all the required files and fonts into one file and copy the file to a disk or network location. You can then unpackage the file onto the destination computer or network and run the presentation. If you want to run the presentation on a computer that does not have PowerPoint installed, you can also include the Microsoft PowerPoint Viewer in the packaged file.

How to Package Your Presentation

To package your presentation for use on another computer, follow these steps:

1. Open the presentation that you want to package.
2. On the **File** menu, click **Pack and Go**.

☞ *By default, the Pack and Go feature is set to the "Installed on First Use" installation state. If this is the first time that you run Pack and Go, you will receive the following message:*

This feature is not currently installed. Would you like to install it now? Click Yes, and when you are prompted, insert the Microsoft Office CD into the CD-ROM or DVD-ROM drive, and then click OK.

3. Click **Next**.
4. Specify the presentation that you want to package, and then click **Next**.
5. Specify the location in which you want to package your publication. You can package the presentation to a floppy disk or directly to another computer on the network. Click **Next**.

☞ *The Pack and Go Wizard splits large presentations across multiple disks if you package your publication to the floppy disk (A:\) drive.*

6. Specify whether you want to include linked files or to embed TrueType fonts, and then click **Next**.
7. Specify whether you want to include the PowerPoint Viewer, and then click **Next**.
8. Click **Finish**, and then click OK when you receive the message that the **Pack and Go Wizard** successfully packaged your presentation.

3.21.5 Add Speaker Notes

Every slide in the presentation can have a special type of output called speaker notes or notes pages. On a note page, you see two objects. The slide on the top part of the page and a text placeholder on the bottom part. The notes page for each slide is an integral part of the presentation. and it is stored in the same file.

Any indication of the presence of notes page text appears only in Normal view. But when you print the presentation, you can choose to print the notes pages.

To enter a note, click the *Click To Add Notes* placeholder below the slide image. The begin typing in the placeholder as if you were typing text in a word processing program. The text will automatically wrap at the right edge of the text box. To start a new paragraph on the notes page, press Enter.

Summary

This chapter presents concepts of *Presentation Package*, MS PowerPoint. This package has innovative ways of working with presentation graphics. It is used for presenting information in a simple and effective manner. PowerPoint also creates entire presentation of slides. All the slides stored in a single file in system. PowerPoint slide refer to each page of visuals in a presentation. You might show the presentation onscreen, post the presentation on a Web site or print on the paper. It also describes different views on a presentation such as normal, slide, outline and slide sorter view. Each view lets your work on a different aspect of the presentation. Drawing tools on the Drawing toolbar are used to add graphic objects to a slide and also can be used to modify individual objects or groups of objects. Inserting a chart can be added to a slide to visually present numerical data in a graph. An organization chart is used to present the mangement structure of a business. It includes preset animation, which is the effect used to display text object during a slide show. Custom Animation dialog box is used to control preset animation, to add an effect to an object on the slide. Finally, a slide display time on the screen can be set during a slide show automatically using the Rehearse timings feature.

REVIEW QUESTIONS WITH ANSWERS

A. Multiple Choice

1. Which of the following is a presentation graphics software
   a. MS-Windows
   b. MS-PowerPoint
   c. MS-Excel
   d. MS-Word

2. Which of the following view in not one of PowerPoint views?
   a. Slide Sorter view
   b. Slide view
   c. Slide Show view
   d. Sorter view

3. Which of the following can be used to create presentation from scratch?
   a. Autocontent wizard
   b. Design templates
   c. Sample presentation
   d. Blank presentation

4. Extension of Power Point file is
   a. .PPT   b. .PPP
   c. .PPS   d. .TMT

5. Which of the following shortcuts is used to insert a New Slide.
   a. Ctrl+M   b. Ctrl+N
   c. Ctrl+O   d. None of the above

6. Actions buttons can be inserted in the slide, by Action Button command of
   a. View menu
   b. Insert menu
   c. Slide show menu
   d. None of the above

7. After a table has been created, which of the following operations cannot be performed?
   a. Insert rows in a table
   b. Delete and insert columns
   c. Split the table into two tables
   d. None of the above

8. To start a slide show
   a. Choose Slide sho<u>w</u> from <u>V</u>iew menu
   b. Choose Rehearse from Slide Sho<u>w</u> menu
   c. Click the Slide Show view button
   d. All of the above

9. Pressing which key moves you to the next slide in the slide show
   a. Space bar
   b. left arrow ⬅
   c. Both (a) and (b)
   d. None of the above

10. Which method can you use to navigate from one slide to another in a slide show?
    a. Press the Esc key
    b. Click the mouse button
    c. Change the channels on the TV
    d. None of the above

B. Descriptive Questions

1. What is the purpose of Presentation Software? Explain the features provided by MS PowerPoint

2. What should be the features of a good presentation package? What role do the presentation packages play in Education?

3. What are the different views, which you can open a presentation using Power-Point?

4. What do you understand by a slide-show?

5. How to animate text and graphic objects?

A. Answers to Multiple Choice

1. b   2. d   3. a   4. a   5. a   6. c
7. d   8. d   9. d   10. b

B. Answers to Descriptive Questions

1. Microsoft PowerPoint 2000 carries a number of features designed to make creating presentations easier. It has new capabilities for collaborating presentations and publishing them on the Web. At the same time, it has become more like its sharing on-screen controls like menus and dialog boxes, and techniques like drag-and-drop editing. It is a powerful presentation processor to communicate your knowledge, information and achievements, and to persuade others with your opinion. PowerPoint has many new features and if you are already familiar with other Office applications, such as Microsoft Word, Excel you will recognize many of these innovations. Here is a list of the new features in PowerPoint 2000.
   - Many additions that make Power-Point easier to use. PowerPoint has improved Open and Save dialog boxes with their Places bars, which makes it easier to get to the presentations you use most. Its new adaptive menus and toolbars give you a

cleaner, simpler screen by revealing only the commands and buttons you use most and temporarily hiding those you rarely use.

- Normal view displays the outline for the entire presentation, a slide, and notes for the slide so that you can see everything you need at once.

- Office Assistant that takes up less space on the screen and offers suggestions for creating better presentations based on the task you are in the midst of carrying out.

- Graphical bullets and numbered list add effectiveness to slides and allow you to create ordered lists that automatically renumber when you add or remove items.

- New Design and Content templates give you more choices for both the appearance of presentations and the contents. Some new templates include animated templates and preset animations.

- The new Clip Gallery is easier to use. You can simply drag images from the gallery onto slides, and you can use the gallery to store sounds and motion clips too.

- PowerPoint slide shows can now shows animated GIFs, the popular and easy-to-create animation files that are used on the Web pages.

- You can save a presentation as a Web page and easily save the page to a Web server. You can send the presentation on the Web for others to view, or you can use the computer with a Web browser to display a presentation from a Web server on the Internet.

- You can save and reopen an HTML version of a presentation and work with it as though you were working on the original PowerPoint file. The HTML version preserves all the formatting and contents, even charts, tables, and other elements on slides.

- Online Meetings allow you to collaborate with others and share and exchange information in real time with people on other sites.

2. The most important thing to remember as you build your presentation is that you should *keep presentation as simple as possible*. Some other useful tips are:

- Limit your bullet paragraphs to a few selected words, if you can. Bullet paragraphs should be like headlines in a newspaper.

- Five or six is the recommended limit for a good presentation. When you have a large number of points to make about one subject, spread them over more than one slide.

- Use as few text levels as possible. Limit text levels to two if so.

- Keep points short and direct.

- Include key words, not long and explanatory sentences.

3. [*Refer section 3.4 to 3.4.6*]

4. [*Refer section 3.18*]

5. [*Refer section 3.16*]

CHAPTER 4

Spreadsheet Packages

The reader will be able to understand in this chapter

- Concept of Workbook, Worsheet and Workspace
- Entering cell address
- Range of cells
- Types of data for MS-Excel
- Data entering facilities using fill series
- Entering formulae

- Entering cell reference using absolute, relative and mixed reference
- Entering worksheet functions such as SUM, COUNT, MIN, MAX, AVERAGE, etc.
- Creating charts, protecting and hiding data in a worksheet
- Import and Export of data charts to other package
- Types of errors that may occur in a worksheet

4.1 INTRODUCTION

A worksheet, also called a *spreadsheet,* is a sheet made up of rows and columns. It is used for planning a project or checking financial position of an organization. The term spreadsheet and worksheet are often used interchangeably. Spreadsheet usually refers to a computer program, where as worksheet refers to the actual document you create by using the spreadsheet program. MS Excel is a popular spreadsheet program, where you design worksheets using this program.

4.2 SPREADSHEET CONCEPTS

4.2.1 What is an Electronic Spreadsheet?

An electronic spreadsheet application accepts data values and relationships between the data values in a tabular format consisting of rows and columns. It allows user to perform calculation on these values. It also manipulates data in a desired format. The first spreadsheet available for the PC was VisiCalc which was a best seller. Visi-Calc was followed by Lotus 1-2-3. The largest selling spreadsheet program is MS Excel.

☞ *Electronic spreadsheet is a software package which shows us data in a tabular form, accepts data in a tabular form (rows and columns) and uses many functions to perform calculations.*

4.2.2 Spreadsheet Terminologies

When you are working with a spreadsheet package you have to know some spreadsheet terminologies. Some such terms are given in the following paragraphs.

Workbook

A workbook is a collection of many worksheets. In a single workbook, you can store information in an organized manner. By default, a workbook opens with three worksheets and it can contain a maximum of 255 worksheets.

Worksheet

A worksheet is a sheet made up of rows and columns. It is used for planning a project or financial documents of an organization. Worksheet refers to the actual document you create by using the spreadsheet program.

☞ *MS-Excel is a popular spreadsheet program, where you design worksheets using this program.*

Chartsheet

Chartsheet is a separate sheet in a workbook that contain only graphs or charts. It is useful when you want to see a chart of tabular data separated from other types of data.

Row

A row is a horizontal block of cells that runs through the entire width of the worksheet. The rows are numbered from top to bottom along the left edge of the worksheet. The first row is numbered 1, the second 2, and so on. There can be a maximum of 65536 rows in an Excel worksheet.

Column

A columns is a vertical block of cells that runs through the entire worksheet. A worksheet contains 256 columns, labeled **A** through **IV**. The first column is **A**, the second is **B** and so on until you reach **Z**. Then comes columns **AA** through **IV**. The last (or rightmost) column of the worksheet, **IV** is the 256th column.

Cells

A cell is the intersection of a row and a column. For example, the uppermost cell is A1 (column A, row 1). Cell E6 is the intersection of column E, row 6. When you select a cell by clicking it with the mouse, or moving to it using the keyboard, it becomes the active cell. (See Figure 4.3)

Formula

It is an order of values, names, cell references, functions and operators in a cell that together give a new values. A formula always begins with = (equal) sign.

Function

Functions are predefined formulas that perform complex calculations by using a specific value in a particular order to give a result.

4.3 STARTING EXCEL

➡ **To start Excel, do this:**

1. Click the Start button on the taskbar, highlight <u>P</u>rograms, click Microsoft Excel. (See Figure 4.1)
2. Microsoft Excel window opens with Tip of the day: box as in Figure 4.2.

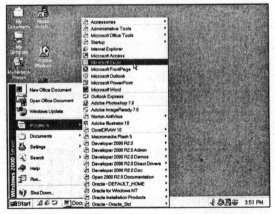

Figure 4.1 Starting Microsoft Excel

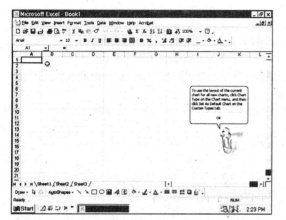

Figure 4.2 Check out Today's Tip dialog box

4.3.1 Elements of Excel Window

Window lets you run a number of applications simultaneously. Each Windows appli-

cation runs in its own application window. Further, Excel can have multiple documents or worksheets open simultaneously.

Figure 4.3 shows the elements of the Excel application window and an open Excel workbook in detail. Various elements of the Excel screen are described in Table 4.1.

Title Bar

At the top of an Excel window, there is the title bar. The left edge of this bar has the application control menu box next to which the name of the open document is displayed. On the right edge of the title bar the *minimize, restore/maximize* and *close* button are placed. Double clicking the title bar of a *minimize/maximize* window restores a window. (See Figure 4.3)

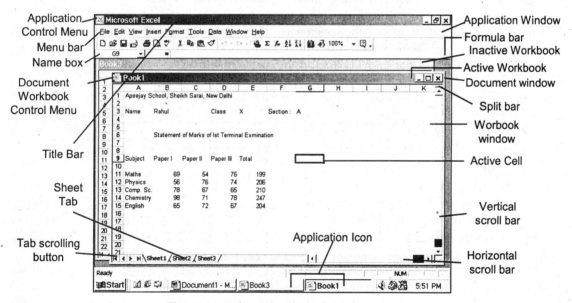

Figure 4.3 Elements of Excel 2000 window

Table 4.1 Elements of Excel Screen

Element	Description
Application window	The window within which Excel runs.
Application icon	The taskbar button of a running application.

(Contd....)

Element	Description
Application control icon	The menu that enables you to manipulate the application window.
Document window	The window in which Excel workbook is displayed.
Mouse pointer	The on-screen *arrow, cross,* or *I-beam* that indicates the current location of the mouse action.
Workbook window	A window within the Excel application window in which a worksheet, chart, or dialog box is shown.
Active workbook window	The Excel workbook window that accepts entries and commands.
Inactive workbook window	A window that contains Excel information, and not affected by commands. Such a window has a gray title bar and is behind the active workbook window.
Workbook bar	A bar of a minimized workbook within the Excel application window.
Workbook control icon	This icon opens a menu that allows you to manipulate the active workbook window.
Sheet tabs	Tabs which allow you to go to a specific sheet in a workbook.
Tab scrolling buttons	It helps you to go quickly through the sheets in a workbook.
Toolbar	A bar containing buttons allowing quick access to commands and procedures.
Formula bar	The area of the screen where you enter *numbers,* or *formulas.* The formula bar is below the menu bar or toolbar.
Status bar	A bar at the bottom of the screen that shows what Excel is prepared to do next.
Indicators	These display modes of operation, such as NUM when the numeric keypad is on.

Menu Bar

The *menu bar* is located just below the title bar as seen in Figure 4.3. It contains all the commands used in Excel grouped under main heads and explained in Table 4.2.

Table 4.2 Menu bar's command groups

Group	Commands
File	Commands relating to file operations such as, saving, opening, printing a file, etc.
Edit	Commands concerned with editing documents such as copy, delete, move, etc.
View	Commands related to controlling the view of the documents such as zoom, etc.

(Contd...)

Group	Commands
Insert	Commands to insert cells, rows, columns, worksheet, chart, etc.
Format	Commands related to formatting cells, rows, columns, sheet, etc.
Tools	Commands related to spreadsheet tools, such as spell checking, etc.
Data	Commands related to database functions of Excel.
Window	Commands related to working within the window.
Help	Commands related to getting help in Excel.

In Excel, the pull down menu opens in two steps. When you click the menu, it opens with the most commonly used options with downward pointing arrow at the bottom

(See Figure 4.4). To see the remaining options, click this downward pointing arrow.

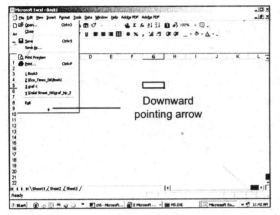

Figure 4.4 Pull down menu

4.3.2 Toolbars

The buttons on the toolbar represent a *command* or a *procedure*. Note that default *Standard* and *Formatting* toolbars are seen just below the menu bar. (See Figure 4.5)

Standard Toolbar Buttons

The buttons on the standard toolbar are as in Table 4.3. The keyboard shortcuts where ever applicable are given in brackets.

Formatting Toolbar

The buttons on the formatting toolbar are explained in Table 4.4. Keyboard shortcuts where ever applicable are given in brackets.

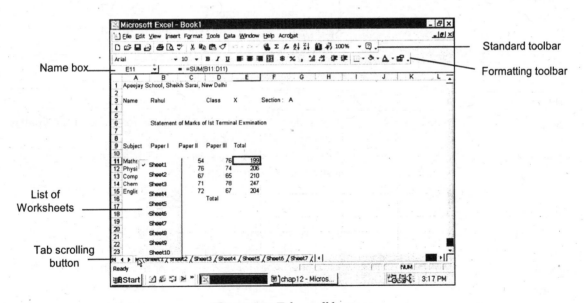

Figure 4.5 Tab scroll buttons

Table 4.3 Standard Toolbar buttons and their functions in Excel 2000

Name	Function
New ($Ctrl$+N)	Creates a new file or workbook.
Open ($Ctrl$+O)	Opens an existing file.
Save ($Ctrl$+S)	Saves the current file.
E-mail	Sends the current worksheet's contents as E-mail message.

(Contd...)

Name	Function
Print ($Ctrl+P$)	Prints the current file/selection.
Print Preview	Print Preview the file.
Spelling ($F7$)	Checks the spelling in the active document file or item.
Cut ($Ctrl+X$)	Cuts the selection to the clip board.
Copy ($Ctrl+C$)	Copies the selection to the clip board.
Paste ($Ctrl+V$)	Paste the contents of the clip board.
Format painter	Copies the format from a selected object or text and applies it to the object or text you select.
Undo ($Ctrl+Z$)	Undoes or reverses the last command or action.
Redo ($Ctrl+Y$)	Redoes or repeats the last command or action.
Insert hyperlink ($Ctrl+K$)	Inserts hyperlink in the document, for HTML
Autosum	Inserts the sum function.
Paste function	Displays the paste function dialog box.
Sort Ascending	Sorts selected cells in ascending order.
Sort Descending	Sorts selected cells in descending order.
Chart Wizard	Creates chart.
Drawing	Display the drawing toolbar.
Zoom	Reduces or enlarges worksheet magnification.
Microsoft Excel Help ($F1$)	Starts office assistant for help

Table 4.4 Formatting toolbar buttons

Name	Function
Font	The drop down list shows the available fonts. Select the desired font or enter the name of the font.
Font size	Enter the font size for the selected text or a number or select the font size from the drop down list.
Bold ($Ctrl+B$ or $Ctrl+2$)	Sets bold text on.
Italic ($Ctrl+I$ or $Ctrl+3$)	Sets italic text on.
Underline ($Ctrl+U$ or $Ctrl+4$)	Sets underline text on.
Align left	Aligns the selected text, numbers, or the objects to the left.
Center	Centers the selected text, numbers, or the object.
Align right	Aligns the selected text, number or the object to the right.
Merge and center	Merge the selected cells and center the text across the cells.
Currency Style	Applies an international currency style to the selected cell.
Percent Style	Displays data in the percent style to the selected cells.
Comma Style	Displays data in the percent style to the selected cells.
Increase decimal	Increases the number of digits shown after the decimal point in the selected cells.
Decrease decimal	Decreases the number of digits shown after the decimal point in the selected cells.

(Contd...)

Name	Function
Increase Indent	Increases the width of the selected cells contents by one character width.
Decrease Indent	Reduces the width of selected cells contents by one character width.
Borders	Adds border to the selected cell or range.
Fill color	Adds, modifies or removes the fill colour from the selected object.
Font color	Formats the selected text with the colour you pick.

4.3.3 Scroll Bar

The scroll bar appears at the *left* for vertical scrolling and at the *bottom right* for horizontal scrolling as seen in Figure 4.3.

- To scroll one cell at a time, click the scroll button with arrows at the corners of the scroll bars.
- To scroll more drag the scroll button in the scroll bar.

4.3.4 Split Bar

The split bar is located at the top of the *vertical* scroll bar and to the right of the *horizontal* scroll bar (See Figure 4.3). Double click the split button on the vertical scroll bar. It splits the sheet horizontally. (See Figure 4.6).

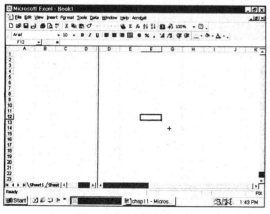

Figure 4.6 Split bar

Double clicking the split button on the horizontal scroll bar would split the worksheet vertically. To size the horizontal scroll bar, point to the left split bar on the horizontal/vertical bar and drag to size the scroll bar.

4.3.5 Tab Scrolling Buttons

These are the arrow buttons to the left of the sheet tabs for scrolling the worksheet. (See Figure 4.5)

- To scroll between sheet tabs, click an arrow for the direction you want to scroll.
- To scroll one sheet tab at a time in left or right direction, click the middle tab scrolling buttons.
- To scroll through a group of sheet tabs in left or right direction, click the tab scroll buttons at the left and right corner (See Figure 4.5).
- To display a list of the sheets in the workbook right click a tab scrolling button to display the menu (See Figure 4.5).

4.3.6 Sheet Tabs

A tab is near to the bottom of a work book window that displays the name of a sheet (See Figure 4.3). Click the sheet tab to move to the next sheet. To display the shortcut menu right click the sheet tab. To scroll through the sheet tabs, use the tab scrolling button.

4.3.7 Name Box

The *name box* is at the left end of the formula bar (See Figure 4.3). It identifies the selected *cell*, *chart item* or *drawing object*. The purpose is as follows:

- To name a selected cell or range.
- To move to a selected name cell, click its name in the Name box. Type the name in the name bar and press (Enter).

4.3.8 Formula Bar

The *formula bar* displays the constant value or formula used in the active cell. The formula bar is also used for editing the cell contents. (See Figure 4.3)

4.3.9 Shortcut Menus

Shortcut menus are meant to display frequently used commands relating to the selected *item* or *object*.

➡ To display Shortcut menus, do this:

Click the right mouse button—the object for which you need a shortcut menu. *Alterna-*

tively, you can use a keyboard, select the item and then press (Shit)+(F10) keys.

Shortcut menus appear at the top of the mouse pointer (See Figure 4.7). It will appear at the top-left corner when activated by a keyboard. To remove a shortcut menu, click outside the menu or press (Esc) key.

4.3.10 Status Bar

Status bar appears at the bottom of the Excel window. It displays information regarding a selected command or an operation in progress. Note that the right side of the status bar shows keys such as (Caps Lock), (Scroll Locks) or (Num Lock). The Status bar displays the sum of any numbers you select (See Figure 4.8). In the middle of the status bar, you can see Sum = 1066.

➡ To control the display of status bar, do this:

1. Click the View menu and choose Status Bar. The option is on when a check mark appears.

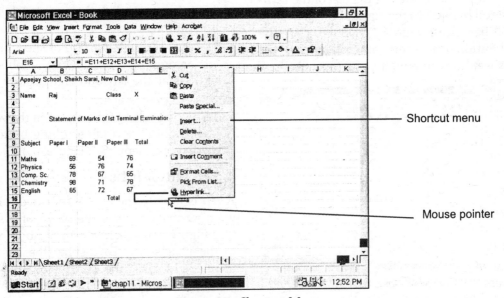

Figure 4.7 Shortcut Menu

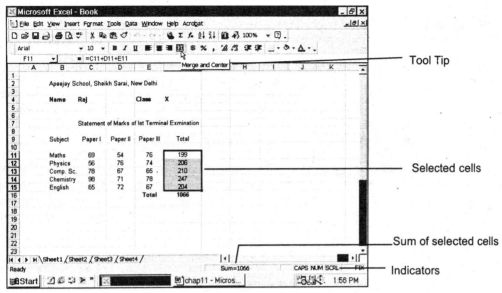

Figure 4.8 Status bar elements

4.4 WORKBOOK WINDOW

Excel makes use of several workbooks and their worksheets. You may therefore have more than one window on-screen. You can however, affect only the active workbook window. If you can see an inactive workbook window open on-screen, you can make it active by clicking any part of it. If you know a workbook window is open, but cannot see it properly, then move the other workbook window using a mouse so that you can see the one you want to click.

4.4.1 Creating a new Workbook

➡ **To create a new workbook, do this:**

1. Click the File menu and choose New... . The New dialog box appears as shown in Figure 4.9.

2. In the New dialogue box, click the General tab and choose workbook and then press (Enter) key. *Alternatively*, press (Ctrl) + (N) keys together.

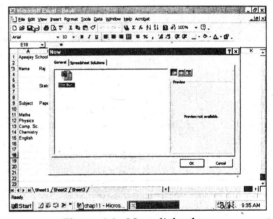

Figure 4.9 New dialog box

4.4.2 Opening a Workbook

➡ **To Open a workbook, do this:**

1. Click the File menu and choose Open... or *Alternatively*, press (Ctrl) + (O). The Open dialog box appears as shown in Figure 4.10.

2. In Dialog box, choose the drive, folder name that contains the workbooks. After finding the required workbook, select it.

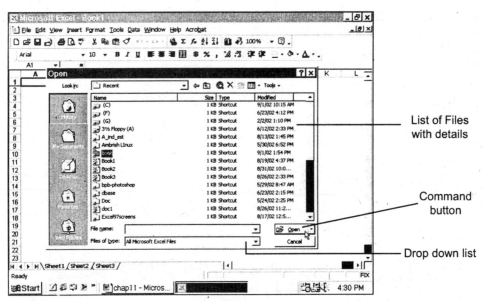

Figure 4.10 Open dialog box

3. Then click OK.

➡ **To Open more than one workbooks simultaneously, do this:**

1. Repeat step 1. and 2. of opening a single workbook.

2. Click the name of one file and then hold down (Ctrl) key and click another file name and then press (Enter) key.

4.4.3 Saving a Workbook

Excel has two commands for saving workbooks. *Save* command used to save an existing workbook; *Save As* command used to save the workbook when you save it for the first time or save the workbook under a new name.

➡ **To save the workbook for the first time, do this:**

1. Click the File menu and choose Save As... . The Save As dialog box appears as in Figure 4.11.

2. In the Save in: box specify the location where you want to save the file.

3. In the File name: box give the name of the file.

4. In the Save as type: box give the type of file.

5. Click OK.

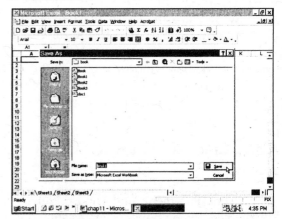

Figure 4.11 Save As dialog box

4.4.4 Closing a Workbook Window

When you finish using worksheet or chart, you close its window. If you have made any changes since the last time you saved the workbook, Excel displays an alert dialog box, as seen in Figure 4.12, asking whether you want to save your work before closing.

➡ To close a file in a workbook, do this:

1. Click the <u>F</u>ile menu and choose <u>C</u>lose. *Alternatively*, click close button on the right edge of the Menu bar or double click the control icon on the left of the title bar. The window closes provided no change has been made to the workbook since it was saved last.

☞ *To close all visible workbooks, hold down* (Shift) *key as you choose File and click Close All. This closes all visible workbooks.*

---

2. If you have made changes to the workbook since the last save, the Alert dialog box appears. In the dialog box, choose *No* if you do not want to save a changed version of the file, or choose *Yes* if you do want to save your changes. Type a new file name and choose OK.

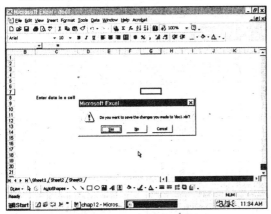

Figure 4.12 Alert dialog box

4.4.5 Quitting Excel

➡ To quit Excel, do this:

1. Click the <u>F</u>ile menu, and choose <u>C</u>lose command. *Alternatively*, click the close

button (x) in the top-right corner or press (Alt)+(F4) or double-click the Control icon at the left of the title bar.

When all workbooks are closed, Excel window closes, and the application is terminated.

4.5 WORKBOOKS AND WORKSHEETS

Excel has many different methods of moving data and selecting specific data in workbooks and worksheets. You will learn these methods in the following sections.

4.5.1 What are Workbooks/ Worksheets?

In Excel, a workbook is a file in which you work and store data. The work is saved as a **.XLS** file. Each workbook can contain many sheets. These sheets may also contain *charts*, *macros*, etc. You can organize various kinds of related information in a single file.

Within a workbook, you can also keep the worksheets containing *formulas*, *database*, *charts*, *slides*, *macros*. Thus, workbooks make it easy to group all the pieces of related jobs you may be doing in Excel.

Each worksheets contains 256 columns and 65,536 rows. The intersection of a row and a column forms a cell in which you can enter data or a formula.

Column headings start at A and as they reach the letter Z column, the headings restart with AA, AB, and so on till IV.

Row headings, down the left side of a sheet, go from 1 to 65,536.

☞ *It is equally easy for formulas to refer to information in another worksheet of the same workbook as it is in the same worksheet.*

Using a Workspace

You can open a group of workbooks in one step by creating a workspace file. A workspace file saves information about all open workbooks, such as their locations, window sizes, and screen positions. When you open a workspace file by using the Open command (File menu), Microsoft Excel opens each workbook saved in the workspace. The workspace file does not contain the workbooks themselves, and you must continue to save changes you make to the individual workbooks.

1. Open the workbooks you want to open as a group.
2. Size and position the workbook windows as you want them to appear the next time you use the workbooks.
3. Click the File menu, click **Save Workspace**.
4. Save Workspace dialog box appears. In the **File name:** box, enter a name for the workspace file.
5. Click Save button. The extension for a workspace file is .xlw. Whenever you want to open the group of workbooks together, open the workspace file.

4.6 WORKING IN A WORKBOOK

We shall now use a workbook for manipulating data stored in various worksheets.

4.6.1 Moving between Workbooks

When you open an Excel file, you really open a workbook that contains multiple sheets. In Excel you can also get multiple workbooks open, each in its own documents window. To work on a workbook you need to *activate* it. Bring to the top; the workbook in which you want to work presently.

➡ **To activate an opened workbook, do this:**

1. Click the **W**indow menu and at the bottom of the menu, select the name of the document window you want to activate.

➡ **To switch between workbooks using a shortcut key, do this:**

1. Press [Ctrl]+[F6] together and switch between open workbook documents.

4.6.2 Inserting and Removing Sheets

If you revise workbooks, you will want to *insert/remove* sheets from the workbook. Excel gives you the flexibility to easily insert and remove sheets.

Inserting a Sheet

You can insert a new sheet in the workbook at any location you desire.

➡ **To insert a sheet into your workbook, do this:**

1. Activate the workbook into which you want to insert the sheet.
2. Select the existing sheet before which you want the new sheet inserted by clicking its sheet tab or by pressing [Ctrl]+[PgUp] or [Ctrl]+[PgDn] as the case may be.
3. Click the **I**nsert menu and choose **W**orksheet. *Alternatively*, Press [Shift]+[F11] to insert a new worksheet.

Deleting a Sheet

When you delete a sheet that contains data, you lose all that data. Also, note that you cannot *undo* or get back a sheet after deletion. Therefore, you should be very careful before you delete a sheet.

➡ **To delete a sheet from a workbook, do this:**

1. Select the sheet you want to delete.

2. Click the Edit menu and choose Delete Sheet. *Alternatively*, position the mouse pointer on the tab of the sheet to be deleted, click the right mouse button and then choose Delete.

4.6.3 Copying and Moving Worksheets in a Workbook

Suppose that you use a budget worksheet in one workbook and the same worksheet is also required for another workbook. You could re-create the worksheet in the new workbook or copy the data from one workbook to another, but it would be much easier if you just copy the entire sheet of other workbook.

Further, you can also move Sheets to new locations. In case you move the sheet from the old location to a new location then a copy of the worksheet is left at the old location.

➡ **To copy/move a sheet, within the workbook using mouse, do this:**

1. Select the sheet you want to *copy* or *move*.
2. If you want to *copy* within the same workbook, press and hold down (Ctrl) key and drag the sheet tab to its new location.
3. However, if you want to *move* the sheet within the original workbook, drag the sheet tab to the location where you want to move the worksheet.

➡ **To copy between workbooks, do this:**

1. Open both the workbooks.
2. Click the Window menu and choose Arrange... Dialog box as seen in Figure 4.13 appears. Select the desired arrangement.
3. *To copy*: Press and hold down (Ctrl) key and drag the sheet tab from one workbook onto the tabs in the other workbook.

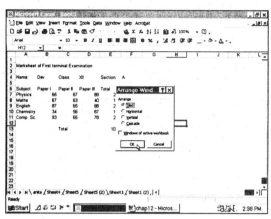

Figure 4.13 Arrange... dialog box

4. *To move*: One sheet to another workbook, drag the sheet tab onto the tabs at the bottom of the other workbook.
5. A black triangle appears above the receiving tabs, to show the location for the copy's insertion. Figure 4.14 shows the triangle above the tabs.
6. Release the mouse button.

☞ *If you want to add a sheet to the end of the workbook, you have to insert it before an existing sheet and then move the new sheet to the end.*

When a sheet is inserted at the new location, then name of the copied sheet will be that of the original sheet name. If a sheet with the same name is already in the workbook, the name is followed by a number in parentheses indicating its copy number.

➡ **To copy/move a sheet between workbooks with menu commands, do this:**

1. Open the workbook from which you want to move a sheet and the workbook to which you want to move this sheet.

2. Activate the sheet you want to move.

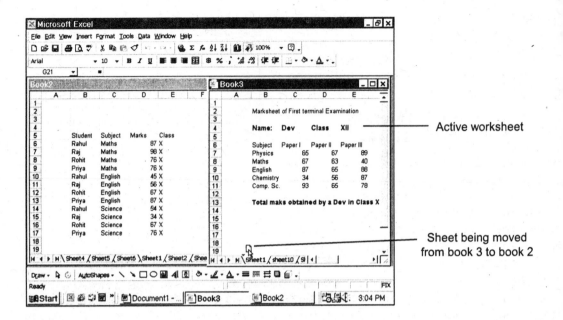

Active worksheet

Sheet being moved
from book 3 to book 2

Figure 4.14 Copying a worksheet between workbooks

3. Click the Edit, menu and choose Move or Copy Sheet... Or *Alternatively* right click the sheet tab and choose Move or Copy... from the shortcut menu. The Move or Copy dialog box appears as in Figure 4.15.

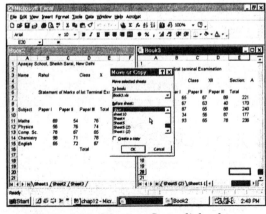

Figure 4.15 Move or Copy dialog box

4. From the To book: in drop-down list, select the name of the workbook to which you want to copy.

5. In the Before sheet: list select the name of the sheet before which you want to position the inserted sheet placed.

6. *To copy*: select the Create a copy check box.
   To move: clear the Create a copy check box.

7. Click OK.

➡ **To create a new workbook and copy the sheet, do this:**

1. Select the sheet you want to copy.

2. Click the Edit menu and choose Move or Copy Sheet... .

3. From the To Book: drop-down list, select (new book).

4. *To copy*: select the Create a copy check box.
   To move: clear the Create a copy check box.

5. Click OK.

4.6.4 Renaming a Sheet

The names assigned to worksheets in a

workbook by default are Sheet 1, Sheet 2, etc. However, you can also name the sheets as per your needs.

➡ To rename a sheet, do this:

1. Select the sheet you want to rename.
2. Double-click the sheet tab. *Alternatively,* Click the F**o**rmat menu, highlight S**h**eet, then choose **R**ename or point to the selected sheet tab, or click the right mouse button; then choose **R**ename. The sheet name is highlighted, as shown in Figure 4.16.

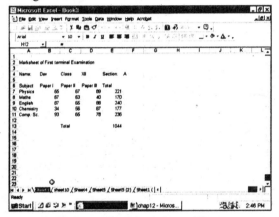

Figure 4.16 Renaming a Sheet

3. Type the new sheet name, using up to 31 characters including spaces.
4. Press (Enter).

The new sheet name appears on the sheet tab.

4.6.5 Selecting and Moving between the Sheets

If you have multiple sheets in a workbook then you need a quick and easy way to select or move between the sheets. For this, when you select a single sheet, that sheet moves to the top of the window and you can work there. Similarly, you can also select multiple sheets. Selecting multiple sheets is useful if you want to insert or delete many sheets.

How to move between Worksheets in a Workbook?

If you want to work within a specific work-sheet, then activate first the workbook that contains the worksheet and then activate the *worksheet* in which you want to work. The name on the tab of the active sheet is bold. You can switch between worksheets by using either the keyboard or a mouse.

☞ *The active sheet is the sheet in which you can operate.*

➡ To move to a worksheets using the keyboard, do this:

Press (Ctrl) + to activate previous (PgUp) sheet.

Press (Ctrl) + to activate next sheet. (PgDn)

➡ To move to a worksheet in a workbook using a mouse, do this:

1. Click the tab scrolling buttons to scroll through the workbook until you can see the name of the worksheet in which you want to work.
2. Click the tab containing the name of the worksheet you want to activate.

4.7 WORKING IN A WORKSHEET

4.7.1 Moving within a Worksheet

An Excel worksheet may have a large number of filled cells. In order to find data on a worksheet, you need to know how to move in a worksheet. You can scroll a worksheet with a mouse or a keyboard.

Scrolling with Mouse

When you scroll a window, imagine that the worksheet stays still but you move the window over the top of the worksheet. To scroll the window with the mouse, use the scroll bars located at the right and bottom of each worksheet (See Figure 4.17). The arrows in

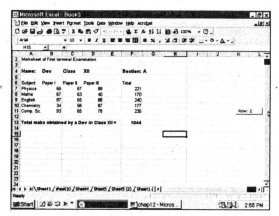

Figure 4.17 Scroll bars

the scroll bars show the direction the window moves over the worksheet. Click the arrow to scroll in that direction.

The vertical and horizontal scroll boxes give you the position in the worksheet. You can also drag the scroll box to move the relative distance in the worksheet.

Scrolling using the Keyboard

When you scroll using a keyboard, the cell selected by you changes as you scroll. To avoid changing the selection, press the (Scroll lock) key and then use the scrolling keys. Now you will find that the selection does not change. Table 4.5 lists the keys and their combination to scroll the window.

Table 4.5 Keys that Scroll the Window

Key	Movement
(↑)	Scrolls up one row.
(↓)	Scrolls down one row.
(←)	Scrolls left one column.
(→)	Scrolls right one column.
(PgUp)	Scrolls up one screen.
(PgDn)	Scrolls down one screen.
(Alt)+(PgUp)	Scrolls right one window.
(Alt)+(PgDn)	Scrolls left one window.

(Contd...)

Key	Movement
(Home)	Moves to the beginning of the row.
(Ctrl)+(Home)	Moves to the beginning of the worksheet.

4.7.2 Selecting Cells and Ranges of Cells

Before you can *enter*, *edit*, or *modify* the contents of a cell, you must select or activate the cell or cells you want to change.

☞ *The single cell that receives the data or formula you enter is the active cell. A selection of multiple cells is referred to as a range.*

The cell defined by a bold border and white background is the active cell. Also, the row number and column letter of the current cell are highlighted. *Commands* affect all selected cells whereas *data* and *formulas* are entered in the active cell. (See Figure 4.18)

Using Go To Command to Move or Select a Cell ((F5) key)

The **G**o To command in the **E**dit menu moves you to any address you request. If you choose a named cell or a range of cells, with Go To, the entire range is selected.

➡ **To use the Go To command, do this.**

1. Click the **E**dit menu and choose **G**o To... or press (F5) or press (Ctrl)+(G). The Go To dialog box appears as in Figure 4.19.

2. In the **R**eference text box, type the cell address or range you want to go to, or select from the **G**o to: list box the named location you want to go to.

3. Click OK or press (Enter).

☞ *If you want to see the active cell, but it is not visible in the window, press (Ctrl)+(Backspace). The window scrolls to show the active cell.*

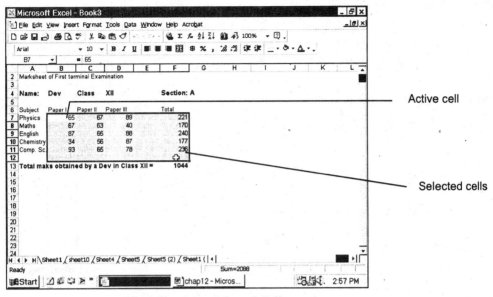

Figure 4.18 Selected Cells

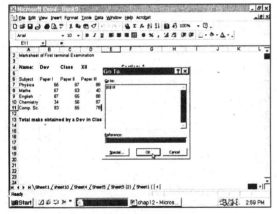

Figure 4.19 Go To dialog box

Selecting a Range of cells

Select a range of cells when you want to apply a command to all the selected cells or enter data into the cells in the range.

➡ **To select a range of cells using the mouse, do this:**

1. Click the cell at one corner of the range.

2. Drag to the opposite corner of the range and release the mouse button. The number box displays the number of rows and columns selected.

3. A rectangular range of cells is selected, as shown in Figure 4.20. Make sure that the pointer is on the correct cell when you release the mouse button.

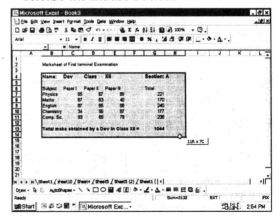

Figure 4.20 ScreenTip display Rows and Column Selected

- If a corner of the range is not displayed, drag the mouse pointer against the document window's edge in the direction you want to move. The window scrolls over the worksheet.

Selecting a Large Range of Cells

➡ **To select a large range of cells using the keyboard, do this:**

1. Select one corner of the range.
2. Click the Edit menu, and choose Go To... Or press (F5).
3. Type the cell reference of the opposite corner in the Reference: text box.
4. Hold down (Shift) key when you click the OK button, or press (Enter). *Alternatively*, type a range address in the Reference: box, such as A5:F12, and then click OK or press (Enter). In this case, the active cell is A5 and the range selected is from A5 to F12.

➡ **To select a large area with a mouse, do this:**

1. Select the cell on one corner of the range. Scroll the window so that the opposite corner appears. (Do not click in the worksheet. The original corner must remain active). or
2. Press and hold down (Shift) key as you click the opposite corner. All cells between the two corners are selected.

➡ **To select a range using the Extend mode, do this:**

1. Select a corner of the range by using the mouse or keyboard.
2. Press (F8) key to enter Extend mode. The **Ext** indicator appears in the status bar. (See Figure 4.21)
3. Select the opposite corner of the range by clicking it or moving to it with the movement keys.

Table 4.6 lists shortcut keys for selecting ranges of cells.

Table 4.6   Shortcut Keys for selecting Range of cells

Key	Extend Selection from Active Cell to
(F8)	Activate Extend.
(Shift) + arrow key	Next cell selected.
(Shift) + (Home)	Beginning of row.
(Shift)+(Ctrl)+ (Home)	Beginning of worksheet (A1).
(Shift)+(Ctrl)+ (End)	End of screen.
(Shift)+ (Spacebar)	Entire row of active cell.
(Ctrl)+(Spacebar)	Entire column of active cell.
(Shift)+(Ctrl)+ (Spacebar)	Entire worksheet.
(Shift)+(Ctrl)+ (PgUp)	Cell in same row one window right.
(Shift)+(Ctrl)+ (PgDn)	Cell in same row one window left.
(Shift)+(Ctrl)+arr ow key	Edge of the next block of data in the direction of the arrow key.

4. Press (F8) again to turn off Extend mode.

4.7.3 Selecting Rows and Columns with Mouse

Some operations are quicker if you select an entire row or column at one time. For example, formatting is simple and more efficient if you select and format the entire row or column instead of formatting each cell in the row or a column (See Figure 4.21).

➡ **To select an entire row/column with a mouse, do this:**

1. Click the *row* or *column's* heading, the complete row or column is selected.

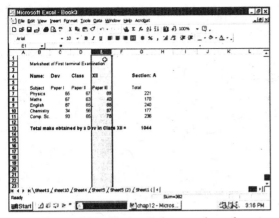

Figure 4.21 Entire Column selected

2. You can select adjacent rows or columns by dragging across the headings or by clicking the first row and pressing the (Shift)+clicking the last, row or column.

3. To select multiple nonadjacent rows and columns, hold down the (Ctrl) key as you click each heading.

4.7.4 Selecting Cells by Type of Contents

Excel has a very useful command that enables you to select cells by contents or the relationship to formulas. This command is useful if you need to select the following:

• Cells containing values within an area of formulas
• Related formulas
• Comments
• A rectangular region that surrounds all touching filled cells
• Array formulas
• Errors
• Embedded, graphical, or charting objects

➡ **To select cells according to their contents, do this:**

1. If you want to check the entire worksheet for a specific cell content then select that single cell, or select a range of cells to check cells within a range.

2. Click the Edit, menu and choose Go To... or press (F5).

3. From the Go To dialog box, click Special... . The Go To Special dialog box appears (See Figure 4.21).

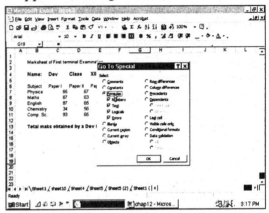

Figure 4.21 Go To Special dialog box

4. Select the option as given in Table 4.7.
5. Click OK.

Table 4.7 Available Options

Option	Explanation
Comments	Select cells containing comments.
Constants	Select cells containing constants of the type specified in the check boxes.
Formulas	Select cells containing formulas that produce a result of the type specified in the check boxes below.
Blanks	Select blank cells.
Objects	Select all graphical objects.
Data Validation	Select only those cells with data validation rules applied.

4.8 TYPES OF DATA ENTERED IN A CELL

There are four distinct types of data that can reside in a cell. These types of data are:

a. text
b. numerals
c. logical values

d. error

4.8.1 Text

Text in a cell can include any combination of *letters, numbers,* and *keyboard symbols.*

- A cell can contain up to 32,000 characters.
- If column width prevents a text string from fitting visually in a cell, the display extends over neighboring cells. However, if the neighboring cells are occupied, the display is truncated.

4.8.2 Numerals

Numerals contain all the decimal digits such as 0 to 9 on which you can do *addition, subtraction, multiplication,* and other mathematical or statistical operations. Numeric calculations is the most common thing that is done with Excel. Therefore, it is important to understand how Excel understands numerals.

- A number may be displayed using *commas, scientific notation,* or one of many built-in numeric formats. The numbers in Excel have two aspects *displaying format* and the *underlying value.* The *display format* is what you see in the cell, and the *underlying value* is the calculated value (which you can see in the formula bar).
- *Date* and *time* are numbers, but with special formatting. If you try to enter 1-9 as a text string. Excel will interpret this as a date and display it as 9-Jan.
- When an unformatted number does not fit in a cell, it is displayed in scientific notation.
- When a formatted number does not fit in a cell, number signs like hash (####) are displayed.

4.8.3 Logical Values

You can enter the logical values namely, TRUE or FALSE into cells. Logical values are often used in writing conditional formulas.

Also, there are many formulas that can return logical values. Thus if you say 3 > 4. The result is FALSE.

4.8.4 Error

An error value is a distinct type of data. For example, if a formula attempts to divide a number by zero, the result is the # DIV/0! Error value.

4.9 ENTERING INFORMATION IN A WORKSHEET

When you see the word *Ready* (See Figure 4.22a) in the status bar then you can enter data in the worksheet. Entering data in Excel worksheet actually consists of 3 steps:

1. Activate the cell in which you want to enter data.
2. Type the data you want to enter.
3. Finalize the data entry by pressing (Enter) key, (Tab), or any one of the arrow keys.

These steps remains the same wether you enter text such as column headings or numbers.

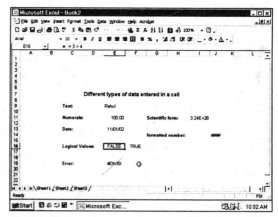

Figure 4.22a Different types of data entered in Cells

➡ To enter the data, do this:

1. Locate the cell in which you want to enter data. Click the desired cell to make it

active. The active cell appears with a dark border and its row and column headings appear to be raised to easily identify the cell address. (See Figure 4.22b).

2. Type your data in the active cell. Two buttons appear in the formula bar: *Enter* button and *Cancel* button. The status bar shows *Enter* to indicate that you are in the process of entering data. (See Figure 4.22b)

Figure 4.22b Entering data in a cell

3. Click the *Enter* button to indicate that you have completed the data typing. You can also press (Enter) key, (Tab) key or any one of the arrow keys to complete the data entry.

4. If you make a mistake before finalizing your data entry, press the (Backspace) key to delete the character to the left of the insertion point. To erase every thing that you have typed, click the cancel button or press (Esc) key.

5. Repeat the above steps to complete the data entry.

Excel provides you with the following two options to enter and edit data:

• You can enter data in the formula bar.

• You can also enter and edit data directly in the cell. If the **E**dit directly in cell feature is turned off, the entry you type appears in the cell but the cursor appears in the formula bar.

To enter and edit data directly in the cell you need to turn on the in-cell editing option.

➡ To turn on in-cell editing option, do this:

1. Click the **T**ools menu and choose **O**ptions... . The Options dialog box appears as in Figure 4.23.

2. In this dialog box click on Edit Tab. Dialog box with Edit tab appears as shown in Figure 4.23.

3. Select the **E**dit directly in cell check box. The option is *on* when a check mark appears.

4. Click OK.

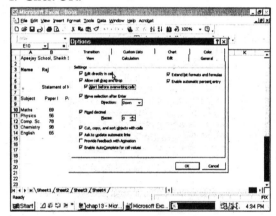

Figure 4.23 Option dialog box with Edit tab

4.9.1 Entering Text

Text entries can include *alphabetical characters, numbers* and *symbols*.

➡ To enter text in a cell, do this:

1. Select the cell, type the text entry, and then enter the text by clicking the Enter box in the formula bar or by pressing (Enter) key.

- To enter numbers as text, type an apostrophe (') followed by the number—for example, '45,000. *Alternatively*, place an equal sign in front of the numbers and enclose the number in quotation marks. For example, to enter the number 45,000 as text, type ="45,000".
- Notice that in a cell with the General format, numbers entered as text will align on the left like text. When you enter a number as text, you can still use the number if it is needed in a numeric formula.

You can quickly format a range of numbers as text in your worksheet by using the Text numeric format.

➡ To use text numeric format, do this:

1. Select the range of cells containing the numbers.
2. Click the Format menu and choose Cells, or press Ctrl + 1 and click the Number tab, and select the Text from the Category list: and click OK (See Figure 4.24).

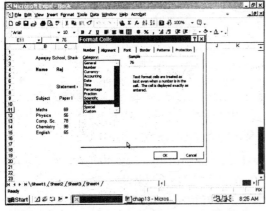

Figure 4.24 Number tab of Format Cells dialog box

4.9.2 Entering Numbers

Numbers are constant values containing only the following characters as given in Table 4.8.

Table 4.8 Special characters for numeric entries

Character	Function
0 through 9	Any combination of numerals.
+	Indicates exponents when used in conjunction with E such as 3E+3 means 3×10^3.
−	Indicates negative number.
()	Indicates negative number.
, (comma)	Thousands marker.
/	Fraction indicator (when fraction is preceded by a space) or date separator.
$	Currency indicator.
%	Percentage indicator.
. (period)	Decimal indicator.
E	Exponent indicator.
e	Exponent indicator.
:	Time separator.
(single space)	Separators of compound fractions (e.g 4 1/2); and date time entries (e.g 1/2/94 5:00).

➡ To enter a number, do this:

1. Select the cell, type the number, and then press Enter key or click the Enter box in the Formula bar.
2. You can enter *integers*, such as 135; *decimal fractions*, such as 135.437; *integer fractions*, such as 1 1/2; or *scientific notation*, such as 1.35437E+2.

As you create worksheets, Excel may display newly entered numbers or formulas as 2.67E+9, for example, or as ########. Scientific notation is another way of representing the *same number*. For example, 2.67E+9 represents 2.67×10^9.

☞ *Entering a number as text enables the number display to exceed the cell's width. If you enter a number in the normal way and the cell is not wide enough to display it, the cell fills with # signs or in some cases may display the number in scientific notation.*

Excel stores both the numbers typed into a cell and the format or appearance in which the numbers should be shown. When you enter a number into a cell, Excel tries to establish how the number should be formatted. For example, Excel accepts and displays the entries listed in Table 4.9 with the formats indicated.

The second example in this Table namely, 7999 Mg Rd., illustrates that if an entry is not a number or date, Excel stores it as text. The entries of the Table 4.9 are displayed in Figure 4.25, as entry would appear in an Excel worksheet.

Excel has a useful feature namely, fixed decimal representation. Using this feature, you can automatically add decimals to every value entered in a worksheet.

➡ **To control the fixed decimal option, do this:**

1. Click the **T**ools menu and choose **O**ption... . The Option dialog box appears as in Figure 4.23.

Table 4.9 Excel's Automatic Formats

Typed Entry	Chosen Format	Result
897	Number, General	897
7999 Mg Rd.	Text, left aligned	7999 Mg Rd
450.09	Number, dollar format	$450.09
54.6%	Number, percent format	5460.00%
2 3/4	Number, fraction	2 3/4
45600	Number, comma format	45,600.00
-678	Number, negative	-678.00
(678)	Number, negative	-678
1/5/99	Date, m/d/yy	01/05/99
4/5	Date, m/d/yy (current year assumed)	05-Apr

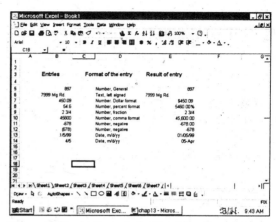

Figure 4.25 Automatic formats for data given in Table 4.9

2. Click the Edit tab in the option box or click the fixed decimal check box so that the check mark does not appear.

3. Click OK.

4.9.3 Entering Date and Time

Excel automatically understands date and time typed in most of the common ways. When you type a *date* or *time*, Excel converts your entry to a serial number. The serial number represents the number of days from the beginning of the century until the date you type. Time is recorded as a decimal fraction of a 24-hour day.

If your entry is recognized as a valid date or time format, you see the date or time on-screen. Correctly entered dates appear in the formula bar with the format **mm/dd/yyyy**, regardless of how the cell is formatted.

For example, if you type **5 Nov 97** in a cell formatted to show numbers with a comma and two decimal places (#,##0.00), you will see that date as **35,739.00.**

If Excel does not recognize the entry as a valid date or time format and you type a text date, such as **Sep 5 99**, Excel treats the entry as text and, in an unformatted cell, aligns it to the left.

➡ To enter a date, do this:

1. Select the cell in which you want to enter the date.
2. Type the date into the cell with any of these formats. For example to enter 10th September 2002 type:

   9/10/02

   10-Sep-02

   10-Sep (The year from the system date is used)

   Sep-02 (Only the month and year are shown)

   9/10/02 09:45

You can also enter the dates as **9/10, 09/10/02, Sep-02**, or **September 10, 2002** (See Figure 4.26). In any of these date formats, you can use either a/, -, or space to separate elements.

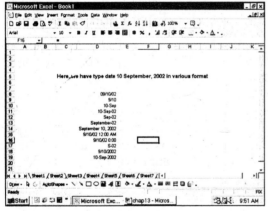

Figure 4.26 Various ways to enter date in a worksheet

➡ To enter the time, do this:

1. Select the cell in which you want to enter the time.
2. Type the time in any of the following formats. For example to enter **1:32   PM**, type:

   13:32

   13:32:45

1:32 PM

1:32:45 PM

6/8/99 13:32

The first two examples are from a 24-hour clock. If you use a 12-hour clock, follow the time with a space and A, AM, P, or PM (in either upper or lowercase).

☞ *Leave a space before the AM or PM. Do not mix a 24-hour clock time with an AM or PM. As the last format shows, you can combine the date or time during entry.*

➡ To enter the current date/time in a cell, do this:

1. To enter the current date select the cell and press Ctrl+⌃;⌄ keys together.
2. To enter the current time select the cell and press Ctrl+⌃:⌄ keys together.

☞ *To format a date in the default date format, select the cell containing the date and press Ctrl+#. To format a time in the default time format, press Ctrl+@.*

4.10 AUTOFILL FEATURE

Excel makes it very easy to enter a series of dates number or text. For example, you can insert column heading like *Jan, Feb, Mar*, etc. or enter number at equal intervals such as 2, 4, 6, 8, etc. very easily.

You can enter the above type of series in two ways:

1. Using the mouse to drag the fill handle.
2. Using a command that gives you the capability to create many types of series.

☞ *Dragging the fill handle to the right and down fills the series in increasing order; dragging the fill handle up or left fills the series in decreasing order.*

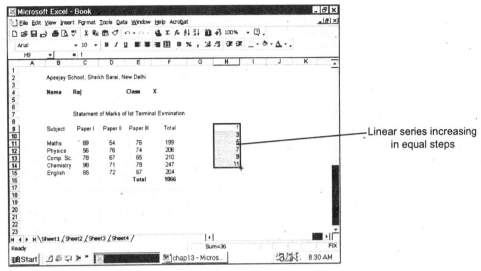

Figure 4.27　Creating a Linear series in equal steps

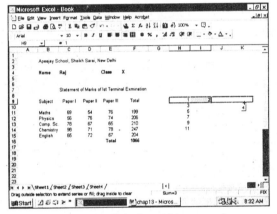

Figure 4.28　Creating a Linear series

4.10.1　Creating a Linear Series

➡ To create a linear series, do this:

1. Enter the first two elements of data in the series in adjacent cells, namely 1 and 3 in cells H9 and H10. (See Figure 4.27). Excel uses these two data items to determine the amount of increment in each step and the starting number for the series.

2. Select these two cells and then drag the fill handle *down* or *right* to fill in increasing and drag the fill handle *up* or *left* to fill

in decreasing order. The fill handle is the small square located at the lower right corner of a selection (See Figure 4.28).

3. Release the mouse button.

The area enclosed with the gray border fills with a series determined by the first two cells you selected.

➡ To use the AutoFill command to fill a series, do this:

1. In the first cell, enter the starting *number* or *date* if you want the range to be filled with values that increment by one. If you want the range filled with values that increment differently, fill the first cell in the range with the initial value and the second cell in the range with the second value that increases or decreases as you want the series to increase or decrease.

2. Select the range of cells containing dates or numbers used as starting values for the series. At the lower-right corner of the selection is the square fill handle.

3. Select the range to be filled by dragging the fill handle with the *right mouse button*.

Release the right mouse button to display the shortcut fill menu shown in Figure 4.29.

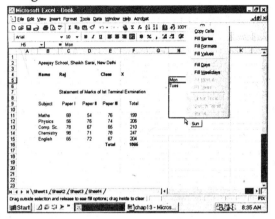

Figure 4.29 Shortcut Fill menu

4. The shortcut menu has the following command options.

Command	Description
Fill Series	Fills the selection with values that increase by one from the value in the first cell.
Fill Days	Fills the selection with days that increase by one starting from the day in the first cell.
Fill Week-days	Fills the selection with weekdays that increase by one beginning with the day in the first cell.
Fill Months	Fills the selection with months that increase by one beginning with the year in the first cell.
Linear Trend	Fills the blank cells in the selection with linear regression (best fit) values. Starting values are not over-written. It is available when more than one cell is filled with a starting value.
Growth Trend	Fills the blank cells in the selection with values calculated from growth (exponential) regression. Starting

(Contd...)

Command	Description
	values are not over written. This command is only available when more than one cell is filled with a starting value.
Series	Displays the Series dialog box.

➡ To create a series using the Fill series command, do this:

1. In the first cell, enter the *first number* or *date*.
2. Select the range of cells you want filled.
3. Click the Edit menu, highlight Fill and choose Series... to display the Series dialog box (See Figure 4.30).
4. Click the Rows or Columns option that matches the type of range you want filled. This is automatically selected to match the orientation of the cells you choose.
5. Select the Trend check box if you want selected values to be replaced by values for a linear or exponential best-fit. This selection limits step 6 to Linear or Growth options.
6. Select one of the following Type options:

Option	Description
Linear	Adds the Step Value to the preceding number in the series.
Growth	Multiplies the Step Value by the preceding number in the series.
Date	Enables the Date Unit group so that the increment applies to a Day, Weekday, Month, or Year.
AutoFill	Creates automatic series that may include text dates and labels.

7. Depending on the kind of series you want to create, use one of the following sets of steps.

➡ To create a Linear or Growth, do this:

1. In the Step value: box enter the step

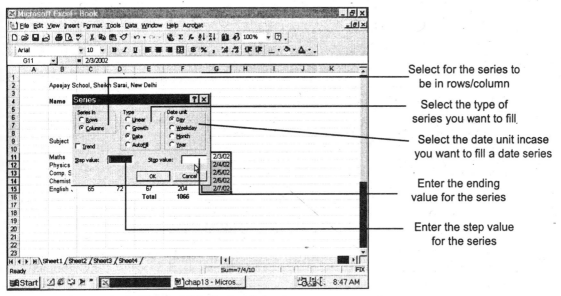

Select for the series to be in rows/column

Select the type of series you want to fill.

Select the date unit incase you want to fill a date series

Enter the ending value for the series

Enter the step value for the series

Figure 4.30 Series dialog box

value. This number is the constant amount by which the series changes from cell to cell. The Step Value may be positive or negative.

2. In the St**o**p value: box enter a value at which you want to stop the fill. This is required only if you think that you highlighted too many cells when you selected the range to fill.

3. Click OK.

➡ **To create a Date Series, do this:**

1. Click the Date unit area of the Series dialog box (See Figure 4.30).

   Select either Day, Weekday, Month, or Year to designate the date increment. Note that *Weekday* gives you dates without *Saturdays and Sundays*.

2. To specify the increment amount, enter the Step value in the **S**tep value box. If the starting value is **12/1/97**, and you choose Month as the Date Unit and 2 as the Step Value, the second date in the series becomes **2/1/98**.

3. To stop the series enter the Stop value in the St**o**p value: box (e.g. **12/1/98**). The stop value indicates the last date in the series.

4. Click OK.

☞ *When the series reaches either the end of the selected range or the St**o**p Value, Excel stops filling the cell. If you use a negative Step Value, the Stop value must be less than the starting value.*

Creating Series of Text and Headings

Excel can extend series of headings which are not dates or numbers. For example, there may be a text headings that includes a number, such as *Quarter1, Task1* (See Figure 4.31).

The text series that Excel recognizes includes the text shown in Table 4.10.

The AutoFill feature in Excel recognizes key words, such as days of the *week, month* names, and *Quarterly* abbreviations. Excel extends a series to repeat correctly, namely, Qtr1 follows Qtr4 and then the series continues.

Table 4.10 Text Series Recognized by Excel

Type	Example
Day	Tuesday, Wednesday, or Tue, Wed
Month	September, October, or Sep, Oct
Text	Project, Task
Text number	Task 1, Task 2, Paragraph 1.2, Paragraph 1.3
Quarterly	Quarter 1, Quarter 2, Qtr 2, Qtr 3, Q1, Q2

➡ **To type in a custom list for use with AutoFill, do this:**

1. Click the <u>T</u>ools menu and choose <u>O</u>ptions... .
2. Select the Custom Lists tab shown in Figure 4.32.
3. Select NEW LIST in the Custom <u>l</u>ist: box.
4. Select the List <u>e</u>ntries: list box, and type each item you want in the list. Press (Enter) to separate items.
5. To add the list to the Custom <u>l</u>ists: list box, click <u>A</u>dd. Your list appears in the Custom <u>l</u>ists: list box.

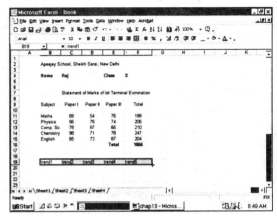

Figure 4.31 Heading that are not Dates or Numbers in a Series

6. Click OK if you have no more lists to enter. If you have additional lists to enter, select NEW LIST from the Custom <u>L</u>ists list box, and then begin typing your list in the List <u>e</u>ntries: list box.

➡ **To add a list that is in a range of cells on the worksheet, do this:**

1. Select the cells that contain the list you want to create. Now follow the step 1 and 2 above.

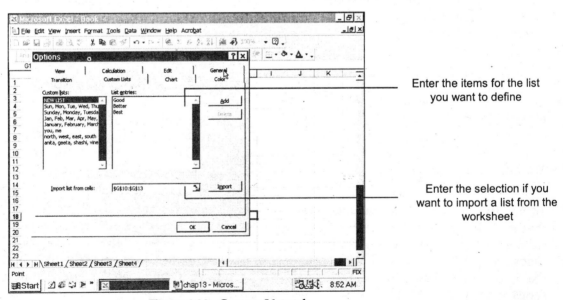

Figure 4.32 Custom Lists tab

2. The selection range appears in the Import list from cells: box you can reselect the list by clicking the arrow on the right.

3. After the selection is final, click Import, and then click OK.

The list you create is stored in Excel. The list can then be used in any other worksheet also.

➡ **To Edit a list, do this:**

1. In the Custom Lists tab, select the list from the Custom Lists: list box, and edit the contents in the List entries: list box.

2. When you finish editing, click Add to add the edited list.

3. To delete a list, select it from the Custom lists: list box, and then click Delete. You will be asked whether you want to delete the list.

4. Click OK.

☞ *AutoCorrect feature working both as a correction tool as it recognize common typing errors and automatically correct text and can also be used as a short hand tool where you enter the abbreviations for long words so that on entering the abbreviation it is replaced with the actual word.*

4.10.2 Entering Data using the Data Form

Data can be entered either by entering it into the individual cells on the worksheet or by using the Data Form.

➡ **To enter data using the data form, do this:**

1. Select any cell in the list.

2. Click **Data** menu and choose **Form**.

3. The **Data Form** dialog box appears as shown in Figure 4.33.

4. Each field name with a corresponding box is displayed.

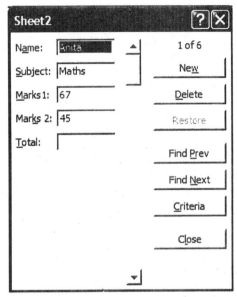

Figure 4.33 Data Form dialog box

5. If you want to add a new data, click the **New** button. A new blank record is displayed. Type the appropriate data entered into each box.

6. After finished entering the data, click the Close button to return to the worksheet.

7. the data you entered in the Data form is added in the list.

4.10.3 Using Data Validation

Validate Data controls the creation of input criteria for a cell or range of cells. It can either prompt the user for the correct information or can display an error message if the data entered does not match the criteria.

➡ **To specify the data validation settings, do this:**

1. Select a cell or range of cells for which you want to validate.

2. Click **Data** menu and choose Validation... .

3. In the Data Validation dialog box, click the Settings tab property sheet (See Figure 4.34).

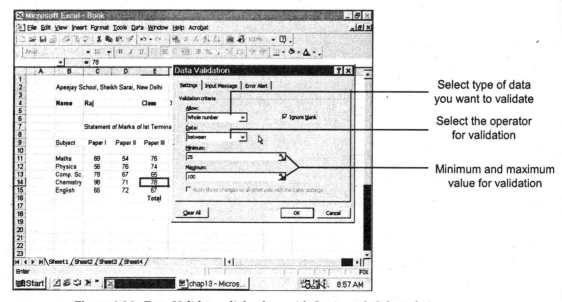

Figure 4.34 Data Validates dialog box with Setting tab Selected

4. Select the type of data to be validated from the **A**llow drop-down list.

5. Select an operator for validation from the **D**ata: drop-down list.

6. Enter the appropriate values in **Mini**mum: and Ma**x**imum: collapsable box.

➡ **To specify an input message, do this:**

1. Click the Input Message tab in Data Validation dialog box after specifying the settings property sheet. (See Figure 4.35).

2. Click the **S**how input message when cell is selected so that the check box is checked.

3. In the **T**itle: box enter a title for the message. This is displayed in Bold in the message box (See Figure 4.35).

4. Type the text of the message in the **I**nput message: box this message is displayed below the title (See Figure 4.35). The message can be upto 255 character long. Press [Enter] to start a new text in the message.

5. Click OK to save your settings.

➡ **To specify an Error alert, do this:**

1. Click the Error Alert tab in the Data Validation dialog box after specifying your settings property sheet (See Figure 4.36).

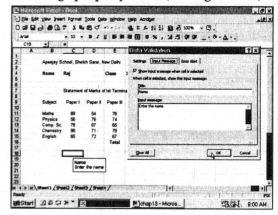

Figure 4.35 Data Validation dialog box with Input Message box Selected

2. Click the **S**how error alert after invalid data is entered, so that the check box is checked.

3. Select a St**y**le: for the message from the drop-down list.

4. Enter a Title for the message in the Title: box.

5. Enter the text for the error message in the Error message: box.

6. Click OK to save your settings.

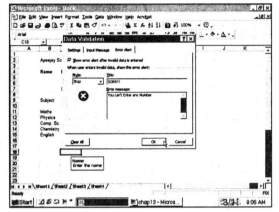

Figure 4.36 Data Validation Dialog Box with Error Alert tab Selected

4.11 EDITING CELL ENTRIES

While editing a cell entry, you can edit the text either in the formula bar or in the cell itself.

4.11.1 Editing Cell Entry in the Formula Bar

➡ **To edit cell entry in the formula bar, do this:**

1. Select the cell containing the data you want to edit.

2. Move the insertion point into the text in the formula bar. Position the pointer in the text you want to edit, and then click. A flashing insertion point indicates where typing and editing take place.

3. Edit the cell entry.

4.11.2 Editing Directly in a Cell

➡ **To edit an entry directly in a cell, do this:**

1. Double-click the cell or press F2 key.

2. Press the arrow keys to move the I-beam that marks the insertion point to where you want to edit.

3. Make the desired changes to the cell entry.

4. Press Enter key to enter the information, or press Esc key to leave the contents unchanged.

4.12 MOVING AND COPYING DATA

4.12.1 Moving and Copying Cell Contents

Cutting and pasting is a valuable function for reorganizing your worksheet. You may *cut out* a range of cells to *paste* them elsewhere. This operation moves cell contents, the format, and any note attached to the moved cells or you can copy a range of cells and paste it into another location. This will copy cell contents which you want to copy and paste.

Moving and Copying Cell Contents by Dragging and Dropping

The easiest and most intuitive way to move or copy a cell or range of cells is to drag the cell or the range of cells to the new location and drop it.

➡ **To move cell's content using drag and drop, do this:**

1. Select the cell or range of cell you want to move.

2. Move the mouse pointer over the selection's border. The pointer changes to an arrow.

3. Drag the pointer and the gray outline of the selection to the new location. Drag past the edge of a window to make the window scroll. Figure 4.37 shows the wide gray border that encloses the area to

be moved. Notice that as you move, you see the range reference where the selection will be pasted.

4. Release the mouse button when the gray outline is where you want to place the selected range.

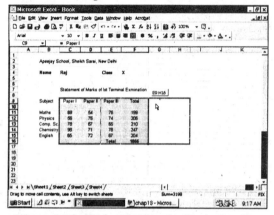

Figure 4.37 Wide Grey Border Enclosing the area to be moved

➡ **To copy cell's contents using drag and drop, do this:**

1. Select the range of cells you want to copy.

2. Hold down the Ctrl key and move the pointer over an edge of the selection. The pointer becomes an arrow with a + (plus) sign.

3. Continue holding down Ctrl key as you drag the edge of the selection to where you want the copy. The copy's location appears enclosed by a wide gray border, as shown in Figure 4.38.

Using the drag-and-drop method, you can make only a single copy. You cannot copy to multiple locations or fill a range.

If you release the Ctrl key before you release the mouse button, the copy operation becomes a move operation. The plus sign next to the arrow disappears. You can press Ctrl key again to switch back to copy operation.

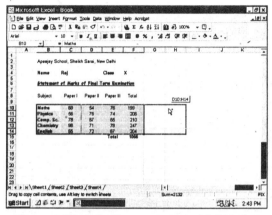

Figure 4.38 Selecting a portion of data to be copied to another place

Moving and Copying Cells with Commands

You can use drag-and-drop technique only when you want to move or copy data between different worksheets, or between panes in a split worksheet. But, when you want to move or copy data to another application such as Word, you cannot use drag and drop technique for this. You can make these operations with menu commands or shortcut keys as given below.

➡ **To move cell's contents using menu command, do this:**

1. Select the cell or range of cells you want to move.

2. Click the Edit menu and choose Cut, or click the Cut button on the Standard toolbar, or press Ctrl+X keys together. The cells you select appear surrounded by a marquee, a moving dashed line.

3. Select the cell at the upper-left corner, where you want the pasted cells.

4. Click Edit menu and choose Paste command, or click the Paste button, or press Ctrl+V keys together.

➡ To copy cell's contents using menu command, do this:

1. Select the cell or range of cells you want to copy.
2. Click the Edit menu and choose Copy. *Alternatively*, click the Copy button on the Standard toolbar, or press Ctrl+C together. The cells to copy are surrounded by a marquee.
3. Select the cell at the top-left corner, where you want the duplicate to appear. Check to see whether other cell contents will be overwritten.
4. Click the Edit menu and choose Paste. *Alternatively*, click the Paste button on the Standard toolbar or click Ctrl+V keys together to paste and retain the copy in memory. Press Enter to paste only one time.

Dragging and Inserting Cells

You can drag and insert a cell or range of cells so that existing cells can move aside. With this procedure, you do not need to insert cells to make room for new data, and then move in the new data. This method is a good way to rearrange a list or move individual records in a database.

➡ To move and insert data, do this:

1. Select the cell or range of cells you want to move.
2. Move the mouse pointer over the selection's border. The pointer changes to an arrow.
3. Press and hold down the Shift key and drag the pointer to where you want the data inserted. The location where the data is inserted appears as a grayed partial cell boundary, as shown in Figure 4.39. As you drag, you also see the range reference where the selection will be inserted.
4. Continue holding down the Shift key as you release the mouse button.

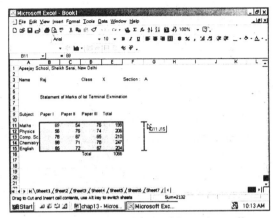

Figure 4.39 Dragging and Inserting cells

5. Release the Shift key.

The cells you dragged are inserted at the location of the grayed boundary.

4.12.2 Filling or Copying cell Contents with Fill Handle

You can save a great deal of data-entry time with Excel's Copy and Fill commands and the many shortcuts that copy or fill. Rather than typing each formula in a worksheet, you can type a few formulas and copy or fill them into other cells. You can also copy the formula and format at the same time.

☞ *To fill multiple rows or columns at one time, select all the original cells, and then use the* Ctrl+*drag procedure to fill at the cells at one time.*

Using the Fill Handle

If you use a mouse and need to fill data or formulas into adjacent cells, use the fill handle which is a black square at the lower-right corner of the selected cell or range. Dragging the fill handle across cells can fill the cells with copies or a data series.

☞ *A data series is a series of data that continues a repeating pattern.*

➡ To fill adjacent cells, do this:

1. Select the cell or range of cells that contains the data or formulas.
2. Drag the fill handle so that the wide gray border encloses all cells to fill. (See Figure 4.40)
3. Release the mouse button.

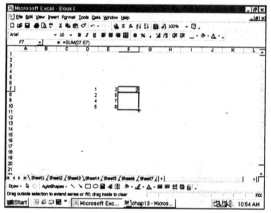

Figure 4.40 Using Fill Handle

Filling formulas into an area produces the same result as copying and pasting. Relative reference formulas adjust as though they were copied. Even if the formula references other spreadsheets, appropriate adjustments will *automatically* be made by Excel.

Using Ctrl + Enter to Fill Cells

You can fill cells as you enter data or formulas if you first select the adjacent cells or ranges to fill. Next, type the formula or value in the active cell. Rather than pressing Enter press Ctrl + Enter. Formulas and values fill into all selected cells just as though you used a Fill or Copy and Paste command. This method also works with nonadjacent multiple selections.

Using across Worksheets

If you have several worksheets that contain similar data or formulas and you have already entered the data, you can copy it to multiple worksheets of a workbook. For example, suppose that you have a monthly budget worksheet that you have created. You want to use the same column and row headings in the other worksheets in the workbook. Instead of re-entering the data, you can fill it across worksheets. You can select to fill the contents, the formats, or both.

➡ To fill data across worksheets, do this:

1. Select the range that contains the data you want to copy.

2. Select the worksheets you want to fill. The data will be copied to all the selected worksheets. Be sure the worksheet that contains the data you want to copy across is on top of all the sheets.

3. Click the Edit menu highlight Fill and choose Across Worksheets. The Fill Across Worksheets dialog box appears (See Figure 4.41).

4. Click All to copy both the contents and formatting.

   Contents to copy just the contents.

   Formats to copy just the formatting.

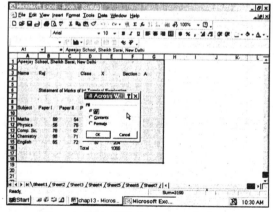

Figure 4.41 Fill Across worksheet

5. Click OK. The data is copied to the same cells in all the selected worksheets.

4.12.3 Using Paste Special Feature

Clicking the **E**dit menu and selecting Paste **S**pecial... command method is useful to copy and paste part of a cell's attributes, such as the format or value, but not both. With this command, you can reorient database layouts into worksheet layouts and vice versa. This command also enables you to combine the attributes of cells by pasting them together.

➡ **To use Paste Special Feature, do this:**

1. Select the cell or range of cells.
2. Click the **E**dit menu and choose **C**opy or click the Copy button.
3. Select the upper-left corner of the worksheet where you want to paste.

   When transporting (flipping) rows and columns, be sure to consider which cells are covered when the pasted area is rotated 90 degrees.
4. Click the **E**dit menu and choose Paste **S**pecial to display the Paste Special dialog box, (See Figure 4.42).

Figure 4.42 Paste Special dialog box

5. Select the characteristics you want transferred as explained in the following table:

Option	Function
All	Transfers all the original contents and characteristics.

(Contd...)

Option	Function
Formulas	Transfers only the formulas.
Values	Transfers only the values and formula results.
Forma**t**s	Transfers only the cell formats.
Comments	Transfers only note contents.
Validatio**n**	Copies data validation rules.
All e**x**cept border	Transfers everything except any borders applied to the selected range.
Column **w**idths	Selects the width of one column to another.

6. Select from the dialog box how you want the transferred characteristics or information combined with the cells being pastes into. Table below gives the different options and their functions.

Option	Function
N**o**ne	Replaces the receiving cell.
A**d**d	Adds to the receiving cell into which they are being pasted.
Subtract	Subtracts from the receiving cell into which they are being pasted.
Multiply	Multiplies by the receiving cell into which they are being pasted.
D**i**vide	Divides into the receiving cell into which they are being pasted.

7. Select the Skip **B**lanks check box if you do not want to paste blank cells which you have selected when you copy a range.
8. Select the Transpos**e** check box to change rows to columns or to change columns to rows.
9. Click OK.

By copying the range of formulas you want to freeze, you can convert formulas into their results so that they do not change. After copying, without moving the active cell, use Paste **S**pecial with the **V**alues and N**o**ne check boxes checked to paste the values over the original formulas.

The Transpose option in the Paste Special dialog box can save time if you use data information in worksheets.

The Transpose option rotates a range of cells between row orientation and column orientation, which is useful for switching between a database row layout and a worksheet column layout. You cannot transpose over the range that contains the original data.

☞ *The Paste Link button in the Paste Special dialog box enables you to link the pasted data to the original source.*

4.13 DELETING OR INSERTING CELLS, ROWS AND COLUMNS

With Excel, you can delete or insert entire *rows* or *columns*. You can also easily delete or insert cells, leaving the surrounding rows and columns unaffected. This technique enables you to add or remove cells without having to change entire rows or columns.

4.13.1 Deleting Cells, Rows or Columns

The Delete command on the Edit menu completely removes *cells*, *rows*, or *columns* from the worksheet. This is different from the Clear command in the Edit menu. The Clear command removes a cell's *contents*, *format*, or *note*, but it leaves the cell intact.

➡ **To delete *cells*, *rows* or *columns*, do this:**

1. Select the cells or range to be deleted, or select cells in the rows and columns to be deleted.

2. Click the Edit menu and choose Delete... . *Alternatively*, press Ctrl + - (minus) keys, or click the right mouse button and select Delete... . The Delete dialog box appears (See Figure 4.43).

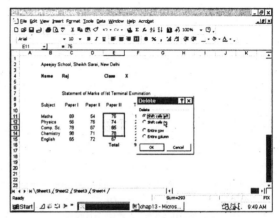

Figure 4.43 Delete dialog box

3. To delete cells, select the direction in which you want remaining cells to move:

Option	Description
Shift cells left	Cells to right of the deleted cells move left.
Shift cells up	Cells below the deleted cells move up.
Entire row	Deletes entire row containing a selected cell.
Entire column	Deletes entire column containing a selected cell.

4. Click OK.

To undo an incorrect deletion, click the Edit menu and choose Undo Delete. *Alternatively*, press Ctrl + Z, or click the Undo button on the Standard toolbar.

4.13.2 Inserting Cells, Rows, or Columns

Sometimes you may need to insert cells, rows, or columns to make room for new formulas or data. You can insert cells, rows, or columns as easily as you can delete them.

➡ **To insert *cells*, *rows*, or *columns*, do this:**

1. Select a cell or range of cells where you need new cells inserted. Or, select cells in the rows or columns where you want to insert new rows or columns.

2. Click the Insert menu and choose Cells... . *Alternatively*, press Ctrl + + (plus) keys or click the right mouse button and select Insert... . The Insert dialog box appears as in Figure 4.44.

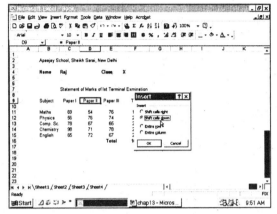

Figure 4.44 Insert dialog box

3. To insert cells, select the direction you want selected cells to be inserted.

The various options to insert cells are:

Option	Function
Shift right	cells Selected cells move right.
Shift down	cells Selected cells move down.
Entire row	Insert a row at each selected cell.
Entire column	col- Insert a column at each selected cell.

4. Click OK.

➡ To insert *rows* or *columns*, do this:

1. Select cells in the *rows* or *columns* where you want to insert new rows or columns.
2. Click the Insert menu and choose Rows to insert rows.
3. Click the Insert menu and choose Columns to insert columns.

4.13.3 Clearing, Inserting or Deleting Cells in Worksheet

After you have drafted and tested the worksheet, you may find that you need to reorganize or restructure the layout of the worksheet. When you restructure, you may need to insert or delete cells, rows or columns.

Shortcuts keys that are very helpful in reorganizing the worksheet layout are given in Table 4.11.

Table 4.11 Shortcut Keys for Changing the Worksheet Layout

key(s)	Action
Del	Clears selected formulas or contents; same as the Edit, Clear, Contents command.
Backspace	Clears the formulas bar; activates and clears the formula bar's contents.
Ctrl + C	Copies the selection so that it can be pasted; same as the Edit, Copy command.
Ctrl + X	Cuts the selection so it can be pasted; same as the Edit, Cut command.
Ctrl + V	Paste at the selected cell; same as the Edit, Paste command.
Ctrl + Z	Undoes last command.
Ctrl + Backspace	Repositions the worksheet so that the active cell is in view.

4.14 FORMATTING A WORKSHEET

Excel has several methods for formatting data as well as the complete worksheet so as to make *reports*, *tables*, and *charts* easier to read and understand. Excel enables you to:

• Change column width.
• Change the height of rows.
• Change numeric and date formats.

4.14.1 Formatting Rows and Columns

In order to improve the appearance of a worksheet or table in it, you can adjust *columns width* and *row heights*. Thus, you can fit more data on a page. If need be, you can even hide confidential data.

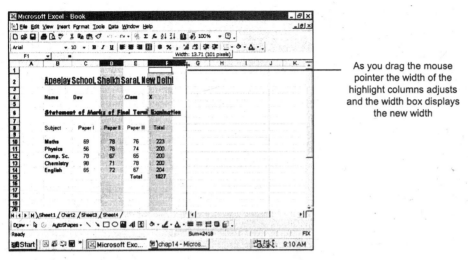

As you drag the mouse
pointer the width of the
highlight columns adjusts
and the width box displays
the new width

Figure 4.45 Changing Column Width with Mouse

How to adjust Column Width?

You can adjust the width of one or more columns to get better appearance in a worksheet. If a column is not wide enough to display a *number*, *date*, or *time*, Excel displays it using # characters in the cell. Therefore, you may need to adjust column widths also to show complete information.

➡ **To change column width with the mouse, do this:**

1. Select the columns for which you need to change the width.

2. Move the pointer onto the column separator to the right of the column heading (See Figure 4.45). The pointer changes to a two-headed, horizontal arrow.

3. Drag the column left or right until the shadow is where you want it. The Width box that appears as you drag the column displaying the numeric value for the column width.

➡ **To change column widths using menu command, do this:**

1. Select cells in the columns that you want to change.

2. Click the Format menu, highlight Column. (See Figure 4.46).

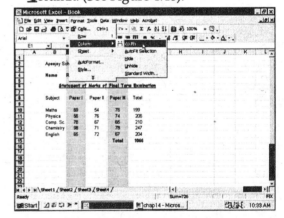

Figure 4.46 Format Column option

3. Use one of the following option to adjust column widths:

Option	Description
Width...	The Column Width dialog box appears (See Figure 4.47). Type the width, and then click OK.
AutoFit Selection	This option adjusts the column width automatically.
Standard Width...	This option would adjust to the default column width for all the selected columns.

4. Click OK.

➡ **To copy a column width, do this:**

1. Select cells in the columns that you want to copy.

2. Click copy button on the standard toolbar.

3. Select the cells where you want to apply this width.

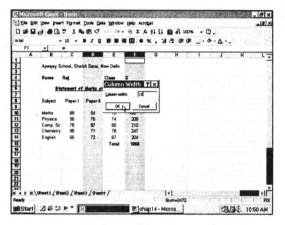

Figure 4.47 Column Width dialog box

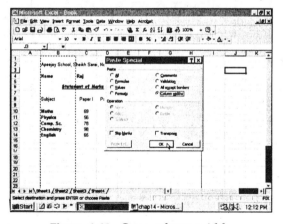

Figure 4.48 Copy column width

4. Click the Edit menu, choose Paste Special. Paste Special dialog box appears. (See Figure 4.48)

5. In this dialog box, choose Column widths from Paste group.

6. Click OK.

4.14.2 Hiding Columns in a Worksheet

If you work on a large worksheet you may not require to print the whole worksheet at one time. For this reason, you can hide columns temporarily so that they do not print or appear on the screen.

➡ **To hide columns, do this:**

1. Select the columns you want to hide.

2. *Using the mouse*: Move the mouse pointer over the column separator line that is on the right of the column you want to hide. The mouse pointer changes to a two-headed pointer. Drag the column separator left until crosses the separator on its left.

3. *Using the keyboard*: Click the Format menu, highlight Column, and choose Hide.

➡ **To unhide a column, do this:**

1. *Using the mouse*: Move the pointer over the column separator on the right of a hidden column. The mouse pointer changes to a two-headed pointer with space between the two heads. (See Figure 4.49). Move the pointer so that its left tip touches the column separator. Drag the column separator to the right, and then release it.

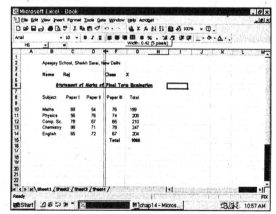

Figure 4.49 Unhiding a column

2. *Using the keyboard*: Select the cells (or columns) between which hidden columns appear. Click the <u>F</u>ormat menu, highlight <u>C</u>olumn, and choose <u>U</u>nhide.

How to adjust Row Height?

You can adjust row height in a worksheet to create enough space for *titles, subtotals, grand totals*, etc.

➡ To change the height of rows using the mouse, do this:

1. Select the rows for which you want to adjust the height.

2. Move the mouse pointer to the line directly under the row header of the row you want to change. The mouse pointer changes to a two headed vertical arrow. (See Figure 4.50).

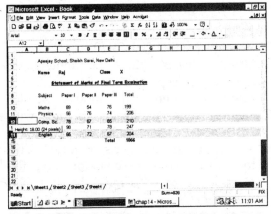

Figure 4:50 Changing row height with a mouse

3. Drag the two-headed arrow pointer up or down until the row is of the required height. Then release the mouse button. The screen tip displays the numeric value for the row height.

➡ To change the height of rows using the menu command, do this:

1. Select a cell in each row you want to change.

2. Click the <u>F</u>ormat menu and then highlight <u>R</u>ow.

3. Click from one of the following options.

Option	Description
<u>H</u>eight...	To display the Row Height dialog box enter the row height and click OK. (See Figure 4.51).
<u>A</u>utoFit	Excel adjusts rows height automatically.

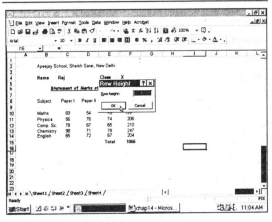

Figure 4.51 Row Height dialog box

4.14.3 Hiding Rows

➡ To hide rows, do this:

1. Select a row or number of rows which you want to hide, in a worksheet.

2. *Using the mouse*: Move the mouse pointer over the row to separate till it *changes* to double arrow. Now drag till the row is hidden or all the selected rows are hidden.

3. *Using the menu commands*: Click the <u>F</u>ormat menu highlight <u>R</u>ow and click <u>H</u>ide.

➡ To unhide rows, do this:

1. *Using the mouse*: Move the pointer over the row number that is under the hidden rows. Move the pointer up slowly until it changes to a double-headed pointer with space in between the two headings. Drag the line down to display the hidden rows.

2. *Using the keyboard*: Select the cells in the row above and below the hide row. Click the **F**ormat menu, highlight **R**ow and click **u**nhide.

3. The hidden rows are displayed.

4.14.4 Formatting all Characters in a Cell or Range of Cells

Generally, you may want to select a cell or range of cells and format their contents with the same *font*, *style*, and *size*.

➡ **To Format entries within a cell or a range of cells, do this:**

1. Select the cell, range, or multiple ranges.
2. Click the F**o**rmat, menu and choose C**e**lls... Or press (Ctrl)+(1). *Alternatively*, right click and choose the **F**ormat Cells... From the shortcut menu. The Format Cells dialog box shown in Figure 4.52 appears.
3. Click the Font tab. The Property sheet as seen in Figure 4.52 appears.
4. Select the font from the **F**ont: list.
5. Select the font style from the F**o**nt Style: list.
6. Select the font size from the **S**ize: list.
7. Select the underline style from the **U**nderline drop-down list. The underline options are *None, Single, Double, Single Accounting,* and *Double Accounting.*
8. Select a colour from the **C**olor drop-down list. Use Automatic for black and white printer.
9. From the Effects group, select any combination of Stri**k**ethrough, Sup**e**rscript or Su**b**script check boxes.
10. The Preview box shows the result of the chosen formatting options.
11. Click OK.

To return the selected cells to the default font style and size, select the **N**ormal Font check box in the Font property sheet.

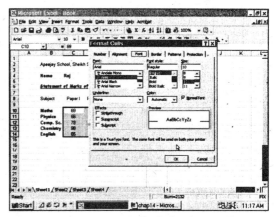

Figure 4.52 Format Cells dialog box with Font tab

➡ **To Format cell entries using the toolbar, do this:**

1. Select cell, ranges, or multiple ranges.
2. Select the Font from the **F**ont: drop down list.
3. Select the Font size, from the Font size drop down list.
4. Click the Bold button to make the entries bold.
5. Click the Italic button to make the entries Italic.
6. Click Underline to make the entries underlined.
7. Click OK.

4.14.5 Numeric Formatting

If you enter a number into a cell, it may not appear with the numeric appearance that you expected. Excel stores all numerals and dates as numbers. The appearance of the numerals or date on-screen is controlled by numeric formatting.

Excel has many predefined *numeric* and *date/time* formats. In addition, you can design your own custom formats. These custom formats can contain characters and symbols that you specify. You can designate the decimal precision you desire, apply any one of the 16 different colours. The format and color can be made to change according to the ranges of values in a cell.

Using Automatic Number Formatting

Numbers, *dates* and *time* are stored in cells as pure numbers without formatting. Excel examines the format of the number you enter, to determine whether the application can format a cell for you.

➡ **To apply a numeric format using the Formatting toolbar, do this:**

1. Select the cell or range of cells you want to format.
2. Click the required formatting button.
   - The formatting toolbar offers buttons for *currency*, *percentage*, or *comma* format.
   - To increase the decimal places, click the Increase Decimal button.
   - To decrease the decimal places, click the Decrease Decimal button.

➡ **To apply a numeric format using the menu commands, do this:**

1. Select the cell or range of cells you want to format.
2. Click the Format menu and choose Cells or press Ctrl+1. In the Format cells dialog box select Number tab property sheet as in Figure 4.53 appears.

☞ *If the active cell contains a number, the Sample area shows you the appearance of the numeric format.*

---

3. In the Category: list, select the type of number format you want to use. This selection determines what appears in the dialog box.
4. If you select *Number, Currency, Accounting, Percentage*, or *Scientific*, you have the following options (See Figure 4.53). Depending on what category you select, you will notice different options.

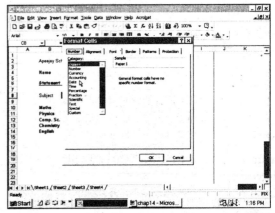

Figure 4.53 Number tab Property Sheet

If you select a Date, Time, Fraction or Special category, select the format you want from the list that appears.

5. Click OK.

Category	Option Displays	Description
Number, Currency, Accounting, Percentage, Scientific	Decimal Places	Enter the number of decimal places you want to appear, or use the spin arrows to scroll to the value you want.
Number	Use 1000 Separator (,)	Check this to use a comma to separate thousands.
Number, Currency	Negative Numbers	Select the style you want to use for negative numbers from this list.
Currency, Accounting	Use a currency symbol	Select a currency format from the Symbol drop-down list.

➡ **To format cells with shortcut keys, do this:**

1. Select the cell or range you want to format.
2. Press one of the following key combinations:

rmat	Shortcut Key
eneral	(Shift)+(Ctrl)+~
umber (two decimal places)	(Shift)+(Ctrl)+!
rrency (two decimal places)	(Shift)+(Ctrl)+$
rcent (no decimal places)	(Shift)+(Ctrl)+%
ientific	(Shift)+(Ctrl)+^

14.6 Formatting Date and Time

xcel can do date and time calculations, but
r this you have to enter date and time in a
ay Excel recognizes. You can type date and
me in cells the way you read or write them.
xcel recognizes date and time entered in
e formats shown in Table 4.12. For exam-
le, if you type the date 1.12.99 into a cell
ith the default General format and then
ress (Enter) key. Excel formats the cell in the
/d/yy date format. Here **m** is month, **d** is
ay and **yy** is year's last two digits.

A date in Excel is the number of days from
e beginning of the century, and a time is
e percentage of a 24-hour clock. The
xamples of Table 4.12 are shown in
igure 4.54.

Table 4.12 Predefined Excel Date and Time Formats

ormat	Example
/d/yy	10/24/02
-mmm-yy	24-Oct-02
-mmm	24-Oct
mm-yy	Oct-02
mmm-yy	October-02
/dd/yyyy	10/24/2002
d-mm-yyyy	24-10-2002
mm AM/PM	8:40 PM (12 hour clock)
mmm:ss AM/PM	8:40:10 PM (12-hour clock)
mm	20:40:10 (24-hour clock)
/d/yy h:mm	10/24/96 20:40 (24-hour clock)

(Contd...)

Format	Example
mm:ss	40:15
mm:ss.0	40:15.0
[h]:mm:ss	20:45:15 (24-hour clock)

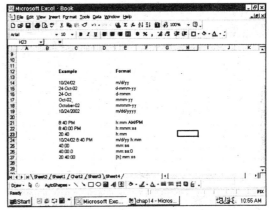

Figure 4.54 Examples of Predefined date and time

4.14.7 Using Predefined Date and Time Formats

You can also display date and time in Excel's
predefined formats. You can select a different colour of cells or decide a format for date
and time within a range.

➡ To change date and time format of a cell, do this:

1. Select the cell or range of cells.
2. Click the F**o**rmat, menu and choose C**e**lls... . The Format cells dialog box appears. Select the Number tab.
3. Select Date or Time from the **C**ategory list.
4. Select a format from the Type list.
5. Click OK.

➡ To automatically enter date/time using shortcut keys, do this:

1. Select the cell.
2. Press one of the following keys:

Shortcut Key	Format Result
Ctrl + ;	Inserts current date.
Ctrl + Shift + :	Inserts current time.
Shift + Ctrl + @	Formats in h:mm AM/PM.
Shift + Ctrl + #	Formats in d-mmm-yy.

4.15 PROTECTING WORKBOOKS IN EXCEL

With Excel, you can protect cells, graphical objects, sheets, windows, and entire workbooks. To prevent unauthorized people from changing the protection status or the display of hidden information, you can use the facility for password.

The procedure for protecting a worksheet and its contents involves two commands:

- The first command formats the cells or objects that you want protected.
- The second command turns on protection for a sheet or the entire workbook.

4.15.1 Protecting and Unprotecting Sheets

➡ **To turn on protection for a sheet or workbook, do this:**

1. Click the Tools menu and choose Protection.
2. Click either Protect Sheet..., Protect Workbook... Or Protect and Share Workbook... .
3. Protect sheet dialog box as in Figure 4.55 appears with different options. Select what you want to protect.
4. If you prefer, enter a password in the Password text box.
5. Click OK.

➡ **To unprotect a cell's contents, do this:**

1. Select the cell or range of cells that you want to unprotect or whose contents you want to hide from the formula bar.

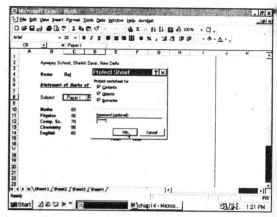

Figure 4.55 Protect Sheet dialog box

2. Click the Format, menu and choose Cells... .
3. Select the Protection tab of the Format Cells dialog box. (See Figure 4.56)
4. Clear the Locked check box to mark the cell or range of cells as the one that can be changed.
5. Click OK.

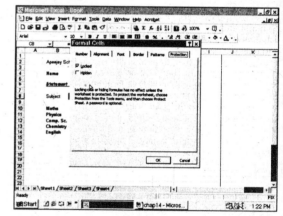

Figure 4.56 Protection tab of the Format Cells dialog box

4.16 USING AUTOFORMATS

You can format your worksheet quickly using any of the 16 predesigned formats as seen in Figure 4.57.

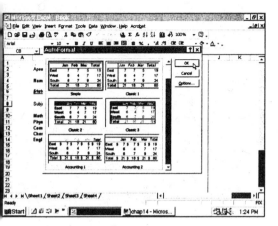

Figure 4.57 The AutoFormat dialog box

4.16.1 Formatting a Table Automatically

You can apply preset formats to the labels, backgrounds, lines, totals and numbers in Excel tables. These formats are designed for tables of information in which labels run down the left column and across the top rows. SUM() functions or totals are shown in the bottom row or the right column.

➡ **To apply an AutoFormat to a table, do this:**

1. Select the range containing the table. If the table is a block of adjacent cells surrounded by clear rows and columns, select a single cell within the table.

2. Click the Format, menu and choose Auto-Format... . The AutoFormat dialog box appears, as seen in Figure 4.57.

3. In this dialog box, all format's sample are shown with the name written at the bottom.

4. Select the format you want from the list.

5. Click OK.

6. If the format does not appear as you expected, click Undo to restore the table to its previous format.

7. To remove the formatting you applied to a table using the AutoFormat command, select None from the list and click OK.

➡ **To use only a part of auto formatting, do this:**

1. Click the Options button in the Autoformat dialog box. The dialog box enlarges to include Formats to apply group of options as seen in Figure 4.58.

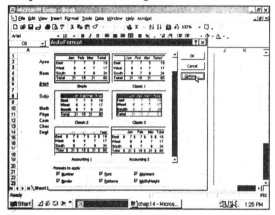

Figure 4.58 Autoformat dialog box with Formats to Apply Group

Option of the Format to apply to group are given below:

Options	Description
Number	To remove a numeric format from the selected sample which you want to use in a table.
Font	To remove any font format from the sample which you do not want to apply in a table.
Alignment	To remove any alignment from the table.
Border	To remove border in a sample which you select for a table.
Patterns	To remove any pattern which is applied on the sample format.
Width/ Height	To change the width and height of the cell.

2. Clear formats in the Formats to apply group that you do not want applied.

3. Click OK.

4.16.2 Using Conditional Formatting

Conditional formatting allows you to specify how cells that meet a specific condition should be formatted.

➡ To use conditional formatting, do this:

1. Select the cells to which the formatting should apply.
2. Click **Format** menu and choose **Conditional Formatting...** .
3. The Conditional Formatting dialog box appears as shown in Figure 4.59.

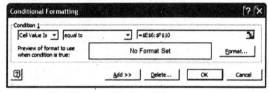

Figure 4.59   Conditional Formatting dialog box

4. Select the Condition 1 drop-down list. The default entry is Cell Value Is. Choose the desired value.
5. Click the down arrow at the right side of the box to see the list of arguments which includes not *between, equal to, not equal to, greater than, less than, greater than* or *equal to.* Select the desired option.
6. Click OK button.

4.17 WORKING WITH FORMULAS

Formulas in Excel always begin with an equal sign (=) and can include following types of data items:

a. *numeric* and text values (constants)
b. arithmetic operator, comparison operators, text operators, functions, parentheses
c. cell references, and names

☞ *By combining these components, you c₁ calculate the result you want by using t₁ information in the worksheet.*

Excel also gives you the option to displa₁ formulas on a worksheet, or the results the formulas.

➡ To control the display of formula resu₁ do this:

1. Click the Tools menu and choo Options... And click the View tab, ar₁ choose the Formulas option. When yc select the option the formulas are di₁ played as seen in Figure 4.60.

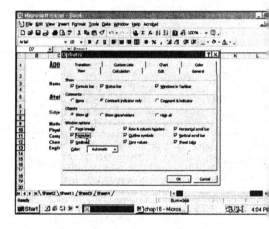

Figure 4.60   View Tab with Formulas Option₁

2. Click OK.

When you display formulas, Excel aut₁ matically doubles the width of all colum₁ (See Figure 4.61). The column widths wi return to their original settings when yc return to displaying the formula result Formulas automatically recalculate and pr₁ duce current results after you update da₁ used by the formulas.

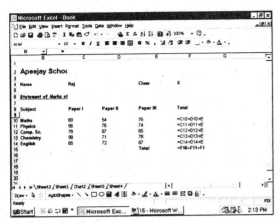

Figure 4.61 Formula displayed in a cells

4.17.1 How to Enter Formulas?

You write a formula with an equal sign (=) and then construct the formula using *values, operators, cell references, functions,* and *names* to calculate the desired result.

You can enter formulas either in the formula bar or in the cell. You can enter a formula using the formula bar by simply typing in it and pressing (Enter). You can also enter a formula directly in the cell and bypass the formula bar.

☞ *Make sure you remember to start the formula with an equal sign (=). If you forget the equal sign, Excel does not interpret the entry as a formula. If you enter B12*D15 (no equal sign), then B12*D15 is actually entered into the cell as text.*

➡ To enter a formula in the formula bar, do this:

1. Select the cell in which you want to enter the formula.
2. Type an equal sign (=) or click the Edit Formula button.
3. Type a *value, cell reference, function,* or *name*.
4. If the formula is complete, press (Enter) or click the Enter box (a check mark) in the

formula bar. If the formula is incomplete, go to step 5.
5. Type an operator. There are many types of operators. The most common operators are math symbols, such as + and –.
6. Return to step 3.

➡ To enter a formula in a cell, do this:

1. Double-click the cell in which you want to enter the formula and type an equal sign (=).
   To use the keyboard, select the cell and press (F2) or click the Edit Formula button. The cell is opened for editing and an equal sign (=) is inserted.
2. Type a value, cell reference, function, or name.
3. If the formula is complete, press (Enter) key. If the formula is incomplete, go to step 4.
4. Type an operator.
5. Return to step 2.

Always separate terms in a formula with operators or parentheses.

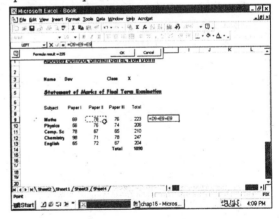

Figure 4.62 Entering a formula in Excel

☞ *If you click the Edit Formula button, Excel automatically inserts an equal sign and displays the results of the formula as you enter it. (See Figure 4.62)*

4.17.2 Moving or Copying Formula

When you move a formula from one cell to other, the cell references within the formula do not change. But when you copy a formula, then

- absolute cell references do not change
- relative cell references will change when you copy a formula

➡ **To move or copy a formula, do this:**

1. Select the cell that contains the formula you want to move or copy.
2. Point to the border of the selection.
3. To move the cell, drag the selection to the upper-left cell of the paste area. Microsoft Excel replaces any existing data in the pasted area.
4. To copy the cell, hold down Ctrl key as you drag the mouse.

☞ *You can also copy formulas into adjacent cells by using the fill handle. Select the cell that contains the formula and then drag the fill handle over the range you want to fill.*

4.18 ENTERING CELL ADDRESSING

Cell references allow you to use values from different parts of a worksheet and execute a desired calculation. You can use any cell or group of cells in a formula.

☞ *The reference of the active cell is displayed in the name box at the left end of the formula bar.*

4.18.1 Entering the Cell Address by Pointing

The easiest method of entering cell references in a formula is by pointing to the cell you want to include in a formula. Although you can type an entire formula, you often can make a typing error or misread the row or column headings. Say for example, you may end up with D52 in a formula when it should be E52.

☞ *When you point to a cell to include it in a formula, you actually move the pointer to the cell you want in the formula. It is found out only when you select the correct cells.*

➡ **To enter a cell reference into a formula by pointing, do this:**

1. Select the cell for the formula.
2. Type an equal sign (=) or click the Edit Formula button.
3. Point to the cell you want in the formula and click, or press the arrow keys to move the dashed marquee to the cell you want in the formula.

   The address of the cell you point to appears at the cursor location in the formula bar.
4. Enter an operator, such as the + symbol.
5. Point to the next cell.
6. Repeat the steps from step 4 to continue the formula, or enter the formula by clicking the Enter box or pressing Enter key.

☞ *The cell reference in a formula changes after you copy the formula to a new location or after you fill a range with a formula. You would usually want formulas to use relative cell references, only.*

4.18.2 Using Cell Addressing in Formulas

You refer to a cell's location with a *relative* reference or an *absolute* reference. Let us understand the difference in the two types of cell references.

Suppose that you are in your office, and you want someone to take a letter to the post office. Using a relative reference, you tell the person. "Go out the front door; turn left cross the road and move two building then turn right and go to the second building." These directions are relative to your office location at the time you give the instructions. If you move to a different location, these directions are no longer valid.

To make sure that the letter gets to the mailbox no matter where you are then you give different set of directions. You must say something like this" "Take this letter to the I.P. Estate post office." No matter where you are when you speak, the post office is at one absolute location: I.P ESTATE.

☞ *Thus, the difference between relative and absolute reference is that in absolute reference, the cell is fixed once for all. In the relative reference it depends on the location where your pointer is.*

Using Relative Addressing

Excel uses relative referencing for cell addresses when you enter a formula.

In Figure 4.63, the formula in cell G9 is = D9+E9+F9. All these references are relative. The formula, translated into English, would read as follows:

"In cell G9, add the number in the 9th column to the left (D9), second column to the left (E9) and the adjacent column on the left (F9)" in the same row.

Suppose you copy formula across Column G, the formulas adjust their cell references to their new positions. The copied formulas are as follows:

Cell Containing FormulaA1 Format

G10	= D10+E10+F10
G11	= D11+E11+F11
G12	= D12+E12+F12

You will notice that the formulas change to give the cell references with relative position from the cell that contains the formula.

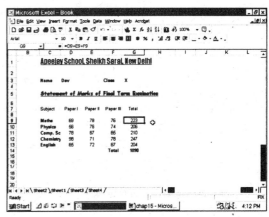

Figure 4.63 Formula with relative reference

Using Absolute Addressing

You use absolute references only to keep the cell reference values from changing as and when you copy a formula to a new location in a worksheets.

➡ **To enter an absolute reference by using the F4 key, do this:**

1. Type an equal sign (=) and the cell reference you want it to be absolute.

2. Press F4, the absolute reference key, until the correct combination of dollar signs appears.

☞ *Indicate absolute references by putting a dollar sign ($) in front of the column letter or row number that you want to freeze or both. (See Figure 4.64)*

---

3. Type the next operator and continue to enter the formula, also.

You can use the F4 key when editing an existing formula. ·

Using Mixed Addressing

In some cases, you may want either the row to stay fixed or the column to stay fixed when copying the cells from one place to other in a worksheet. In such cases, use a mixed reference. Such references contain both absolute and relative reference. For example, the reference $B5 prevents the column from changing, but the row changes relative to a new copied location. The dollar sign prevents the column from changing. In B$5, just the opposite occurs. The column adjusts to a new location but the row always stays fixed at 5 because the dollar sign prevents the row from changing.

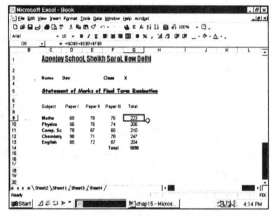

Figure 4.64 Formula with absolute reference

You can create mixed references the same way as you can create absolute references. Type the dollar signs or specific row and column numbers without brackets or press F4 key. Each press of F4 cycles the cell reference to a new combination.

☞ *Each time you press* F4, *Excel cycles through all combinations of relative and absolute references. Press* F4 *four times, for example, and you cycle from B22 through $B$22, B$22, $B22, and B22.*

Referring to Other Sheets in a Workbook

You can refer to other sheets in a workbook by including a sheet reference as well as a cell reference in a formula. For example, to refer to cell A1 on Sheet6, you would enter Sheet6!A1 in the formula.

You can use the mouse to enter a reference to a cell or range of cells on another worksheet in a workbook.

➡ **To refer to cell or range in a different worksheet, do this:**

1. Start entering the formula in the cell where you want the result to appear.
2. Click the sheet tab for the worksheet you want to refer to.
3. Select the cell or range that you want to refer to. The complete reference, including the sheet reference, appears in the formula bar (See Figure 4.65).

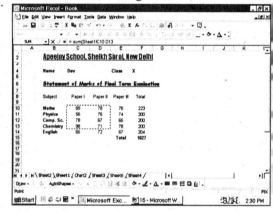

Figure 4.65 Referring a cell or range of cells in another worksheet

4. If the sheet name includes spaces, Excel surrounds the sheet reference with single quotation marks.
5. Finish the formula and press Enter key.

Entering 3-D References

You can use 3-D references to refer to a cell range that includes two or more sheets in a workbook. A 3-D reference consists of a sheet range specifying the beginning and ending sheets, and a cell range specifying the cells being referred to. Let us see an example of a 3-D reference:

```
=SUM(Sheet1:Sheet6!$E$1:$E$6)
```

This reference sums up the values in the range of cells $E$1:$E$6 in each of the sheets from Sheet1 to Sheet6, and adds the sums together resulting in a grand total.

➡ **To use the mouse to enter the reference, do this:**

1. Click for entering the formula in the cell where you want the result to appear.
2. Click the sheet tab for the first worksheet you want to include in the reference, hold down the (Shift) key and click the last worksheet you want to include in the reference, and then select the cells you want to refer to.
3. Finish the formula and press (Enter) key.

☞ *Notice the exclamation mark (!) that separates the sheet reference from the cell reference. If you have named the sheet, simply use the sheet name and then the cell reference. If the sheet name included spaces, you must surround the sheet reference with single quotation marks.*

4.19 FUNCTIONS IN EXCEL

Functions are the predefined formulas that perform calculations on specific values, called arguments. Each function takes specific types of arguments, such as *numbers*, *references*, *text*, or *logical values*. You can enter the arguments, enclosing them in parentheses i.e. ( ), after the function name. Functions use these arguments in the same way that algebraic equations use variables. For example, the SUM function adds values or range of values, and the PMT function calculates the loan payments based on an interest rate, the period of loan, and the principal amount of loan. Excel includes many functions that can be divided into the following categories:

1. Mathematical
2. Logical
3. Statistical
4. Date and time
5. Text
6. Financial
7. Database
8. Engineering
9. Information
10. Lookup and Reference

All these different types of functions are explained in the following Sections.

4.20 ENTERING WORKSHEET FUNCTIONS

You can enter a function in two ways in a worksheet.

a. You can type the function name and the required arguments in the formula bar. To use this method you need to remember the name of the function and the arguments to be passed.
b. Paste the function—This is an easier method because Excel inserts the function and asks you to fill in the parameters only.

➡ **To enter a function directly, do this:**

1. Activate the cell.
2. Type the function and the argument in the formula bar.

4.20.1 Using the Paste Function

Use the Paste Function to make your job much easier. The Paste Function guides you through the process and explains each function as well as each argument within a function.

➡ **To insert a function and its arguments into the worksheet, do this:**

1. Select the cell where you want to enter the function. If you are entering a formula in the formula bar, move the insertion point to where you want the function inserted.

2. Click the Insert menu and choose Function or click the Paste Function button in the standard toolbar, to display the Paste Function dialog box. (See Figure 4.66)

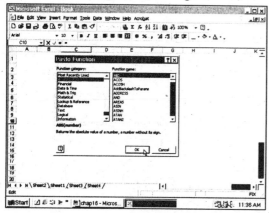

Figure 4.66 Paste Function dialog box

3. Select the type of function you want from the Function category list. These categories segment the large number of functions into smaller lists. If you are unsure of the category, select Most Recently Used or All.

4. Click the Specific function that you want from the Function name: list box. Read the description in the lower part of the dialog box to verify that this is the function you want.

☞ *Scroll quickly to a function by clicking in the list and typing the first letter.*

5. Click OK.

6. The Paste Function displays palette under the Formula bar as seen in Figure 4.67. Enter the arguments in each argument text box. You can type the cell references or numbers, click the cell to enter, or drag across multiple cells to enter. Notice the description of each arguments as you select the text box.

If you want to use range names in an argument text box, type the range of cell's name or select Insert, Name, Paste.

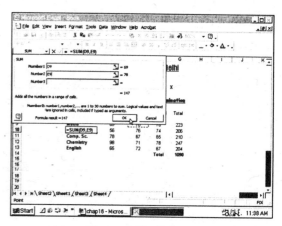

Figure 4.67 Palette

You can also create more complex functions where each argument is a function by itself. Click button next to the argument name and enter the desired formula.

7. Click OK to complete the function and insert it in a cell.

You can also choose Cancel if you decide not to insert the function.

☞ *In the Paste Function, use the Most Recently Used category to quickly get to functions you use very often.*

4.20.2 Editing Function

After you enter functions into a formula in the formula bar if need be, you can edit them in two ways. You can use Paste Function to step through the functions in a formula, or you can manually edit the formula and functions.

➡ To edit functions using the Paste Function, do this:

1. Select the cell containing a function.

2. Click the Insert menu and choose Function or click the Paste Function button in the Standard toolbar. The Paste Function dialog box appears and shows the first function in the formula.

3. Change any arguments necessary in the first function.

4. When you finish making changes, click OK.

➡ **To edit functions manually, do this:**

1. Select the cell containing a function.

2. Press F2 key to activate the Formula bar or click in the Formula bar.

3. Select the argument in the formula you want to change.

4. Enter the new argument by typing, dragging, pasting a name, or inserting a function.

5. Press Enter.

You can move across arguments by pressing Ctrl+→ or Ctrl+← keys. To select as you move, hold down Shift key.

☞ *Select a term or argument in the formula bar by double-clicking it.*

4.20.3 Text Functions

Text functions convert all uppercase letters in a text string to lowercase. And all lowercase letters convert to uppercase

Syntax

LOWER(text)

Text: is the text you want to convert to lowercase. LOWER does not change characters in text that are not letters.

Syntax

UPPER(text)

Text: is the text you want to converted to Uppercase.

Examples

UPPER ("uppercase") equals "UPPERCASE"

LOWER ("UPPERCASE") equals "uppercase"

4.20.4 Mathematical Functions

Excel includes many math and trigonometry functions. Mathematical functions are used to perform wide variety of simple or complex calculations such as totaling the value for a range of cells, rounding of a number. Trigonometry functions are used when we want to know the sin or cosine values, etc.

SUM( )

Adds all the numbers in a range of cells. (See Figure 4.68)

Syntax

SUM(number1,number2,...)

Where **number1, number2,** ... are upto 30 arguments for which you want the total value or sum.

• Numbers, logical values, and text representations of numbers that you type directly into the list of arguments are counted.

• If an argument is an array or reference, only numbers in that array or reference are counted. Empty cells, logical values, text, or error values in the array or reference are ignored.

• Arguments that are error values or text that cannot be translated into numbers would cause errors.

Examples

SUM (3, 2) equal 5

SUM ("3", 2, TRUE) equals 6 because the text values are translated into numbers, and the logical value TRUE is translated into the number 1. (See Figure 4.68)

Unlike the previous example, if A8 contains "text" and A9 contains "text1", then:

SUM (A8, A9, 2) equals 2 because references to nonnumeric values in references are not translated. (See Figure 4.68)

If cells A2:E2 contain, 5, 15, 30, 40 and 50, then

SUM (A2:C2) equals 50
SUM (B2:E2, 15) equals 150 (See Figure 4.68)

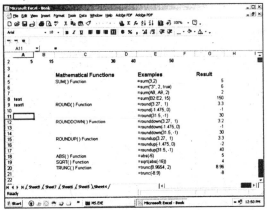

Figure 4.68 Mathematical functions and their results

COUNTIF

Counts the number of cells within a range that meet the given criteria.

Syntax

COUNTIF(range,criteria)

Range: is the range of cells from which you want to count cells.

Criteria: is the criteria in the form of a number, expression, or text that defines which cells will be counted.

Example

If cells A6:B6 contain, 32, 43, 42, 32 and 50, then
COUNTIF(A6:B6) equals 2
CRITERIA type 34 equals 2 (See Figure 4.68)

Round( )

Round( ) function rounds a number to a specified number of digits. (See Figure 4.68)

Syntax

ROUND(number,num_digits)

Where **number**— is the number you want to round.

Num_digits specifies the number of digits to which you want to round a number.

- If num_digits is greater than 0 (zero), then number is rounded to the specified number of decimal places.
- If num_digits is 0, then number is rounded to the nearest integer.
- If num_digits is less than 0, then number is rounded to the left of the decimal point.

Examples

ROUND (3.27, 1) equals **3.3** (See Figure 4.68)

ROUND (−1.475, 0) equals **−1**

ROUND (31.5, −1) equals **30**

Rounddown( )

Rounddown( ) function rounds a number down towards zero. (See Figure 4.68)

Syntax

ROUNDDOWN(number,num_digits)

Where **number**— is the number you want to round.

Num_digits specifies the number of digits to which you want to round a number.

- If num_digits is greater than 0 (zero), then number is rounded down to the specified number of decimal places.
- If num_digits is 0, then number is rounded down to the nearest integer.
- If num_digits is less than 0, then number is rounded down to the left of the decimal point.

Examples

ROUNDDOWN (3.27, 1) equals **3.2** (See Figure 4.68)

ROUNDDOWN (−1.475, 0) equals **−1**

ROUNDDOWN (31.5, −1) equals **30**

Roundup( )

Roundup( ) function rounds a number up away from 0 (zero). (See Figure 4.68)

Syntax

`ROUNDUP(number,num_digits)`

Where **number**— is the number you want to round.

Num_digits specifies the number of digits to which you want to round a number.

- If num_digits is greater than 0 (zero), then number is rounded up to the specified number of decimal places.
- If num_digits is 0, then number is rounded up to the nearest integer.
- If num_digits is less than 0, then number is rounded up to the left of the decimal point.

Examples

`ROUNDUP (3.27, 1)` equals **3.3** (See Figure 4.68)

`ROUNDUP (-1.475, 0)` equals **-2**

`ROUNDUP (31.5, -1)` equals **40**

ABS( )

`ABS( )` function returns the absolute value of a number. The absolute value of a number is the number without any + or – sign.

Syntax

`ABS(num)`

Where **num** is the real number of which you want the absolute value.

Examples

`ABS(5)` equals **5**

`ABS(-5)` equals **5** (See Figure 4.68)

SQRT( )

`SQRT( )` returns a positive square root of a number. (See Figure 4.68)

Syntax

`SQRT(num)`

Where **num** is the number for which you want the square root. If number is negative, SQRT returns the #NUM! error value.

Examples

`SQRT(16)` equals **4**

`SQRT(-16)` equals **#NUM!**

But if you want to find the square root of negative number then you have to give function like this:

`SQRT(ABS(-16))` equals **4** (See Figure 4.68)

TRUNC( )

`TRUNC( )` function truncates a number to an integer value by removing the fractional part of the number. (See Figure 4.68)

Syntax

`TRUNC(num,num_digits)`

Where **num** is the number you want to truncate.

Num_digits is a number specifying the precision of the truncation. The default value for num_digits is 0 (zero).

Examples

`TRUNC(8.9)` equals **8**

`TRUNC(-8.9)` equals **-8**

`TRUNC(8.9654, 2)` equals **8.96**

4.20.5 Logical Functions

Logical functions are used when we want to check whether a given condition is true or false.

IF( )

`IF( )` function used to determine whether a condition specified with in braces is true or false. It returns one value if a specified condition evaluates to TRUE and another value if it evaluates to FALSE. (See Figure 4.69)

Syntax

`IF(logical_test,value_if_true,value_if_false)`

Where

`Logical_test` is a value or expression

that can be evaluated to TRUE or FALSE. For example, A10 = 100 is a logical expression.

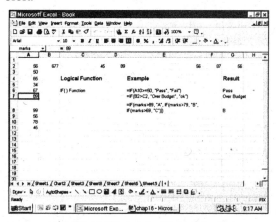

Figure 4.69 Logical functions

Value_if_true is the value that is returned if logical_test is TRUE. For example, if the value in cell A10 is equal to 100, the expression evaluates to TRUE.

Value_if_false is the value that is returned if logical_test is FALSE. For example, if the value in cell A10 is not equal to 100, the expression evaluates to FALSE.

Examples

On a Marksheet, cell A10 contains a formula to calculate the result. If the result of the formula in A10 is greater than or equal to 50, then the following function displays "Pass". Otherwise, the function displays "Fail". (See Figure 4.69)

`IF(A10>=50,"Pass","Fail")`

Suppose an expense worksheet contains in B2:B4 the following data for "Actual Expenses" for January, February, and March: 1000, 500, 500. C2:C4 contains the following data for "Predicted Expenses" for the same periods: 800, 800, 975.

You can write a formula to check whether you are over budget for a particular month, generating text for a message with the following formulas:

`IF(B2>C2,"Over  Budget","OK")equals "Over Budget"`

`IF(B3>C3,"Over          Budget","OK") equals "OK"`

We can also use nested IF function:

`IF(Marks>89,"A",IF(Marks>79,"B",`

`IF(Marks>69,"C",IF(Marks>59,"D","F ")))))`

In the above example, **Marks** in the name of the cell **A7** (See Figure 4.69), if the first logical_test (Marks>89) is TRUE, "A" is returned. If the first logical_test is FALSE, the second IF statement is evaluated, and so on.

☞ *When averaging cells, keep in mind the difference between empty cells and those containing the value zero, especially if you have cleared the Zero values check box on the View tab (Options command, Tools menu). Empty cells are not counted, but zero values are.*

TRUE( )

TRUE( ) returns the logical value TRUE and it takes no arguments.

Syntax

TRUE( )

FALSE( )

FALSE( ) function is same as TRUE( ) but it returns the logical value FALSE.

Syntax

FALSE( )

4.20.6 Statistical Function

Statistical functions are used to perform statistical analysis on ranges of data. It includes simple as well as complex statistical functions such as *average, min, max, standard deviation, slopes* etc.

MAX( )

Max function returns the largest value in a set of values stored in a cells.

Syntax

`MAX(number1,number2,...)`

Where **number1,number2,...** are upto 30 numbers for which you want to find the maximum value.

- You can specify arguments that are *numbers, empty cells, logical values,* or *text representations of numbers.* Arguments that are error values or text that cannot be translated into numbers cause errors.
- If the arguments contain no numbers, MAX returns 0 (zero).

Examples

If A1:A5 contains the numbers 10, 7, 9, 27, and 2, then:

`MAX (A1:A5)` equals **27** (See Figure 4.70)

`MAX (A1:A5, 30)` equals **30**

MIN( )

Min function returns the smallest number in a set of values.

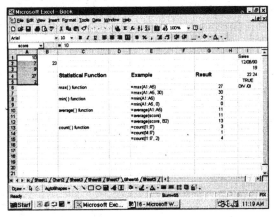

Figure 4.70 Statistical functions

Syntax

`MIN(number1,number2, ...)`

Where **number1,number2,...** are upto 30 numbers for which you want to find the minimum value.

- You can specify arguments that are *numbers, empty cells, logical values,* or *text representations of numbers.* Arguments that are error values or text that cannot be translated into numbers cause errors.
- If the arguments contain no numbers, MIN returns 0.

Examples

If A1:A5 contains the numbers 10, 7, 9, 27 and 2 then:

`MIN (A1:A5)` equals **2** (See Figure 4.70)

`MIN (A1:A5, 0)` equals **0**

Average( )

The Average function returns the average (arithmetic mean) of the arguments which are passed in function as an argument. (See Figure 4.70)

Syntax

`AVERAGE(number1,number2,...)`

Where **number1, number2,...** are upto 30 numeric arguments for which you want the average.

Notes

- The arguments must be either numbers or names, or references that contain numbers.
- If an array or reference argument containing text, logical values, or empty cells, such values are ignored; however, cells with the value zero are included.

☞ *When averaging cells, keep in mind the difference between empty cells and those containing the value zero, especially if you have cleared the Zero values check box on the View tab (Options command, Tools menu). Empty cells are not counted, but zero values are.*

Examples

If A1:A5 is named Scores and contains the numbers, 10, 7, 9, 27 and 2 then:

AVERAGE (A1:A5) equals **11** (See Figure 4.70)

AVERAGE (Scores) equals **11** Here **Scores** is the name of range. (See Figure 20.5)

AVERAGE (A1:A5, 5) equals **10**

AVERAGE (A1: A5) equals **SUM (A1:A5)/COUNT (A1:A5) equals 11**

If C1:C3 is named OtherScores and contain the numbers 4, 18, and 7, then:

AVERAGE (Scores, OtherScores) equals **10.5**

Count( )

Count function counts the number of cells that contain numbers and numbers within the list of arguments. Use COUNT to get the number of entries in a number field in a range or array of numbers. (See Figure 4.70)

Syntax

COUNT(value1, value2,...)

Where **value1, value2,...** are upto 30 arguments that can contain or refer to a variety of different types of data, but only numbers are counted.

- Arguments that are *numbers*, *dates*, or *text* representations of numbers are counted. Arguments that are error values or text that cannot be translated into numbers are ignored.
- If an argument is an array or reference, only numbers in that array or reference are counted. Empty cells, logical values, text, or error values in the array or reference are ignored. If you need to count logical values, text, or error values, use the COUNT function.

Examples

In the following example, the column I1 to I6 contain the following values: (See Figure 4.70)

```
I1   Sales
I2   12/8/90
I3   19
I4   22.24
I5   TRUE
I6   D/V/0!
```

COUNT (I1:I7) equals **3** (See Figure 4.70)

COUNT (I4:I7) equals **1**

COUNT (I1:I7, 2) equals **4**

4.20.7 Date and Time Function

With date and time functions, you can analyze and work with date and time values in formulas. For example, if you need to use the current date in a formula, you can use the TODAY ( ) function, which returns the current date.

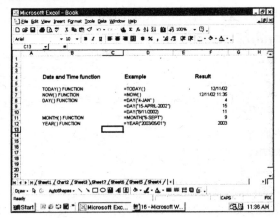

Figure 4.71 Date and Time functions

Today ( )

It returns the current date of the system. (See Figure 4.71)

Syntax

TODAY( )

Now()

Returns the current date and time. (See Figure 4.71)

Syntax

`NOW( )`

Day()

It returns the day of a date passed as a arguments. The day is given as an integer ranging from 1 to 31. (See Figure 4.71)

Syntax

`DAY(serial_number)`

Where **serial_number** is the date of the day you are trying to find. Dates may be entered as text strings within quotation marks.

Examples

`DAY("4-Jan")` equals **4** (See Figure 4.71)

`DAY("15-Apr-2002")` equals **15**

`DAY("8/11/2002")` equals **11**

`DAY("2001/10/10")` equals **10**

Month()

It returns the month of a date which is passed as a arguments. The month is given as an integer, ranging from 1 (January) to 12 (December). (See Figure 4.71)

Syntax

`MONTH(serial_number)`

Where **serial_number** is the date of the month you are trying to find.

Examples

`MONTH("6-Sept")` equals **9** (See Figure 4.71)

`MONTH("2004/04/01")` equals **4**

Year()

Returns the year corresponding year to a date. (See Figure 4.71)

Syntax

`YEAR(serial_number)`

Where **serial_number** is the date of the year you want to find.

Examples

`YEAR("7/7/1999")` equals **1999**

`YEAR("2003/05/01")` equals **2003** (See Figure 4.71)

DAYS 360

The number of days between two dates based on a 360-day year (twelve 30-day months), which is used in some accounting calculations. Use this function to help compute payments if your accounting system is based on twelve 30-day months.

Syntax

`DAYS360(start_date,end_date,method)`

Start_date and end_date are the two dates between which you want to know the number of days. If start_date occurs after end_date, DAYS360 returns a negative number.

Example

`DAYS360("1/30/2008","2/1/2008")` equals **1**

If cell D10 contains the date 1/30/2008 and cell D11 contains the date 2/1/2008, then: DAYS360(D10,D11) equals 1

4.20.8 Text Function

With text functions, you can use text strings in formulas. You can also change the case of the string, find out the length of a text string or join two strings etc.

Concatenate()

Joins two or more text strings into one text string. (See Figure 4.72)

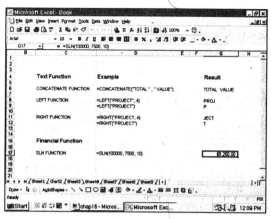

Figure 4.72 Text functions

Syntax

`CONCATENATE (text1,text2,...)`

Where **text1, text2,...** are 1 to 30 text items to be joined into a single text item.

The **"&"** operator can also be used to join text items.

Examples

`CONCATENATE("Total"," Value")` equals `"Total Value"`. (See Figure 4.72)

If you use & operator to join strings then

`"Total"&" "&"Value"`

LEFT( )

LEFT returns the first character or characters in a text string, based on the number of characters specified as arguments. (See Figure 4.72)

Syntax

`LEFT(text,num_chars)`

Where **text** is the text string.

num_chars specifies the number of characters to be extracted. By default, it is assumed to be 1.

Examples

`LEFT("PROJECT",4)` equals `"PROJ"` (See Figure 4.72)

If A1 contains "SUBJECT", then:

`LEFT(A1)` equals `"S"`

RIGHT( )

It is same as LEFT but it returns the last character or characters in a text string, based on the number of characters specified as arguments. (See Figure 4.72)

Syntax

`RIGHT(text,num_chars)`

Where **text** is the text string.

num_chars specifies the number of characters to be extracted.

Examples

`RIGHT("PROJECT",5)` equals `"OJECT"` (See Figure 4.72)

`RIGHT("PROJECT")` equals `"T"`

4.20.9 Financial Function

Financial functions perform common business calculations For example, determination of the payment for a loan.

SLN( )

Returns the straight-line depreciation of an asset for one period. (See Figure 4.72)

Syntax

`SLN(cost,Last_value,life)`

Where **Cost** is the initial cost of the asset.

Last_value is the value at the end of the depreciation.

Life is the number of year in which the asset is being depreciated (the useful life of the asset).

Example

Suppose you purchased a Car for **1,00,000** that has a useful life of 10 years and a salvage value of **7,500**. The depreciation allowance for each year is:

`SLN(100000, 7500, 10)` equals **$9,250** (See Figure 4.72).

PMT( )

Suppose you want to buy a car and you want to calculate your monthly installment you can use the **PMT()** function built in Excel.

Example

1. Activate a cell.
2. Click the <u>I</u>nsert, menu and choose <u>F</u>unction or click the Paste Function button, in the standard toolbar, to display the **Paste Function** dialog box.

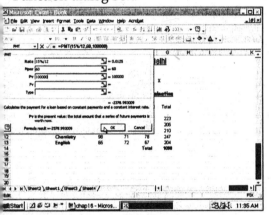

Figure 4.73 PMT Function dialog box

3. Select the Financial function from the Function <u>c</u>ategory list and **PMT()** from the Function <u>n</u>ame: list.
4. The dialog box open as in Figure 4.73.

The argument require by the function are as follows:

Argument	Description
Rate	is the interest rate for the loan.
Nper	is the total number of payments for the loan.
Pv	is the present value, or the total amount that a series of future payments is worth now; also known as the principal.
Fv	is the future value, or a cash balance you want to attain after the last

(Contd...)

Argument	Description
	payment is made. If Fv is omitted, it is assumed to be 0 (zero), that is, the future value of a loan is 0.
Type	is the number 0 (zero) or 1 and indicated when payments are due.

Set type equal to	If payments are due
0 or omitted	At the end of the period
1	At the beginning of the period

Notes

a. The payment returned by PMT includes principal amount and interest.

b. Make sure that you use specific units for *rate* and *Nper*. If you make monthly payments on a four-year loan at an annual interest rate of **15** percent, use **15%/12** for rate and **4*15** for Nper. If you make annual payments on the same loan, use 15 percent for rate and **4** for Nper.

The following formula returns the monthly payment on a 1,00,000 loan at an annual rate of 15 percent that you must pay off in 60 months:

PMT (15%/12, 60, 1,00,000)
equals 2378.99

For the same loan, if payments are due at the beginning of the period, the payment is:

PMT (15%/12, 60, 1,00,000, 0, 1)
equals 2349.62

The following formula returns the amount someone must pay to you each month if you loan that person 5,000 at 12 percent and want to be paid back in five months:

PMT (12%/12, 5, -5000) equals
1,030.20

You can use PMT for in your PPF account to determine payments to annuities other than loans. For example, if you want to save Rs. 5,00,000 in 18 years by saving a constant amount each month, you can use PMT to determine how much you must save. If you assume you will be able to earn 12 percent interest on your savings, you can use PMT to determine how much to save each month.

```
PMT (12%/12, 18*12, 0, 5,00,000)
equals
Rs 659.75
```

that is if you pay Rs 659.75 per month in 18 years you will get Rs 5,00,000 after 18 years.

The above examples illustrate the use of financial functions. There are many more complex functions which are very useful for accountants, engineers and other professionals.

VLOOKUP

The function VLOOKUP searches for a value in the leftmost column of a table, and then returns a value in the same row from a column you specify in the table.

☞ *Use VLOOKUP instead of HLOOKUP when your comparison values are located in a column to the left of the data you want to find.*

Syntax

```
VLOOKUP(lookup_value,table_array,c
ol_index_num,range_lookup)
```

Lookup_value is the value to be found in the first column of the array. Lookup_value can be a value, a reference, or a text string.

Table_array is the table of information in which data is looked up. Use a reference to a range or a range name

- If range_lookup is TRUE, the values in the first column of table_array must be palced in ascending order:..., -2,-1,0,1,2 ..., A-Z, FALSE, TRUE; otherwise VLOOKUP may not give the correct value. If range_lookup is FALSE, table_array does not need to be sorted.
- You can put the values in ascending order by choosing the **Sort** command from the **Data** menu and selecting **Ascending**.
- The values in the first column of table_array can be text, numbers, or logical values.
- Uppercase and lowercase text are equivalent.

HLOOKUP

The function HLOOKUP searches for a value in the top row of a table or an array of values, and then returns a value in the same column from a row you specify in the table or array.

☞ *Use HLOOKUP when your comparison values are located in a row across the top of a table of data, and you want to look down a specified number of rows.*

Syntax

```
HLOOKUP(lookup_value,table_array,r
ow_index_num,range_lookup)
```

Lookup_value: is the value to be found in the first row of the table. Lookup_value can be a value, a reference, or a text string.

Table_array: is a table of information in which data is looked up. Use a reference to a range or a range name.

- The values in the first row of table_array can be text, numbers, or logical values.
- If range_lookup is TRUE, the values in the first row of table_array must be placed in ascending order: ...-2, -1, 0, 1, 2,..., A-Z, FALSE, TRUE; otherwise,

HLOOKUP may not give the correct value. If range_lookup is FALSE, table_array does not need to be sorted.

- Uppercase and lowercase text are equivalent.
- You can put values in ascending order, left to right, by selecting the values and then clicking **Sort** on the **Data** menu. Click **Options**, click **Sort left to right**, and then click **OK**. Under **Sort by**, click the row in the list, and then click **Ascending**.

4.20.10 Goal Seek (What-If Analysis)

Goal Seek is part of a suite of commands sometimes called what-if analysis i.e. process of changing the values in cells to see how those changes affect the outcome of formulas on the worksheet.

➡ **To use the goal seek feature, do this:**

1. Click the **Tools** menu and choose **Goal Seek...** . The **Goal Seek** dialog box. (See Figure 4.74)

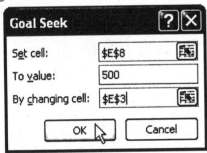

Figure 4.74 Goal Seek Dialog box

2. In **Set cell:** box, enter the reference for the cell that contains the formula.
3. In **To value:** box, type the new value you want in above cell reference.
4. In **By changing cell:** box, enter the reference for the cell whose value you want to adjust.

5. Click OK. Now it will show the status of Goal Seek as seen in Figure 4.75.

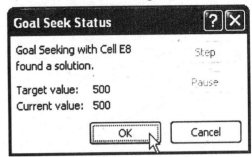

Figure 4.75 Goal Seek Status Dialog box

☞ *With Goal seek, you specify the value you want a formula to calculate, and then Excel changes the data in the formulas cell reference to tell you what values you need to achieve that goal.*

4.21 HOW TO CREATE A CHART?

You can create two types of charts namely, *embedded charts* and charts that appear in a *chart sheet*.

4.21.1 Embedded Chart

An *embedded chart* appears in a worksheet next to tables or text. Figure 4.76 shows an embedded chart.

☞ *Embedded charts are required when you want a chart side-by-side with the data for the chart, such as in a report.*

4.21.2 Chart in a Chart Sheet

A chart can also appear in its own chart sheet within a workbook (See Figure 4.77). Thus, you are able to work with the chart sheet separately from the data worksheet. If you insert a chart in a sheet, you add the chart to the active workbook and save it along with the workbook.

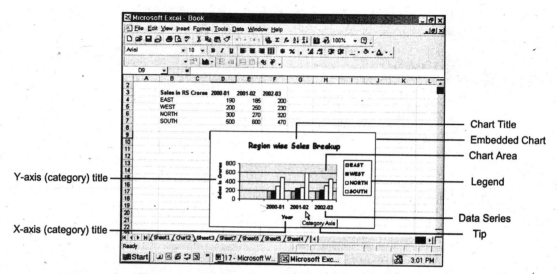

Figure 4.76 Embedded Chart with Chart Elements

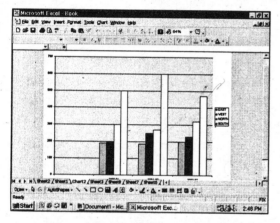

Figure 4.77 Chart in a Chart Sheet

☞ *If you need to print a chart on its own, cre-ating the chart on a chart sheet is the best approach.*

4.21.3 Chart Wizard

You can create both embedded charts and charts in chart sheets by using the Chart Wizard. The Chart Wizard guides you through the process of creating the chart step-by-step and gives you a preview of the chart before completing it, so that you can make any changes.

Alternatively, if you select data and press the F11 key then Excel insert a chart in a chart sheet, using the default chart type. Thereafter, you can use the chart commands to modify the chart.

4.22 CHART TERMINOLOGY

An Excel chart may contain objects that you may modify individually. Figure 4.76 showed some of these objects. Table 4.13 describes each object. Note that if you move mouse pointer over an object in a chart, a tip appears to give description of the chart object.

Table 4.13 Parts of an Excel Chart

Object	Description
Axis (x-axis and y-axis)	The horizontal or x-axis along the bottom of most charts is also referred to as category axis. The vertical or y-axis against which data

(Contd...)

Object	Description
	points are measured is also referred to as value axis. This axis contains the scale against which data is plotted.
Data point	A single piece of data.
Data series	A collection of data points.
Legend	The name of each data series is used as a legend title.
Marker	An object that represents a data point in a chart such as bars, pie and symbols. Markers that belong to the same data series appear as the same shape, symbol and colour.
Plot area	The Rectangular area bounded by the two axes.
Text	Text associated with data points or free-floating text that can be moved easily. The box containing the text can be resized.
Tick mark	A division mark along the category (X) and value (Y and Z) axes.
Toolbar	A special toolbar is available with charting tools.
Tip	A box that identifies the object which the mouse pointer is pointing to.

4.23 CREATING A CHART USING CHART WIZARD

Before you use the Chart Wizard button, select the data in a worksheet that you want to chart. The Chart Wizard allows you to select the data you want to chart, but it is easier to do this before starting the Chart Wizard. Include the row and column headings if you want them to appear in the chart as category and legend labels.

➡ **To create a chart with the Chart Wizard, do this:**

1. Select the data you want to chart.

2. Click the <u>I</u>nsert, menu and choose <u>C</u>hart... . or click the Chart Wizard button on Standard toolbar. The dialog box as in Figure 4.78 appears.

Figure 4.78 Chart Wizard step 1 of 4–Chart Type Dialog Box

This dialog box has two tabs Standard Types and Custom Types. Click the tab from which you want to select the chart type. From the <u>C</u>hart type: drop down list and click to select the chart type.

From the Chart sub-<u>t</u>ype: select from the different variation of the Chart type. To see how the chart will look like, Press and Hold to <u>V</u>iew Sample button. After selecting the Chart type, click <u>N</u>ext > button.

3. The Chart Source Data dialog box appears (See Figure 4.79).
   Verify that the data range is correct in the Chart Source Data dialog box.
   Click the Collapse Dialog button, select the data range with the mouse or keyboard, and click the Expand Dialog button to redisplay the dialog box.

4. You can also work with the data series in the Chart Source Data dialog box. Click the Series tab to display the dialog box shown in Figure 4.80. Here you can add and remove data series and modify the range of cells containing the Category (X)

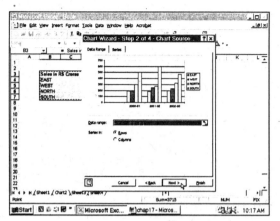

Figure 4.79 Chart Wizard–step 2 of 4–Chart Source Data dialog box

axis labels. To add a data series, click the **A**dd button. Now click in the **N**ame box and then click the cell in the worksheet containing the name for the new series.

Click the **V**alues: box and select the cells containing the values for the new data series. To remove a data series, select the series you want to remove in the Series list and click **R**emove.

After you select the range, click **N**ext > to move to Step 3 of 4 Chart Wizard.

5. Modify or add various chart options in the Chart Options dialog box, as shown in Figure 4.81, and click **N**ext>. The third Chart Wizard dialog box (refer to Figure 4.81) enables you to add or modify several optional features in a chart. You can add titles to the chart and axes, modify or remove the category axis, remove the value axis, and add or remove gridlines.

You can also add or remove a legend and change the placement of the legend. Data labels can be attached to data points and a data table showing the source data for the chart can be added. After you specify the option click **N**ext >.

6. The Chart Location dialog box shown in Figure 4.82 appears. Select one of the following:

As new **S**heet: option to create a chart on a separate chart sheet. You can enter a title for the new sheet in the text box next to this option. Otherwise, the new sheet will be given a generic name such as Chart1 or Chart2.

As **O**bject in: option to embed the chart in a worksheet. By default, the chart will be embedded in the worksheet containing

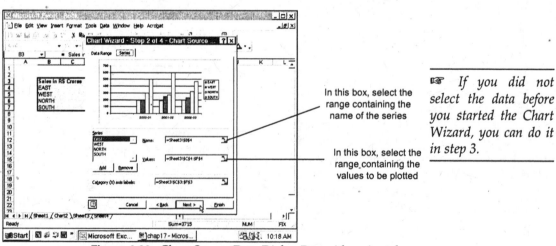

In this box, select the range containing the name of the series

In this box, select the range containing the values to be plotted

☞ *If you did not select the data before you started the Chart Wizard, you can do it in step 3.*

Figure 4.80 Chart Source Data Dialog Box with series tab

the source data. You can embed the chart in another worksheet by selecting the sheet from the As **O**bject in: drop-down list to the right of the option. To create the chart in a separate chart sheet, select the As New Sheet option.

7. Click **F**inish to create the chart.

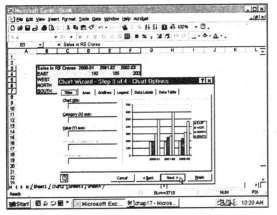

Figure 4.81 Chart Wizard dialog box Step 3 of 4 Chart Option

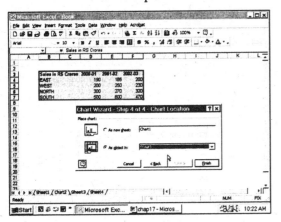

Figure 4.82 Chart Wizard Step 4 of 4 Chart Location dialog box

4.24 HYPERLINKS

Hyperlink is a shortcut, coloured, underlined text or a graphic that specifies the link to a location that is stored on a Web, MS-Word or any other location. When we click this link the specified file would open.

➡ **To create a hyperlink, do this:**

1. Click the **I**nsert menu and choose Hyperlink... or press Ctrl+K or select a **H**yperlink... from the shortcut menu. The Insert Hyperlink dialog box appears (See Figure 4.83)

Hyperlink to a New File:

- In Link to: Group, choose Create **N**ew Document. Create New document's options appear as in the Figure 4.83.

- In the Name of new **d**ocument: text box, type the name of the new file.

- If you want to change the path of the file you will change it by clicking on the **C**hange... button.

- Under the when to Edit Option: click the option for opening a file now or later.

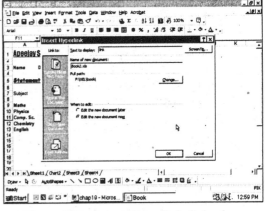

Figure 4.83 Insert Hyperlink dialog box

Hyperlink to an Existing File:

- In Link to: Group, choose E**x**isting file or Web page. Existing file or Web page's options appear as in the Figure 4.84.

- If you want to select a file from recently used files, then under the Select from list: group, click the file list and choose the file *or* if you do not know the file path, you select the **F**ile... button under Browse for: option. The

Link to File dialog box appears. Here, locate the file name and click OK, *or if you know the name and path of the file, you type it in the Type the file or Web page: text box.*

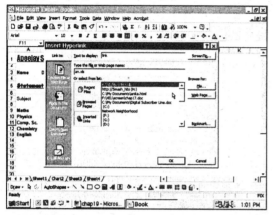

Figure 4.84 Hyperlink created to an existing file

Hyperlink to a Web page:

- In Link to: Group, choose Existing file or Web page. Existing file or Web page's options appear as in the Figure 4.85.

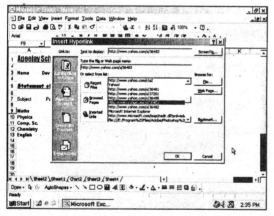

Figure 4.85 Hyperlink to a Web page

- If you want to select the Web page from the list of Web pages, then under the Select from list: group, click Browsed Pages and select the Web page from list *or* if you want to search the Web page by using the Web

browser, click **W**eb Page... button under Browse for: option. Open the Web page you want to link to and switch to Excel *or* if you know the name of the Web page, you type it in the Type the file or Web page: text box.

2. To assign the screen tip, click on the Screen Ti**p**... button. The Set Hyperlink ScreenTip dialog box appears as shown in Figure 4.86.

3. Type the screen tip in the ScreenTip text: box and then click OK.

4. Click OK in the Insert Hyperlink dialog box.

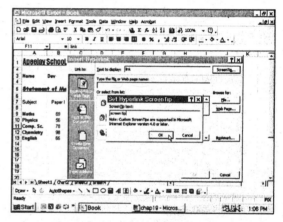

Figure 4.86 Dialog box for set Hyperlink Screen Tip

Hyperlinked text is now displayed shown in coloured and underlined text. If you click this text your specified file or Web page will open. If you remove this link, right click and choose **H**yperlink and then choose sub menu **R**emove Hyperlink.

4.25 AUTOFILTER

Autofilter is used to find specific values in rows in a list by using one or two comparison criteria for the same column.

➡ **To use AutoFilter, do this:**

1. Select any cell in the list to be filter.

2. Click **Data** menu highlight **Filter**. A sub menu appears. Select **AutoFilter**.

3. Each Column heading in the data, a drop-down list appear as shown in Figure 4.87.

4. Click the down arrow to the right of the field name you want to filter.

5. The drop-down list appears allows you to display all records in the list, such as display the top 10 records, create a custom filter, or select an entry that appears in one or more records in the list. (See Figure 4.87)

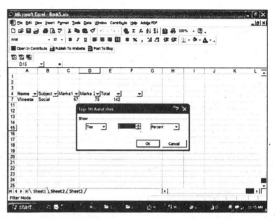

Figure 4.88 Top 10 filter dialog box

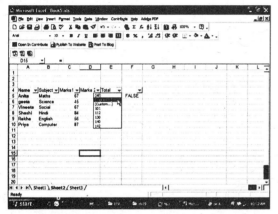

Figure 4.87 Using AutoFilter in the field

6. For example, here to select Top 10 option from the drop-down list. It works only if there are values stored in that column.

7. Top 10 filter dialog box appears as shown in Figure 4.88. Select the **percent** in the list.

8. Click OK button. It shows the results of top percent in the list. (See Figure 4.88)

4.25.1 Using Advanced Filter

Advanced filter can be used to create a list of unique values.

➡ **To create a list of unique values, do this:**

1. Select the portion of the list to be extracted from.

1. Click **Data** menu highlight **Filter**. A sub menu appears. Select **Advanced Auto-Filter**.

2. The **Advanced Filter** dilaog box appears as shown in Figure 4.89.

Figure 4.89 Advanced Filter dialog box

3. Click to Copy to another location option to select it.

4. In the **List range:** $A$4:$E$10 is entered in the box.

5. Click the Collapse dialog button at the right of the Copy to box. Select the range to copy the selected cells.

6. Click the **Unique records only** option check box.

7. Click OK button.

8. The unique records are copied to selected cells.

4.26 DATA TABLE

A data table is a range of cells that shows how changing certain values in the formulas affects the results of the formulas. Data tables provide a shortcut for calculating multiple versions in one operation and a way to view and compare the results of all of the different variations together on the worksheet.

4.26.1 One-variable data tables

The first thing you must do is to create a base model and tell your Data Table which formulas from your base model you want to test. This is easily done from inside the Data Table by placing a formula to reference the formula in the base model.

Let us say that we wish to purchase a new tractor for work on our family farm. We need to know that if interest rates fluctuate we can still afford to pay for the tractor. So we need to know what our loan repayments will be, what our total repayments will be and how much interest we are paying.

1. In B3, type the amount of loan = 30,000

2. In B5, type the Interest Rate = 7%

3. In B7, type the Term of Loan (year) 10

4. In B12, type the Number of payment (per year) 12

5. In B11, type the Amount of Payment. Calculate the rate of interest. i.e.
   =PMT (B5/12, B9 * B7, B3)* -1

6. In B13, apply formula i.e. Amount of payment = Number of payment x Term loan.

7. In B14, apply formula i.e. Total paid - Amt of loan

The results for the above example is shown in Figure 4.90.

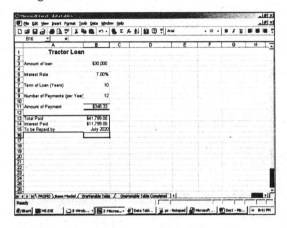

Figure 4.90 One variable data table

4.27 SCENARIO

Excel's Scenario Manager is a tool that can be used to different projected outcomes of data by changing different cells within a Worksheet.

☞ *A scenario is a specific set of values that Excel can save for you and automatically substitute into your Worksheet.*

This means that you could have a spreadsheet displaying numerical data that is relevant to a certain date, month, topic or whatever and using the Scenario Manager. You can enter different values into the worksheet to forecast the outcome of the data. These values (or Scenarios) can be retained for future use and are stored in a hidden part of the workbook which can be retrieved by asking the Scenario Manager to show the Scenario that uses those specific values.

For Scenarios to work correctly, you should first set up a table on a worksheet in Excel.

4.27.1 Adding Scenarios

There is no limit to the number of Scenarios that you can apply to your worksheet model.

➡ **To add scenarios, do this:**

1. Click the **Tools** menu and choose **Scenarios** to display the **Scenario Manager** dialog box. (See Figure 4.91)

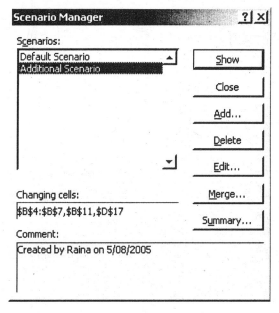

Figure 4.91 Scenario Manager dialog box

2. Click **Add...** button

3. The **Add Scenario** dialog box is displayed. Type the **Scenario name:** in the list box. (See Figure 4.92)

4. Click the **Changing cells:** box, enter the reference for the cells that you want to change. The highlighted cells applied formula. (See Figure 4.93)

5. Again click the Collapse Dialog box.

6. Under **Protection**, select the options you want.

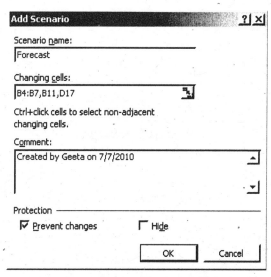

Figure 4.92 Add Scenariodialog box

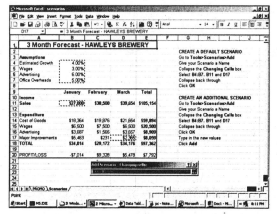

Figure 4.93 Changing cells get highlighted

7. Click OK.

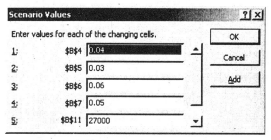

Figure 4.94 Scenario values

6. The **Scenario Values** dialog box appears as shown in Figure 4.94.

7. Enter the values in each cells you want to change.

8. To save the changes, click OK button.

9. The new applied value get changed in the worksheet data. (See Figure 4.95))

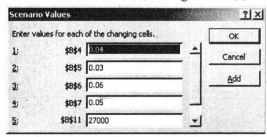

Figure 4.95 The new value get changed in the worksheet data

4.28 IMPORT AND EXPORT OF DATA

Data in an Excel workbook may need to be accessed by another application or you may need to have the data from another application in an Excel workbook. When data from Excel is sent to another application, such as Word, the data is said to be exported from Excel. When data from another application, such as Web browser, is sent to Excel, the data is said to be imported into Excel. To import and Export data to and from Excel enables you to share your Excel data across applications.

4.28.1 Importing Data from Text Files

Excel provides automatic help when importing text files. There are two common formats for data that is arranged in rows and columns in a text file, a delimited text file and a fixed width text file. A delimited text file uses a special character or delimiter, which is often a comma or a tab, to separate one column from the next.

➡ **To import a text file, do this:**

1. Click the **File** and choose **Open...** . The **Open** dialog box appears as shown in Figure 4.96.

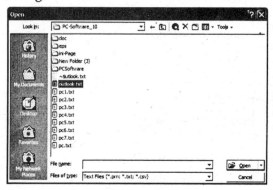

Figure 4.96 Open dialog box

2. Locate the folder you want to import the text in the **Look in**: drop-down list.

3. Click the down arrow to the right of the **Files of type:** box. Select the *Text* Files. And then click Open.

4. The **Text Import Wizard - Step 1 of 3** dialog box appears as shown in Figure 4.97.

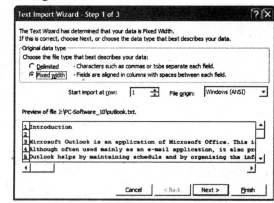

Figure 4.97 Text Import Wizard Step 1 of 3 dialog box

5. Choose any one of the file type that describes data whether the file is **Delimited** or **Fixed** width.

6. Click **Next**.

7. The **Text Import Wizard** - Step 2 of 3 dialog box is displayed as shown in Figure 4.98.

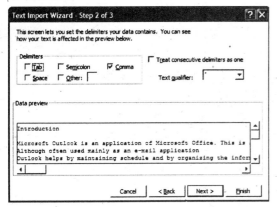

Figure 4.98 Text Import Wizard Step 2 of 3 dialog box

8. If the file is delimited, the Step 2 dialgo box allows you to set what character should be used as the delimiter. You also can select the Text qualifer, which typically is the quotation mark.

9. Click **Next**.

10. The Text Import Wizard Step 3 of 3 dialog box is shown in Figure 4.99.

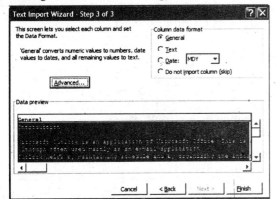

Figure 4.99 Text Import Wizard Step 3 of 3 dialog box

11. Select the data from under Column data format.

12. Click **Finish** button.

13. You can the imported text file in the Excel worksheet as shown in Figure 4.100.

Figure 4.100 Imported text file displayed in the worksheet

4.28.2 Placing Excel Data on the Web

By using the publishing and saving features of Excel, you can save an Excel workbook or part of it in HTML format, and make it available on an HTTP site, in a Web server or in network server.

➡ To save Excel data as a Web page, do this:

1. Open the workbook which you want to save as a Web page.

2. Click File menu and choose Save as Web Page... . The **Save As** dialog box appears as shown in Figure 4.101.

3. In Save: group select Entire Workbook to save entire workbook as a Web page.

4. Select Selection: sheet, when you want to save a selected cells as a Web page.

5. Click on the Change Title... button to change the title for the Web page.

6. In File name: text box give it the file name.

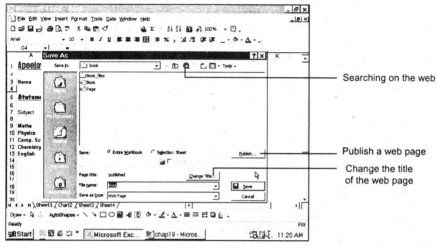

☞ *The application of Excel has expanded the horizon of its utility because of linking and embedding including hyperlinks over the Web.*

Figure 4.101   Save As dialog box

7. In the Save as type: choose the Web page option from list.

8. Click O.K. to save file as a Web page.

To see the preview of the Excel data in Web form, click File menu and choose Web Page Preview. The preview of the saved data is shown in Figure 4.102.

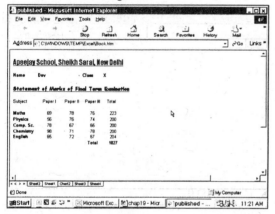

Figure 4.102   Preview of Excel data using Web browser

4.28.3 Exporting Data Text Files

You can export the data in an Excel worksheet to a text file.

➡ **To export a worksheet, do this:**

1. Click the **File** menu and choose **Save As**.
2. Enter a name for the file in the file name box.
3. Click the down arrow to the right of the **Save as type:** box.
4. The option you select from the list depends on the application to use the file.
5. Table 4.14 explains some of the text file options found in the list.

Options	Description
Text (tab delimited)	Columns are separated by tabs
CSV (comma delimited)	Columns are separated by commas
Formatted Text (Space delimited)	Columns are a fixed width

6. After you made selection from the list. Click **Save** button.

4.28.4 Importing Data from a Web Page into Excel

There are mnay ways to import data from a Web page into Excel. Depending on which method you choose, some of the data might display differently in Excel than it does on the Web page.

Simply copying and pasting is one way to import data from a Web page into Excel. Select the data you want to import and right-click on any of the cells. From the shortcut menu that appears, click Copy. Click the appropriate cell on the worksheet into which you want to import the copied data and click the Paste button on the Standard toolbar. The data from the Web page is copied into the worksheet.

Data from a Web page can be imported into Excel using drag and drop. First select the data to be imported from the Web page and then click the selected data and drag it to the desired cell in Excel.

You can import data from a Web page into Excel from the Web browser by clicking the Export to Excel toolbar button. When you click the Export to Excel button, a read-only copy of data immediately appears in Excel. Using the Save permanently as an Excel worksheet.

4.29 TYPES OF ERRORS

To use formulas in Excel, you will likely need to lean how to correct or hide formula errors. The first thing you should know is what each error type means. Once you understand what each error value means, correcting the formula becomes a LOT easier.

Hide Zeros

To hide zeros on the Workbook level go to Tools menu highlight Options and the choose View - Zero Values.

Eror Values

#VALUE! - You are trying to perform a calculation or function with an improper type, e.g. taking the absolute value of a string

#DIV/0! - You are dividing by zero

#NAME? - The function you are using is unknown

#REF! - The cell you are refering to is no longer a valid cell address

#NUM! - The numeric result in that cell is too big

#N/A - Several different situations can cause this

#NULL - A null or 'no data' is in that cell

Summary

This chapter presents concepts of *Spreadsheet Package* namely, MS Excel. It is one of the most versatile and popular spreadsheet program. First, we discussed workbook. In MS Excel each file is termed as a workbook. Each workbook consists of sheets. A sheet in Excel is divided into rows and columns and each intersection point of a row and a column is termed as a cell. Cells are used for storing data. Next, we discussed worksheet. You can enter and edit data on several worksheets and perform calculations based on data from multiple worksheets. Workspace file saves information about all open workbooks, such as locations, windows sizes etc. It also includes many formatting features, including basic options found on the formatting toolbar. Conditional formatting allows you to specify how cells that meet a specific condition should be formatted. It includes many functions that makes the task for creating a worksheet much easier. Functions perform complex mathematical, financial and logical operations. In Excel, data can be entered either by entering into the individual cells on the worksheet or by using Data form. Data validation feature allows you to specify the exact data that can be entered into a cell. Import and export data to and from Excel enables you to share your Excel data across different applications. And finally, charts are visually appealing and make it easy for users to see comparisons, patterns and trends in data.

REVIEW QUESTIONS WITH ANSWERS

A. Multiple Choice

1. The first electronic worksheet was known as
   - a. VisiCalc
   - b. Lotus 1-2-3
   - c. Microsoft Excel
   - d. None of the above

2. Which of the following is not a tool for analyzing spreadsheet data?
   - a. What-if analysis
   - b. Mail merge
   - c. Goal seeking
   - d. Sorting

3. The combination of the column letter and row number for a cell in an Excel worksheet is called a
   - a. cell cross
   - b. cell identification number
   - c. cell reference
   - d. cell identify

4. In its default setting, a workbook is made up of sheets and the number can be extended to:
   - a. 3, 255
   - b. 3, 225
   - c. 19, 255
   - d. 16, 225

5. To fill multiple rows or columns at one time, press
   - a. (Ctrl) key
   - b. (Ctrl)+(shift) key
   - c. (Shift) key
   - d. (Alt) key

6. Shortcut fill menu contain
   - a. Fill week-days
   - b. Fill series
   - c. (a) and (b)
   - d. None of these

7. Formulas with absolute references are references that always

8. a. refer to the different cells, regardless of the location of the formula
   - b. produce 0 as the default
   - c. refer to the same cells, regardless of the location of the formula
   - d. none of the above

9. Cell address A$4 in a formula means it is a
   - a. relative cell reference
   - b. absolute cell reference
   - c. mixed cell reference
   - d. all of the above

9. The **Today()** function enters the current
   - a. system time in a cell
   - b. system date and time in a cell
   - c. system date only
   - d. none of the above

10. Which of the following is not a financial function?
    - a. FV()
    - b. NPV()
    - c. SUM()
    - d. PMT()

11. In a new Worksheet, cell A1 contains, 5, cell A2 contains 7 and cell A4 contains 9. If cell B1 contains = **COUNT(A1:A4)**, the following result will be displayed in cell B1:
    - a. 9
    - b. 3
    - c. 4
    - d. 5

B. Descriptive Questions

1. Describe the process of opening, saving, closing a workbook in Excel 2000.
2. Differentiate between workbook and worksheet.
3. Why use Conditional formatting in Excel? Expalin.
4. What is Autofilter? How do you apply Autofilter to a worksheet?
5. Discuss the step to enter a formula in Excel worksheet.

6. What is the difference between reltive and absolute cell reference.
7. What are 3D references. How are they useful in business?
8. Describe basic features of functions in Excel. Write functions for displaying date and time.

A. Answers to Multiple Choice

1. a 2. b 3. c 4. a 5. a 6. c
7. c 8. c 9. c 10. c 11. b

B. Answers to Descriptive Questions

1. [*Refer section 4.4.2 to 4.4.4*]
2. [*Refer section 4.5*]
3. [*Refer section 4.16.2*]
4. [*Refer section 4.24*]
5. [*Refer section 4.17.1*]
6. [*Refer section 4.18.2*]
7. [*Refer section 4.18.2*]
8. [*Refer section 4.20.7*]

CHAPTER 5

Outlook Express

The reader will be able to understand in this chapter
- Creating e-mail account

- Sending and receiving E-mail Messages
- Managing and Organizing E-mail

5.1 INTRODUCTION

MS Outlook Express is an application package of MS Office. This is a powerful tool of *Personal Information Management* (PIM) program that helps a person in organizing his schedule, keep track of contacts and communicate with others. Generally, people have several appointments to keep and tasks to accomplish in a day, week, or month.

Although often used mainly as an e-mail application, it also provides a calendar, task and contact management, note taking, a journal and web browsing. Outlook helps by maintaining schedule and by organizing the information in a structured and readable manner. By having this facility, one can keep a track of meetings, e-mail messages, and notes with a particular contact. This organization consists of Outlook's Calendar, Contacts, Tasks and Notes. Contact information can be found via Find option, which can be accessed from the calendar, e-mail, and other Outlook components. PIMs give an opportunity to individuals and workgroups to organize, find, view, and share information in the most convenient way.

5.2 STARTING OUTLOOK

Like other Office program, you can start Outlook using the Start Menu.

➡ **To start Outlook, do this:**

1. Click the **Start** menu highlight **All Programs** highlight Micorsoft Office and then choose **Outlook Express** as shown in Figure 5.1.

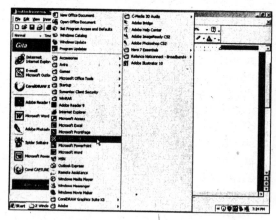

Figure 5.1 Starting Outlook Express

2. The **Outlook Express** windows opens as shown in Figure 5.2.

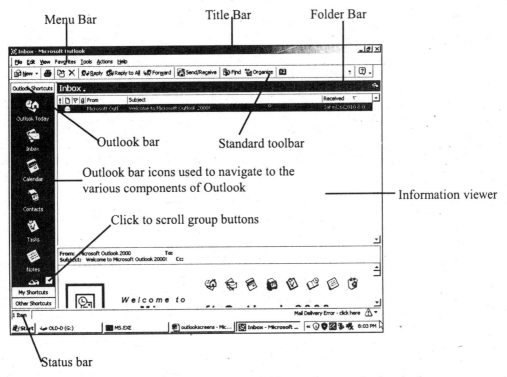

Menu Bar   Title Bar   Folder Bar

Outlook bar   Standard toolbar

Outlook bar icons used to navigate to the various components of Outlook

Information viewer

Click to scroll group buttons

Status bar

Figure 5.2 Outlook displays the Inbox folder marking pg 2 of outlook express

5.2.1 Outlook Window

The Outlook window is similar to other Windows programs. It has a title bar, a menu bar, a toolbar, a status bar, and Minimize, Maximize/Restore, and Close buttons. An Inbox email messages box appears. The icons in the vertical Outlook Bar, to the left of the Inbox Information viewer, represent shortcuts to frequently used Outlook folders and features. These are explained below.

Title Bar: It shows the name of the Outlook feature you are currently working with.

Menu Bar: This provides access to a list of commands available in Outlook, and displays an area where you can type a question to get information.

Standard Toolbar: It contains buttons you can use to select common commands, such as Save and Print.

Folder Banner: This is the horizontal bar just below the Standard Toolbar. The Outlook navigation arrows, an icon for the active folder and the name of the active folder is displayed in the Folder banner. When the folder name is clicked, the Folder list shows the available folders and subfolders.

Navigation Pane: It provides access to the features included in Outlook. You can click the down arrow button on the Outlook bar to browse through the features.

Information Viewer: It displays the Outlook feature you are currently working with. The Information viewer is the main Outloook window in which e-mail messages, contact and calendar items, tasks, and other information are displayed. (See Figure 5.2)

The Outlook bar–It includes Outlook Shortcuts, My Shortcuts and Other Shortcuts. These three groups that provide you with quick access to the functions you use.

5.2.2 Working with the Outlook Bar

Each Information viewer displays the Outlook Shortcuts Bar at its left edge. Click the shortcut icons in the Outlook Bar to select which Information viewer you want to use.

☞ *If the Outlook Bar is not displayed, click the View menu and select Outlook Bar.*

The Outlook Bar contains three default groups.

(a) Outlook Shortcuts
(b) My Shortcuts
(c) Other Shortcuts

It display only one group at a time. Click the name of the group to display that group's shortcuts. The Information viewer does not change, only the shortcut listing. The name of each shortcut identifies an Outlook folder. Click a shortcut and the Information viewer changes to show the information contents of that folder.

Using Outlook Shortcuts Group

This group contains shortcut icons that provide access to most of the standard Outlook folders.

Shortcut	Description
Outlook Today	It displays day at-a-glance by displaying your appointments for the next few days, the number of new messages in your Inbox, and a list of your tasks. This is customizable.
Inbox	It displays the Inbox Information viewer that lists

(Contd...)

Shortcut	Description
	the headers of messages you have received that are in the Inbox folder. The number in parentheses at the right of the icon name is the number of unread messages.
Calendar	It displays the Calendar Information viewer that shows Calendar items, such as appointments and events.
Contacts	It displays the Contacts Information viewer where you can keep track of business and personal contacts.
Tasks	It displays the Tasks Information viewer that shows Task items, such as personal tasks, tasks you have assigned to others, and tasks assigned to you.
Notes	It displays the Notes Information viewer where you can quickly record reminders.
Deleted Items	It displays the Deleted Items Information viewer that contains any items you delete from other Outlook folders.

Using My Shortcuts Group

This group contains shortcut icons that provide access to folders containing email messages you are preparing to send or have sent and to the Outlook Update Web page.

Shortcut	Description
Drafts	Keeps copies of unfinished messages until you are ready to complete and send them at a later date. The number in parentheses at the right of the icon name is the number of drafts in the Drafts folder.
Sent Items	Keeps copies of messages that you have sent.
Outbox	Temporarily stores messages that you have told Outlook to send, but are still waiting to be sent. This folder is mainly used when working offline.
Journal	Automatically tracks all specified items as they occur in Outlook.
Outlook Update	Outlook is set up to automatically connect to the Internet. This shortcut accesses the Microsoft Web page regarding information about Outlook. The Web page URL is: http://officeupdate.microsoft.com/welcome/outlook.htm

Using Other Shortcuts group

This group contains shortcut icons that access your Windows folder structure.

Shortcut	Description
My Computer	It displays Windows environment, providing you access to your hard drive

(Contd...)

	and any mapped network drives. This Information viewer can be used to print lists of folders and files.
Personal	This shortcut is available to those running Windows NT. It provides access to personal folders on your hard drive.
My Documents	This shortcut is available to those running Outlook under Windows 98. It provides access to the My Documents folder.
Favorites	It displays uniform resource locators (URL's) and provides access to Web sites from the Favorites menu in Internet Explorer.

Customizing the Outlook Bar

The default Outlook Bar gives only basic access to your Outlook and Windows folders. The Outlook Bar can be customized to suit your personal needs.

You can make the Outlook Bar narrower or wider by moving the pointer onto the border between the Outlook Bar and the Folder List. When the pointer icon changes to a pair of vertical lines with left- and right-pointing arrows, press the mouse button and drag to the left or to the right.

You can choose to have small icons, instead of the default large icons, displayed in the Outlook Bar. This choice is selected separately for each Outlook Bar group. To have small icons in an Outlook Bar group, select that group, then right-click within the Outlook Bar group (not on an icon). From the submenu, select Small Icons.

You can change the order of the icons in a group so that those you use most often are close together. Point onto the shortcut icon you want to move and press the mouse button. Drag up or down. As you drag, a black bar appears between icons. Stop dragging when a bar appears at the position where you want the icon. Release the mouse button and the icon moves to the new position.

You can change the names of the Outlook Bar shortcuts to something that seems more appropriate. Outlook Bar groups can be deleted as well as shortcut icons within groups.

You can also add shortcut icons to a group and create new groups. In addition to creating shortcuts to Outlook's folders, you can create shortcuts to files and folders within the Windows file system.

5.2.3 Renaming an Outlook Bar Group

➡ **To renaming an Outlook bar, do this:**

1. In the Outlook Bar, right-click the group name you want to change.
2. From the submenu, select **Rename Group**. The group name button changes to white with the name selected.
3. Edit the group name in the normal way, then press the (Enter) key. The group now displays the new name.

5.2.4 Adding a group

The Outlook Bar has three default groups of shortcut icons. The maximum number of groups allowed is twelve.

➡ **To add a group, do this:**

1. Right-click any group name and select **Add New Group** from the submenu. A button appears at the bottom of the Outlook Bar with the temporary name "*New Group*" highlighted.

2. Change the name to the reflect what you want the group to be called and press the (Enter) key.

☞ *Each new group created always appears below the existing group buttons in the Outlook Bar. There is no way to change the order of group buttons.*

5.2.5 Removing a group

You can remove any group from the Outlook Bar, including the default groups.

➡ **To remove group, do this:**

1. Right-click the name of the group you want to remove and select Remove Group from the submenu.
2. Outlook asks you to confirm that you want to remove the group.
3. Click Yes to remove the group.

☞ *When Outlook asks you to confirm that you want to remove the group, it does not name the group you have selected. Be sure the group you selected is really the one you want to delete. After you have removed the group, you can not undo the process.*

5.2.6 Creating a Shortcut to an Outlook Folder

1. Select the Outlook Bar group into which you want to add a shortcut icon.
2. Be sure the Folder List is displayed. If not, click the **View** menu and select **Folder List**.
3. If necessary, expand the folder list so that the name of the folder for which you want to create a shortcut icon is visible.
4. Drag and drop the folder into the Outlook Bar group, releasing the mouse button when a bar appears at the position where you want the icon.

5.2.7 Creating a shortcut to a Windows Folder or file

You can create a shortcut to any folder or file in your Windows folder structure.

1. Select the Outlook Bar group into which you want to add a shortcut icon.
2. Right click the Outlook Bar group select **Outlook Bar Shortcut...** . The **Add to Outlook Bar** dialog box appears as shown in Figure 5.3.

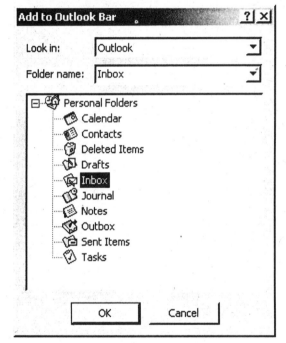

Figure 5.3 Add to Outlook bar

3. Click the drop-down **Look in:** list and select **File System**. This list shows your Windows desktop structure.

☞ *The folder structure includes Network Neighborhood. You can expand it to see folders on a local area file server to which you have access to and create shortcut icons on the Outlook Bar to those folders.*

4. Expand the list to display the folder for which you want to create a shortcut.

5. Select the folder.
6. Click OK. The shortcut icon appears in the Outlook Bar.

5.2.8 Removing a shortcut icon from the Outlook Bar

1. Right-click the shortcut icon you want to remove and select Remove from Outlook Bar from the submenu.
2. Outlook asks you to confirm that you want to remove the selected shortcut icon. Click Yes.

5.2.9 Moving a shortcut icon to Another group

You can also move a shortcut icon from one group to another.

1. With the group displayed, point on the icon that you want to move and press the mouse button.
2. Drag on to the group button that you want the icon to move to. That group appears. As you drag the mouse into the group area, a black bar representing the icon you are dragging appears.
3. Drag the icon where you want it to be with in the new group, then release the mouse button.

☞ *Whether you are dragging a shortcut icon within a group, or from one group to another; if you drag onto a group name and then release the mouse button, Outlook gives you are warning message stating that you can not do that. Click OK to close the message. Try the process again, only be sure not to release the mouse button while you are pointing onto a group name.*

5.3 CREATING AN E-MAIL ACCOUNT

To send and receive emails using Outlook Express, we first need to set up an email account. This is able by providing certain details to the software so that it can connect to the email server (the computer which stores the email), log in at the designated account and download/send all messages. Thus, need to create an account in Outlook Express to download and send emails.

The steps of creating new email accounts in Outlook Express and using these accounts to send and receive emails.

5.3.1 Setting up new E-mail Accounts in Outlook Express

Let us look at the steps which we need to follow for setting up an email account in Outlook Express.

➡ To create an account, do this:

1. Click on **Tools** in the menu bar and then go to **Accounts...** . (See Figure 5.4)

Figure 5.4 Highlighting Accounts options

2. **Internet Accounts** dialog box appears as shown in Figure 5.5.

3. Click on the **Mail** tab. If you are starting Outlook Express for the first time, there would not be any email accounts listed on this window.

4. To add a new mail account, click on the **Add** button. A sub menu options appears. Then click **Mail...** as shown in the Figure 5.6.

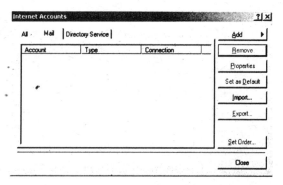

Figure 5.5 Internet Accounts dialog box

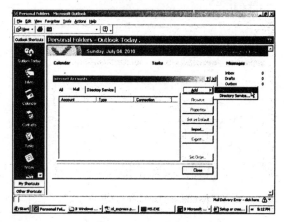

Figure 5.6 Selecting Mail

5. The **Internet Connection Wizard** dialog box appears. Enter your name in the **Display name:** field and click on the **Next** button. (Figure 5.7)

6. The wizard now asks for your email address. Enter the full email address and click on the **Next** button. (Figure 5.8)

7. In the next window, you need to feed in three important bits of information - the *incoming* and *outgoing email servers and the type of the incoming email server*. It is likely that the incoming email server is POP3. (See Figure 5.9)

8. The last information that you need to enter to complete the setup of the new account is the username and password for that email account. These login

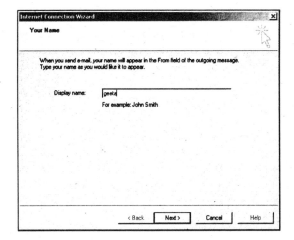

Figure 5.7 The Internet Connection Wizard dialog box

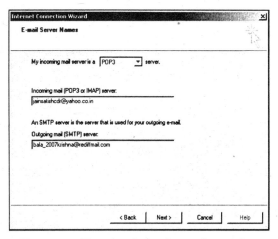

Figure 5.9 Entering incoming and outgoing e-mail

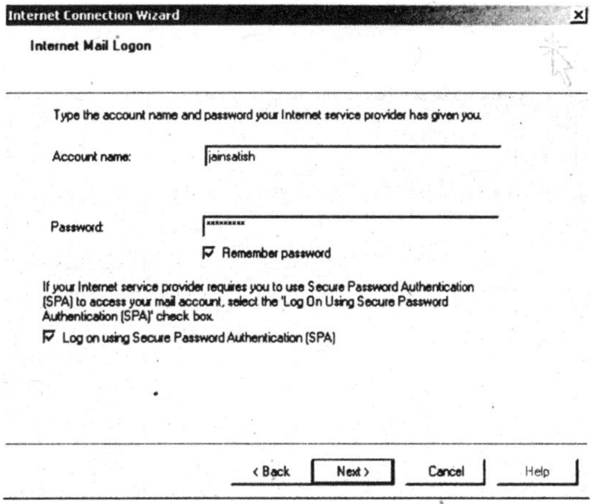

details would have been given to you by your ISP or you would have set these online using a control panel.

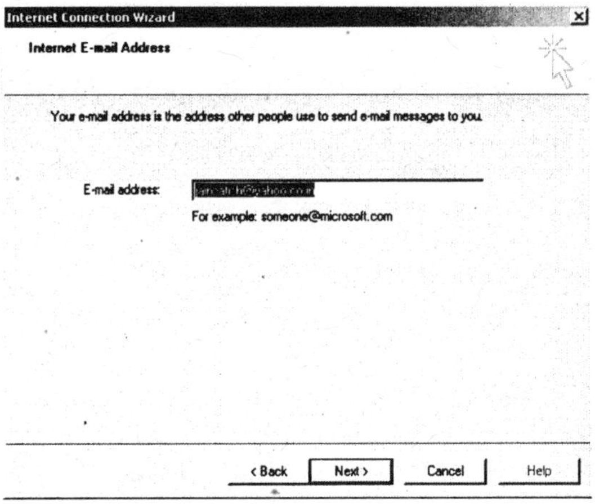

Figure 5.10 Enter account name and password

Figure 5.8 Entering e-mail address

After completing the fields for **Account Name** and **Password**, click on the **Next** button. (See Figue 5.10)

9. The Internet Connection Wizard asks, which method do you want to use to connect to the Internet? (See Figure 5.11) Select any one of the options, and then click **Next**.

10. In the following window, click on the **Finish** button to complete the process of setting up a new email account in Outlook Express. (See Figure 5.12)

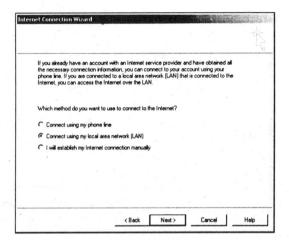

Figure 5.11 Choosing internet connection options

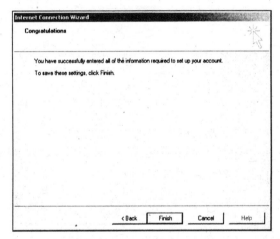

Figure 5.12 Click Finish buttons

11. You will now see the new email account has been added to the **Accounts list**. The account is referred by its server name. (See Figure 5.13)

5.4 CREATING AND SENDING AN E-MAIL MESSAGE

Electronic mail (e-mail) is the electronic equivalent of writing a letter, addressing an envelope, and putting it in the mailbox for delivery. E-mail use has risen in the last few years because of its abilty to deliver a message within seconds anywhere around the world.

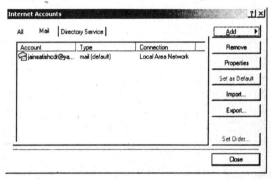

Figure 5.13 Email account added in the account list

To send and receive e-mail, you need to be connected to a *mail server*. You can think of the mail server as the post office. It is the computer with the network connection that receives your messages and directs your outgoing messages to other computers on a network. The computer is used to create your messages and read the messages you have received. This is known as the *mail client*.

5.4.1 Sending an Email using Outlook Express

➡ **To create a new e-mail message, do this:**

1. Click the **File** menu and choose **New**. A sub menu appears, select **Mail Message**. Or click the **New Mail Message** button on the Standard toolbar. Alternatively, press (Ctrl)+(N) keys together.

2. Enter the receipient addresses in the **To...** text box. If you enter multiple recipient addresses are entered separated by a semicolon and one space.

3. If you want to send a copy of the message to someone besides the recipient, enter the address in The **Cc...** text box.

2. The new message window's title bar appears. It displays Untitled - Message (Plain Text) until you enter text on the Subject line. The subject line then appears in the title bar of the message window. (See Figure 5.14)

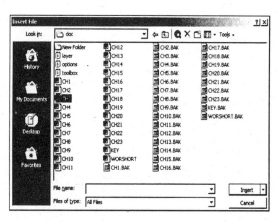

Figure 5.15 Insert File dialog box

6. Outlook Express will send the message and the attached file(s) to the e-mail address(es) you specified.

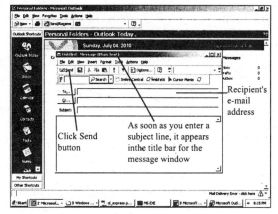

Figure 5.14 Message window with untitled opens

3. Type the body of the message in the message window below the subject line.

4. Click **Send** button on the Standard tool-bar.

5.4.2 Attaching a File to a Message

You can attach a file to a message you are sending. Attaching a file to a message is useful when you want to include additional information with a message.

➡ **To attach a file, do this:**

1. In the **Mail Message window**, click **Insert File** on the Standard toolbar.

2. The **Insert File** dialog box appears as shown in Figure 5.15.

3. Choose the name of the file you want to attach. After choosing the file name, click the **Insert** button.

4. In the Look in box, select the disk and the folder that contains the file.

5. Click Send to send the message.

5.4.3 Receiving an E-mail

To read an E-mail message which you have received do the following steps:

➡ **To receive an E-mail, do this:**

1. Move the mouse pointer over the **Mail** button on the **Standard toolbar** screen. Then click the left mouse button on it.

2. Immediately, a pull-down menu appears next to the Mail button

3. Inside the pull-down menu, click on the **Read** Mail option.

Immediately, MS Outlook Express logo appears on the screen for a few seconds. Finally, the Outlook Express window opens up on your screen.

4. To view all the E-mails you have received, move the mouse-pointer over the Inbox option inside the **Folders** box and click the left mouse-button. An Inbox-Outlook Express widnow appears giving details of all E-mail messages sent to your address.

5. If you wish to read the contents of a particular mail, move the mouse-pointer over it and double-click the left mouse button. Immediately, a message box opens up on screen displaying the contents of the message.

5.5 ADDRESS BOOK

The Address Book is used to store the names and e-mail addresses of people you send mail. When you are creating a message to someone with an entry in your Address Book.

➡ **To open address book in the message window, do this:**

1. Click the **Tools** menu and choose **Address Book....**.

2. The **Select Names** dialog box appears as shown in Figure 5.16.

3. Select the name in the **Name** box and then click **To->** or **Cc->** buttons. To enter the selected name in the appropriate text box in the **Message Recipients** section.

4. Click OK to the the Select Names dialog box after choosing names.

5. The names displayed in the text boxes in the message window will appear underlined, indicating they were selected from the address book.

6. When you send the message, the e-mail address stored in the address book for the displayed name is used to deliver the message.

5.5.1 Adding a Name to the Address Book

Adding names will help you start to build a useful Address Book. Also, if you share your e-mail address with other and they send e-mail to you. You can add names to your Address Book using the messages you receive.

➡ **To add a name to the address book, do this:**

1. Click the **Tools** menu and choose

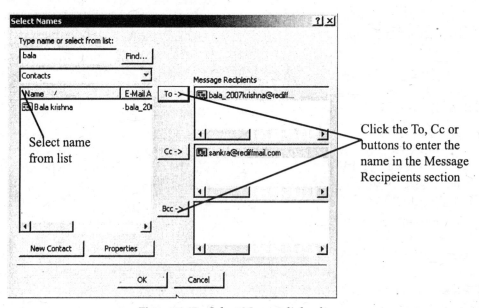

Figure 5.16 Select Names dialog box

Address Book... . Alternatively, press Ctrl+Shift+B. On the Standard toolbar, click the Address Book button.

2. The **Address Book** dialog box appears as shown in Figure 5.17.

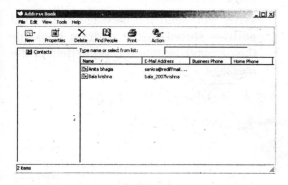

Figure 5.17 Address Book dialog box

3. In the **Address Book** dialog box, click the **New** button on the toolbar, and then select **New Contact**. The **Properties** dialog box appears as shown in Figure 5.18.

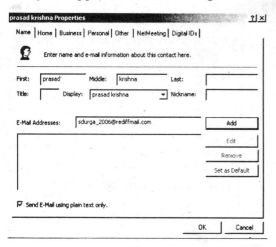

Figure 5.18 Properties dialog box

4. On the **Name** tab, type the contact's name information in the Name boxes. The name you entered in the e-mail information is added in the properties dialog box.

5. Type the contact's e-mail address and then click the **Add** button. It added in the E-mail addresses list box. Click OK.

6. The e-mail information is added in the Address book.

5.6 MANAGING AND ORGANIZING E-MAIL

New and innovative techniques for better managing and organizing their inbox and overcoming the e-mail overload.

Outlook 2000 has serveral powerful strategies that can help you with the mail you do and do not want. By organizing your Inbox, you will be able to quickly find what you need, when you need it. Whether you choose to sort the Message list in the Information viewer, add a filter to screen only e-mail that meets a certain criteria, or organize your mail by adding fields to the Information viewer.

☞ *Outlook makes it easy to group similar messages. You can create and use folder, to organize messages and set up rules that will automatically handle messages without having to do a thing.*

5.6.1 Sorting E-mail

Outlook lets you sort by single column or multiple columns. For example, if you select the column heading that is the exclamation mark (!) icon (located below the folder banner), all your important messages will be listed at the top of the Message list. Or if you click the From button, the messages will be sorted in alphabetical order by first name of the person who sent you the message. To sort by more than one column, select the column headings in reverse order.

☞ *For example, to sort e-mail first by date, then by sender, click the From button first and then the Received button.*

In addition, to sorting your e-mail using the column headings, you can sort e-mail using the Sort dialog box.

➡ **To sort e-mail using the Sort command, do this:**

1. Click the **View** menu and choose **Current View**. A sub menu appears. Select **Custom Current View**.

2. The **View Summary** dialog box appears as shown in Figure 5.19.

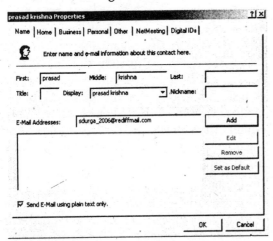

Figure 5.19   View Summary dialog box

3. In the **View Summary** dialog box, click the **Sort...** button. The **Sort** dialog box appears as shown in Figure 5.20.

4. In the **Select available fields from:** drop-down list at the bottom of the dialog box, select the field set containing the fields that you want to use for sorting.

5. In the Sort Items by drop-down list, select an item from the list, such as *From, Subject, Received*, and then choose either the **Ascending** or **Descending** option.

6. Click OK twice to close the dialog boxes and see your changes.

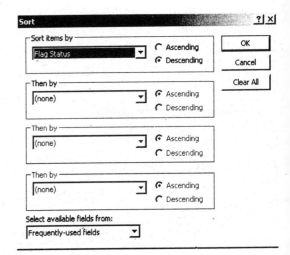

Figure 5.20   Sort dialog box

5.6.2   Filtering E-mail

Using a filter, you can temporarily hide the items that do not need. With fewer items in your folder, you can quickly find the message you need. When you remove a filter, the hidden items are visible again.

➡ **To set up a filter, do this:**

1. Open the folder you want to filter.

2. Click the **View** menu and choose **Current View**. A sub menu appears. Select **Custom Current View**.

3. The **View Summary** dialog box appears. (See Figure 5.19).

4. Click the **Filter** button. The **Filter** dialog box appears as shown in Figure 5.21.

5. In the **Search for the word(s):** drop-down list, type the words you want to locate. To look for two or more words or phrases, enclose the words in quotation marks.

6. In the **In:** drop-down list, select a field to search. For, select *Frequently-Used text fields, subject field and message body*.

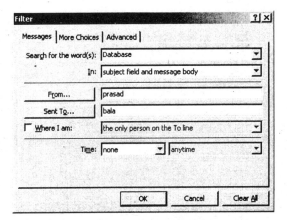

Figure 5.21 Filter dialog box

7. To find all the messages sent by one person, type the person's name in the **From...** list. To find all the messages sent to you by more than one person, separate the names with commas. Click the From button to display a list of e-mail names to choose from.

8. To find all the messages you have sent to a recipient, type the name of the person in the **Sent To...** list. To find all the messages you have to more than one person, separate the nams with commas. Click the Sent To button to display a list of e-mail names to choose from.

9. To find messages where your name is listed on a particular line, such as the **To** or **Cc** line, select the **Where I am:** check box, and then select an option from the drop-down list.

10. To locate a message based on time criterion, select an option from the Time drop-down box, and then specify a time criterion in the drop-down lsit.

The Filter dialog box, shown in Figure 5.19 includes three tabs: *Messages, More Choices* and *Advanced*. The Messages tab lets you specify options to temporarily hide items that you do not need. This limited view

makes it easier to read relevant e-mail because it removes all the irrelevant messages.

5.6.3 Adding Fields to the Information Viewer

The Column headings in Outlook's Folder list are set by default and display fields that are frequently used. To add or remove columns, and you can rearrange the order of the columns to make it easier to organize and manage your e-mail messages.

➡ **To add columns to a Folder list, do this:**

1. Click the Inbox shortcut on the Outlook bar.

2. Open the folder in which you want to add a column.

3. Click the **View** menu and choose **Current view**. A sub menu appears. Select **Customize Current View**.

4. The View Summary dialog box appears. (See Figure 5.19)

5. Click the **Fields** button. The **Show Fields** dialog box appears, as shown in Figure 5.22.

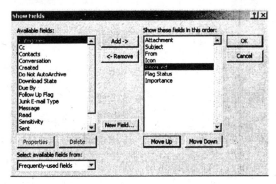

Figure 5.22 Show Fields dialog box

6. In the **Available fields:** list, select a field name, such as Categories etc., and then click the Add button.

7. To change the order of the field names, select the field name in the **Show these fields in this order:** list, and then click the Move Up button or the Move Down button depending on where you want to position the field name.

8. Click OK twice to close the dialog box and see your changes.

5.6.4 Using the Organize Page to Manage E-mail

You can easily organize and manage e-mail using a collection of tools that Outlook keeps the Organize page.

➡ **To organize page, do this:**

1. Click the Organize button on the Standard toolbar.

2. The Organize page opens at the top of the Information viewer as shown in Figure 5.23.

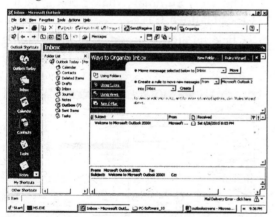

Figure 5.23 Organize page offers several ways to manage e-mail messages

3. You can create new folder or move messages to an existing folder in the **Using Folders** tab.

4. In the **Using Colors tab**, you can color-code e-mail messages, which will make them easy to identify in your Inbox.

5. The **Using Views** tab lets you change Inbox views. one moment you see *Message with AutoPreview*, or you see *By Sender* with a single click.

6. The Junk E-mail applies filters to weed out junk and adult content messages. You can also open the Rules Wizard and create a rule to automatically mangage the messages you receive.

5.6.5 Creating a New Folder

Creating a new folder is a very simple task. If you want to keep your Inbox manageable. To add folders to your Inbox, you should consider what type of messages you will be receiving or who will be sending messages to you. For example, if you exchage e-mail with your accountant,, then you may want to create a folder called Investments. Or. if you have a friend who sends you funny e-mail, then might want to store them in a folder.

Once you have a folder set up, you can create a rule, which messages automatically carries out when an item arrives in your Inbox. For example, when a message arrives from your friend, it is directly into the folder.

➡ **To create a new folder using the Organize page, do this:**

1. Click the Inbox shortcut on the Outlook bar.

2. On the Standard toolbar, click the Organize button. The Ways to Organize Inbox page will display at the top of the Information viewer.

3. Select the **Using Folders** tab. The **Using Folder tab** appears.

4. Click the **New Folder** button at the top of the box. The **Create New Folder** dialog box appears as shown in Figure 5.24.

5. In the **Name:** box, type a name for the new folder.

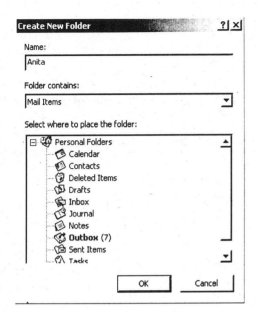

Figure 5.24 Create New Folder dilaog box

6. The **Folder contains:** drop-down list shows **Mail Items**.

7. In the **Select where to place foler:** list, select an existing folder in which you want to keep new folder.

8. To add a shortcut to the folder it send to **My Shortcuts** on the Outlook bar. Click OK button. (See Figure 5.25)

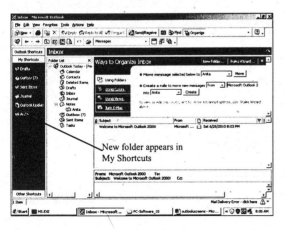

Figure 5.25 Add folder in My shortcuts items

5.6.6 Organizing Messages in Folders

To move a message from Inbox to new folder, select the message(s) you want to move in the Information viewer. You can move more than one message by pressing Ctrl and then clicking each message. Message do not have to be in any particular order when you select them.

1. In The Ways to Organize Inbox page, click **Using Folder**. The **Using Folder** tab appears as shown in Figure 5.26.

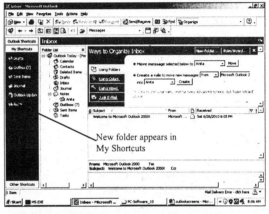

Figure 5.26 Move a message to a different folder by using the move message feature in Organize page

2. In the Move message selected below to drop-down list, select the name of the folder to which you want to move the message(s) (See Figue 5.26)

3. Click the Move button.

5.6.7 Organizing E-mail by Topic

As the number of messages grows in Outlook, you are not able to view related items. The Usign Views tab of the Organize page lets you quickly change the view of messages. To choose 10 different view, including *By Sender*, *Conversation Topic*, and *Message Timeline*. When you select a new view, the messages in the information viewer are reorganized. For example, if you view messages By Sender, the name of each sender will appear on a separate line with a plus (+) sign next to the name.

➡ **To choose a new view for your message, do this:**

1. Click the Inbox shortcut on the Outlook bar.
2. On the Standard toolbar, click the Organize button. The **Ways to Organize Inbox page** will display at the top of the Information viewer.
3. Click **Using Views** to select it. The **Using Views** tab appears.
4. In the **Change your view:** drop-down list, select a view. The message in the Information viewer will display according to the view you select.

Summary

In this chapter you leart the fundamentals of working with *Outlook 2000*. First, we discussed how to share the information with other users and integrate data from others. It also explores the features of Outlook that are used for e-mail. To create New Mail Message button, the Outlook Standard toolbar to create and send an e-mail message. And also receiving a message from the Inbox folder. Add names to the Address Book to facilitate entering e-mail addresses in messages box. Finally, organize your email files to prevent corruption and speed up how Outlook accesses files.

REVIEW QUESTIONS WITH ANSWERS

A. Multiple Choice

1. The Outlook Today shortcut can be found in the

   a. Folder list   b. Inbox
   c. Outlook Bar   d. Status Bar

2. Press _____ to move the insertion point to the end of a message.
   a. F3   b. End
   c. Ctrl + End   d. Ctrl + Alt + End

3. You can press _____ to display the Appointments Calendar in Day view.
   a. Alt + M   b. Alt + R
   c. Alt + W   d. Alt + Y

4. You can locate specific data in Outlook by choosing Advanced Find in the _____ menu.
   a. Edit   b. View
   c. Tools   d. Actions

5. Text, such as your name and your phone number, that is automatically added to any message you send is called a
   a. file   b. list
   c. shortcut   d. signature

B. Descriptive Questions

1. What is the use of Organize a Messages in folders?
2. What is the use of Address Book?
3. Differentiate between Cc and Bcc in Outlook Express?

A. Answers to Multiple Choice

1. a 2. c 3. d 4. c 5. d

B. Answers to Descriptive Questions

1. [*Refer section 5.6.6*]
2. [*Refer section 5.5*]
3. [*Refer section 5.4.1*]

CHAPTER 6

Computer Viruses

The reader will be able to understand in this chapter
- What is Computer Virus?
- Types of Viruses
- Prevention and Cure from virus

6.1 INTRODUCTION

6.1.1 What is Computer Virus?

A computer virus is a small block of coded instruction that obtains control of a PC's CPU and directs it to perform unusual and often destructive actions.

6.1.2 How does it Spread?

Computer virus is spread unknowingly from one infected computer to another via e-mails and instant messaging.

6.2 TYPES OF VIRUSES

Viruses are classified in the following types:
(a) Trojan Horse
(b) Time and Logic Bombs
(c) Melissa and SKA Virus pertaining to MS Word files

6.2.1 Trojan Horse

A Trojan Horse is a program that invades a computer system by secretly attaching itself to a valid program downloaded into the computer. It may be used to locate password information, or it may alter an existing program to make it easier to gain access to it.

☞ *A virus is called a Trojan horse that continues to infect programs over and over again.*

It also pretends to do something useful or interesting. But when run, it produces some harmful effects like scrambling FAT (File Allocation Table) or formatting the hard disk.

6.2.2 Time and Logic Bombs

A Time and Logic bomb is a program that destroys data; for example, it may reformat the hard disk or randomly insert garbage into data files.

☞ *A time bomb as the name suggests, is triggered by an event. It can format the hard disk on a given date or slow down computer every Friday or make a ball bounce around the screen.*

A logic bomb may be brought into a personal computer by downloading a public-domain program that has been tampered with. Once executed, the logic bomb usually does its damage right away, whereas a software virus slowly invades a system and attaches itself to other programs too.

6.2.3 Melissa and SKA Virus

Melissa virus attacks MS Word documents and spreads very fast. This virus affects MS Word documents by installing itself to Normal.doc and disabling the macro protection message and infects all the Word files opened or created subsequently. The message generated by the virus says "Here is a document you asked for ...don't show anyone else".

A new virus called Melissa spreads around the world rapidly, infecting many computers and bringing down networks. It was a Word Macro virus and used Microsoft Outlook to send infected documents across the Internet. The Melissa virus belongs to the so called Class Infectors and resides in the module "This Document." The module is renamed by the virus to Melissa. When an infected document is opened in Word, the virus removes the Tool/Macro menu item and then turns off three options: Confirm Conversion, Virus Protection and Save NormalPrompt.

When an infected document is opened in Office 2000, it sets several registry keys and then proceeds to execute the most dangerous part of the code. Using Microsoft Outlook, the virus finds the first 50 entries from the user's Address Book and sends the infected document as an attachment to those selected recipients. This means that if a mailing list is one of those first 50 entries, more than 50 users would receive the virus. The subject line in all the sent messages read, "Important Message from—UserName."

☞ *This somewhat virgin virus literally brought companies and the Internet users to their knees. Mail servers around the world were bogged down handling the sudden influx and explosion of messages.*

Melissa has two kinds of impact. First the initial snowball effect and then the ripple effect. If the end users open the attachment that causes the problems, corporate systems are flooded with resource-hogging e-mails, in exponentially increasing numbers. As the snowball gets momentum, more e-mail servers are affected.

There is another virus called SKA which increases the size of the file and changes the extension of the files to .ska. These viruses delete the Microsoft Document files or change their contents.

6.3 PREVENTION AND CURE

The saying "Prevention is better than cure" should be the guiding principle for organisations to control virus spread. There are various things one can do to prevent viral infection in a computer system. These are:
(a) Limit sharing of software.
(b) Limit transitivity.
(c) Limit functionality.
(d) Use the Scanner and virus remover.

6.3.1 Limit Sharing of Software

One can limit sharing by limiting information flow so as to form a post office set of communicating information domains in a network system. In such a system, a virus will spread only to those domains which are in the transitive flow path from its initial source.

6.3.2 Limit Transitivity

In a system with unlimited information paths, limited transitivity may have an effect. If users do not use all available paths, but since there is always a direct path between any two users, there is always the possibility of infection. As an example, in a system, with transitivity limited to a distance of 1, it is safe to share information with any user you trust without having to worry about whether the user has wrongly trusted another user.

6.3.3 Limit Functionality

Although isolationism and limited transitivity offer solutions to the infection problem they are not ideal solutions in the sense that widespread sharing is generally considered a valuable tool in computing.

The third option for absolute prevention is limited function. Most real-world users do not exploit the general purpose capabilities provided to them, and it would be a substantial advantage for the defender if limited function could be applied. However, all modern software packages allow general purpose function, including most application programs such as databases, spreadsheets, editors and mail systems etc.

6.3.4 Virus Scanner and Remover

You should install the latest anti-virus software and update it regularly. The anti-virus programme should ideally start by default when the computer is switched on. The system should also be equipped with the ability to self-repair the damage caused by virus attacks.

Virus scanners are products designed to help identify viruses within files, boot sectors, master boot sectors, memory, and other hiding places, name them, and eventually remove them. The capability to detect and identify a virus is probably the most important feature of a scanner.

Summary

In this chapter we discussed how virus spread in Computer. We also dicussed various types of viruses and how to prevent them.

REVIEW QUESTIONS WITH ANSWERS

Descriptive Questions

1. "Prevention is Better than Cure"-is very much valid in the context of computer viruses. Discuss
2. What is "Virus Attack"? Give their characteristics.
3. List the precaution to be taken to keep the Computer(s) "Virus-Free".

Answers to Descriptive Questions

1. Normally a computer if attacked by a virus, will contain some damaged files of data. This is inherent. In many a cases, the only remedy is to format the hard disk. It may not be able to damage the hardware, but the loss of data may be very expensive for an organization specially if no backup is kept aside. Therefore, a better way to safe guard the computer against the computer virus attack is to keep it away from the access by unauthorized persons. If possible, do not allow any outside pen drive or file being imported in the machine. Thus, *prevention is always better than cure.* Because if one removes virus using virus removers, still it is possible that some of the files might retain virus attached. This may again damage the system.
2. Virus attack means destroying or currupting program or data files stored on a permanent storage device such as hard disk. There are only two ways in which a virus can enter the computer. These are:
   (a) When the computer is booted by a virus infected disk.
   (b) The second is when you execute a virus infected program.

   Once a virus enters in a computer it can spread in the following two ways:

(a) As a memory resident virus which loads itself in RAM and either waits like a time-bomb for doomsday, or infects your files gradually over a period of time.

(b) As a direct-action virus which either infects a set of files or all of them and becomes dormant again. This type of virus turns the control back to the original file and does not reside in memory.

Virus Characteristics

Virus do not want to give any indication of their presence. And the maximum programming time of virus creators is spent making the virus as transparent or undetectable as possible till it has done damage of spreading far and wide. The only reason a virus gets detected at all is because of its bugs, that is programming errors or shortcomings. Since no programmer can be perfect, no virus can really escape user's eye if one is bent on catching it young.

3. Following precautions must be taken to reduce the chances of a machine being infected by a virus.

(a) Do not boot computers from disks that have been in any other computer.

(b) If the system is to boot from a disk, make sure that the boot disk is labeled to identify the machine it belongs to, and enforce a policy that restricts the use of that disk to that machine only.

(c) Consider creating a virus scanning machine for employee use. The ideal machine contains a menu-driven product that can scan a disk in with the press of a key. All employees could be required to scan all disks/pen drives they bring from home before taking them to their office.

(d) Any software lending library, shared computer, or training room is a potential virus transmission site. At even greater risk is the friend who may visit a user experiencing difficulties, get a virus on their diagnostic disk, and then move on to another user, infecting that user's machine in the process.

APPENDIX

Windows XP

INTRODUCTION

Windows XP is one of the later versions of Windows desktop operating system for the PC. Windows XP brings a new, more personalized look to the desktop that will also make it easier for users to scan or import images. It is meant to acquire music files on the Web and transfer them to portable devices. Windows XP will allow different family members to use their own desktop and personal set of files. The Start menu has been redesigned to make the most-used programs easiest to find. Windows XP comes in a professional version and a Home Edition version.

Main Features in Windows XP

- **Sharing computers:** Windows XP Professional makes sharing a computer easier than storing personalized settings and preferences for each user.

- **Fast User Switching for Multiple User of a Computer:** User Switching from one user to another is easy without logging off and on.

- **Store User Names and Passwords:** With Windows XP Professional, we can store different user names and passwords for connecting to different sites and resources. Names and Passwords saved as part of our user profile, which we can take to different computers.

- **Files and Settings Transfer Wizard:** With the help of Files and setting transfer wiz-

ard, we can move our personal settings and data files from old computer to new one.

- **Desktop cleanup Wizard:** With the help of Desktop Cleanup Wizard, we can remove those shortcuts that we do not use from desktop.

- **Personal screen saver:** With this feature, we use our own photographs as a screen saver.

- **Copying Files and Folders to a CD:** If we have a CD Rewritable (CD-RW) or CD Recordable (CD-R) drive, we can copy photos, music, or data to a CD. This is the easy way to back up information.

- **Network Setup Wizard:** With the help of network setup wizard we can create a small office network for increasing productivity.

- **Internet Connection Sharing:** Internet Connection Sharing helps in connecting office network computers to the Internet even if all the computers did not have a direct Internet Connection.

- **Internet Connection Firewall (ICF):** The Internet Connection Firewall provides a protection on computers directly connected to the Internet. It is also available for LAN (Local Area Networks).

- **Online Help:** Windows XP provides extensive help on all the features in operating system.

- **Remote Assistance:** This feature allows you to remotely view and control a computer for any support task. For any computer problem, You can even chat online as you work through the problem.

- **Compatibility:** This feature provides up-to-date, comprehensive, compatibility information to users.
- **Remote Desktop:** With Remote Desktop, you can access a Windows session that is running on your computer when you are at another computer.
- **Search Companion:** With Windows XP Professional Search Companion, you can search for objects, pictures, music, documents, printers, computers, etc.
- **Windows File Protection:** Windows File Protection prevents the replacement or removal of protected system files. It runs in the background and protects all the files installed by the Windows setup program.
- **System restore:** In the event of a system problem, System restore feature, restore computer to a previous state without losing personal data files.
- **Compressed Folders:** Using the Compressed Folders feature in Windows XP Professional, you can decrease the amount of drive space folders occupy.
- **ClearType:** Choosing ClearType for your screen fonts makes the words on your computer screen look as smooth as the words on a page. This is for laptop computers.
- **File associations:** With Windows XP Professional, you can specify that files with certain file name extensions always open in the same program.
- **Offline files and folders:** With Windows XP Professional, you can make network files available offline, so you can work on them when you are not connected to your network.

BASIC ELEMENTS OF OPENING SCREEN OF WINDOWS XP

The different parts of the Windows opening screen are as marked in Figure A.1 and discussed in the following paragraphs.

The Desktop

The Desktop is the work area on a Windows screen where you are made to work. It is called the *Desktop* because Windows uses your whole screen in a way that is similar to the way you use the top of your desk. As you work in Windows, you move items on the Desktop, retrieve and put away items and perform many other day-to-day tasks.

Icons and their Types

An icon is a graphic object that shows a program or a file on your monitor. The different types of icons are described in the successive sub-sections.

System Icons

System icons are displayed along left edge of the screen. These objects are created automatically by Windows XP during its installation.

The five system icons are explained in the following table.

System Icon	Function
My Computer	This icon lets you browse through the resources connected to your computer.
My Documents	This icon represents a folder that is used by many programs as a default location for starting the documents.
Internet Explorer	This icon starts Internet Explorer.
My Network Places	This icon opens a Window displaying the names of each server or computer in your own work group.
Recycle Bin	This icon provides temporary storage for files and folders that you delete.

System
Icons

Shortcut
Icons

Desktop

Start
button

Program
Icon

Taskbar

Figure A.1 Different parts of the Windows XP screen

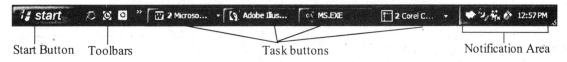

Start Button   Toolbars   Task buttons   Notification Area

Figure A.2 Different Parts of the Taskbar

Shortcut Icons

These are the icons with small arrows in the lower left corner. A shortcut icon provides easy access to some objects on your system, such as a *program*, a *document*, or a *printer*, etc. The shortcut icon only contains information about the location of the object but not the object itself.

☞ *Deleting a shortcut icon does not delete the program from the hard disk for that shortcut.*

Program, Folder and Document Icons

These are non–system icons without arrows and they represent the actual objects they describe.

☞ *Thus, if you delete such an icon you are deleting the object itself, from the hard disk. So be very careful!*

The Taskbar

Along the bottom of the screen as seen in Figure A.2 is the Taskbar. The taskbar can also be displayed along the side or the top of the screen.

The different parts of the taskbar (as seen in Figure A.2) are explained in the following table.

Taskbar Elements	Function
Start button	It is located at the left end of the taskbar. Clicking the start button brings up the start menu as seen in Figure A.3.
Toolbars	Toolbars represent a set of related icons. When clicked these buttons or

(Contd...)

icons activate certain functions or tasks. For example, the Quick launch toolbar provides icons for launching Internet Explorer and Microsoft Outlook. (See Figure A.2)

Task buttons
Task buttons are displayed in the center portion of the Taskbar. A button appears for each program you have started or each document you have opened. You can click these buttons to move from one open Program or Folder to another. (See Figure A.2)

Notification area
The right corner of the Taskbar has the notification area in which Windows provides information about the status of your system. It displays the time and also contains shortcuts that provide quick access to programs, such as Volume Control. Other shortcuts can appear temporarily. For example, the printer icon appears after a document has been sent to the printer and disappears when printing is complete.

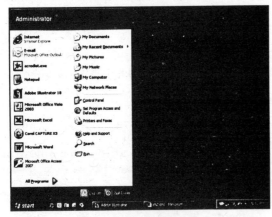

Figure A.3   Start menu

Customization of Taskbar

There is no reason to customize the Taskbar. But if you really want to customize the taskbar and change its properties then follows the undermentioned steps.

➡ **To customize the Taskbar, do this:**

1. Right Click on unoccupied area of the task bar and then choose Properties. The Taskbar and Start Menu properties dialog box appears as shown in Figure A.4.

Figure A.4   Taskbar Properties dialog box with Taskbar Options Tab

2. In this dialog box, click on Taskbar Options Tab to change the settings ON or OFF. If check mark appears it means option is ON otherwise option is OFF.

Select *Lock the taskbar* check box, if you want the taskbar to fix in a position from where it cannot moved to a new location on the desktop. It also locks the size and position of the toolbars so that it cannot be changed.

Select *Auto-hide the task bar* check box, if you want to hide the taskbar. When you want it to reappear then move the mouse pointer over the taskbar location.

Select *Keep the taskbar on top of other windows* check box, if you want taskbar to appear always on top whether any program is open or not.

Select *Group similar taskbar buttons* check box, if you want the different buttons of the same program into one button.

Select *Show Quick Launch* check box, if you want to display the Quick Launch bar on the taskbar.

Select *Show the clock* check box to show the system clock on the taskbar.

Select *Hide inactive icons* check box when you want to hide the unused icons from the notification area of the taskbar.

3. After changing the setting according to you need, click on the **A**pply button and then OK button to save the settings.

Start Menu

Start menu appears when you click on the Start button on the Taskbar as seen in Figure A.3. The Start menu provides you with more customization options. It shows you who is logged on. It automatically adds the most frequently used programs to the top-level menu. It enables you to move any programs you want to the Start menu. Items such as My Pictures and My Documents folders and Control Panel are also now available from the top level.

All Programs

It displays the **Programs menu** which contain many application programs you can run.

My Recent Documents

It displays the **Document menu** that contains the list of the documents you have recently opened. To open the recently used documents, choose it from the list of this menu.

Control Panel

It allows you to install software and change different setting of Windows such as Date, Time, Keyboard, Mouse, Password, Display, Sound settings.

Printers and Faxes

It allows you to see the current status of the printers and Faxes.

Help and Support

It displays online help which is a set of screens of information about Window itself and the accessories that comes with it.

Search

It displays a window by which you can find Files, folders, computers, people, pictures etc.

Run

It allows you to run any program by typing name and location of that program.

Log Off

If your computer is on a local area network, this command closes all the programs, disconnects your computer from the network, and prepares your computer to be used by someone else for logging on.

Turn off Computer

It displays the Turn off Computer dialog box. Choose Turn off if you are ready to switch off computer. Choose Restart to restart your computer. Choose Stand by if you want to put your computer to low power state.

Customization of Start Menu

➡ **To customize the Start menu, do this:**

1. Right Click on unoccupied area of the task bar and then choose P**r**operties. The Taskbar and Start Menu properties dialog box appears as shown in Figure A.4. In this dialog box, click Start Menu Tab to customize the start menu. (See Figure A.5)

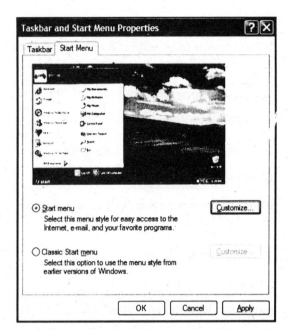

Figure A.5 Taskbar Properties dialog box with Start Menu Programs Tab

2. In this Tab, Select *Start menu* option to select the default Start menu.

   Select the *Classic Start menu* option to select the style from an earlier version of Windows.

   If you want to make additional selections for the Start menu style, click Customize... . It includes specifying the items you want to display on the Start menu, clearing your list of recently used programs, documents, and Web sites, etc.

3. After that click on the Apply button and then OK button to save the changes.

DIFFERENT TYPES OF WINDOW DISPLAYS

There are three types of window openings namely, *application window, document window* and *folder window*. Details of each is given in the following sub sections.

Application Window

Application window contains a program which you are running and working with, namely, the Window that shows Microsoft Word, Excel, Paint, etc. Most of the work that you do will be in application window. Figure A.6 shows a typical application window, also called a *parent window.*

Document Window

Document window contains a document you are working on *within* an application window. Most of the applications allow you to have multiple documents window open at a time (See in Figure A.6). The document window is also referred to as child window.

Folder Window

Opening My Computer, or any of the folder you move to the desktop produces a Folder window (See Figure A.7). The window's Title bar displays the name of the open folder. Just below the title bar, is the Menu bar and Toolbar. At the bottom of the window lies the status bar which displays the number of objects in the folder, the number of objects hidden, and the amount of disk space occupied by the folder.

Elements of a Window

Following elements form part of a window as shown in Figure A.8.

Borders

The four edges that define the perimeter of a window are called borders. Borders also give a way to change the size of the window.

Title Bar

Just below the top border of the window is

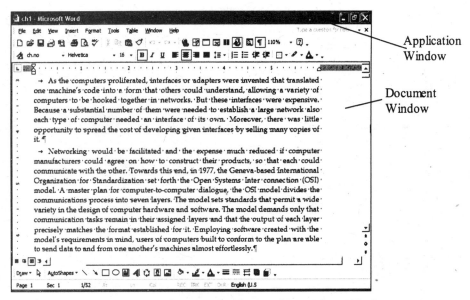

Figure A.6 Application Window and Document Window

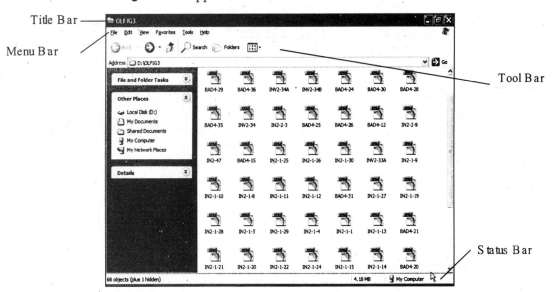

Figure A.7 Folder Window

the Title bar. It displays the name of the program or the document. For example, Wordpad's Title bar shows the name of the document being edited. It is also used for moving the window.

Control Box

Control box is a small icon located on the left side of the Title bar. The Control box performs two functions. These are:

- It opens the Control menu as seen in Figure A.8 whenever you click the Control

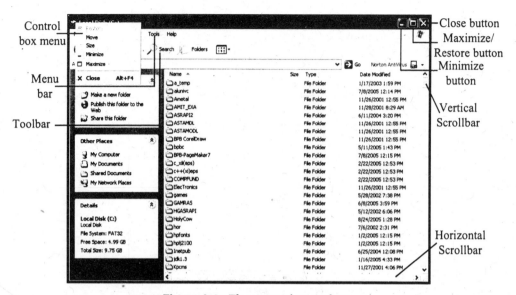

Figure A.8 Elements of a window

bar. In most of the programs the command on a Control menu lets you control the size of the window. But some programs may have special items on their control menus.

- Control box for a program or document will close the window that terminates the program or closes the document when you double click it.

☞ *Pressing* Alt+- *keys together opens the Control box of the active **document** window.* Alt+ Spacebar *opens the Control box of the active application window.*

Close Button

At the right edge of the Title bar is a square containing an × called the Close button. Clicking the Close button closes a *document* or folder, or terminates a program (See Figure A.8).

Minimize, Maximize and Restore Buttons

The three small buttons at the right end of the Title bar as in Figure A.8 with small graphics in them are the *Minimize* button, *Maximum* or *Restore* button, and the *Close* buttons. These are control buttons with which you can quickly change the size of a window or close the window.

- Clicking the *minimize* button reduces the window to a button on the Task bar. Once *minimized*, the window no longer takes space on the desktop but the program in it continues to run.
- Clicking the *maximize* button enlarges the window to occupy the whole Desktop. When the window is *maximized*, the *minimized* and *restore* buttons appear.
- Clicking the restore button causes a window to assume an intermediate size, i.e. neither minimized nor maximized. In this case, the *minimized* and *maximized* buttons appear.

Scroll Bars, Scroll Boxes and Scroll Buttons

If a window is not long enough to display its contents completely, *vertical scroll bar* appears along the right edge. Similarly, if the window is not wide enough, a *horizontal scroll bar* appears along the bottom of the window.

☞ *Scroll bars offer an easy way to navigate through a window with the mouse. They also provide useful information about the contents of the window.*

Scroll bars have small rectangular boxes called scroll box (See Figure A.8). The position of this box within the scroll bar tells you where you are within the window itself. If the scroll box is at the top of the scroll bar, it means you are at the top of the document.

Scroll buttons appear along the top and bottom edges of the vertical scroll bar and along the left and right edges of the horizontal scroll bar.

Menu Bar

The row of words just below the Titlebar constitute the *Menubar*. The *Menubar* appears only in an application window and not in a document window. Each word on the Menubar represents a menu which opens up when you click it (See Figure A.8). The names of the menus may vary from program to program but they have some common headings such as File, Edit, Window, and Help.

Choosing Menu Commands

Choosing a menu command involves two steps:
• Click to open it.
• Selecting the required command from the menu.

➡ **To open a menu do this:**

Using the mouse click the menu name.
Or using the keyboard, press Alt+(under-

lined letter in the menu name). For example, to open the Edit menu press Alt+E keys together (See Figure A.9).

After a menu is opened, you can select a menu command as follows:
• By typing the underlined letter in the command name (e.g. t for cut in Figure A.9)
• By clicking on a command's name.
• By pressing the ↓ arrow or ↑ arrow keys to highlight the desired command name and then pressing Enter.

To close a menu without selecting any command, press the Esc key or click anywhere outside the menu.

Special Indicators in Menus

When you open a menu you would notice (See Figure A.10) that many of the commands have additional words or symbols next to the command name. These additional words or symbols next to the command name indicate the following:

Grayed (Dimmed) Command Name

When a command is displayed as *grayed*, or *dimmed* (See Figure A.9), it means that this choice is not currently available for selection. A command can be dimmed for many reasons. For example, if a window is already Maximized, the Maximize command on the Control menu will be dimmed because this choice does not make sense.

Ellipses(...)   Ellipses next to a command (See Figure A.10) means that you will be asked for additional information before it is executed on selecting such a command. A dialog box appears on the screen, asking you to provide additional information.

Check Mark (✔) A check mark preceding a command (See Figure A.10) means the command is a

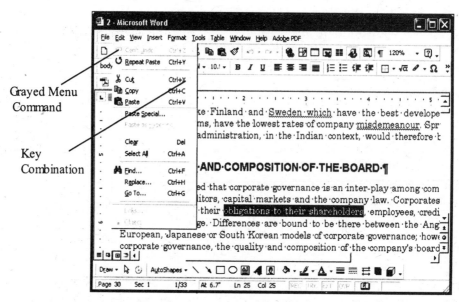

Figure A.9   Edit Menu Open

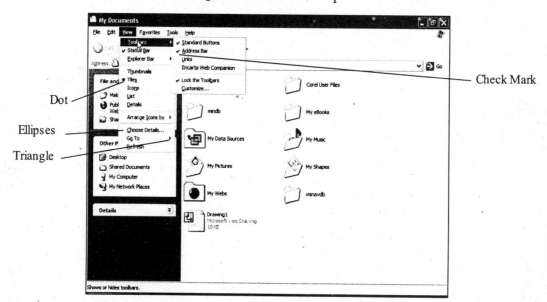

Figure A.10   Special Indicators in Menu

toggle that is activated (turned on). A toggle is a command that is alternately turned *Off* and *On* each time you select it. Each time you select one of these commands, it switches from *On* to *Off* or *Off* to *On*. If there is no check mark, then the command or setting is *Off*.

Triangle (➤) A triangle to the right of a menu command (See Figure A.10) means that the command has additional choices to choose from. This is also called a *cascading menu*. You make selections from a cascaded menu in the same way you would from a normal menu.

Dot(•) A dot to the left of the command means that the option is currently selected and is an exclusive option among several related options (See Figure A.10). Only one of these options can be selected at a time. The dot indicates the current setting.

A Key Combination Some menu commands list keystrokes that can be used for opening the menu and choosing that command (See Figure A.9). These are also called *shortcut keys*.

Shortcut Menus

Pressing the right mouse button shows a small menu related to the currently selected object or the one the mouse is pointing to (See Figure A.11). This menu is at times also referred to as *pop up* menu. For example, if you right click the Taskbar, you get a menu of commands relating only to the Taskbar.

Figure A.11 Shortcut/Popup Menu

Dialog Boxes

A Dialog box will appear when you select a command with an ellipsis(...) after it. Dialog boxes appear on your screen when Windows or its Application program you are

using needs more information to execute the command. The various dialog box elements are as follows:

Dialog box tabs Some of the dialog boxes (See Figure A.12) have multiple option pages. You select the page you are interested in by clicking its icon at the top of the dialog box. Using the keyboard, press (Ctrl)+(tab) to flip through the option pages.

Moving between Dialog Box Elements

Dialog boxes often have several sections in them as seen in Figure A.12. You can move between the sections in three ways:

• By clicking on the section you want to change.
• Using the keyboard, you can press the (Tab) key to move between sections and press the (Spacebar) to select them.

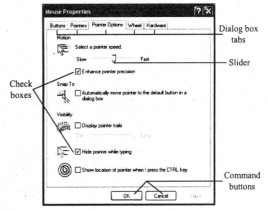

Figure A.12 Dialog box Tabs

Entering Information in a Dialog Box

The dialog boxes have following eight different types of sections where you need to enter information (See Figure A.12 and A.13).

• Text boxes
• Check boxes
• Option buttons
• Command buttons

• List boxes
• Sliders
• Spinners

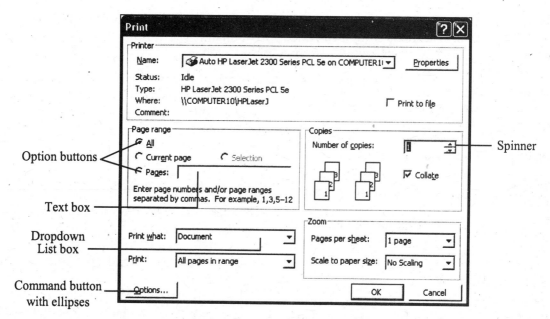

Figure A.13 Dialog box elements

Text Boxes   Text box is also called an *Edit box* and it is where you type in the information (See Figure A.13). To enter information in the text box, click the text box. The insertion point appears in the text box. The insertion point indicates the place where the character you type will appear.

- If the text box is empty, the insertion point appears at the left side of the box.
- If the box already contains text, the insertion point appears at the point where you clicked the mouse.

Check Boxes   Check boxes are small square boxes (See Figure A.12). Each check box is independent of all other check boxes in the dialog box. To select a check box item, click the box or anywhere in the text next to the box and similarly, to deselect repeat the same procedure. A check box when selected displays an (×) or (✔) sign within the box. Some check boxes have three states — *checked, unchecked*, and *partly checked*. A gray (in place of a black) check mark means that certain condition applies to it and some of the selections do not apply.

Option Buttons   Option buttons are also called *radio buttons* and present a set of mutually exclusive options (See Figure A.13). Option buttons are always present in groups of two or more and may either be round or diamond shaped. You may select any one option from the group but not more than one. To select the option, click the button or any where in the text next to the button.

Command Buttons   Command buttons are like option buttons and are used to execute a command immediately. They are rectangular and not square or circular in shape. An example of a command button is the OK button found on almost every dialog box. (Figure A.12)

List Box   A List box presents a list of options or items from which you can select. To make a selection from a list box, using the mouse, click on it or using the keyboard highlight the desired option and then press (Enter) key to choose it. (See Figure A.13)

Sliders A slider works like a sliding control. Moving it in one direction increases some value, moving it in the other direction decreases the same value (See Figure A.12).

Spinners A spinner is a pair of arrows used to increase or decrease the value in a text box (See Figure A.13). To increase the value in the text box, click the up arrow and to decrease the value click the down arrow.

SIZING AND MOVING THE WINDOW

➡ **To change the size of a window do this:**

1. Position the pointer on the border of the window to be moved. Press and hold the left mouse button and move the border to resize the window (See Figure A.14). For example, to make the window wider, drag the *left* or *right* border. To make a window taller drag the top or bottom border. To make a window both wider and taller, you can drag one of the corners.

Figure A.14 Border being dragged to resize the window

➡ **To move a window do this:**

1. Drag its Title bar i.e position the mouse pointer in the Title bar, press and hold down the left mouse button as you move the window.

Switching Between two Windows

You may have different Application windows open at the same time. In such a case, the window on the top is called the *active window* i.e window in which you are working and it is also called the *foreground window*. The Active window's titlebar is normally displayed in one colour, while the titlebars of all inactive windows are displayed in another colour. In addition, Taskbar button for the active window appears to be pressed in the taskbar.

➡ **To change the active window use any one of the following methods:**

- Click the Taskbar button for the window you want to switch to.
- Press and hold the [Alt] key. Then press [Tab] key to bring up the Window Task Switcher.

  The Task Switcher displays an icon for each running program and draws a box around the icon of the active window. Continue holding [Alt] key and pressing [Tab] until the window that you want to be active.

Arranging Windows on the Screen

If you have many windows open at one time, arranging them becomes important. Windows XP provides two ways to arrange the different windows.

- Cascade Arrangement
- Tile

➡ **To arrange windows in cascade do this:**

1. Right click an unoccupied area of the Taskbar. (press [Ctrl]+[Esc] keys if the taskbar is not visible). Highlight arrangement and choose the Cascade.

In a cascade, from the shortcut menu, in both active windows you can easily switch by clicking any Title bar—as well as by clicking the Taskbar.

➡ **To arrange windows in tile arrangement do this:**

1. Right click the unoccupied area of the taskbar.
2. From the shortcut menu choose Tile Windows Horizontally or Tile Windows Vertically.

➡ **To minimize all open windows, do this:**

1. Click on the **Show Desktop** button on the taskbar. All the open windows will appear as buttons on the taskbar.
2. To restore all windows to their previous state, click again on the **Show Desktop** button.

☞ *If the Quick Launch bar is not displayed in task bar then right-click an empty area on the taskbar, Click to Toolbars, and then click Quick Launch. A check mark appears when the Quick Launch is displayed on the task bar.*

Working with Document Window

Document window appears inside program windows. It is designed to hold documents, not programs. Document windows can be *maximized, restored, minimized, moved,* and *sized,* but they have to remain within the program window.

CONFIGURING WINDOWS XP

To use Windows XP effectively, you have to configure or reshape Windows and the other programs that you run to work with your computer's hardware. You do this using the following features:

Feature	Function
Properties	These are the settings for many different objects in your computer's hardware and software.

(Contd...)

Feature	Function
Control Panel	This lets you see and change many properties and other settings.
Wizards	These are programs that help automate the process of installing hardware, software and configuring software.

Properties

Every object in Windows XP—the hardware components of your computer, software programs, files, and icons—has *properties.* These properties are settings that determine how that object works. For example, a file has properties such as *filename, size* and *the date* the file was last modified.

➡ **To change the properties of an object do this:**

1. Right click the object, the shortcut menu is displayed as seen in Figure A.15.
2. From the shortcut menu click Properties. The Properties dialog box appears.

The properties that you can change depend upon this object you have selected.

Figure A.15   Shortcut Menu to change the property of an object

Control Panel

Control Panel is a window that displays specialized tools for a number of programs that let you control your–computer, looks and behaviour of Windows, and the software you have installed. Some of these tools help you adjust settings that make your computer more fun to use. For example, use Mouse to replace standard mouse pointers with animated icons that move on your screen. Other tools help you set up Windows so that your computer is
easier to use.

In Windows XP, Control Panel can be display in two views i.e.

(a) Category view that groups together similar items.

(b) Classic view that display all items individually.

☞ *You can switch between the different views of Control Panel with the help of window pane shown in the left side of the Control Panel window.*

➡ To open Control Panel do this:

1. Click the Start button and then choose Control Panel. The Control Panel window appears as seen in Figure A.16 or Figure A.17 (It will depend on the view selected by you).

The various icons available in the control panel are as follows:

Accessibility Options

Accessibility Properties dialog box lets you configure Windows's keyboard, sound, display, mouse, and other options, for people with disabilities. This icon appears only if you installed Accessibility options when you installed Windows.

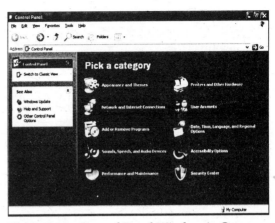

Figure A.16 Control Panel Window in Category view

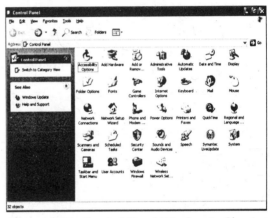

Figure A.17 Control Panel Window in Classic view

Add Hardware

Add Hardware Wizard detects and configures devices connected to your computer i.e. printers, keyboard, mouse, disk drives, modem, etc. To add new hardware click this icon in Control Panel.

Add or Remove Programs

Add or Remove Programs Properties dialog box helps you to install new programs from CD-ROM, floppy disk, or a network, or uninstall programs you no longer use. This dialog box also adds Windows updates from the Internet, add or remove Windows components. To change Add/Remove Properties click this icon.

Administrative Tools

Following types of administrative tools appear in Windows XP:

Component Services used by the system administrator to control and administer COM+ programs from a graphical user interface.

Computer Management used to manage local or remote computers from a single, consolidated desktop utility. It combines several Windows XP administrative tools into a single console tree.

Data Sources Open Database Connectivity (ODBC) is a programming interface that enables programs to access data in database management systems.

Event Viewer is used to view and manage logs of system, program, and security events on your computer. It gathers information about hardware and software problems, and monitors security events.

Local Security policy is used to configure security settings for the local computer.

Performance is used to collect and view real-time data about memory, disk, processor, network, and other activity in a graph, histogram, or report form.

Services is used to manage the services on your computer, set recovery actions if a service fails.

Automatic Updates

Automatic Updates checks for updates that can help protect your computer against the latest viruses and other security threats. If you turn on Automatic Updates, you do not have to search for updates online. Windows automatically downloads and installs them for you.

Date and Time

The Date/Time Properties dialog box lets you set the date, time, and time zone where you are located. To change Date/Time Properties, click the Date/Time icon in the Control Panel.

Display

Display Properties dialog box controls the appearance, resolution, screen saver, and other settings for your display monitor. To change display properties click the display icon in Control Panel window.

Folder Options

With Folder Options, you can specify how your folders function and how content is displayed. To change folder options settings, open Folder Options in Control Panel. Or, to open Folder Options from a folder window, click Tools, and then click Folder Options.

Fonts

Fonts window lets you install new screen and printer fonts. To change Fonts, click Fonts icon in Control Panel window.

Game Controllers

Game Controllers dialog box lets you add, configure and customize game controllers. To change Game controller Properties click Game controllers in Control Panel Window.

Internet Options

Internet Options dialog box contains settings for your web browser and Internet connection. To change Internet Properties click Internet Options icon in Control Panel.

Keyboard

Keyboard dialog box contains settings that control your keyboard and the cursor. To change keyboard properties click Keyboard icon in Control Panel window.

Mail

Mail dialog box lets you add new E-mail accounts, change setting for the files that Outlook Express used to store E-mail messages and documents. It can also be used to setup multiple profiles of E-mail accounts.

Mouse

Mouse Properties dialog box lets you define the buttons on your mouse. It lets you choose how fast you need to double-click, what your mouse pointer looks like on-screen, and whether moving the mouse leaves a trail. To change mouse properties click mouse icon in Control Panel window.

Network Connections

Network dialog box contains settings, you use when configuring a local area network. It also contains settings for connecting to the Internet. To change Network properties click Network Connections icon in Control Panel window.

Network Setup Wizard

Network Setup Wizard guides you through setting up your home or small office network.

Phone and Modem Options

Phone and Modem Options is used to install a telephony client, or install and configure a modem.

Power Options

Power Options dialog box contains controls to be set when Windows automatically turns off your monitor, hard disks, and other computer components to save electricity. To change Power Management Properties click Power Options icon in Control Panel.

Printers and Faxes

Printers and Faxes is used to install and share printing resources across your entire network.

QuickTime

QuickTime contains the QuickTime hardware and software settings.

Regional and Language Options

The Regional and Language Options dialog box lets you tell Windows the time zone, currency, number format, and date format you prefer to use. To change Regional settings, click Regional and Language Options icon in Control Panel window.

Scanners and Cameras

You can use Scanners and Cameras to install scanners, digital still cameras, digital video cameras and image-capturing devices.

Scheduled Tasks

Scheduled Tasks regulate any script, program, or document to run at a time that is most convenient for you

Security Center

Windows Security Center checks the status of your computer for the three security essentials Firewall, Virus protection software and Automatic updates. If a problem is detected, the Security Center sends you an alert and provides recommendations for how to better protect your computer.

Sound and Audio Devices

With the Sounds and Audio Devices you can assign sounds to some system events.

Speech

Speech dialog box is used to control voice properties, speed, and other options for text-to-speech translation.

Symantec LiveUpdate

Symantec LiveUpdate dialog box contains the setting of LiveUpdate.

System

The System dialog box lets you to change advanced settings for each hardware component of your computer. You can also optimize the performance of your computer. To change system properties click the system icon in Control Panel window.

Taskbar and Start Menu

It contains the setting of taskbar and start menu. You can also customize the taskbar and start menu with the help of Taskbar and Start Menu icon of the Control Panel.

User Accounts

User Accounts windows lets you create or change properties of user accounts, and to manage your stored passwords.

Windows Firewall

A firewall helps to keep your computer more secure. Windows Firewall dialog box lets you adjust Firewall setting.

Wireless Network Setup Wizard

Wireless Network Setup Wizard lets you to set up a wireless network in your home or small office.

WIZARD IN WINDOWS XP

Windows like many other Microsoft programs, includes many *Wizards*, programs that take you step by step through the process of creating or configuring something. For example, the Network Setup Wizard leads you through the many steps required to set up a Dial-Up Networking connection to an Internet Service Provider (ISP).

☞ *Wizards include instructions for each step, telling you what information you must provide, and making suggestions regarding what choices to make.*

Most Wizards display window after window of information and questions, with *Back, Next,* and *Cancel* buttons at the bottom of each window. Figure A.18 shows a Wireless Network Setup Wizard.

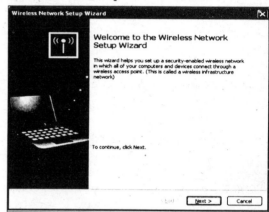

Figure A.18   Wireless Network Setup Wizard

Fill out the information requested by the Wizard, and then click the Next button to continue. If you need to return to a previous Wizard window, click the Back button. To exit the Wizard, click the Cancel button. The Wizard's last screen usually displays a *Finish* button, since there is no "next" screen to see.

RUNNING A PROGRAM

The easiest and the most commonly used way to run the application is with the Start button.

➡ **To run a program with the Start button do this:**

1. Click the Start button. The Start menu appears as seen in Figure A.19.

2. Highlight the All **P**rogram menu item that displays the list of programs comes up as in Figure A.19. Selection that has a pointer to the right of its name is a *Program group*. A Program group is a collection of Programs and related document files. When you choose a Program group, it opens a menu listing the items in the program group.

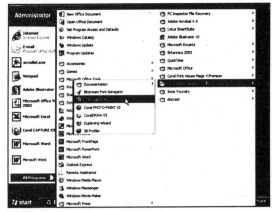

Figure A.19 The Start Menu With Program Item and Program Groups

3. From the Program menu item list, click the program you want to run. Or highlight the Program group that contains the program you want to run and click the desired program item.

THE SEARCH FEATURE

With the help of Search Companion of Windows XP, you can search for all types of objects, from pictures, music, and documents, to printers, computers, and people. You can search in your own computer, other computers that are connected to your computer using network, and the Internet. You can also choose to search with the help of an animated screen character. Search Companion also has an indexing service that maintains an index of all the files on your computer, making searches faster.

In Search Companion, you can specify several search criteria. For example, you can search files and folders by name, type, and size, file based on when you last worked on it or files containing specific text.

➡ To use the Search Feature do this:

1. Click the Start button and then click on **S**earch.

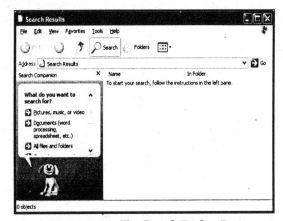

Figure A.20 The Search Dialog Box

2. The Search Result dialog box appears, as in Figure A.20. In the left pane of the window, click All files and folders link. Left pane will change and appears as seen in Figure A.21.

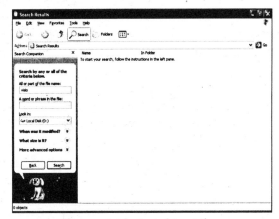

Figure A.21 Searching Files

3. Type the full file name or a part of it in All or part **of** the file name box of the file or folder, or type a word or phrase that is in the file.

In **L**ook in: drop down list, click the drive, folder, or network you want to search.

Click When was it modified? if you want to give.

Click What size is it? if you know.

Click More advanced options to specify additional search criteria.

4. Finally click on Sea**r**ch button to search.

FONT MANAGEMENT

How does Windows handle printers? When you print something from an application, a Windows *printer driver* (Printer Control Program) for the current printer formats the material to be printed to a form understood by the printer and sends it to printer and then the printer prints it.

You can have several printers installed on your system. Each such installed printer has a *printer driver* in the Windows *printers folder*. You can have different physical printers or different modes on the same printer. For example, some printers handle both Hewlett Packard's PCL (Printer Control Language) and the Adobe Postscript language. So you can have two printer drivers installed, one for PCL and one for Postscript but have one physical printer.

The *default printer* indicates that anything you print goes to the default printer unless you specifically tell your program to use a different printer. In the Printers folder, you can make any of your printer the default.

Windows also provides *spooling*. It means, that your PC stores document data on disk until the printer can accept it. When you print a document from an application, the information to be printed is stored temporarily in the *queue* (storage for print jobs)

until it can be printed. If you print a long document to a slow printer, spooling lets you continue working with your application while the printer works. ("spool" stands for Simultaneous Printer Operation On-Line).

Fonts

Modern computer screens and printers can display text in a variety of *typefaces* and *sizes*, as illustrated in Figure A.22.

- *Monospaced* typefaces—all the characters are the same width, like on a typewriter.

- *Proportionally spaced* typefaces—different characters are different widths like the typeface used in a book.

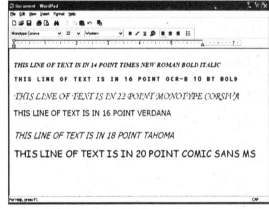

Figure A.22 Some of the Different types of Fonts Supported by Windows XP

Most typefaces are available in different *sizes*, with the *sizes* measured in printer's points, that is 1 inch equals 72 points. Commonly used sizes are 10-point and 12-point. Fonts are provided in several variations, such as normal, **bold,** *italic,* and ***bold-italic***.

Font and Typeface are commonly used interchangeably. Font refers to the set of all characters and numbers in a given size and normal. For example New Times Roman 10-point is a font and the typeface is New Times Roman.

Windows comes with a small set of fonts, but many programs and printer drivers include fonts of their own. Once a font is installed, any Window based program can use it.

TrueType Fonts

Computer printers and screens print and display characters by printing or displaying patterns of black and white dots. The size of the dots depends on the resolution of the device, ranging from 72 to 100 dots-per-inch on screens, from 300 to 1200 dots-per-inch on laser printers.

TrueType stores each typeface not as a set of bitmaps, but as a set of formulas the system can use to *render* (draw) each character at any desired size and resolution. This means that TrueType fonts look the same on all devices, and that can be used in any size.

Installing and using Fonts

Windows provides a simple way to install and use fonts.

➡ **To view the fonts installed on your system, do this:**

1. Open the folder C:\Windows\Fonts in a Folder window or alternatively in Control Panel Windows Click on Fonts Icon. The window as in Figure A.23 appears.

2. TrueType fonts have a T_T icon but older fonts have an A icon.

3. To install a new font click the File menu and choose Install New Font... . The Add fonts dialog box as in Figure A.24 appears.

In the Drives and Folder boxes, select the drive and folder where the files are located for the new font or fonts.

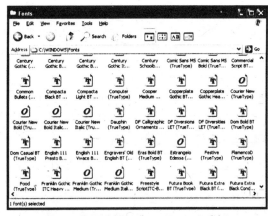

Figure A.23 Window Fonts Folder

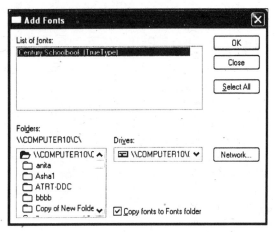

Figure A.24 Add Fonts Dialog Box

4. In the List Of Fonts box, select the font(s) you want to install.

5. Windows copies the fonts files into its font folder (C:\Windows\Fonts).

6. Click Ok, and Windows installs the fonts you want.

To delete a font or fonts, select the fonts you want to delete and click the File menu and choose Delete.

You choose a font in three steps.

1. The name of the font (the name of the typeface).

2. The style (regular, **bold**, *Italic*), and the point size.

3. True Type fonts are available in any size and style, and are identified by the T_T logo before the font name. Older fonts are available in only a few fixed sizes and styles.

DISPLAY PROPERTIES

The settings which are related with computer or desktop is the display properties. The display properties include wallpaper, screen saver, colour, font etc. The display properties can be set through Display Properties dialog box.

➡ **To show the display properties dialog box, do this:**

1. Click on the Start button then click on <u>C</u>ontrol Panel. In Control Panel window, double click on Display icon to open it. *Alternatively*, right click at an empty space on the desktop and then choose P<u>r</u>operties. This will show the Display Properties dialog box on the screen. (See Figure A.25)

Wallpaper

Wallpaper is the background pattern or picture against which desktop menus, icons and other elements are displayed and moved around. A wallpaper image can be in **jpeg** format or a **gif** format. A wallpaper image may be centered, stretched, or tiled.

➡ **To set the wallpaper on the desktop, do this:**

1. In Display Properties dialog box, select Desktop Tab to set wall paper. In Bac<u>k</u>ground: list, select the background from the list which you want to use. (See Figure A.26).

2. Click on the <u>B</u>rowse... button to select background from the different drives.

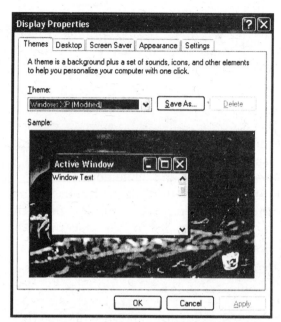

Figure A.25   Display Properties dialog box

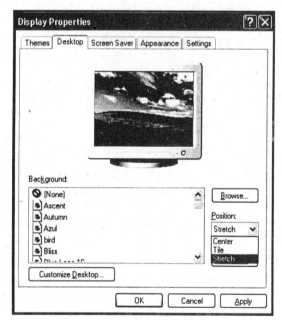

Figure A.26   Setting the wallpaper in Desktop

3. Select the position of the wallpaper from the <u>P</u>osition: drop down list.

4. Click on the <u>A</u>pply button to apply all the setting and then click OK to accept the changes and close the dialog box.

Screen Savers

Screen saver is an animated image that is activated on the PC monitor when user walks away from the computer and leaves the monitor on. The main purpose of the screen saver is to prevent the burning of an image into the phosphorus material inside the monitor.

➡ **To set the screen saver, do this:**

1. In Display Properties dialog box, select Screen Saver Tab. (See Figure A.27)

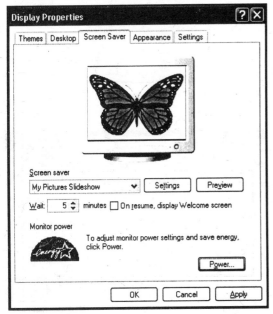

Figure A.27 Display properties with Screen Saver Tab

2. Select the desired screen saver from the drop down list from the <u>S</u>creen Saver group.

3. You can also set the time in <u>W</u>ait: section under the <u>S</u>creen Saver group.
   To see the preview of the selected screen saver click on the Pre<u>v</u>iew button.

4. To apply all the settings, click on the <u>A</u>pply button and then click on the OK button to close the dialog box.

☞ *In Windows XP, you can also use personal pictures as a screen saver. For this, you have to select My Pictures Slideshow from the list of pictures under Screen saver group.*

ClearType Font Setting

This is the very special feature of Windows XP. Setting ClearType for your screen improves font resolution, so your existing spreadsheets, word processing documents, and Web pages displayed on your computer screen look as smooth as the words on a page. ClearType is basically design for flat screen monitors, so it is ideal for portable computers and other flat screen monitors.

➡ **To set ClearType font, do this:**

1. In Display Properties dialog box, select Appearance Tab. (See Figure A.28)

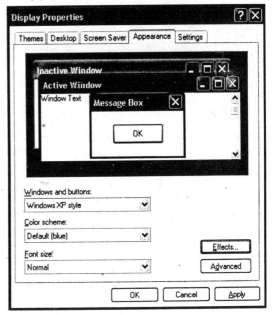

Figure A.28 Display properties with Appearance Tab

2. In this dialog box, click on <u>E</u>ffects... button.

3. In the Effects dialog box, select ClearType from Use the following method to smooth edges of screen fonts check box.

4. Then, click OK button and finally click the <u>A</u>pply button to apply all the settings and the click on the OK button to close the dialog box.

Cleanup Unused Desktop Icons

This feature is new in Windows XP. With the help of Desktop Cleanup Wizard you can remove shortcuts that you do not use from your desktop. The wizard automatically runs every 60 days, or you can start it yourself whenever you want.

➡ **To Remove unused desktop icons, do this:**

1. In Display Properties dialog box, select Desktop Tab. (See Figure A.29)

2. In this dialog box, click Customize <u>D</u>esktop... button.

3. A dialog box Desktop Items appears as seen in Figure A.29.

4. Under **Desktop cleanup** group, click <u>C</u>lean Desktop Now. Follow the directions in the Desktop Cleanup Wizard. The Desktop Cleanup Wizard displays a list of desktop icons that have not been used for 60 days or more, enabling you to remove those icons that you do not want on your desktop.

WINDOWS XP ACCESSORIES

Windows XP provides some utility software packages such as system tools, games, calculator, media player, paint brush etc. in the Accessories group.

➡ **To open the Windows Accessories, do this:**

1. Click on the Start button. Highlight

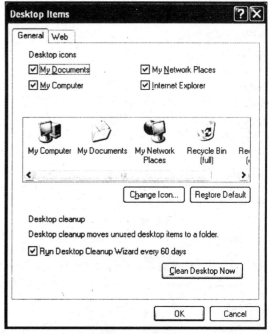

Figure A.29 Display properties with Desktop Items dialog box

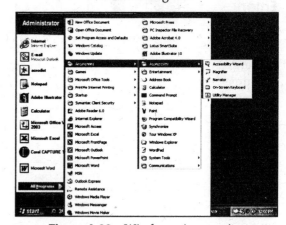

Figure A.30 Windows Accessories

the All <u>P</u>rogram menu and then choose Accessories. (See Figure A.30)

Accessibility

Accessibility Wizard

The Accessibility Wizard guides you to customize computer tools that are designed to help meet vision, hearing, or mobility needs.

Accessibility options (such as StickyKeys, ShowSounds, and Mousekeys) help users with disabilities to make full use of the computer. Some of the options, such as MouseKeys, may be of interest to all users. Once the Accessibility tools are set up, they can be accessed through Control Panel and the Accessibility menu.

Windows includes the following programs to enhance accessibility:

(a) *Magnifier* expands a portion of the screen for easier viewing.

(b) *Narrator* uses text-to-speech technology to read the contents of the screen aloud. This is useful for people who are blind.

(c) *On-Screen Keyboard* provides the ability to type on-screen using a pointing device (i.e. mouse).

(d) *Utility Manager* enables users to check an Accessibility program's status and start or stop an Accessibility program.

Entertainment

Entertainment tools such as Sound Recorder, Volume Control, Windows Media Player, etc. allow you to play audio, video, or animation files and to control the settings for multimedia hardware devices. To hear sound when you use Media Player, you must have a sound card, installed on your PC.

Recording Sounds with Sound Recorder

If you have a microphone attached to the sound card, you can use Sound Recorder available in Windows XP to make voice recordings, which can then be added to other documents. And if sound card has a *Line In Connector*, you can connect a stereo receiver or other sound source to it and use Sound Recorder to make recordings from that source.

➡ To make sound recording, do this:

1. To Open Sound Recorder, click Start, and then highlight All Programs, highlight Accessories, choose Entertainment, click Sound Recorder. The Sound Recorder window appears, as shown in Figure A.31.

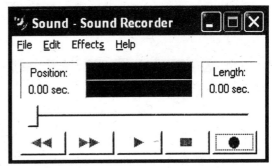

Figure A.31 Sound Recorder window

2. Choose Properties from the File menu. In the Properties dialog box that appears. Click Convert Now... button to display the Sound Selection dialog box.

   Choose the file format and attributes i.e. sampling rates you want. Higher sampling rates require more disk space but provides better quality of sound.

3. Click the Record button and start recording.

   As you record, the green line expands and contracts like in an oscilloscope to indicate sound levels. You can see how much time has elapsed. The maximum recording length is 60 seconds.

4. When you finish the recording, click the Stop button.

5. To save the recording as a files open the File menu, and choose Save and then name the file if you have not done so.

Sound Recorder saves its documents as *wave* files and gives them the filename extension as **.WAV**.

Controlling Sound Volume

The Volume Control Program allows you to control the loudness of your computer's various sound sources.

To open Volume Control by itself, click the Start button, and highlight All Programs, highlight Accessories, choose Entertainment, click Volume Control. The Volume Control window appears, as seen in Figure A.32.

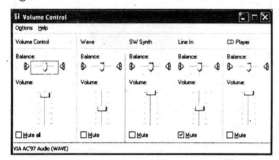

Figure A.32 Volume Control window

Windows Media Player

Windows Media Player is used to play any multimedia sound or video file.

➡ **To play a multimedia file using Windows Media Player, do this:**

1. Start Windows Media Player by clicking the Start button, and then highlight All Programs, highlight Accessories choose Entertainment, click Media Player. Media Player window appears, as shown in Figure A.33.

2. Open the File menu and choose Open and use the Open dialog box to open the file you want to play.

   If the file you open is a video clip, a window displaying the first frame of the video appears.

☞ *You can also open Media Player and open a media file by right-clicking that file's icon in a folder window and choosing Open.*

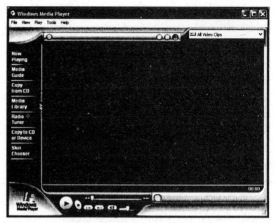

Figure A.33 Media Player

3. Click the Start button to begin playing the media file.

Address Book

Address Book provides a convenient place to store contact information for easy retrieval by programs such as Microsoft Outlook Express, Internet Explorer, NetMeeting, etc. You can search for people and businesses, create groups of contacts for mailing lists, and send and receive electronic business cards.

➡ **To open the address book, do this:**

1. Click on the Start button. Highlight the All Program menu and then choose Accessories, click on Address Book.

Address book provides following features:

(a) It stores important information about people.

(b) It find people by using Internet directory services.

(c) It can create groups of contacts for mailing lists.

(d) It can share your Address Book with other users.

(e) It sends and receives business cards.

Calculator

The calculator available in Windows XP is useful for doing calculations while you are working in any other window. The Calculator has two options, namely the standard calculator and scientific calculator. The Standard Calculator that does simple arithmetic, and a more complicated Scientific Calculator, that can be used by scientists, engineers and chartered accountants.

➡ **To use the Calculator, do this:**

1. Click Start button, Choose All **P**rograms, highlight Accessories, and then choose Calculator.
2. The Calculator program opens in Standard View. (See Figure A.34) To use the Scientific Calculator, open the **V**iew menu and choose **S**cientific.

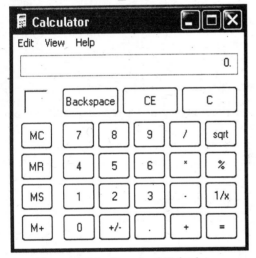

Figure A.34 Standard Calculator

The Standard Calculator (shown in Figure A.34) can be used to add, subtract, multiply and divide. You can also take square roots, calculate percentages and find multiplicative inverses.

The Scientific Calculator is considerably larger, more powerful, than the Standard Calculator. It has many functions that can be used for more advanced scientific calculations.

Notepad

The Notepad is also one of the products in Accessories group. It can be used for writing notes, e-mail messages, etc. It is useful for editing and storing all textual data.

Starting Notepad

➡ **To start Notepad, do this:**

1. Click the Start button, highlight **P**rograms menu item and choose Accessories and then choose Notepad. The Notepad window appears as in Figure A.35.

Figure A.35 Notepad

2. To open a new file in the Notepad, open the **F**ile menu and choose **N**ew.
3. To open an existing file, open the **F**ile menu and choose **O**pen... . In the open dialog box, that appears, specify the name and location of the file you want to open. Click **Open** button.
4. Notepad can open files with the extensions **.BAT, .SYS, .INI**, and **.TXT** as these files are all in ASCII code.

➡ **To close a Notepad file do this:**

1. Close the Notepad application.

2. To close the Notepad application, click the **File** menu and choose **Exit** or press Alt+F4 keys together.

Paint

Paint is a graphical program that can be used for drawing pictures. MS–Paint is a bit-mapped program. Its drawing consists of a series of pixels. The computer's screen is divided into very small dots called *pixels* (pels) that can be controlled by you.

☞ *A bit is similar to a light switch that can be either on or off so each dot on the screen can either be on or off. Thus a drawing is created by a matrix of dots or pixels that are on or off.*

Starting Paint

➡ To start the Paint program do this:

1. Click the Start button, highlight Programs choose Accessories and then choose Paint. Paint opens with a new file as seen in Figure A.36.

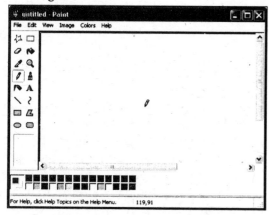

Figure A.36 The Paint Screen

Basics of Drawing Created in Paint

The general procedure for making a drawing in Paint is as follows:

1. *Select a drawing tool*: Each drawing tool is used for a particular kind of object. The toolbox on the left side of the screen has the drawing tools. To select a tool, click the tool you want to use. (See Figure A.36)

2. *Choose a line width from the line-size box*: Click the width you want to use.

3. *Choose a foreground colour*: Foreground colour is used for line borders of shapes and text.

   To choose a foreground colour, point to the appropriate box in the colour/pattern palette, and then *click the left mouse button.*

4. *Choose a background colour*: Background colour is used to fill the inside of enclosed shapes and background of text frames. It also appears where you use the eraser.

   To choose a background colour, use the mouse to point to the appropriate box in the palette, and then *click the right button of the mouse.*

WordPad

WordPad is a word processor inbuilt with Windows XP. It does not have word processing facilities as much as MS Word.

➡ To start WordPad do this:

1. Click the Start button highlight Programs menu item and choose Accessories and then choose WordPad.

2. The WordPad Opening Screen appears as in Figure A.37. Various elements of the WordPad screen are marked in this figure. With WordPad, you can open and edit a document.

☞ *WordPad does not offer many of the advanced features that you get in MS-Word. But it does offer many of the formatting tools that you need to create a letter, memo, etc.*

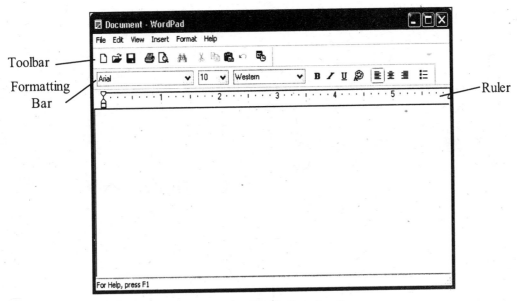

Figure A.37 WordPad's Opening Screen

Elements of WordPad Window

The WordPad window has the following elements as marked in Figure A.38 and explained in the following sections.

Toolbar—Wordpad's toolbar, contains buttons for issuing commonly used commands. To see what a particular button does, move your mouse pointer over the button. A short description appears just below the mouse pointer, and a more detailed description appears on the status bar.

Format bar—Like the toolbar, the format bar provides one-click access to formatting commands. Most of WordPad's formatting options are available on the format bar.

Ruler—The ruler provides an easy way to change tab and margin settings.

Opening and Saving Files with WordPad

With WordPad, you can open and edit a document.

➡ To Open a document in WordPad do this:

1. Open the File menu and choose Open or press Ctrl+O. The open dialog box appear as in Figure A.38.

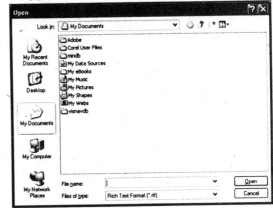

Figure A.38 WordPad's Open Dialog Box

2. In the open dialog box choose the name location and type of the document you want to open.

➡ To save a document do this:

1. To name a document or when saving it for the first time click the File menu and choose Save As... . The Save As dialog box appears as in Figure A.39. The Save As dialog box specify the name and location of the files.

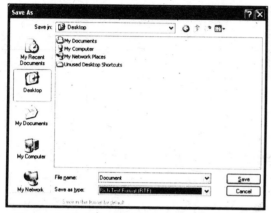

Figure A.39 WordPad's Save As dialog box

2. To Save an existing document, open the File menu and choose Save or click the save icon on the toolbar.

WordPad supports the following file formats in which you can save the file.

Format	Description
Rich Text Format	In the Rich Text Format (.rtf) formatting is retained but the files are much larger than .doc files.
Text Document	When you save a file in a plain text format (with extension .txt), you lose all formatting, but you retain all text in the ANSI character set a standard set of codes used for storing text.
Text Document — (MS-DOS Format)	In MS-DOS text format (with extension .txt), you lose all formatting, but you preserve all text in Microsoft's extended ASCII character set, which includes various accented characters.
Unicode Text Document	Unicode allows you to use characters from practically every language.

Printing the WordPad Document

➡ To print WordPad document do this:

Click the Print button, on the toolbar, or click File menu and choose Print, or press Ctrl+P. The Print dialog box appears as in Figure A.40, in which you can select the printer, the pages you want to print, and the number of copies.

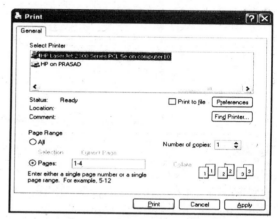

Figure A.40 WordPad's Print Dialog box

You can also preview the document before you print it.

➡ To preview your document, do this:

1. Click the Print Preview button, on the toolbar, or open the File menu and choose Print Preview.

2. The WordPad window shows approximately how the printed page will appear.

3. Click the Zoom In button to get a closer look. Click Print to begin printing, or click Close to return to the regular view of your document.

System Tools

System Tools option under Accessories, provides a set of tools for computer system management. It includes disk defragmenter, disk cleanup, backup, scheduling, etc.

Disk Defragmenter

Disk Defragmenter consolidates fragmented files and folders on your computer's hard disk, so that each file occupies a single, contiguous space on the volume. As a result, your system can gain access to your files and folders and save new ones more efficiently. By consolidating your files and folders, Disk Defragmenter also consolidates the volume's free space, making it less likely that new files will be fragmented.

➡ **To open Disk Defragmenter, do this:**

1. Click Start button, Choose All Programs, highlight Accessories, highlight System Tools, and then choose Disk Defragmenter. Disk Defragmenter will open up as shown in Figure A.41.

Figure A.41 Disk Defragmenter

To start defragmentation, click on the Defragment button.

Disk CleanUp

You can use Disk CleanUp to free up space on your hard disk by removing temporary Internet files, removing installed components and programs that you no longer use, and emptying the Recycle Bin.

➡ **To open Disk Cleanup, do this:**

1. Click Start button, Choose All Programs, highlight Accessories, highlight System Tools, and then choose Disk Cleanup.

2. Choose the drive which you want to clean and then click OK.

☞ *Disk Cleanup helps to free space on your hard drive. Disk Cleanup searches your drive, and then shows you temporary files, cache files, and unnecessary program files that you can safely delete. You can direct Disk Cleanup to delete some or all of those files.*

Task Scheduler

Task Scheduler is a tool that enables you to regulate tasks (such as Disk Defragmenter) to run regularly, when it is most convenient for you. Task Scheduler starts each time you start Windows and runs in the background.

➡ **To add scheduled task, do this:**

1. Click Start button, Choose All Programs, highlight Accessories, highlight System Tools, and then choose Scheduled Tasks. Scheduled Tasks window appears as seen in Figure A.42.

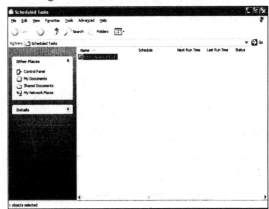

Figure A.42 Scheduled Tasks

2. To add a scheduled task double click the Add Scheduled Task icon and follow the instructions of Scheduled Task Wizard.

MY COMPUTER ICON

My Computer icon lets you browse through all the resources attached to your PC. When you click on My Computer icon, a window appears as shown in Figure A.43.

Computer's information is divided into three parts:

(a) **File Stored on this Computer:** Displays files and folders shared between the user of the computer.

(b) **Hard Disk Drives:** Displays the hard disk drives of the computer.

(c) **Devices with Removable Storage:** Displays floppy disk, CD-ROM, Zip drive, etc.

MY NETWORK PLACES

My Network Places is the gateway to all available network resources, just as My Computer is the gateway to all the resources stored on PC system. Launching My Network Places opens a Window of your immediate workgroup. (See Figure A.44)

FILE MANAGEMENT IN WINDOWS XP

Files and folders are two of the most fundamental concepts of the Windows operating system. You create and organize files and folders as soon as you save your work in a PC.

File

A file is any collection of related information that is given a name and stored on a disk so that it can be read and manipulated whenever required.

☞ *A file can contain any kind of information: a program or application or a document; a part of a document, such as a table or a graphic; a sound or a piece of music, etc.*

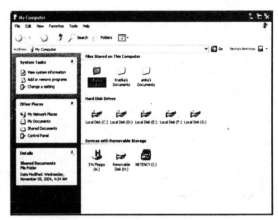

Figure A.43 My Computer window

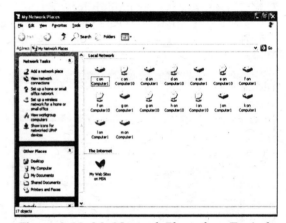

Figure A.44 My Network Places for a Typical small Local-Area Network

Folder

As you work in Windows you would see that a hard disk contains hundreds of files even before you start creating your own files. It would be impossible to keep track of all these files if they are not arranged properly. In Windows, the fundamental device for managing files is a *folder*.

☞ *A folder is a special kind of group of files that contains a list of other files or subfolders. The files on the list are said to be in the folder.*

A folder can be either open or closed. When it is closed, all you see is its name and the folder icon. When a folder is open, it has its own window, and the files contained in the folder are shown in the window.

The Folder Tree

The power of arranging the folder system lies in the fact that it is hierarchical.

☞ *Hierarchical means that folders can contain other folders. This feature allows you to organize and keep track of a large number of folders.*

If Folder *A* is *inside* Folder *B*, then Folder *A* is a *subfolder* of *B*. Any folder can contain as many subfolders as you want, but each sub-folder (like each file) is contained in only one folder. And so, a diagram showing which folders are contained in which other folders looks something like a family tree. This diagram is called the *folder tree*, or the *folder hierarchy*. Windows Help calls it the *folder list*.

At the top of the folder tree is the founder of the Folder family, namely the desktop. Next to the desktop are *My Computer*, etc. and additional files and folders that you might have copied to the desktop. Underneath My Computer are icons representing all of your system's storage media: *hard drives, floppy drives, CD-ROMs* etc.

Basic file and folder operations are the following:

*   Selecting
*   Creating
*   Naming
*   Opening

Selecting Files and Folders

Windows works on the rule, *select* and *do*. It means, you first have to select the file or folder you want to use. Files and folders are represented in Folder and Windows by icons, with the name of the file or folder printed underneath its icon.

➡ **To select all the items in a folder do this:**

*   Open a Folder. Click the **E**dit menu and choose Select **A**ll. Or press ⌨Ctrl+Ⓐ keys together on the keyboard.

Creating Files and Folders

➡ **To create a new File/Folder do this:**

1. In the Folder window click the **F**ile menu and choose Ne**w**. *Alternatively*, right click an empty area of the Desktop and choose Ne**w**.
2. In both the cases, a submenu lists the new objects you can create: *folders, shortcuts*, and a variety of types of files (See Figure A.45).

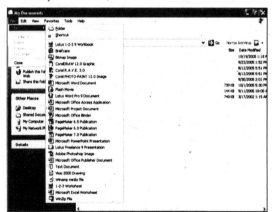

Figure A.45 Submenu Indicating the New Objects created

3. Select an element of the list. Windows XP creates the selected object.

Naming and Renaming Files and Folders

➡ **To rename a file or folder, do this:**

1. Select the file/folder you want to rename. Click the **F**ile menu and choose Rena**m**e. *Alternatively*, right click the file/folder and choose Rena**m**e from the context

menu or press F2 key. *Alternatively*, in the left task pane click Rename this file/folder.

2. A box appears around the current name, and the entire name is selected. Type the new name in the box and press Enter (See Figure A.46).

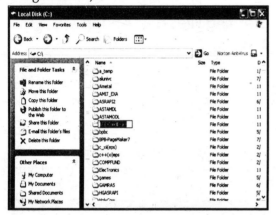

Figure A.46 Renaming a folder BPB-CorelDraw

To edit the old name instead of typing the new one, Click inside the name-box at the place where you want to begin typing or deleting.

Opening Files and Folders

Any object in a Windows Explorer or Folder window can be opened by single-clicking (*in Web style*) or double-clicking its icon (*in Classic style*).

Moving or Copying Folders and Files

Under File and Folder left task pane, click Move this file or Move this folder. After that In Move Items dialog box, click the new location for the file or folder, and then click Move. (See Figure A.47)

Deleting Files and Folders

➡ **To delete file(s) and folder(s) do this:**

1. Select the file or folder to be deleted.
2. Click this file or folder from left task pane.
3. Click **Yes** in the dialog box.

Alternatively, you can right click the objects and then choose **Delete** from the context menu. The dialog box as in step 2 above appears.

☞ *Objects deleted from your computer go to the Recycle Bin folder. You can recover them by double clicking the Recycle Bin folder, if desired.*

Figure A.47 Moving a folder

THE RECYCLE BIN

Files and folders deleted from your hard disk drives are not actually deleted but transferred to the *Recycle Bin*. The Recycle Bin icon appears on the desktop and looks like a waste paper basket. When you open the icon, a Recycle Bin window opens, displaying the files and folders that have been deleted since the Recycle Bin was last emptied. In effect, the Recycle Bin works like a folder.

Note the following for the Recycle Bin:

- Like a folder, it contains objects, and can be viewed in either a Folder window or a Windows Explorer window.

- Objects can be moved in and out of the

Recycle Bin, just as you do with any other folder.

- Unlike a folder, the Recycle Bin is not contained on a single drive. Each of your computer's hard disk drives maintains its own *Recycled folder*, and the contents of all of the Recycle folders are visible whenever you open the Recycle Bin.

- Folders that have been sent to the Recycle Bin are not considered part of the folder tree. Therefore, they do not appear in a Windows Explorer window's left-pane map and they cannot be opened. To examine the contents of a folder that is in the Recycle Bin, you must first move the folder to another location.

☞ *Files in the Recycle Bin cannot be opened, edited, or worked on. The Recycle Bin cannot be used as a workspace. You can only put things in the Recycle Bin or take things out and copy them in a separate location.*

Emptying the Recycle Bin

Deleting the old files clears useless files so that you do not confuse them with useful files. It reclaims the diskspace occupied by unwanted files. Once a file is in the Recycle Bin, you are not going to open it or work on it by mistake. But a file in the Recycle Bin still takes disk space. The space is reclaimed only by emptying the Recycle Bin.

➡ **To empty the Recycle Bin do this:**

1. Open the Recycle Bin from the desktop.
2. Open the File menu and Choose Empty Recycle Bin or in the left pane of the Recycle Bin Click Empty Recycle Bin. Dialog box appears as in Figure A.49 asking you to confirm your choice. (See Figure A.48)
3. Click **Yes**. Windows empties the Recycle Bin.
4. Close the Recycle Bin.

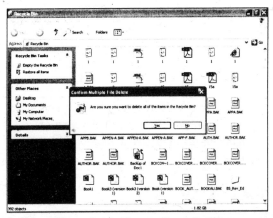

Figure A.48 Empty Recycle Bin

Alternatively, right-click the Recycle Bin and choose Empty Recycle Bin from the Shortcut menu.

☞ *Deleting objects from an ordinary folder on the hard disk transfers them to the Recycle bin and deleting files and folder from Recycle bin actually delete them from the hard disk.*

➡ **To delete selected objects from the Recycle Bin do this:**

1. Open the Recycle Bin.
2. Select the objects to be deleted.
3. Click the Delete button on the toolbar, or press the (Delete) key on the keyboard.
4. Dialog box appears, asking whether you really want to delete these objects. Click **Yes**.

Recovering Objects from the Recycle Bin

➡ **To recover an object from the Recycle Bin do this:**

1. Open the Recycle Bin.
2. Select the object(s) you want to recover.
3. Click the File menu and choose Restore. *Alternatively*, click Restore the selected items from the left task pane.

The object returns to the folder it was deleted from—the address given in the Original Location column of the Details view. If the object is a folder, all of its contents return with it.

☞ *You can use Restore even if the object was deleted from a folder that no longer exists. A folder of the appropriate name will be created to contain the restored object.*

Resizing the Recycle Bin

By default, the maximum size of the Recycle Bin on any hard disk is 10 percent of the size of the drive itself. For example, a 1 GB hard disk has a maximum Recycle Bin size of 100 MB. If you delete an object that causes the Recycle Bin to exceed this size, Windows XP warns you with an error message. But you can resize the Recycle Bin as per your working.

➡ **To resize the Recycle bin do this:**

1. Right-click the Recycle Bin icon on the desktop, and choose Properties from the context menu; or, select the Recycle Bin in Folder or Windows Explorer window and click the Properties button on the toolbar. The Properties dialog box appears as in Figure A.49.

2. The Properties dialog box contains a Global tab, and a tab for each hard disk on your system. To change the maximum size setting for all the hard drives at once, set the new maximum size of the Recycle Bin (as a percentage of total drive space) by moving the slider on the Global tab. Then click OK. Skip the remaining steps.

3. To reset the maximum Recycle Bin size for only a single drive, select the Configure Drives Independently using radio button on the Global tab.

4. Now click the tab showing the drive you want to change.

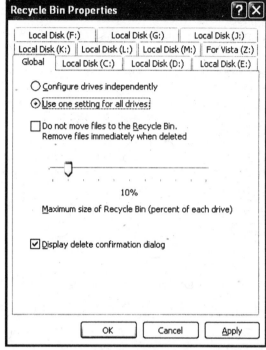

Figure A.49   Properties Dialog Box For Recycle Bin

5. Set the slider on that tab.
6. Click OK.

Bypassing the Recycle Bin

If you want to delete a file or a folder without sending it to the Recycle Bin press and hold down the (Shift) key when you select Delete. But there is no way in Windows to recover a deleted file that has bypassed the Recycle Bin.

☞ *If you have the Norton Utilities for Windows, you can use its Unerase program to recover deleted files that are not in the Recycle Bin. However, you must do this very quickly before another file overwrites the space occupied by the previous file.*

SHORTCUTS

A shortcut is a small file that is linked to a

program, document, folder, or an *Internet address.* The file is represented by an icon with an arrow in its lower left corner.

Shortcut is linked to a file or folder, that file or folder can be located anywhere—on a local hard disk or CD-ROM drive or on a floppy disk.

Creating a Shortcut

A shortcut can be created in the following two ways:
- by using cut and paste or
- by using the Create Shortcut wizard.

☞ *A shortcut is a pointer to an object, and not the object itself. This means that you can create and delete shortcuts without affecting the object it is linked to a file.*

➡ **To create a shortcut using copy and paste do this:**
1. Right click the items for which you want to create a shortcut.
2. From the context menu choose **Copy**.
3. Now right click on the desktop and choose **Paste** from the context menu.

➡ **To create a shortcut using the create shortcut wizard do this:**
1. Right-click the desktop, from the Context menu choose **New**, and then choose **S**hortcut.
2. Wizard for Create Shortcut appears, as seen in Figure A.50.
3. Click the B**r**owse... button. In the Browse for Folder dialog box, locate the item for which you want to create a shortcut.

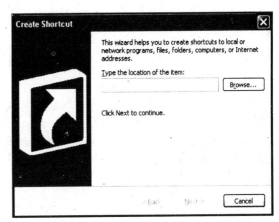

Figure A.50 Create Shortcut Wizard

4. Click **N**ext > type a name for your shortcut, click **Finish**, and your shortcut will appear.

Renaming a Shortcut

When you create a shortcut, Windows gives it a default name based on the underlying object.

➡ **To change the shortcut name do this:**
1. Right-click the shortcut.
2. From the context menu, choose **Rename**.
3. Type the name you want to use.

Deleting a Shortcut

➡ **To delete a shortcut do this:**
1. Select the icon and press the [Del] key. *Alternatively,* right click the shortcut to be deleted and choose **Delete** from the context menu.
2. Windows asks you for conformation before deletion.

Glossary

@ function A built-in formula that performs a specialized calculation.

Absolute cell address A cell address or range name in a formula that always refers to the same cell or range. To make a cell address absolute, prefix the row and column with a dollar sign ($); for example, $AX$2.

Access Key A key combination, such as Alt+F, that moves the focus to a menu, command, or control, without using the mouse. For example, to move the focus to a menu command, press Alt plus the designated character for the menu, and then press the designated character for the command. In contrast, a shortcut key is a function key or a key combination, such as F5 or Ctrl+A, that carries out a menu command.

Action The basic building block of a macro, a self-contained instruction that can be combined with other actions to automate tasks.

Action list A list of all actions you can use with a macro. The list appears when you click the arrow in the Action column of the Macro window.

Action Query A query that copies or changes data. Action queries include append, delete, make-table, and update queries. Append and make-table queries copy existing data; delete and update queries change existing data.

Action row A row in the upper part of the Macro window in which you enter macro names, actions, cor ditions, and comments associated with a particular macro or macro group.

Active area The part of the current worksheet into which you have entered data or have formatted cells. The active area starts at cell A1 and ends at the lowest and rightmost filled or formatted cell.

Active partition The disk partition from which your computer starts, usually the Primary DOS partition.

Active window The active window is the window that is currently accepting input from the keyboard and mouse. This window appears "on top" of other windows, hiding parts of other windows that overlap.

Add-in A Visual Basic procedure and any objects the procedure opens, which are stored in a database and can be added to or removed from the Microsoft Access user interface by using the Add-in Manager. Some add-ins, such as Microsoft Access wizards, are installed with Microsoft Access. You can also create your own add-ins or buy them from third-party vendors.

Add To Favorites Button Creates a shortcut to the selected file or folder, and then adds the shortcut to the Favorites folder. The original file or folder does not move.

Address Information that tells you and Windows 98 where to find a piece of information such as e-mail address; file address; I/O address; memory address; UNC address; URL.

Address book Windows 98 utility that is so designed that you can store names and addresses of your friends and clients, etc.

Address box Box appearing on the Address Bar toolbar in a Folder window or Windows Explorer window, in which the name of the open folder appears.

Address toolbar Toolbar that can appear in Folder windows and Windows Explorer, and includes only the Address box.

Address toolbar Toolbar that can appear on the Taskbar, containing a box in which you can type a URL to view a web page.

Alias Visual Basic. An alternate name you give to an external procedure to avoid conflict with a Visual Basic keyword, public variable, constant, or a name not allowed by the Visual Basic naming conventions.

Allocation The assigment of memory locations during the creation of graphical objects.

Anchored range A range in which one corner is fixed. You can adjust the other corner with the pointer-movement keys. To anchor a range, press the period key (.).

Application program Software designed for a specific purpose such as pay calculation, processing of examination results, stores accounting and inventory control, etc.

Application window One of the two main types of windows used by Windows; the other type is called a *document window*. An application window contains the application's menu bar and work area. An application window may contain multiple document windows.

Applications Specific uses for a program. With Word, for example, you can create letters, mailing lists, proposals, resume, timetables, etc.

Ascending order Database records or other worksheet data that can be sorted in either ascending or descending order. Ascending sorts labels in alphabetical order and values from lowest to highest.

ASCII File It is a document file in the universally recognized text *format* called ASCII (American Standard Code for Information Interchange). An ASCII file contains characters, spaces, punctuation, carriage return, and sometimes tabs and an end-of-file marker, but it contains no formatting information.

Attachment A file appended to an e-mail message for transport via the Internet or an on-line service. Any type or format of file can be attached to an e-mail message. Some organizational networks parse attached files from e-mail messages, sometimes unknown to the message recipient. Some networks impose a byte size limit on incoming message attachments, typically between 1-2 MB.

Attribute A characterstic (or property) of a disk file. Also used in DTP for the scharacteristic of a font.

Autoexec.BAT file A special-purpose batch file (set of commands) that is automatically carried out by the MS-DOS operating system whenever the computer is started or restarted.

Autoformat A collection of forms that determine the appearance of the controls and sections in a form or report. You can apply an autoformat to a form or report by clicking AutoFormat on the toolbar, or you can select an autoformat when you create a form or report with a wizard.

Automatic link A link from an Object Linking and Embedding (OLE) object in Microsoft Access to an OLE server that automatically updates the object in Microsoft Access when the information in the object file changes. In contrast, a manual link requires you to take action to update the object in Microsoft Access.

Automation A way to work with an application's objects from another application or development tool. Formerly called OLE Automation. Automation is an industry standard and a feature of the Component Object Model(COM).

Automation object An object supplied by a component that supports Automation. For example, the Microsoft Access application object is an Automation object. Automation objects may also be referred to as "ActiveX objects" or simply "objects"

AutoNumber data type A field data type that automatically stores a unique number for each record as it is added to a table. Three kinds of numbers can be generated: sequential (increment by 1), random, and Replication ID (used by the Replication Manager to ensure the integrity of data in replicated databases). Numbers generated by an AutoNumber field can not be deleted or modified.

Backup Alternate facilities of programs, data files, hardware equipments, etc., that are used in case the original one is destroyed, lost, or fails to operate.

Backup File A duplicate of another file, which you create for safekeeping. A specail kind of backup file, .bak, is automatically created by Word when you save the file you have been editing. You can not edit a .bak file.

Bandwidth The data handling capacity of any Internet or computer network connection. Bandwidth is measured at two levels:

1) kilobits per second (Kbps) and 2) meagbits per second (Mbps). Common low-end connection bandwidth are 14.4-56.6 Kbps; high bandwidth are between 1.5 Mbps and 45 Mbps.

Bar graph   A graph that shows numeric data as a series of vertical bars of different height evenly spaced along the x-axis. Each bar reflects the value of a single worksheet cell. The x-axis of a bar graph has labels that identify what each bar represents. The y-axis is scaled numerically, depending on the worksheet values being graphed.

Baud   A measurement (in bits per second) of the speeed with which information is transmitted between two computer devices, a computer and a printer, for example. If the transfer rate of a computer is 9,600 baud, 9,600 bits of information can be transmitted between the computer and the printer each second.

Baud rate   The speed of data transmission, usually in bits per second.

Binary   Belonging to a system of numbers having 2 as its base. A bit, which is binary digit, has a value of 0 or 1.

Bios (Basic Input Output System)   Bios is responsible for handling the details of input/output operations including the task of relating a program's logical records to a peripheral device physical records.

Bit   The smalletst, most basic unit of information recognized by a computer. Eight bits represent a single byte (which represents a character). Because computer work with binary logic, a bit can exist in one of two states: *on* or *off*. Thus, a bit is represented on a computer as either a zero (0) or a one (1). The term "bit" is a contraction of the terms "BInary" and "digiT".

Bit Mask   A value used with bit-wise operators (And, Eqv, Imp, Not, Or, and Xor) to test, set, or reset the state of individual bits in a bit-wise field value.

Bitmap   Graphics format in which a picture or character is stored as a grid of dots. Standard Windows bitmap files have the extension .bmp.

Bits-per-second (bps)   The average number of data bits transferred per second by an Internet connection. Bits are measured in units of thousands (kilobits per second, or Kbps) and millions (megabits per second, or Mbps).

Block   A group of related items (records, characters, etc.) handled as a unit during input and output. A section of program coding is treated as a unit.

Block   A portion of text ranging in length from one word to several pages. During editing, you mark blocks in order to move, copy, or delete text.

BMP file   Graphics file in bitmap format (a Windows standard format for graphics files) with the extensions **.bmp**.

Bookmark   A property of a Recordset object or a form that contains a binary string identifying the current record.

Bookmark   A method for recording, organizing, and retrieving the address (URLs) of Web pages in a Web browser. Some Web browsers call this feature *Favorites* or a *Hotlist*.

Boolean   An expression that can be evaluated either true (nonzero) or false (0). You can use the keywords True or False to supply the values of 1 and 0, respectively. The field data type Yes/No is Boolean and has the value of 1 for Yes and 0 for No. Several property sheet settings are Boolean, including Yes/No, True/False, and On/Off.

Boot   Bring the operating system into your computer's memory to begin its working. To reboot is to return the program that starts your operating system. A boot program is a short set of instructions used to load a larger program.

Boot disk or boot drive   Disk drive from which Windows loads on startup.

Boot record   The section on a disk that contains the minimum information MS-DOS needs to start the system.

Bootstrapping   When the computer is turned on or is rebooted from the keyboard with (Ctrl)+(Alt)+(Del) keys pressed together, it loads enough of its operating system into memory to get started; it pulls itself up by its bootstraps program.

Border   Any of the four sides of a window. The borders of most windows can be *dragged* inward or outward with the mouse to resize the window.

Bounced mail   An e-mail message that is returned to the sender after it fails to reach the intended recipient.

Bound column The column in a list box or combo box that is bound to the field specified by the control's ControlSource property.

Bound Control A control on a form or report that gets its contents from a field in the underlying table, query, or SQL statement. (The control's Control Source property is set to a field name in the table, query, or SQL statement). For example, a text box that displays an employee's last name is bound to the LastName field in the Employees table.

Bound object frame A control on a form or report used to display and manipulate. OLE objects that are stored in tables.

Break mode Temporary suspension of program execution while in the development environment. In break mode, you can examine, debug, reset, step through, or continue program execution. Break mode can be entered by encountering a breakpoint during program execution, pressing Ctrl + Break during program execution, encountering a Stop statement or untrapped run-time error during program execution.

Browse To look through files and directories. When using some dialog boxes, you can use the *Browse button* to view a list of files and directories and select the file you want.

Browser Software that interprets the markup of HTML files posted on the World Wide Web, formats them into Web pages, and displays them to the user. Some browsers can also open special programs to play sound or video files in Web documents if you have the necessary hardware.

Buffer An area in memory set aside to speed up the transfer of data, allowing blocks of data to be transferred at one time.

Build Button A button on a toolbar, property sheet, or dialog box that you can click to start a builder that helps you perform a task, such as creating an expression or an event procedure.

Built-in toolbar A toolbar that is part of Microsoft Access when it is installed on your computer. In contrast, a custom toolbar is one you create for your own application.

Byte data type A data type used to hold small positive integers ranging from 0 to 255.

Cache Area on disk (usually a folder) for the temporary storage of information. Browsers store recently viewed web pages in a cache, in case you want to see them again. Windows also maintains caches for CD-ROMs and removable disks.

Cache memory A small buffer storage, smaller and faster than main storage (often made of Static RAM), that is used to hold a copy of instructions and data in main storage that are likely to be needed next by the processor and that have been obtained automatically from main storage such as hard disk. It is used to increase the speed of processing by making current programs and data available to the CPU at a rapid rate.

Calculated control A control on a form or report that displays the result of an expression rather than stored data. The value is recalculated each time a value in the expression changes.

Calculated field A field defined in a query that displays the result of an expression rather than stored data. The value is recalculated each time a value in the expression changes.

Cell The intersection of a column and a row in an Excel worksheet. The cell is the basic unit of a worksheet.

Cell address A cell's location in the grid of worksheet/column/row intersections. The cell address consists of the worksheet letter, a colon, and the column letter plus the row number.

Cell pointer The highlighted rectangle in the worksheet display area that marks the current cell. You can move the cell pointer with arrow keys and a number of other keys on the keyboard.

Character A single digit, letter, punctuation mark, space, or other symbol which the computer can read or write.

Character string Any group of contiguous characters (letters, numbers, punctuation marks, special symbols, etc.) enclosed in quotation marks and used in formulas and macros.

Chart A graphical representation of data in a form or report. (In previous versions of Microsoft Access, charts were referred to as graphs).

Chat Room Group of people communicating together using Internet Relay Chat or another online chat system.

Check box   Box onscreen that can either be blank or contain a check mark (or ×,) usually appearing in a dialog box. FrontPage Express comes with form templates to put check boxes on web page forms. Also, a control that indicates whether an option is selected. A check mark appears in the box when the option is selected.

Client   A computer on a network that requests data or files from a server computer. Also, any network or Internet-specific software application residing on a client PC that communicates with a server.

Clipboard   The name given to the memory area assigned to temporary storage duties for information transfer between applications. It is the temporary storage space in memory for storing cut-and-paste information.

Clipboard file   File saved by Clipboard Viewer, with the extension .clp.

Close button   Button in the upper-right corner of a window. Clicking this button closes the window and (possibly) exits the program.

Collating sequence   The collating sequence determines how labels are sorted (numbers before letters, letters before numbers, or by character value). By default, Excel sorts numbers before letters; you can choose a *different* collating sequence when you run Install for Excel.

Collection   An object that contains a set of related objects. An object's position in the collection can change whenever a change occurs in the collection; therefore, the position of any specific object in a collection may vary.

Column   The visual representation of a field in a datasheet, the query design grid, or the filter design grid. In a datasheet, a column is a vertical stack showing the value of a field in every record. In the query and filter design grids, a column is a vertical stack of information, such as the field name and the sort order, about each of the fields included in the query or filter.

Column selector   A horizontal bar at the top of a column that you click to select an entire column in the query design grid or the filter design grid.

combo box   A control that is like a list box and a text box combined. In a combo box, you can type a value or click the arrow so that you can click an item in the list that drops down.

Comma format   A global or a local format that adds commas to numbers larger than 999 and places negative values in parentheses.

Command   An instruction transmitted to your computer when you press specified keys.

Command bar   In Microsoft Access, toolbars, shortcut menus, and menu bars and their menus have been combined into a single new functionality, called "toolbars" in the user interface, and "command bars" in Visual Basic. Command bars can be one of three types: menu bar, toolbar, or pop-up menu. Each type can include built-in and custom commands. The menu bar type replaces the existing menu bars. The toolbar type replaces the existing toolbars. The pop-up menu type replaces the existing drop-down menus or menu bars (such as the Edit menu) and the existing shortcut (right-click) menus.

Command button   Button that you can click to perform a command. A control that runs a macro, calls a Visual Basic function, or runs an event procedure. This is sometimes called a push button in other applications.

Command line   The string of characters used to start an application. For example, you enter a command line when you start Microsoft Access by clicking the Windows Start button and then clicking Run.

Command Prompt Only mode   Windows startup mode in which Windows loads all drivers, but starts an MS-DOS command prompt, not the full Windows system. Also called MS-DOS mode.

Commands and Settings button   A button in the File Open dialog box that displays commands that you can use to specify how to list and search for files.

Comparison operator   An operator used to compare two values or expression—for example, < (less than), > (greater than), and = (equal to).

Compile time   The time during which Visual Basic prepares code for execution. Modules automatically compile before they run.

Compound control   A control and an attached label; for example, a text box with an attached label.

Compound logical operator The logical operators #NOT#, #OR#, and #AND#. The operator #NOT# negates a logical expression; #OR# and #AND# join two logical expressions.

Compressed pitch A printing mode in which characters print smaller than standard characters.

Compression ratio A multiplicative factor that estimates how much file space can be squeezed onto a physical disk drive using the compression technology of the DBLSPACE facility in DOS 6 and Dos 6.2.

Condition Part of the criteria that a field must meet for searching or filtering. Some conditions are complete when used with a field; for example, the field sent with the condition yesterday. Other conditions must be used with a field and a value, for example, the field Author with the condition equals with the value Jane. Author equals, by itself, would be incomplete.

Conditional Expression An expression that Microsoft Access evaluates and compares to a specific value—for example, If... then and Select Case statements. If the condition is met, one or more operations are carried out. If the condition is not met, Microsoft Access skips the operations associated with the expression and moves to the next expression. You can use conditional expression in macros and Visual Basic code.

CONFIG.SYS A special text file that controls certain aspects of operating-system behaviour in MS-DOS and OS/2. Commands in the CONFIG.SYS file enable or disable system features, set limits on resources (for example, the maximum number of open files), and extend the operating system by loading device drivers that control hardware specific to an individual computer system.

Configuration An initial set of system values, such as the number of buffers DOS will use, the number of simultaneously open files it will allow, and specific devices that will be supported.

Connection string A string expression used to open an external database.

Console The combination of your system's monitor and keyboard.

Constant A representation of a numeric or string value that does not change. True, False, and Null are constants. You can use constants in expressions in tables, queries, forms, reports, and macros. In a Visual Basic module, you can use the *Const* statement to declare your own constants. A constant may be a string or numeric literal, another constant, or any combination that includes arithmetic or logical operators. Microsoft Access also provides intrinsic constants that supply fixed values for action arguments and function values (such as the values returned by the Var Type function). These constants can be viewed in the Object Browser.

Continuous form A form that displays more than one record on the screen in Form view. You can create a continuous form by setting a form's Default View property to Continuous Forms.

Control A graphical object, such as a text box, a check box, a command button, or a rectangle, that you place on a form or report in Design view to display data, perform an action, or make the form or report easier to read.

Control codes ASCII codes (from 0 to 31) that do not display a character but perform a function, such as beeping or deleting a character.

Control commands Commands issued to the computer when you press a key (or keys) while holding down the control key.

Control Key Ctrl A key, often represented by the caret symbol (^), used with other keys to command the computer to perform specific functions.

Control Menu The menu in the upper-left corner of an application or a window. It contains commands to move, resize, and close the application or window and is designated by an icon rather than by a menu name.

Control Panel The top three lines of the Excel display area. The control panel is where you enter data and give commands to Excel. It also displays information about the current cell and displays indicators that reflect what Excel is doing at any given moment. Also, Windows that displays icons for a number of programs that let you control your computer, Windows 98, and the software you have installed.

Conventional memory Physical memory located below the 640K addressing limit of MS-DOS.

Country code Part of the Internet's Domain Name System (DNS), country codes are two-letter codes appended to domain extensions that indicate the nation in which an Internet server—or, in the case of e-mail addresses, an individual—resides.

Criteria A set of limiting conditions, such as = "Denmark" (meaning equal to Denmark) or > = 30000, used in creating an query or filter to show a specific set of records.

Criteria range The criteria range contains selection criteria that tell Excel which records in the input range to search for during a database query. The criteria range must contain exact copies of the field names from the input range.

Currency data type A data type that is useful for calculations involving money or for fixed-point calculations in which accuracy is extremely important. This data type is used to store numbers with up to 15 digits to the left of the decimal point and 4 digits to the right.

Current directory The directory in which file operations initiated from a command prompt or a Run line will be carried out unless another directory is specified.

Current record The record in a record set that you modify or retrieve data from. Only one record in a record set can be the current record; however, a record set may have no current record.

Cursor The underscore character (_) that shows the position of the next character to be typed when you are entering data or editing an entry in the control panel. In READY and POINT modes, the cursor appears in the current cell.

Custom dialog box A modal pop-up form you create to ask the user for additional information or to display a message.

Custom properties dialog box A custom property sheet that allows users to set properties for an ActiveX control.

Custom toolbar A toolbar that you create for your application. In contrast, a built-in toolbar is part of Microsoft Access when it is installed on your computer.

Data Information stored or processed by the computer.

Data-definition query An SQL-specific query that can create, alter, or delete a table, or create or delete an index.

Data disk A disk that contains only data; no room has been reserved for system files.

Data file A group of related pieces of information, called records, stored together on a disk. A record consisting of a mailing list. For example, a record might contain all the information about a single addressee. One field within that record might contain the name, another the street address, another the city, etc.

Data label Values or words that appear next to above, or below the data points on a graph.

Data range The range of cells containing the data records to be sorted or graphed.

Data type The attribute of a variable or field that determines what kind of data it can hold. For example, the Text and Memo field data types allow the field to store either text or numbers, but the Number data type will allow only numbers to be stored in the field. Number data type fields store numerical data that will be used in mathematical calculations.

Database A collection of data and objects related to a particular topic or purpose. A database can contain tables, queries, forms, reports, macros, and modules.

Database objects Tables, queries, forms, reports, macros, and modules.

Database replication The process of reproducing a database so that two or more copies (replicas) of the same database can stay synchronized. Changes to the data in a replicated table in one replica are sent and applied to the other replicas.

Database table A collection of related data arranged in rows and columns in a worksheet. An Excel database table consists of fields and records; fields are arranged in columns and records in rows.

Database window The window that appears when you open a Microsoft Access database. It contains Tables, Queries, Forms, Reports, Macros, and Modules tabs that you can click to display a list of all objects of that type in the database.

Datasheet Data from a table displayed in a row-and-column format.

Datasheet view A window that displays data from a table, form, or query in a row and column format. In Datasheet view, you can edit fields, add and delete data and search for data.

Date data type A data type used to hold date and time information.

Default A pre-set value or condition in a program, which you can change or allow to stand.

Default print settings The print settings Windows uses unless you tell it to use different settings.

Defragmentation Rearranging the location of files stored on a disk into contiguous clusters in order to make the data in those files more quickly retrievable.

Delimiter In data files, special characters, such as comma or space, used to separate values or data entries.

Design grid The grid that you use to design a query or filter in query Design view or in the Advanced Filter/Sort window. For queries, this grid was formally known as the QBE grid.

Design view A window that shows the design of a table, query, form, report, macro, or module. In Design view, you can create a new database objects and modify the design of existing ones.

Design view—forms To open a form in Design view, go to the Database window, click the Forms tab, click the form you want to open, and then click Design. If the form is already open, you can switch to Design view by clicking View on the toolbar.

Design view—queries To open a query in Design view, go to the Database window, click the Queries tab, click the query you want to open, and then click Design. If the query is already open, you can switch to Design view by clicking View on the toolbar.

Design view—reports To open a report in Design view, go to the Database window, click the reports tab, click the query you want to open, and then click Design. If the report is already open, you can switch to Design view by clicking View on the toolbar.

Design view—tables To open a table in Design view, go to the Database window, click the Tables tab, click the table you want to open, and then click Design. If the table is already open, you can switch to Design view by clicking View on the toolbar.

Desktop toolbar Toolbar that can appear on the Taskbar, containing a button for each icon on the desktop.

Destination General term for the name of the element you go to from a hyperlink.

Detail section (forms) Displays records from the form's record source. This section usually contains controls bound to the fields in the record source but can also contain unbound controls, such as labels that identify a field's contents.

Detail section (reports) Use to contain the main body of the report. To place controls in the detail section, use the field list or the toolbox. To hide the detail section (for example, to create a summary report).

Device driver A special program that must be loaded at the time of booting to use that device.

Dial-up Connection A method for connecting to the Internet via a modem over analog or digital phone lines. Internet Service Providers (ISPs) provide dial-up accounts, which are economical, but substantially slower than direct connections. Dial-up connections are prone to line noise and abrupt interruptions.

Dialog box Special kind of window that allows you to change settings or give commands in a program. Most dialog boxes include OK and Cancel command buttons.

Direct connection A method for establishing an Internet connection without a modem, usually over a high-speed, fiber-optic connection. Direct connections are substantially faster and more reliable than dial-up connections, but they are also much more expensive to install and operate. Direct connections do not involve a dial-up process.

Direct Memory Access (DMA) Very fast tranfer of data between commputer memory and a peripheral device (e.g., a disk drive) using a dedicated high-speed I/O channel.

Directory An onscreen list of the file names on your disk.

Directory tree A graphic depiction of the directories and subdirectories that represent the organization of files on a disk.

Disable control A control that appears dimmed on a form, can not be tabbed to, and would not respond to typing or clicking. You disable a control by setting its Enabled property to No.

Disk optimizer A program (such as DEFRAG.EXE in DOS 6) that rearranges the location of files stored on a disk in order to make the data in those files quickly retrievable.

Display adapter An add-in hardware board that sends video output signals to your monitor corresponding to the current contents of video memory.

Document window A window inside an application window. Each document window contains a single document or other data file. In some applications, there can be more than one document window inside an application window. Document windows are also called child windows.

Domain extension The three character suffix appended to an Internet serverd domain name under the Doamin Name System. There are six domain extensions: COM (Commerical organization), NET (network services provider), EDU (educational organization), GOV (government agency or branch), MIL (military organization), and ORG (non-profit organization).

Domain name The official address of an organization or individual on the Internet. Domain names, along with the other elements of the Domain Name System, allow client computers to reference, locate, and communicate with Internet servers.

Domain Name System (DNS) The computer naming and addressing convention of the Internet devised in the early 1970s. The DNS provides a user-friendly method of allowing client computers to access server computers by specifying a domain name, such as `www.domain.com`. Without a domain name, you must know the equivalent numerical IP address, such as 198.115.182.23, for the server computer.

DOS memory Some items used to refer to the first 64K of conventional memory that is used by typical DOS applications.

Download The transfer of data or files from a server computer to a client computer via a network.

Drag To drag an object means to position the *mouse pointer* on the object, then press and hold the active mouse button, then move the mouse to a new position, and release the mouse button.

Drag-and-drop Method of moving or copying information from one file to anther, or to another location in the same file.

Drop-down list box A *list box* that is designed to open, much like a *drop-down menu*. In a *dialog box*, a drop-down list box appears as a single line of text with a downward-pointing arrow to its right. When you *click* the arrow, the list opens.

Drop-down menu Menu that appears when you click a command on a menu bar. FrontPage Express comes with form templates to put drop-down menus on web page forms.

DSL (Digital Subscriber Line) Refers collectively to all flavors of Digital Subscriber Line, a type of high-speed (multi-megabit per second) connection to the Internet that operates over standard copper phone lines. DSL connections are available as both symmetric and asymmetric connections. The problem with DSL is that it requires your home or office to be within a specific distance of your local telephone compnay switching station (typically less than 20,000 feet).

Dynamic data exchange An established protocol for exchanging data between windows-based applications.

E-mail (electronic mail) A messaging service of the Internet. Although e-mail currently supports only text messages, any type of file can be appended to and sent along with an e-mail message.

Empty The state of an uninitialized variant variable. Variants that are Empty return a Var Type of 0. Empty is not the same as Null, which is a variable state indicating invalid data. Variables containing zero-length strings ("") are not Empty, nor are numeric variables having a value of 0.

Enabled database A database created with a previous version of Microsoft Access that has been opened in Microsoft Access 97 without converting its format. To change the design of objects in an enabled database, you must open it in the version of Access in which it was originally created.

Error Message A statement that appears on your screen when your computer is unable to continue processing. The message tells you what the problem is and how to solve it.

Event An action recognized by an object, such as a mouse click or key press, for which you can define a response. An event can be caused by a user action or a Visual Basic statement, or it can be triggered by the system. Using properties associated with events, you can tell Microsoft Access to run a macro, call a Visual Basic function, or run an event procedure in response to an event.

Event procedure A procedure automatically executed in response to an event initiated by the user or program code, or triggered by the system.

Excutable file Any "runnable" application program with a file extension of . COM, .EXE, or .BAT. The term is sometimes extended to include files that don't run by themselves but do contain program code, such as .OVL and .PIF files.

Explode To separate and lift out one or more slices of a pie chart for emphasis.

Explorer bar Left pane of a Windows Explorer window, usually displaying a folder tree.

Exploring window Window displayed by the Windows Explorer program.

Expression Builder A Microsoft Access tool you can use to create an expression. It is available by clicking the Build button wherever you want to create an expression (for example, in many property boxes, in the Field or Criteria rows in query Design view, or in a Module window). The Expression Builder includes a list of common expression that you can select.

Extended DOS partion A hard-disk DOS partion, beyond the first hard disk drive C:, which can be divided into further logical disk drives (D:, E:, and so on).

Extended memory manager Any device driver (e.g., HIMEM.SYS) that manages and facilitates the use of extended physical memory.

Extension The one to three characters after the period following the base name in a file specification.

External Database A database other than the one that is currently open. An external database can be used as the source of a table to be imported or linked, or as the destination for a table to be exported from the current database. An external database can also be the destination for a table that is the result of a make-table query based on a pass-through query.

External table A table outside the open Microsoft Access database.

Field Categories in a database record. For example, in a phone book record, the fields would be name, address, and phone number. In an Excel database table, fields are labeled columns.

Field data types The set of data types you can choose from for a field in a Microsoft Access table. Microsoft Access has nine field data types: Auto-Number, Currency, Date/Time, Hyperlink, Memo, Number, OLE Object, Text, and Yes/No.

Field selector A small box o bar that you click to select an entire column in a datasheet.

Folder Special kind of file that contains a list of other files. Folders can contain other folders.

Folder Icon Icon that represents a folder.

Folder Options Command on the Start Settings menu that helps you configure your desktop, Folder windows, and Windows Explorer windows.

Folder tree Diagram showing which folders are contained in which other folders. Also called a *folder hierarchy or folder* list.

Folder window Window displaying the contents of a folder. The My Computer icon on the desktop displays a Folder window when opened.

Font All the characters in a typeface of a given size and style.

Font set A collection of font sizes for one font customized for a particular display and printer. Font sets determine what text looks like on the screen and when printed.

Footer One or more identifying lines printed at the bottom of a page. A footer might be printed on the first page, all pages, every even page, or every odd page, and it might be centered or aligned with the left or the right margin.

Formatting For documents, the elements of style and presentation that are added through the use of margins, indents, and different sizes, and styles of type. Formatting, especially in word processing, is intrinsic to a document in the sense that a certain appearance is, by default, built into the margins, spacing, and typeface of every document.

Formula A mathematical expression that performs calculations on values in the worksheet. Formulas can contain numbers and arithmetic operators, as well as cell addresses, range names, and @functions.

Front-end/back-end application An application consisting of two database files. The "back-end" database file contains the tables. The "front-end" database file contains all other database objects (queries, forms, reports, macros, and modules) and links to the tables in the back-end database. Typically the back-end database is located on a network server, and copies of the front-end database are installed on individual users computers.

FTP Full form as File Transfer Protocol. It is Internet service that provides a directory-based text interface for accessing tens of millions of files of all formats stored on hundreds of thousands of FTP servers worldwide. An FTP server can be accessed via either dedicated FTP software or a Web browser. A dedicated FTP application is required for uploading files. When using a Web browser, the FTP address must be preceded by `ftp://`.

Function procedure A procedure that returns a value and that can be used in an expression. You declare a function with the Function statement and end it with the End function statement.

Global menu bar A special custom menu bar that replaces the built-in menu bar in all windows in your application, except where you have specified a custom menu bar for a form or report.

Global shortcut menu A special custom shortcut menu that replaces the built-in shortcut menu for the following objects; fields in table and query-datasheets; forms and form controls in Form view, Datasheet view, and Print Preview; and reports in Print Preview. If you have specified a custom shortcut menu for a form, form control, or report, that custom shortcut menu is displayed instead of the global shortcut menu.

Globally unique identifier (GUID) A 16-byte field used to establish a unique identifier for replication. GUIDs are used extensively to identify replicas, replica sets, tables, records and other objects.

graph A visual way to present data. A graph can often illustrate trends and projections more clearly and effectively than worksheet numbers.

graph file A file in which you store a graph for use outside of Excel. The graph file can then be printed or edited by other software programs, such as MS-Word or Lotus Freelance Plus. Graph files cannot be retrieved or printed from within Excel.

Graph window A part of the worksheet display that shows the current graph. You establish a graph window by moving the cell pointer to the column at which you want the window to start.

Group account A collection of user accounts in a workgroup, identified by group name and personal ID (PID). Permissions assigned to a group apply to all users in the group.

Group footer Used to place information, such as a group name or group total, at the end of a group of records. To create a group footer, click Sorting and Grouping on the view menu, select a field or expression, and set the GroupFooter property to Yes.

Group level The depth at which a group in a report is nested inside other groups. Groups are nested when a set of records is grouped by more than one field or expression. The first field you sort or group on is level 0, and as many as 10 group levels are possible. In other database products, group levels are sometimes referred to as break levels.

Header A line of text that Excel prints below the top margin of each page. Also, header is a hypertext or hypermedia navigational anchor within a Web page that can be either 1) a text block, 2) an image, or 3) multiple anchors within a single image (image map).

Help file · A file of textual inforation containing helpful explanations of commands, modes, and other on screen tutorial information.

Hidden attribute A bit in a file specification used to indicate whether the file in question is to be hidden from view and from all commands that search the DOS directory table.

High-low-close-open (HLCO) graph A graph that plots up to four data points as a series of vertical lines. HLCO graphs are typically used to track the performance of a stock equity over time. They plot the high, low, closing, ad opening prices of the stock. They are also called stock market graphs.

Highlight Emphasize, a character, word, or block of text by making it either brighter or dimmer than the surrounding text.

HIMEM.SYS The extended memory (XMS) manager used by both DOS and Windows.

Hyperlink data type A field data type you use for fields that will store hyperlinks. Hyperlink fields contain text or combinations of text and numbers stored as text that are used as a hyperlink address. A hyperlink address can have up to three parts (each part can contain up to 2048 characters) and uses the syntax.

Hypermedia The fusion of hypertext and multi-media. Hypermedia is available in the form of audio, video, animation, and special image and multimedia data types on the World Wide Web. Hypermeida information is located, downloaded, and consumed in the technical framework of the Web's hypertext navigation system, which includes Web browsers and the HTTP transfer protocol.

Hypertext A system of organizing and navigating information used on the World Wide Web. Hyper-text information is organized into an interconnected web of linked text and image. Hypertext documents (called web pages) contain navigational anchors (commonly called hyperlinks) that allow you to naviage to another part of the same document or to a different hypertext document. You activate a link by clicking with a mouse. Web pages are created using the HyperText Markup Language (HTML).

Hyphen Help A MS-Word feature that finds places where hyphenation would improve the appearance of your text. You decide whether to hyphenate that word or not.

Index A Microsoft Access feature that speeds up searching and sorting in a table. The primary key of a table is automatically indexed. Fields whose data type is Memo, Hyperlink, or OLE Object can not be indexed.

Indexes window A window in which you can view or edit a table's indexes, or create multiple-field indexes.

Input/Output Input refers to any information coming into the computer. Output refers to processed information going out of a computer.

Input range The range Excel searches when it is performing a **Data Query** command. The input range must include the field names of the database tables being searched as well as the data records themselves.

Integer data type A fundamental data type that holds integers. An Integer variable is stored as a 16-bit (2-byte) number ranging in value from -32,768 to 32,767. The type-declaration character is % (ANSI character 37).

Internal command One of the following memory-resident commands that are part of the DOS COMMAND.COM file:

BREAK,	ERASE,	SET,
CALL,	EXIT,FOR,	SHIFT,
CD,	GOTO,	TIME,
CHCP,	IF,	TYPE,
CHDIR,	LH	VER,
CLS,	LOADHIGH,	VERIFY,
COPY,CTTY,	MD,	VOL, and
DATA,	MKDIR,	REN,
DEL,	PATH,	RENAME,
DIR,	PAUSE,	RMDIR,
ECHO,	PROMPT,	REM,

Internet A worldwide network of thousands of smaller computer networks and millions of commercial, educational, government, and personal computers. The internet is like an electronic city with virtual libraries, storefronts, business offices, art galleries, and so on.

Internet Service Provider (ISP) An organization that maintains a gateway to the Internet by leasing a high bandwidth, dedicated, and persistent connection to an Internet backbone. Commercial ISPs sub-lease low, mid, and high bandwidth access to the Internet to individuals and organizations.

Intranet A network within an organization that uses Internet technologies (such as the HTTP or FTP protocols). You can use an intranet to move between objects, documents, pages, and other destinations using hyperlinks.

Intrinsic constant A constant supplied by Micro-soft Access, Visual Basic for Applications. These constants are available in the Object Browser by clicking <globals> in each of these libraries.

IP Address   Also known as an Internet Protocol address, the numeric address, such as 163.142.84.6, of a computer on the Internet. This numeric address is equivalent to the domain name, such as domain.com or domain.edu. Internet domain name servers translate domain names to IP addresses.

ISDN (Integrated Services Digital Network)   A type of Internet connection that can be obtained as either a dial-up or direct connection. ISDN offers faster transmission speeds (between 64 Kbps and 128 Kbps) than conventional analog dial-up modems. ISDN is a digital connection, requiring a special digital modem and phone line.

Justification   The alignment of text within given margins. The left margin is justified as you enter your text. Word wrap justifies the right margin by adding small spaces between words.

Label   Any cell that begins with a letter or a label-prefix character is a label.

Legend   Legends explain the patterns, symbols, and colors used to identify the **A** through **F** data ranges on a graph. The legends and patterns, symbols, and colors appear beneath the graph.

Line/Border width button   Changes the width of the selected control's border.

Line graph   A graph that represents worksheet values as a continuous line, a sequence of symbols, or both. Line graphs are generally used to show one or more values changing over time. The x-axis defines a specific period of time; the y-axis is a numbered scale.

Link(OLE/DDE)   A connection between an OLE object and its OLE server, or between a dynamic data exchange (DDE) source document and a destination document.

Link (tables)   To establish a connection to data from another application so that you can view and edit the data in both the original application and in Microsoft Access. You can also link tables from other Microsoft Access databases so you can use them without opening the other database. In previous versions of Microsoft Access, this process was referred to as attaching.

Linked table   A table stored in a file outside the open database from which Microsoft Access can access records. You can add, delete, and edit records in a linked table, but you can not change its structure.

List box   A control that provides a list of choices. A list box consists of a list and an optional label.

Literal   A value that Microsoft Access uses exactly as you see it. For example, the number 25, the string "Hello", and the date #01-05-95# are all literals. You can use literals in expressions, and you can assign literals to constants or variables in Visual Basic.

locked   The condition of a record, recordset, or database that makes it read-only to all users except the user currently modifying it.

Logical operator   Used in formulas to test for equality, inequality, and other conditions. The logical operators are: <,<=, >, >=, =, <>, #NOT#, #OR#, and #AND#. A logical formula evaluates to either TRUE (1) or FALSE (0).

Long data type   A fundamental data type that holds large integers. A Long variable is stored as a 32-bit (4-byte) number ranging in value from -2,147,483,648 to 2,147,483,647.

Long label   A label that is longer than the column width of the cell. If the cells to the right of the long label are blank, Excel displays the entire long label. Otherwise, Excel truncates the long label display. You can see the entire long label in the control panel when you highlight the cell that contains the label.

Lookup field   A field that displays one of the following types of lists:
A list that looks up data from an existing table or query. You can select a value in the list to store in the field. Any updates to the table or query are reflected in the list.
A list that stores a fixed set of values that would not change. You can select a value in the list to store in the field.

Looping macro   A set of macro instructions that executes repeatedly. The macro commands {BRANCH} and {FOR} can create a loop in a macro.

LPT port   A parallel communications port. Windows supports up to three such ports, which are named LPT1, LPT2, and LPT3.

Macro A set of instructions for automating an Excel task. Macros include key-strokes, macro commands, values, and labels. They can duplicate simple keyboard operations but can also be self-contained applications; any Excel task you can perform can be automated with a macro.

Macro command A special Excel command that has meaning only within a macro. A macro command tells Excel to perform a built-in programming function. Each macro command consists of a keyword and its arguments (if any), enclosed in braces.

Macro library A file that contains Excel macros. When a macro library is in memory, you can run the macros in the library from any active file.

Main Form A form that contains one or more subforms.

Make-table query An action query that creates a new table from the result set of an existing query.

Memo data type A field data type. Memo fields can contain up to 65,535 characters.

Memory cache Data stored in a very fast type of memory (usually Static-Column RAM chips) that provide faster access to standard memory (usually Dynamic-RAM) locations.

Menu A screen display that list options or commands from which you can choose.

Menu bar The horizontal bar below the title bar that contains the names of menus. A menu bar can be the Microsoft Access built-in menu bar or a custom menu bar. You can click a menu name on a menu bar to display the list of commands.

Menu bar macro A macro containing AddMenu actions that you can use to create:
A custom menu bar for a form or report.
A custom shortcut menu for a form, report, or control.
A global menu bar.
A global shortcut menu.

Menu pointer The highlight you use to select a menu item and display its description. To select a menu command, use the pointer-movement keys to move the pointer and then press (Enter) key, or type the first letter of the command.

Microsoft Access object An object defined by Microsoft Access that relates to Microsoft Access itself, its interface, or an application's forms and reports. You use Microsoft Access objects, such as the Form and Report objects, to represent elements of the interface that are used to enter and display data, such as forms and reports, in code.

Minimize To reduce an *application window* or *document window* to an *icon*.

Minimize button The downward-pointing arrow at the right side of a window's *title bar*. Clicking a window's minimize button reduces the window to an *icon*.

Minimized window Window that is not displayed, so that only the window's button on the Taskbar appears on the screen.

Mixed cell address A cell address in which part of the address is relative and part is absolute. A dollar sign ($) precedes the part of the address that is absolute. When a mixed cell address is used in a formula and the formula is copied, the relative part of the address adjusts to the new location while the absolute part stays the same.

Modem A device used by a computer to communicate with other computers over telephone lines or coaxial cable. There are two general types of modems: 1) digital and 2) analog. On the Internet, analog modems are used to login to an ISP to gain access to the Internet. The term "modem" is a contraction of the terms "MOdulate" and "DEModulate".

Module A collection of declarations, statements, and procedures stored together as one named unit. Microsoft Access has two types of modules: standard modules and class modules. Form and report modules are class modules containing code that is local to the form or report. Unless explicitly made private to the module in which they appear, procedures in standard modules are recognized and can be called by procedures in other modules in the same database or in referenced databases.

Module level Describes any variable or constant declared in the Declarations section of a module or outside a procedure. Variables or constants declared at the module level are available to all procedures in a module.

Mouse   Device for moving the mouse pointer on the screen and selecting the item the pointer points to.

Mouse keys   Accessibility option that enables you to use the numeric keypad to control the pointer.

Mouse pointer   The screen symbol representing the symbolic location of the mouse. When in graphic mode, the mouse pointer is generally an arrow. When in text mode, it appears as a solid movable rectangle.

MS-DOS mode   Mode in which Windows exists and you see only the DOS prompt. Also called Command Prompt Only mode.

Named graph   A collection of graph settings identified by a name. Using a named graph causes the named graph's settings to replace the current graph settings.

Netscape Navigator www.netscape.com A freeware Web browser available from Netscape Communications Corporation. Netscape Navigator supports JavaScript, Java, and many multimedia and streaming data formats via the use of plug-ins. Unlike Internet Explorer, Navigator does not support ActiveX.

Node   A generic term that can represent an element of a computer network (PC, server, or sub-network).

Notepad   Windows 98's built-in text editor.

Online service   A commercial proprietary computer network. Major online services offer service throughout the United States and Internet access. Online service networks are separate from the Internet in general and ISPs. One of the general misperceptions about online services is that they are synonymous with the Internet. Examples of online services are America Online and CompuServer.

OR search   You conduct an OR search on a database when you want Excel to find records that match any criterion in the criteria range.

Output range   The range into which Excel copies extracted records.

Page   A portion of the database (.mdb) file in which record data is stored. Depending on the size of the records, a page (2K in size) may contain more than one record.

Page Break   A place in text where one page ends and another begins. You can direct Word to palce a page break between two blocks of text so that they will print on separate page.

Page footer (forms)   Displays the date, page number, or any information you want at the bottom of every page. A page footer appears only on printed forms.

Page footer (reports)   Use to place information, such as page summaries, dates, or page numbers, at the bottom of each report page. To add or remove the page footer, click Page Header/Footer on the View menu.

Page header (forms)   Displays a title, column headings, or any information you want at the top of every page. A page header appears only on printed forms.

Page header (reports)   Use to place information, such as column headings, dates, or page numbers, at the top of each report page. To add or remove the page header, click Page Header/Footer on the view menu.

Password   A sequence of characters that allows entry into a restricted system or program.

Pie chart   A graph in the form of a circle divided into slices, where each slice stands for a value in the A range. Pie charts show what proportion of the total each graphed value represents; if one value is twice as large as another, it gets a slice that is twice as large.

Plus pointer   The pointer that appears when you move the pointer to the left edge of a field in a datasheet. When the plus pointer appears, you can click to select the entire field.

Point   Unit of measure referring to the height of a printed character. A point equals 1/72 of an inch, or approximately 1/28 of a centimeter.

Pointing   Moving the cell pointer or highlight to a cell; menu choice; file, graph, or range name; or help screen choice.

Portrait mode   A printer orientation in which the printer prints across the short dimension of the page, from the top to the bottom.

Primary DOS partition   The first, logically named disk portion of a hard disk. Contains the boot record and other DOS information files.

Primary key When you sort a database, you select a primary key to tell Excel what field to base the main sort on.

Print range A range you tell Excel to print. A print range can be a cell, a single range, or a list of ranges. Print ranges can include named graphs also.

Printer control code Code used in printer setup strings. Printer control codes vary from one printer to another.

Printer driver The software program that manages the control interface between your computer and a particular printer.

Protect You protect a worksheet, file, or range to avoid accidentally erasing or changing cell contents and settings accidentally.

Radio button One of a group of round buttons that can either be blank or contain a dot, usually appearing in a dialog box. FrontPage Express comes with form templates to put radio buttons on web page forms.

RAM disk An area of random access memory (RAM) that acts as if it were a disk drive. All data in this area of memory is lost when the computer is turned off or warm booted. It is also known as a virtual disk.

Random access memory (RAM) Semi-conductor-based memory that can be read and written by the microprocessor or other hardware devices. The storage locations can be accessed in any order. The term RAM is generally understood to refer to volatile memory, which can be written as well as read.

Range A cell or a group of contiguous cells in the worksheet file.

Range name The name you give to a single cell or to a range of cells. A range name can be up to 15 characters long.

Re-director That part of the network software that translates a virtual resource request from the user to real resource on a server.

Read-ahead Extra information Windows reads from the disk and stores in memory, so that the information will be instantly available if Windows needs it.

Read-only attribute A file with this attribute setin cannot be updated or deleted, but can still be read.

Recalculation The process Excel uses, after a cell entry has changed, to update worksheet values that depend on other cells. Formulas that contain references to changed cells are automatically recalculated if the default recalculation setting is Automatic (the initial setting).

Record In a Excel database, a record is contained in a single row and a field in a column.

Record A collection of data about a person, a place, an event, or some other item. A record is represented as a row in Datasheet view of a table, query, or form.

Record Number box A small box that displays the current record number in the lower-left corner in Datasheet view and Form view. To move to a specific record, you can type the record number in the box and press (Enter) key.

Record selector A small box or bar to the left of a record that you can click to select the entire record in Datasheet view and Form view.

Record set The collective name given to table-, dynaset-, and snapshot-type recordset objects, which are sets of records that behave as objects.

Recycle Bin Special folder in which Windows 98 stores files and folders you have recently deleted.

Recycled folder Folder that contains part or all of the Recycle Bin.

Reference An identifier that serves as an alternate name for a variable. A reference is defined in terms of an existing name for the variable and becomes an alias of that name. It provides a means, whereby the names of the data objects can, in effect, be passed to and returned by the functions and operators.

Refresh Redisplay a window using updated information.

Regional settings Windows settings that control how numbers, dates, times, and currency amount appear.

Relative cell address A cell address in a formula that changes when you copy the formula to a different part of the worksheet file.

Repeating label Beginning a label with a back-slash (\) followed by a character or character string causes the character or string to be repeated for the width of the column. Repeating labels are often used to draw lines in the worksheet.

Report A Microsoft Access database object that presents information formatted and organized according to your specifications. Examples of reports are sales, summaries, phone lists, and mailing labels.

Report Footer Use to place information, such as a report summary, grand total, or date, at the end of a report. To add or remove the report footer section, choose Report Header/Footer on the view menu. To hide the report footer, set its height property to 0.

Report Header Use to place information, such as a title, date or report introduction, at the beginning of a report. To add or remove the report header, choose Report Header/Footer on the view menu. To hide the report footer, set its height property to 0.

Report window A window in which you work with reports in Design view, Layout Preview, or Print Preview.

Requery To rerun a query underlying the active form or datasheet in order to reflect changes to the records, display newly added records, and eliminate deleted records.

Result set The set of records that results from running a query or applying a filter. In some cases, you can update the data in the underlying table or tables when you make changes to a result set.

Scanner Device that digitizes pictures (or anything on paper) for use by your computer.

Scroll Move the screen view (or "window") up, down, to the right or to the left. You can scroll one line, one column, or one whole screen at a time.

Scroll bar Vertical or horizontal bar running along the right side or bottom of a window, allowing you to scroll the information displayed in the window.

Scrolling The use of program-specified keys to quickly move through a word processing document or spreadsheet to locate the desired material.

Search and Replace A process typical of application programs such as word processors in which the user can specify two strings of characters— one string for the program to find and replace with the second string. For example, a program might be instructed to find the word *company* and replace it with the word *corporation*.

Search engine Web site that helps you find information on the Web by searching the full text of the World Web for the words or phrases you type.

Search page A search page provides a way to find and go to other Internet sites or to documents on an intranet. Many search pages provide different ways to search, such as by topic, by keyword, or by matches to user queries. Others simply provide a well-organized list of hyperlinks to selected Internet sites or to documents on an intranet. You can open the search page from the Web toolbar in an MS-Office program.

Secondary key You select a secondary key when you need to specify the sort order of records whose primary keys are the same. For example, if First Name is the primary key, you would need to specify Last Name as the secondary key to put Santosh Jain ahead of Santosh Sharma in a database sort.

Section A part of a form or report, such as a header, footer, or detail section.

Section selector The box to the left of a section bar in form or report Design view. Click this box to select the section. Double-click this box to open the section's property sheet.

Select query A query that asks a question about the data stored in your tables and returns a result set in the form of a datasheet without changing the data. Once the result set is displayed, you can view and, in some cases, make changes to the data in the underlying tables. In contrast, action queries do make changes to your data.

Server A computer on a network that archives and makes available data and files to client computers and other server computers. Multiple client computers can simultaneously access a single server computer.

Setup string A series of characters that controls printer settings such as font size, line spacing, or other printer characteristics.

Shortcut key A function key or key combination, such as F5 or Ctrl+A, that allows you to carry out a menu command. In contrast, an access key is a key combination, such as Alt+F, that moves the focus to a menu, command, or control, without using the mouse.

Shortcut menu A list of commands that is displayed when you click the right mouse button on a toolbar, property sheet, control, object, or screen region (such as a title bar or window background). The commands listed depend on what you click on.

Single data type A fundamental data type that holds single-precision floating-point numbers in IEEE format.

Sizing handle In form or report Design view, one of the small squares displayed on the edge of a selected control that you click and drag to resize the control.

Snap To grid A tool that you can use to align new or existing controls to the grid in forms or reports.

Snapshot A static image of a set of data, such as the records displayed as the result of a query. Snapshot-type Recordset objects can be created from a base table, a query, or another recordset.

Sort key Specifies a field on which to base a sort.

Sort order The order in which records are displayed—either ascending (A to Z or 0 to 100) or descending (Z to A or 100 to 0).

Spelling checker Software that checks every word in a document against an electronic dictionary of correctly spelled words.

Spreadsheet A structure used for numeric or financial calculations. Spreadsheets contain columns and rows that intersect to form a pattern of boxes, called cells, each of which can hold a value.

Stacked bar graph A bar graph in which related bars are placed on top of each other (stacked) rather than placed side by side. The height of the stack of bars usually represents a total.

Start button Button labeled Start that usually appears at the left end of the Taskbar. When clicked, the Start button displays the Start menu.

Start command DOS program that switches to Windows to open a program or a file.

Start menu Menu displayed by clicking the Start button on the Taskbar. It contains commands and additional menus listing most of the programs that you can run on your computer.

Start Menu folder Usually C:\Windows\Start Menu, the folder that controls what appears on the Start menu, Programs menu, and their submenus.

Start page When you start a World Wide Web browser, the start page is the first page that appears in the browser. You can set this location to any Web site you want, or to a document on your computer hard disk. A start page may contain hyperlink to other documents on your computer, on the network, or on the web.

Startup folder Folder that contains programs that Windows runs automatically when you start Windows. Usually C:\Windows\Start Menu\Programs\Startup.

Startup menu Menu that appears if you press F8 while Windows 95 or 98 is loading.

Statement A syntactically complete unit that expresses one specific kind of operation, declaration, or definition. Usually, a statement consists of one line in a procedure or declarations section. In most cases, however, you can include more than one statement on a line by separating the statements with a colon (:).

Status bar A horizontal bar at the bottom of the screen that displays information about commands, toolbar buttons, and other options.

Structure The framework of a worksheet, as opposed to the data the worksheet manipulates. Worksheet structure includes titles, labels, and the formatting specifications that control the worksheet's appearance.

Submenu A list of additional commands available when you select a main menu command. Many menu commands bring up a submenu. Some submenu commands, in turn, bring up additional submenus.

Subquery An SQL SELECT statement inside another select or action query. You can use a subquery as an expression in a field cell, or to define criteria for a field.

Subreport A report contained within another report.

Subroutine A set of macro instructions that perform a specific task.

Switch A parameter included in DOS commands, usually preceded by the slash (/) symbol, which clarifies or modifies the action of the command.

Tab control A control that contains multiple pages on which you can place other controls, such as text boxes or option buttons. When a user clicks the corresponding tab, that page becomes active.

Tab order The order in which the focus moves in a form from one field or button to the next as you press the (Tab) key.

Table The fundamental structure of a relational database management system. In Microsoft Access, a table is an object that stores data in records (rows) and fields (columns).

Table properties Attributes of a table that affect the appearance or behavior of the table as a whole. Table properties are set in table Design view, as are field properties.

Table window A window in which you work with tables in Design view or Datasheet view.

Tagged Image File (TIF) The TIF Format (sometimes known as TIFF) is a graphics format used by most scanner and page layout applications.

TCP/IP (Transfer Control Protocol/Internet Protocol) The universal data transmission protocol for the Internet. TCP/IP is actually a collection of over 100 individual data transfer protocols. Any computer that connects to the Internet must be running TCP/IP.

Template A worksheet that contains the structure of an application but does not contain the data to be manipulated.

Text box In a dialog box, a box in which you type information needed to carry out a command. The text box may be blank or may contain text when the dialog box opens.

Text data type A field data type. Text fields can contain up to 255 characters or the number of characters specified by the FieldSize property, whichever is less.

Text file A file containing only alphabets, numbers, and symbols. A text file is an ASCII file and contains no formatting information, except possibly for linefeeds and carriage returns.

Title Rows or columns frozen in place on the top, left, or top and right of the worksheet display. Titles always remain in view as you scroll through the worksheet.

Title bar The bar that appears at the top of a window and displays the window's name.

Toggle button A control that acts as an on/off button. A toggle button can display either text or a picture and can stand alone or be part of an option group.

Toolbar A bar that contains a set of buttons, menus, or other controls that you can click to carry out common menu commands.

Toolbox The set of tools you use in Design view to place controls on a form or report. You can show or hide the toolbox by clicking Toolbox on the view menu. When the Help window has the focus, the toolbox is not displayed. Click anywhere in the application window to make the toolbox reappear.

ToolTips Brief descriptions of the names of buttons and boxes on toolbars and in the toolbox. A ToolTip is displayed when the mouse pointer rests on the button or combo box.

Topic The subject of a dynamic data exchange (DDE) conversation between two applications. For most applications that use files, the topic is a filename. A special topic that most applications recognize is System. You can use the System topic to obtain information about the application, such as the other topics it supports.

Totals query A query that displays summary calculations, such as an average or sum, for values in various fields from a table or tables. Strictly speaking, a totals query is not a separate kind of query, rather, it extends the flexibility of select queries.

Transaction A series of changes made to a database's and schema. Mark the beginning of a transaction with the Begin Trans statement, commit the transaction by using the CommitTrans statement, and undo all your changes since the BeginsTrans statement by using the Rollback statement.

Transfer protocol A common set of data transmission standards for exchanging information between computer networks or two computers. All Internet transfer protocols are subsets of the TCP/IP suite of data transfer protocols. Sometimes referred to as a transmission protocol.

TrueType fonts (Windows) Fonts under Windows 3.1 and higher that can be sized to any height to appear the same on the printed page as they appear on your screen. Depending on your printer, a True-Type font may be generated as a bitmap or as a soft font.

Upload The transfer of data or files from a client computer to a server computer via a network.

URL (Uniform Resource Locator) The address of any Internet-based information when accessed via a Web browser. Neither Netscape Navigator nor Microsoft Internet Explorer require you to type the transfer protocol.

Value A number, or a formula that evaluates to a number. Values begin with a number or one of the following symbols: + – @ .

Variable In Excel, a worksheet cell that contains one of a set of values you enter into the cell. Changes to the value in the cell are reflected elsewhere in the worksheet file.

View button A button located at the far left of the toolbar in the Table, Query, Form, and Report windows. You can click the button to change to the view displayed by the picture on the button, or you can click the arrow next to the button to display a list of different views to choose from. The list of views displayed depends on whether you are in a Table, Query, Form, or Report window.

Virus A small block of coded instructions that obtains control of your computer's CPU and directs it to perform unusual and often destructive actions.

Volume label A one to eleven character name for identifying a disk. You can assign whatever label you want to a disk during a FORMAT operation or after formatting with the LABEL command.

Web page A document made available via a Web server. Web pages are constructed with the Hypertext Markup Language (HTML) and are navigated via hyperlinks. Multiple Web pages are assembled in a non-linear navigation scheme. A group of Web pages belonging to an individual, company, or organization is called a Web site.

Web site A collection of Web pages potentially offering text, images, animation, audio, video or special multimedia data types, such as Java or ActiveX.

What-if graphing The process of changing worksheet values and seeing the effect of the changes reflected in a graph.

What-if analysis The process of changing worksheet values and seeing the effect of the changes in the worksheet file.

What-if scenario A calculation that uses variables in formulas to determine potential outcomes of different hypothetical situations.

Wildcard character A keyboard character that can be used to represent one or many characters; usually encountered with operating systems as a means of specifying more than one file by name. In MD-DOS, for example, the question mark (?) wild card character can be used to represent a single character, and the asterisk (*) can be used to represent any number of characters.

Wizard It is an online coach you use to create documents. When you use a wizard to create a document you are asked questions about your document preferences and the wizard creates the document according to your specifications. The Answer Wizard allows you to pose questions about an operation or feature to get more information. The TipWizard monitors your actions as you work and provides tips for improving your effectiveness with Microsoft Word. The TipWizard appears above the ruler at the top of the document window.

Word A group of bits or characters considered as an entity and capable of being stored in one storage location. Also fixed-size storage areas that form the primary memory of a computer system.

Word-wrap It is the automatic placement of a word on the next line. When you type text and reaches the right margin or indent, Microsoft Word checks to see whether the entire word you typed fits on the current line. In case that is not, Microsoft Word automatically places the word on the following line.

Word addressable storage A storage device in which each numbered address location is used to store a fixed number of characters (equal to its word

- length in bytes). For such a storage device, storage space is always allocated in multiples of word-length.

Word length   A measure of the size of a word, usually specified in units such as characters or bits. Each location of a computer system can store a fixed number of characters or bits called its word length.

Word processing   The use of computers to create, view, edit, format, store, retrieve, and print text materials for human communication.

Word Viewer   Program that can display document files in Microsoft Word format.

WordPad   Windows 98's built-in word processor.

Work area   The area of an *application window* or *document window* where you enter data. Also known as *workspace*.

Workgroup   Group of computers on a local area network.

Working folder   Folder in which a program reads and writes files, unless another folder is specified.

Worksheet   A grid of 256 columns by 8192 rows.

You use the worksheet to enter and manipulate spreadsheet data and database table entries.

World Wide Web   Also called the Web, www, and W3, an interlinked collection of hypertext documents (Web pages) residing on Web servers and other documents, menus, and databases, available via URLs (uniform resource locaters). Web documents are marked for formatting and linking with HTML (hypertext markup language), and Web servers use HTTP (hypertext transport protocol) to deliver Web pages. It is a non-proprietary, platform-independent, open document architecture based on ISO standard. It works equally well on stand alone computers, LANS, WANS, and the global Internet, on all major desktop computing platforms (UNIX, Mac, PC, OS/2). Today the Web is the fastest growing service of the Internet, offering over 400 million pages and millions of multimedia files.

XY graph   A graph that displays cell values as points. XY graphs use both a scaled x-axis and a scaled y-axis, so each point on the graph has an X value and a Y value. XY graphs are used to show how two different types of data are correlated. They are also known as scatter charts.

Index

GUJARAT UNIVERSITY
BCA First Year 2009

Subject Name: PC Software

Time : 3 Hours   *Max. Marks : 70*

Instructions:
1. **Attempt all questions**
2. **All questions carry equal marks**
3. **Draw diagrams when necessary**

1.   A.   Answer the following:
    (i)   Explain the use of wildcard with example   3
    (ii)   What does the following DOS Command do?   2
       (a)   C:\windows\type test.txt
       (b)   C:\windows\delete a:*.doc
    (ii)   Differentiate: DOS based PC & Windows based PC.   2

    B.   Do as directed
    (i)   Differentiate: TODAY( ) & NOW () functions in MS Excel   2
    (ii)   List out different types of cell references in MS Excel. Explain any   3
       two in detail.
    (iii) What are the advantages of formula in MS Excel? How one can   2
       enter it in a cell?

OR

    A.   Answer the following:
    (i)   Define Operating System. List out any four roles of it. Also give
       the name of any four popular operating systems.   3
    (ii)   Explain COPY and MOVE commands in DOS with example.   2
    (iii) What is file? What do you mean by naming convention of a file?   2

    B.   Do as directed
    (i)   What is a chart? Explain pie chart in detail.   2
    (ii)   Which are the different types of errors in MS Excel? Explain any   3
       two with example
    (iii) What is the use of paste and paste special?   2

2.   A.   Answer the following: (any ten)   **10**
    (i)   What is icon?
    (ii)   What is the use of Recycle bin?
    (iii) Explain the significance of Desktop
    (iv)   What is the utility of My Computer?
    (v)   Define: Client & Server.
    (vi)   What does SCANDISK command do in DOS?

(vii)   Write any one method to delete a folder from windows explorer.

(viii)   What is the use of search option of a Start menu in windows operating system?

(ix)   How one can create a shortcut for any application on Desktop?

(x)   What is taskbar?

(xi)   What do you mean by disk de-fragmentation?

(xii)   What is Network Neighborhood?

(xiii)   What is workstation?

B.   Answer the following: (any two)   **4**

(i)   What are computer viruses? Give any four ways by which they can spread?

(ii)   Give any four viruses name & explain the harmfulness of any two.

(iii)   How one can prevent and cure a computer from computer viruses?

(iv)   List out any eight symptoms of computer viruses.

3.   A.   State as True/False   **4**

(i)   In MS Word, F4 key is used for Spelling & Grammar checking.

(ii)   Macro is available under Tools menu.

(iii)   In Page Setup, gutter margin is used for binding.

(iv)   In MS Word, the default tab stop value is 0.5"

(v)   In MS Word, by default view is normal view.

B.   Answer the following (any five)   **10**

(i)   What is the use of mail merge facility in MS Word? Which two files are used for it?

(ii)   Differentiate: Auto Text & Auto Correct.

(iii)   Explain endnote & footnote with example.

(iv)   In MS Word, what is the utility of replace command? Under which menu it is available?

(v)   What do you mean by bookmark & comment?

(vi)   Explain hanging paragraph with example.

(vii)   In MS Word, what is template? What is the extension of a template file?

(viii)   What is hyperlink? How one can create it in a document?

4.   A.   Answer the following in MS Excel. (any four)   **4**

(i)   Define Worksheet.

(ii)   What is the user of freeze panes under window menu?

(iii)   What does UPPER() function do?

(iv)   What is the use of data consolidation?

(v)   What do you mean by merge cell?

(vi)   What types of data one can enter in a worksheet?

(vii)   What will be the output for = ROUND (12.35,-1)

B.   Answer the following (any five)   **4**

(i)   Explain the use of SUM() and SUMIF() functions

(ii)   What is Macro? Write down the steps to creat it.

(iii) What do you mean by Auto filter and Advanced filter?

(iv)   Explain formatting and conditional formatting.

(v)   Differentiate HLOOKUP() and VLOOKUP().

(vi)   What is Goal Seek and Scenario.

(vii) What is the use of data form and data validation?

(viii) Define Cell and Range.

5.   A.   Answer the following (any five)   **10**

(i)   What is presentation? What types of presentation are available in Auto Content Wizard of MS PowerPoint?

(ii)   Explain the utility of Pack and Go facility of MS PowerPoint.

(iii) What is custom show?

(iv)   List out different types of views in MS PowerPoint, Explain in any two.

(v)   What is custom animation? How one can apply it?

(vi)   What is a slide? List out any four layouts of it.

(vii) What is the use of Rehearse timing?

(viii) Write any two methods for inserting a new slide in MS PowerPoint presentation.

B.   Answer the following (any two)   **4**

(i)   What is the use of MS Outlook Express? State the significance of address book of it.

(ii)   Explain Outbox & Sent items box of MS Outlook Express.

(iii) What is the importance of Drafts box in MS Outlook Express?

(iv)   Differentiate cc & bcc in MS Outlook Express.

Notes